All the People

A HISTORY OF US

BOOK ONE   The First Americans
BOOK TWO   Making Thirteen Colonies
BOOK THREE   From Colonies to Country
BOOK FOUR   The New Nation
BOOK FIVE   Liberty for All?
BOOK SIX   War, Terrible War
BOOK SEVEN   Reconstructing America
BOOK EIGHT   An Age of Extremes
BOOK NINE   War, Peace, and All That Jazz
BOOK TEN   All the People
BOOK ELEVEN Sourcebook and Index

On August 28, 1963, two thousand buses, 21 chartered trains, and about 250,000 people arrived in Washington, D.C. to demonstrate for civil rights. They gathered at the Lincoln Memorial to hear speakers from all over the country. One of the speakers was Martin Luther King, Jr., who started his speech from prepared notes but then began to speak from his heart. It was his "I Have A Dream" speech, which has become one of the most famous American speeches of all time. Bruce Davidson, a photographer, took the picture that you see on the cover. Read more about that inspiring day in Chapter 20 of this book.

OXFORD
UNIVERSITY PRESS

A HISTORY
OF
US

All the People

Since 1945

Joy Hakim

OXFORD
UNIVERSITY PRESS

Oxford University Press

Oxford   New York

Auckland Bangkok Buenos Aires
Cape Town Chennai Dar es Salaam Delhi Hong Kong Istanbul
Karachi Kolkata Kuala Lumpur Madrid Melbourne Mexico City Mumbai
Nairobi São Paulo Shanghai Singapore Taipei Tokyo Toronto

and an associated company in
Berlin

Published by Oxford University Press, Inc.,
198 Madison Avenue, New York, New York 10016
Oxford is a registered trademark of Oxford University Press

Library of Congress Cataloging-in-Publication Data is available
ISBN: 978-0-19-973502-0 (cloth)
ISBN: 978- 0-19973553-2 (paper)

*The illustrations used herein were drawn from many sources, including commercial photographic archives and the holdings of major museums and
cultural institutions. The publisher has made every effort to identify proprietors of copyright, to secure permission to reprint materials protected by
copyright, and to make appropriate acknowledgments of sources and proprietary rights. Sources of all illustrations and notices of copyright are
given in the picture credits at the end of the volume. Please notify the publisher if oversights or errors are discovered.*

5 7 9 8 6
Printed in the United States of America on acid-free paper

The quote in the caption is from *Heritage,* the magazine of the New York State Historical Society, Cooperstown, NY. Used by permission. The
words on page 5 (opposite) are from "This Land Is Your Land," words and music by Woody Guthrie. Copyright © 1956 (renewed), 1958 (renewed), and 1970 by Ludlow Music, New York, N.Y. Used by permission. The extracts on pages 73 and 87 from *Colored People* by Henry Louis
Gates, Jr., are copyright © 1994 by Henry Louis Gates, Jr. Reprinted by permission of Alfred A. Knopf, Inc. The poem on page 79 is from "On
the Bus With Rosa Parks" by Rita Dove. Copyright © 1999 by Rita Dove. Used by permission of W.W.Norton & Company, Inc. The extract on
page 86 is from *Warriors Don't Cry* by Melba Pattillo Beals. Copyright © 1994 by Melba Pattillo Beals. Reprinted by permission of Pocket Books.
The poem on page 147 is "Mexico Is Sinking" by Guillermo Gomez-Peña. Copyright © 1986 by Guillermo Gomez-Peña.
First published in *High Performance*, no. 35, 1986. Reprinted by permission of *High Performance*.

Bernard Curtis Brown II, who was 11, loved school, basketball, and his family.
He was proud to have been chosen—with two other outstanding students,
Asia Cottom and Rodney Dickens (all from Washington, D.C.)—
to go on a dream trip to California.
No one knew it, but hijackers were on the plane he boarded.
They would crash the plane into the Pentagon, killing the three boys, their
teachers, everyone else aboard, and many on the ground.
This book is dedicated to all those who died on September 11th, 2001,
with the hope that good will come from the awfulness of that day.

Celebrating the centennial of the
Statue of Liberty, 1986

This land is your land
This land is my land
From California
To the New York island,
From the redwood forest
To the Gulf Stream waters,
This land was made for you and me.

—Woody Guthrie, © 1956

Contents

Dr. Martin Luther King, Jr.

To become the instrument of a great idea is a privilege that history gives only occasionally.
—Dr. Martin Luther King, Jr.

	PREFACE: About Democracy and Struggles	9
	FEATURE: BUILDING AMERICA	10
1	The Making of a President	13
2	A Major Leaguer	18
3	A (Very Short) History of Russia	23
4	A Curtain of Iron	27
5	The Marshall Plan	30
	FEATURE: ISRAEL AND AN AMERICAN PEACEMAKER	34
6	A "Lost" Election	36
7	Spies	40
8	Tail Gunner Joe	44
9	Liking Ike	49
10	Houses, Kids, Cars, and Fast Food	54
11	French Indochina	60
12	Separate but Unequal	64
	FEATURE: JIM CROW IN THE FAR NORTH	66
13	Linda Brown—and Others	68
	FEATURE: GETTING INTEGRATED	73
14	MLKs, Senior and Junior	74
15	Rosa Parks Was Tired	78
16	Three Boys and Six Girls	83
17	Passing the Torch	88
	FEATURE: A SOLITARY CHILD	90
18	Being President Isn't Easy	93
19	Some Brave Children Meet a Roaring Bull	97
20	Standing with Lincoln	101
21	The President's Number	105
22	LBJ	109
23	The Biggest Vote in History	112
24	Salt and Pepper the Kids	116
25	A King Gets a Prize and Goes to Jail	120
26	From Selma to Montgomery	124

27 War in Southeast Asia   **128**
FEATURE: AN UNWILLING GUEST AT THE HANOI HILTON   **131**

28 Lyndon in Trouble   **133**
FEATURE: A FARMING VILLAGE IN VIETNAM   **136**

29 Friedan, Schlafly, and Friends   **137**

30 As Important as the Cotton Gin   **144**

31 Picking and Picketing   **147**

32 "These Are the Times That Try Men's Souls"   **153**
FEATURE: CIVIL RIGHTS FOR NATIVE AMERICANS   **156**

33 Up to the Mountain   **157**

34 A New Kind of Power   **161**

35 The Counterculture Rocks   **165**

36 Nixon: Vietnam, China, and Watergate   **170**
FEATURE: MERCURY, GEMINI, AND APOLLO   **176**

37 A Congressman and a Peanut Farmer   **179**

38 Taking a Leading Role   **182**

39 Living on the Edge   **191**

40 The End of the Cold War   **194**

41 A Quilt, Not a Blanket   **198**
FEATURE: THE NEW TECHNOLOGY   **201**

42 Is It Me or We?   **203**
FEATURE: PICTURING OURSELVES   **206**

43 The Land That Never Has Been Yet   **208**

44 A Boy from Hope   **211**

45 Politics and Values   **214**
FEATURE: COVERING UP...OR JUST PLAIN LYING   **217**

46 Electing the 21st Century's First President   **218**

47 Of Colleges and Courts   **221**

48 Big Ideas   **226**
FEATURE: WATCH THAT BRIEFCASE!   **229**

49 Catastrophe, War, and a New Century   **230**

50 New York and the American Way   **236**

If the United States, like the countries of the Old World, are also to grow vast crops of poor, desperate, dissatisfied, nomadic, miserably-waged populations, such as we see looming upon us of late years . . . then our republican experiment, notwithstanding all its surface-successes, is at heart an unhealthy failure.

—Walt Whitman, *The Tramp and Strike Questions*, 1892

President Barack Obama at the Oval Office

The American revolution is still going on—not because we ourselves are wise and good and helpful but because it embodies an idea that reaches everybody and will never lose its force.

—Bruce Catton,
20th-century historian

You know—we've had to imagine the war here, and we have imagined that it was being fought by aging men like ourselves. We had forgotten that wars were fought by babies. When I saw those freshly shaved faces, it was a shock. "My God, my God—" I said to myself, "it's the Children's Crusade."

—Kurt Vonnegut,
Slaughterhouse-Five, 1962

I believe that we are lost here in America, but I believe we shall be found....I think that the true discovery of America is before us. I think the true fulfillment of our spirit, of our people, of our mighty and immortal land, is yet to come.

—Thomas Wolfe

51	War in Iraq	**238**
52	Blowing in the Wind	**244**
53	The Iraq War Continues	**252**
54	A Very Brief History of a Very Complex Place	**256**
55	The Great Panic	**260**
56	Both Lucky and Ready	**265**
	FEATURE: NOT YOUR ORDINARY PARENTS	**268**
57	Yes, We Can!	**270**
	FEATURE: JOINING THE SUPREMES	**275**
58	Where Are We Going? It's Up to Us.	**276**
	FEATURE: "A CALL TO ACTION"	**281**
	CHRONOLOGY OF EVENTS	**282**
	MORE BOOKS TO READ	**284**
	PICTURE CREDITS	**286**
	INDEX	**288**
	A NOTE FROM THE AUTHOR	**295**
	ATLAS	**297**

Sit-in at a Woolworth's lunch counter in Jackson, Mississippi, 1963

PREFACE
About Democracy and Struggles

"What next?" says poor President Truman in 1946, as he faces the problems of a world shattered by war.

For more than a century, western Europe's nations had dominated the globe. Now, in 1945, they were exhausted. Two awful wars had been fought on their territory. Their peoples had suffered horribly. After World War II, it was as if there were a vacuum. We filled the vacuum. We had become the world's most powerful nation.

Our economy had been changed, and strengthened, by the war. We had acted quickly and with imagination. Using something we called "know-how," we had built

World War II began in 1939 when Germany invaded Poland. The United States entered the war after December 7, 1941, when Japan attacked Pearl Harbor. The war came to an end when Japan surrendered in August of 1945.

All of America's citizens threw themselves into winning the war. But when the war was won, many found there was another battle for freedom still to be waged at home. Left: African-American trackwomen on the B & O Railroad, 1943.

9

FOR COLORED ONLY

In 1945, most schools and employers, and even the government, discriminated against women and people of color. Some businesses and public organizations were for white Protestants only. Immigration laws didn't treat people equally. Were those things fair? Have they changed? Are more changes needed? (Those are some of the questions this book raises. You can try to come up with answers.)

See book 5 of A History of US *to read about Elizabeth Cady Stanton.*

tanks, ships, airplanes, and bombs better and faster than anyone thought possible. Women, blacks, and others—who were not always treated according to America's creed of fairness—worked as hard as anyone else. Many fought and died for their nation. Then, when the black soldiers came home, they were often not allowed to vote. Women workers were paid less than men for doing the same job. Was that fair?

Those citizens began to demand equal rights, which was their right as Americans. Anyone who read the Declaration of Independence knew *all men are created equal.* Elizabeth Cady Stanton had changed that to *all men and women are created equal.* Did *all* really mean all? Did it mean

Building America:

The Liberty Bell is old, and it has a bad crack. It last rang out in 1846, on George Washington's birthday, and cracked beyond repair. And yet, in our minds, it sounds loud and clear, because it stands for a set of ideas—political ideas—and they are America's gift to the world.

We are a nation built on ideas (instead of on a sameness of birth and background). One of our national ideas is that what you believe is no business of the president or the government. The Founders called that *freedom of conscience*, or *freedom of religion.* Jefferson wrote of "a wall of separation between church and state."

We have another great idea. It is the idea that *we, the people*, can be responsible for ourselves. We can run our own government. We can pick our own leaders. That is called *democracy.*

Democracy had been tried before our constitution was written. More than 2,000 years earlier, a small Greek city-state named Athens tried democracy, and it worked marvelously well. Most Athenians were prosperous and happy; their sculpture, plays, and writings have rarely been surpassed. But Athenian democracy had flaws. Slaves did the hard work, women did not vote, and there was no protection for minorities when the voting majority made a poor decision. (The Athenians made a bad mistake when they voted to sentence the philosopher Socrates to death because he didn't believe in their democratic ideas.)

We improved on the Greek idea of democracy. We worried about protecting individuals and minorities

An Idea-Centered Nation

from what is called "the tyranny of the majority." But we didn't establish a perfect democracy. Our constitution begins with the words "We the people," but we didn't mean *all* the people. Like the Greeks, we allowed slavery, and women couldn't vote.

Still, ours was the best constitution any nation had ever written. Our Founders—who were thinking men—had read widely; they used the best ideas they could find from history in planning our nation. They studied the republican government of ancient Rome, they studied England's Magna Carta and its Glorious Revolution, and they studied the Iroquois confederacy. They read the words of writers on government, especially England's John Locke. They understood that a fair government is a process. It doesn't happen all at once.

That process began right away, when some of the new citizens of the new nation demanded a bill of rights. So James Madison wrote ten amendments to the Constitu-tion—called the *Bill of Rights*—that guaranteed rights such as freedom of speech and of religion and of the press. That was very unusual in the 18th century (it still is).

It may seem surprising to you that freedom and self-government are unusual. But they are. After our constitution went into effect, in 1789, other nations began looking at America to see if democracy would work. A Frenchman named Alexis de Tocqueville (duh-TOKE-vil) came to this country to see for himself. He said America was a laboratory for democracy. Tocqueville said that what was happening here was "in-teresting not only to the United States, but to the whole world."

Mankind was watching and taking notes. Soon some other nations became democratic. But there was something that was spoiling things in the United States; it was like a worm in a good apple. No, it was worse than that; it was clearly evil— even though it was common practice in many places. Jefferson called it a "cruel war against human nature itself." Yet he and his friends had not done away with it. It was slavery.

Getting rid of slavery was hard. It involved property rights (slaves were property to some people); it hit slave owners in their pocketbooks. Finally, a civil war was fought to end slavery. It would have been better, and

The Liberty Bell's home is in Philadelphia, where the Constitution was drafted and proclaimed the guiding law of the land.

wiser, if we could have done it without a war. But slavery was wrong; we needed to get rid of it, and we did.

How about women? The 15th Amendment said that all citizens have the right to vote. Were women citizens? The 15th Amendment didn't say. The men who were running the country (and some women) didn't seem to think they were. So women had to protest, picket, and even go to jail until, in 1920, another amendment—the 19th—gave them the right to vote.

By this time, people began to no-tice that democracies don't usually go to war with each other, and so we learned that it was important to encourage democracy elsewhere.

But some people didn't understand. They seemed to think that democracy just meant the absence of all controls. Have you heard anyone say, "This is a free country, isn't it?" when they want to do something they shouldn't do? Well, total freedom isn't what democracy is about. That is *anarchy,* and it leads to disaster. Democracy is responsible government. It has controls established by *we the people*.

Remember, creating a free, fair government is a process, and not an easy one. Improving that government is a process without end. One thing is clear: in a government of the people, the people have to pay attention. If citizens don't get involved in their government, they can lose their precious rights. In a democracy, if you want to change things, you have to be part of the process. As Jefferson said, "If a nation expects to be ignorant and free, in a state of civilization, it expects what never was and never will be."

We do a better job of taking part in our government than most people realize. In this book you will see some Americans risk everything, even their lives, to help make our democracy what it was meant to be: a government for *all the people*.

In 1947, this cartoon suggested, the communist vulture has replaced the stork and threatens to drop Baby Chaos among the European nations crippled by war if Dr. U.S. Congress doesn't step on the gas and come to their rescue.

During the first half of the 20th century we fought two horribly destructive world wars and an economic depression. What we didn't fight was segregation and unfairness at home.

all people of every color and description? Most Americans thought so.

But some people said those words in the Declaration without really listening to them. The U.S. government often did the same thing. Our nation wasn't guaranteeing basic human rights to all its citizens. Habit and selfishness were standing in the way of fairness—and no one did much about it. That was going to change. It would take a struggle to overcome the demons of bigotry—a struggle that continues today. You will read about it in this book.

You'll read about another struggle, too: America *vs.* the Soviet Union (also known as the U.S.S.R.—the Union of Soviet Socialist Republics—or Soviet Russia, or, often, just Russia). The Soviet Union was the second most powerful nation in the world. We had been allies and friends during the war. But there was something about the Soviet Union that made us nervous. It was a communist nation with a totalitarian government.

Totalitarianism is a political idea; *communism* is an economic idea. In a totalitarian government, the leaders have total control. They tell people what they can do and say, and punish them if they do otherwise. Totalitarianism is the opposite of free government.

Communism is a method for controlling work and distributing a nation's farm produce, manufactured goods, and services. Under communism, the government owns almost everything—land and business and industry. Citizens work for the government, not for themselves.

Under *capitalism,* citizens do work for themselves. Businesses are mostly owned by individuals or corporations. If you check Article 1, Section 8, of the Constitution, you will see the responsibilities of Congress in our capitalistic nation.

Totalitarianism and democracy are enemies. Communism and capitalism are rivals. After two world wars, we were fearful of rivals. Soviet Russia wasn't the only communist dictatorship. China and Cuba would soon become two others. Could we all live together on the same planet? Or would there be a World War III? It is with those worries that this book begins. It is 1945, and we are about to begin a war of nerves with the communist nations.

1 The Making of a President

Harry Truman aged about 13. He got his first pair of glasses at age six—they cost $10, a lot of money in 1890.

"Mr. President," a boy asked Harry S. Truman, "were you popular when you were a boy?"

"No," said Truman. "I was never popular. The popular boys were the ones who were good at games and had big, tight fists. I was never like that. Without my glasses I was blind as a bat, and to tell the truth, I was kind of a sissy. If there was any danger of getting into a fight, I always ran."

The boy, and his classmates, applauded. Maybe some of them had run from fights and understood that it takes some bravery to admit it. Maybe they wondered about the popular boys in Harry Truman's class. He had become president of the United States; what had happened to his schoolmates? And how exactly did he get to be president? And what was it like running the world's most powerful nation? Well, Truman would answer as many of their questions as he could.

Vice President Harry S. Truman became president near the end of World War II, after President Franklin Roosevelt died. It was, as he said, an accidental presidency. He had been a senator—a quiet, hardworking senator—who seemed an ordinary, likable man. Then, to his surprise, Roosevelt asked him to be vice

After he retired, Harry Truman spent a lot of time sharing his experiences with children. He especially liked to tell them stories from American history. "I'm mostly interested in the children. The old folks...they're too set in their ways and too stubborn to learn anything new, but I want the children to know what we've got here in this country and how we got it, and then if they want to go ahead and change it, why, that's up to them."

Mr. Truman goes to Washington (in 1935). "I am hoping to make a reputation as a senator," he wrote his wife, Bess, back in Missouri. "But you'll have to put up with a lot if I do because I won't sell influence."

The wartime Truman Committee investigated companies producing weapons and other supplies. Truman uncovered many abuses and saved the government millions of dollars.

He held to the old guidelines: work hard, do your best, speak the truth, assume no airs, trust in God, have no fear. Yet he was not and had never been a simple, ordinary man. The homely attributes, the Missouri wit, the warmth of his friendship, the genuineness of Harry Truman, however appealing, were outweighed by the larger qualities that made him a figure of world stature, both a great and good man, and a great American president.

—David McCullough, *Truman*

president. He was just getting settled in that job when, suddenly, he was president. He felt, he said, as if a bull had fallen on top of him.

When most Americans looked at President Harry Truman they sighed. He certainly was ordinary: more like a next-door neighbor than a president. He refused to even try to be sophisticated. Why, except for a year in France as an army captain in World War I, he'd hardly been anywhere. He'd been a farmer, a bank clerk, a shopkeeper, and a county administrator—all in Missouri. When he arrived in Washington, at age 50, you could almost see the rough edges. Sometimes he lost his temper and didn't think much about what he was saying. But he was never mean, or dishonest.

In fact, his honesty was legendary. When he wrote letters home to his mother and sister, as he did almost every day, he paid for the stamps himself. The *franking privilege*—which allows senators and presidents to send their mail free—was meant for government business, he said. He never used it for his personal letters. He lived modestly on his salary, and he didn't use his position to earn extra money. When a Republican who was a political rival left his briefcase at the

In 1905, Harry (right) had a good job in a Kansas City bank. Then his father's farm failed, and Harry had to give up the bank to help run the farm that belonged to his grandmother (sitting, with Harry's mother, outside the Young family farmhouse).

White House, some of Truman's Democratic aides wanted to go through it and see what it held. President Truman was horrified. He would not do a sneaky thing like that.

But when he was president, some people made jokes about him and acted as if he were a hayseed, although a few people noticed that he was very good at making decisions. Later, a historian wrote of him, "With more fateful decisions than almost any president in our time, he made the fewest mistakes." A senator said he was usually wrong about all the little things, but right about all the big ones.

Harry Truman was president during clamorous times. An army of men was returning from military to civilian life; they needed jobs and homes. People were moving from farms to cities faster than ever before. Could those cities become good places for everyone living in them? Europe and Japan were devastated. How would they rebuild? People of color were being treated unfairly. Would that continue? How would we change from making tanks and bombs to making dishwashers and automobiles? And what about Russia? The Russian leader, Joseph Stalin, had made promises he wasn't keeping. Truman the president had to answer those and many other questions. He said that knowing history helped him do the job.

Harry Truman could have been a history teacher; he knew a whole lot about the subject. His interest began when he was a boy and his father read a book to him about the ancient Greeks and Romans. He found he loved stories about people, especially real people. So, as soon as he could read himself, he started on biographies. Andrew Jackson became a special hero of his. Jackson was the kind of man Harry wanted to be: a man of action who represented the common people. A man who was independent, free-thinking, and not at all stuck up.

Truman was born on a farm in Jackson County, Missouri (which was named after Andrew Jackson);

Harry Truman rides the cultivator over a field of young corn. The Young farm was over 600 acres, one of the biggest in the county, and Harry had to work very hard. He took it well, but he didn't enjoy milking cows. He liked the hogs best, and gave them pet names—one was called Carrie Nation (who was she?).

When he was a boy, Harry Truman read a book by an ancient Greek author named Plutarch. The book is called *Lives.* Plutarch wrote about people in pairs, contrasting Greek and Roman personalities. His book is lively and full of interesting dialogue and stories of historical events. Truman read it again and again throughout his life. You might like it, too.

Bess Wallace aged 16. Her mother didn't think Harry was good enough for Bess; the first time he proposed she turned him down.

Grandfather Solomon Young in his seventies, when Harry was a little boy. He was "quite a man, a great big man," Harry remembered, and in the summer took Harry riding all over the countryside in a high-wheeled cart.

most people in Jackson Country felt as he did about the seventh president. When Harry was six, the family moved to nearby Independence. There, Harry discovered the public library and started reading all kinds of books. He never stopped.

He was soon forming his own opinions, and he didn't always agree with those around him. Reading gave him information; it allowed him to think for himself. There was one president whom everyone in Truman's family hated. Really hated. They could hardly talk about him without getting angry. But the more Harry Truman read about that president, the more he admired him.

It was the Civil War president. It was Abraham Lincoln. People hated Abraham Lincoln? They certainly did. You see, Harry Truman was a boy at the end of the 19th century, when many men and women could remember the Civil War. They hadn't cooled down. Harry Truman's parents and grandparents remembered the war as if it had just happened.

Truman's grandparents, both sets of them, had come to Independence, Missouri, in the 1840s, during the early pioneer days, when Missouri was a border state—and a slave state. They came from Kentucky by steamboat, newly married, bringing slaves they got as wedding presents. They weren't unusual; most of their neighbors were slave owners, too. They were decent people who worked hard and tried to live a good life. They didn't think slavery was wrong. (Do you think some things we do now will be judged harshly in the future? What things?)

One of Truman's grandfathers, Solomon Young, was a pioneer who led wagon trains and herds of cattle across the Overland Trail—to California and Oregon and Mormon Utah. Independence was called the jumping-off place; it was the last town before the wagon trains started on the trails west. Everything west of Missouri and east of California was known as "the

Harry's father and mother, Martha and John Truman, as newlyweds. They gave Harry the middle initial S when he was born—but it didn't stand for any name.

Great American Desert." It took some courage to venture out into that desert. Each journey to California and back took Grandfather Young about a year. On one trip he bought most of the land that eventually became the city of Sacramento. It was a family tale—how, if he had kept it, they might have all been rich. But if Solomon Young's grandson Harry Truman had been rich—well, maybe he wouldn't have worked hard and become president of the United States.

Now back to the Civil War. The Kansas–Missouri region was one of the hottest and meanest regions before and during that war. It was in Kansas that the abolitionist zealot John Brown got out his hatchet and chopped some people to bits. And he wasn't the worst of the killers, not at all. There were some terrible things done—on both sides.

One morning in 1861, Truman's Grandmother Young was on her farm (her husband, Solomon, was away) when a band of Union raiders galloped into the yard, ordered her to cook a big meal for them, killed all her chickens and 400 hogs, set fire to the barns, and then rode off with the freshly butchered meat, 13 mules, 15 horses, and the family silver. While all this was going on, 11-year-old Martha hid under the kitchen table.

Two years later, Martha and the rest of the family were marched to a Yankee fort where they were kept prisoners. Their home—a white-pillared plantation house—was burned to the ground by Union soldiers. Are you surprised that Martha Young hated Yankees and President Lincoln?

Martha was Harry Truman's mother. She grew up to be a strong woman who played the piano well, had a good education, and said what she thought—which was a trait that she passed on to her son. (He was a good piano player, too.) Once, when she came to visit the White House, the only empty bed was Lincoln's famous one. Now, most White House guests feel very privileged if they can sleep in the very bed where Abraham Lincoln slept, but not Martha Truman. She said if that was the only bed, why, she'd just sleep on the floor. She was well known for her sense of humor, but this time her son knew she wasn't kidding. He found another bed for her.

During the war, many well-known actors, singers, and comedians entertained the troops—including Vice President Truman, who played under the keen eye of movie star Lauren Bacall at Washington's National Press Canteen in 1945.

John Brown was a violent zealot who claimed he was inspired by God to help the slaves. See books 5 and 6 of *A History of US* for details.

A *trait* is a special characteristic, something that distinguishes you from others. Usually it has something to do with your personality—like plain speaking, or lying, or being optimistic.

17

2 A Major Leaguer

Even at college, said his wife, Jackie Robinson "walked straight, held his head up, and was proud not just of his color, but his people."

Jim Crow (which is discussed a lot in book 7 of *A History of US*) is a term used for rules and practices that discriminate along color lines.

Blatant means "obvious."

Negro-league ballplayers weren't badly paid. Their average was certainly less than that of white players, but for most of them it was still a lot more than they would have gotten in an ordinary job.

Out of 438 known all-star black *vs.* white games, blacks won 309 and whites won 129.

In 1945, we were a Jim Crow nation. It was nothing to be proud of, but that's the way it was. In the South, everything was segregated: schools, buses, restaurants, hotels, even phone booths. The rest of the country wasn't as blatant about it, but there was plenty of separation and prejudice.

In the U.S. armed services, blacks were allowed to die for their country—as long as they did it in segregated regiments.

And when it came to the national pastime—which is what baseball is called—there were the major leagues, the minor leagues, and there were the Negro leagues (for ballplayers of color).

Those who approved of Jim Crow segregation said that things were "separate but equal." They were separate all right. But they were rarely equal. And they certainly were not on the ballfield.

The major leaguers played in fine ballparks, traveled first class, and slept in decent hotels. The Negro leaguers? Well, they put up with a lot: shoddy conditions, no ballparks of their own (they rented what they could find), travel any way they could make it, and—usually—lower pay (except for the incredible Satchel Paige, who in 1942 managed to make more money than anyone in any league).

One thing the Negro leagues did have in abundance was talent. When black players played all-star games against white teams they usually won. Just think about it, and you can see how insane the system was. All those good ballplayers and no one letting them play in the majors! There were plenty of whites who understood that; and there were plenty of whites without prejudice.

One of them was the general manager of the Brooklyn Dodgers. His name was Branch Rickey. Rickey decided he was going to change baseball. He was going to make it the national pastime for all Americans.

But he knew it wouldn't be easy. Fighting prejudice never is. Rickey was the right man for this job. He had founded baseball's system of farm teams back in the 1920s. That means he came up with the idea of taking over minor-league teams (which had been independently owned, just like the major-league clubs) and using them to develop ballplayers for the major leagues. Branch Rickey was used to scouting good players. He knew how to pick them. He was also a shrewd businessman. Black ballplayers (then) were a pool of inexpensive talent. They played an exciting, hustling kind of baseball. And they would bring a huge new black audience to the majors.

If Rickey was going to change baseball and some of the nation's attitudes by integrating the Brooklyn Dodgers, he knew he would have to find a ballplayer who was not only a great athlete, but, even more important, a great person. When he found Jack Roosevelt Robinson he had just the man he was looking for.

Jackie Robinson was a spectacular athlete. He had earned letters and trophies in four sports at the University of California at Los Angeles (UCLA). He was very smart and did well in school. And he had the strength to fight for his beliefs. As an officer in the army, Robinson refused to move when a bus driver asked him to sit in the back of the bus (where blacks were expected to sit). That got Jackie in trouble, but he wouldn't back down. He faced a court martial (a military court) for disobedience. But the young lieutenant had acted within his rights; the army dropped the charges against him.

In 1943 Bill Veeck (VEK) tried to buy the Philadelphia Phillies and sign up black players. An editorial in the *Sporting News* scolded him for the very idea. As long as Judge Kenesaw Mountain Landis was baseball commissioner there wasn't much chance of it. He was a bigot. Soon after he died, in 1944, Branch Rickey began looking for black players. The new commissioner, A. B. "Happy" Chandler, former governor of Kentucky, said, "If a black boy can make it on Okinawa and Guadalcanal, hell, he can make it in baseball."

When some Dodgers said they wouldn't play on the team with a black man, Rickey traded them away.

Branch Rickey signs up Robinson. "Baseball people are generally allergic to new ideas," said Rickey. "It took years to persuade them to put numbers on uniforms.... It is the hardest thing in the world to get big-league baseball to change anything....But they will...eventually. They are bound to."

Mack Robinson, one of Jackie's older brothers, was a world-class sprinter who finished second to American track star Jesse Owens in the 1936 Berlin Olympics. (Jesse Owens is someone to read more about, in book 9 of *A History of US* and elsewhere. His is quite a story.)

Late, late as it was, the arrival in the majors of Jack Roosevelt Robinson was an extraordinary moment in American history. For the first time, a black American was on America's most privileged version of a level field. He was there as an equal because of his skill, as those whites who preceded him had been and those blacks and whites who succeeded him would be. Merit will win, it was promised by baseball.

—A. Bartlett Giamatti,
Take Time for Paradise

Some people thought him a troublemaker, but Branch Rickey was impressed. Here was a man of courage, he believed.

Rickey asked Robinson to come to New York. He said he wanted to talk about a new Negro team. Then, in his office, Branch Rickey told Jackie the truth: he wanted him to break baseball's color line. Both men knew the first black ballplayer in the major leagues wouldn't have it easy. Rickey told Robinson that if he wanted the job—no matter what happened to him—he had to promise not to fight back. He would have to take abuse and hold his tongue. At all times he would have to be a gentleman.

Robinson was the first UCLA student ever to win letters in four different sports. He beat his own brother's national long-jump record and also won tournaments in tennis and golf.

"Mr. Rickey, do you want a ballplayer who's afraid to fight back?"

"I want a player with guts enough not to fight back," said Rickey.

Robinson had never backed away from a fight. He knew that if someone insulted him it would be very difficult to do what Rickey asked: to "turn the other cheek." But he agreed; he gave his word. He was going to do something bigger than anything he'd done before; it was more important than his feelings. It was for his people and for all people.

The two men talked for three hours. Still, neither of them realized how much courage Jackie Robinson would actually need. He had tough times ahead of him. He was going to be spiked, spat on, sent death threats, hit with pitches, and called awful names. How would you have responded?

Branch Rickey began by sending Jackie Robinson to Brooklyn's leading farm team, the Montreal Royals. The Royals'

Of his four college sports, Robinson liked baseball the least. But when he left the army in 1944, the Negro-league Kansas City Monarchs offered him the job of shortstop, and he took it.

manager, Clay Hopper, had grown up with prejudice. He had never had a black friend. He begged Branch Rickey not to make him coach Jackie Robinson. Rickey knew he was a good coach; he told him to do his job. By the end of the season Hopper had learned a lesson: most prejudice comes from ignorance. He told Robinson, "You're a real ballplayer and a gentleman. It's been wonderful having you on the team."

On April 15, 1947, Jackie Robinson, up from Montreal, batted in Brooklyn for the first time as a major leaguer. He was put out four times that day. He didn't do much better the rest of the week. Had Rickey made a mistake?

Then, when the Dodgers went to Philadelphia to play the Phillies, even Rickey was stunned by what happened. The Phillies' manager, Ben Chapman, spewed hate language and encouraged his players to do the same. "At no time in my life have I heard racial venom and dugout abuse to match the abuse that Ben sprayed on Robinson that night," said one of Branch Rickey's aides. "I could scarcely believe my ears," said Robinson.

Jackie Robinson took a deep breath and kept his word. The abuse wasn't all verbal. Runners were sliding and cutting him with

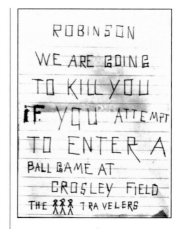

ROBINSON
WE ARE GOING
TO KILL YOU
IF YOU ATTEMPT
TO ENTER A
BALL GAME AT
CROSLEY FIELD
THE 🏃🏃🏃 TRAVELERS

Robinson gritted his teeth and stuck it out through all the abuse. "I'm not concerned with your liking or disliking me," he said. "All I ask is that you respect me as a human being."

I think sports…teach a guy humility. I can see a guy hit the ball out of the ballpark, or a grand slam home run to win a baseball game, and that same guy can come up tomorrow in that situation and miss the ball and lose the ball game. It can bring you up here but don't get too damn cocky because tomorrow it can bring you down there. See? But one thing about it though, you know there always will be a tomorrow.

—Buck O'Neil, first black coach in big-league baseball

Jackie Robinson steals home. Black baseball was different. "In our baseball," said Buck O'Neil, "you got on base if you walked, you stole second, you'd try to steal, they'd bunt you over to third and you actually scored runs without a hit."

I slid into him this one time and really cut him badly....I could see he was bleeding the same color blood as me. I just stood there and felt ashamed of myself, like a real jerk.

—Richie Ashburn, star outfielder for the Philadelphia Phillies

their spikes, pitchers were throwing at his head. It was too much for his teammates—even those who hadn't wanted a black player on the club. "You yellow-bellied cowards," yelled a Dodger player. "Why don't you pick on somebody who can answer back?"

"If you guys played as well as you talked, you'd win some games!" hollered another Dodger.

Sometimes actions bring unexpected results. The poor sportsmanship of some other teams brought the Dodgers together. They were behind their new teammate now.

Soon Robinson was swinging—and connecting. And when it came to base running? Hardly anyone has ever done it the way Jackie Robinson did. He gave pitchers the jitters. And when he stole home? Well, have you ever seen anyone steal home? There isn't much in baseball that is more exciting. Robinson was a fantastic base stealer.

In his rookie season, Jackie Robinson finished first in the league in stolen bases and second in runs scored. He tied for the team lead in home runs. Dodger fans began cheering and cheering. The nation's most important sports paper, the *Sporting News* (which had said that Rickey was unwise to bring a black to the majors), named him rookie of the year. In September, the Brooklyn Dodgers won the National League pennant. And, at the end of the season, Branch Rickey told his star, "Jackie, you're on your own now. You can be yourself." Robinson no longer had to keep quiet, and he didn't.

Jackie Robinson had won the affection and respect of his fellow ballplayers and of the nation. He was the first; he took the punishment, he made it easy for those who followed. Baseball was now the national pastime for all the people.

In his first season Jackie helped set new attendance records at the ballparks. "A life is not important," he said, "except in the impact it has on other lives."

3 A (Very Short) History of Russia

Vladimir Lenin led the second Russian Revolution in 1917. "It is true that liberty is precious," he said. "So precious that it must be rationed." What did he mean?

In order to understand American history in the 20th century, you need to know some Russian history. Does that sound strange? Well, things were happening in Russia that would decide much that happened in the United States. Partly it was because we were obsessed with Russia, which means we couldn't get that country out of our minds. Partly it was because there were real dangers to the world from communist Russia's dictatorship.

After World War II we were determined to be mightier than the Soviet Union. Because of that, we spent vast sums of money on our military forces. We built huge stockpiles of expensive weapons—more than enough to blow up the world. We persecuted some of our own citizens because of fear of communist ideas. Sometimes we even seemed to lose faith in our way of life because we mistakenly thought Russian communism was more powerful.

Now for that Russian history. In 1917, during World War I, Russia had a revolution. For centuries, Russia had been a feudal society controlled by tsars—who were like emperors. The word *tsar* (ZAR) comes from *caesar,* which was the title of ancient Rome's great leaders.

A **dictator** is a ruler who makes people do what he wants (it doesn't matter what they want).

The official name for Lenin's nation was the Union of Soviet Socialist Republics, or the U.S.S.R. Russia was the largest of a group of states, or republics. None were free, independent republics. The union lasted until 1991.

Yassen Gregorovich

Exile means to banish someone from his or her home or country.

Oust means to throw out.

Stalin's opponents were either killed or sent to a *gulag*. To learn about life in those prisons, read *One Day in the Life of Ivan Denisovich* by Alexander Solzhenitsyn, a short, unforgettable book.

What the Russian peasant wanted was his own land. The communists said that peasants and workers would now be the owners and masters.

Many of Russia's tsars were selfish tyrants with absolute control over their people. The Russian people wanted something better: they wanted the things that all people want—peace, opportunities, and freedom. Alexander Kerensky led a revolution in 1917. When Vladimir Ilyich Lenin heard that news in Switzerland, where he had been exiled by the tsar, he headed home to Russia. Lenin—who was the head of a radical political party called the Bolsheviks—ousted Kerensky in a second revolution a few months after the first. Kerensky was a moderate. Lenin was not. He formed a commu-

Kerensky was a tall, handsome lawyer with the gift of the gab. But it didn't save him from exile when Lenin took over the government.

nist government. It was an experiment. Communism had never been tried in a whole nation before. Lenin had to use force to make it work. He soon created a vicious, unfree, totalitarian government. When Lenin died, Joseph Stalin took over. He was worse than Lenin, and worse than any of the tsars. He killed millions of his own people. Russians who protested were murdered, or sent to prison camps in Siberia. Most never came home again. Meanwhile, Stalin and his followers were telling the rest of the world that the Soviet Union was turning into a wonderful, perfect society. It was hard for outsiders to find out the truth. There was no free press; the government controlled all the media. Many people believed the experiment was working.

Communism, to those who hadn't tried it, seemed like a fine economic plan. Most of the ideas for modern communism came from a 19th-century thinker named Karl Marx. Marx wanted to make the world better. He looked at capitalism and saw that, without regulation, wealth soon piled up in a few hands and left many people miserable. There was something even more disturbing: money power usually led to political power. So the poor had double troubles. They had no money and no political power. Marx said capitalism was doomed. And, during the worldwide Depression of the 1930s, it seemed as if he was right.

Under Marx's economic system, people are supposed to work hard and give their products to the government, which is then expected to distribute things fairly to everyone as needed. People don't get paid according to how much they work, but rather according to how much they need. Unfortunately, Karl Marx didn't know a lot about human

Russia's disastrous military defeats in World War I led to strikes, food riots, street demonstrations, and mutiny of troops in Petrograd (St. Petersburg) in February 1917. In March Tsar Nicholas II was forced out of power. For a time, a provisional (temporary) government shared power with a group that represented workers. In July rioting broke out again as the Bolsheviks (the hardline communists) tried to take power. Above: Troops loyal to the government fire machine guns against revolutionaries on the Nevsky Prospekt, Petrograd's main street. The Bolsheviks were defeated, but not crushed. Led by Lenin, they succeeded in seizing power in October 1917. Within weeks, the whole country was in a state of civil war.

nature. Most people need a reason to work hard.

Russia, China, and several other nations tried communism. There was neither economic nor political freedom in any of them. Work and pay were decided by the government. And there was no leaving if you didn't like the system. The communist nations were huge police states.

FRESH AS A DAISY

on a sultry
Arkansas night

thanks to your

Electric Room Air Conditioner!

Things didn't turn out the way Marx had predicted. In communist countries, productivity was low and government distribution was not fair. In Russia, the government became terribly inefficient and wasteful. Perhaps communism didn't get a good test, as some said, but, mostly, the experts who had hoped for great things from Karl Marx's ideas were disappointed.

There was something else that surprised a lot of experts: capitalism wasn't doomed. If Karl Marx could have risen from his 19th-century grave he would have been astonished to find that in the United States, in the second half of the 20th century, capitalism helped a great many people pursue happiness. Free markets brought cars, washing machines, nice clothes, and TV sets to most Americans. But none of that was clear in 1945. We didn't understand ourselves, and we certainly didn't understand the Soviet Union. Some people thought Russia was the hope of the future. Some were terrified of communism without really knowing why. Others feared that communists were about to take over the United States. It was very confusing.

Many in the U.S. of the early 1950s feared that Stalin, the world's strongman, had the upper hand everywhere. This cartoon is titled *But What Part Shall the Meek Inherit?*

By the 1950s, America—unlike the Soviet Union—was a wonderland of modern consumer goods. On average, the national standard of living was the highest on earth (although large numbers of Americans lived in poverty, especially in the South and in cities).

(?) *What if we'd spent all our military money on things to make our cities, schools, and towns safer and more prosperous? Would Russia have attacked us, as we feared? Would Russia have taken over in western Europe and the Middle East? What do you think? (No one knows the answers to those questions, but it is fun to think about them.) Historians have a big advantage. It is called hindsight. We know how things came out. Some 40 years after World War II, Russian communism collapsed because the system proved unworkable.*

4 A Curtain of Iron

Churchill (above) told President Truman that his speech in Fulton, Missouri, would be about "the necessity for full military collaboration between Great Britain and the U.S. in order to preserve peace in the world."

Britain's great wartime leader, Winston Churchill, had something to say, but no one was listening. So, in 1946, when President Truman asked the former prime minister to speak at tiny Westminster College in Fulton, Missouri, Churchill didn't hesitate. He said yes.

Churchill wanted to talk about Russian communism. Many people did not know what to think about Stalin and Soviet Russia. During World War II (which ended in 1945), Russia was the ally of Britain and the United States. No people fought harder against the Nazis than the Russians. No nation suffered war losses as enormous as Russia's. When the war ended, everyone hoped for friendship between the new superpowers: Russia and America. Around the world, many people believed that Russian communism was an acceptable form of government.

Winston Churchill thought differently. Churchill had warned of Adolf Hitler and Nazism long before most Britons or Americans took them seriously. Once again, he wanted to tell the world of a dangerous dictator and an ominous form of government. "A shadow has fallen upon the scenes so lately lighted by the Allied victory," he said at that small Missouri college. The shadow he was talking about was vicious totalitarian rule. "From Stettin in the Baltic to Trieste in the Adriatic an *iron curtain* has descended across the Continent," Churchill continued.

I do not believe that Soviet Russia desires war. What they desire is the fruits of war and the indefinite expansion of their power and doctrines. ...I am convinced that there is nothing they admire so much as strength and there is nothing for which they have less respect than for weakness, especially military weakness.

—Winston Churchill

Ominous means "threatening."

A *totalitarian* government has total control over its citizens' lives.

The continent
Churchill was referring to was Europe.

27

The curtain of iron was blocking out truth and freedom. Nations behind that curtain were prisoners of Russia.

When World War II ended, the armies of the winning Allied powers—the U.S., the U.S.S.R., and Great Britain—moved through Europe, freeing the nations that had been conquered by Hitler's Nazis. The Allies promised to help the liberated nations. They promised to help them hold open elections and form free governments. After that, the Allied armies were supposed to leave (which was what we did).

BERLIN, 1961

THE IRON CURTAIN

IRON CURTAIN COUNTRIES

For a short time in 1956, Hungary revolted against Soviet rule; these Hungarians burned Stalin's portrait in the streets.

Russia wouldn't go. Soviet armies stayed in control in Poland, Romania, Bulgaria, Czechoslovakia, Hungary, Yugoslavia, Latvia, Lithuania, Estonia, and East Germany. There were no free elections there. Elsewhere—in nations like Italy and France—the communist parties were growing strong. Joseph Stalin bragged that the whole world would eventually go over to communism.

But most people didn't stay behind the iron curtain willingly. At every Soviet border, armed guards kept peoples captive. Iron curtains would soon extend over several Asian countries. Some east European countries, like Hungary and Yugoslavia, attempted to rebel and become independent. The Hungarians were crushed and their leaders killed. The president of Yugoslavia, Marshal Tito (TEE-toe), was as crafty as Stalin himself, and he managed to keep the Soviet Union at arm's length. But even Yugoslavia was not really a free country. It had only one political party, and that was communist.

President Truman decided the United States would come to the aid of any nation endangered by communism. We would not let Soviet Russia expand further. We began by sending $400 million in emergency aid to Greece and Turkey. That program of assistance was called the Truman Doctrine. It was the beginning of a *cold war* against Russia. The Cold War lasted more than 40 years.

[Communism] is based upon the will of a minority forcibly imposed upon the majority. It relies upon terror and oppression, a controlled press and radio, fixed elections, and the suppression of personal freedoms. I believe that it must be the policy of the United States to support free peoples who are resisting attempted subjugation by armed minorities or by outside pressure.

—Harry Truman, announcing the Truman Doctrine to Congress

After the war, Germany was split in two. East Germany stayed under Soviet control, and West Germany got a free, democratic government. The old capital of Germany, Berlin, was also divided between east and west (*see map inset opposite*). In 1961, the Russians built a concrete wall in the middle of Berlin and topped it with barbed wire to keep people from running away to freedom.

29

5 The Marshall Plan

President Truman sends Secretary of State George Marshall off to London to attend the Conference of Ministers, 1947.

The idea behind the Truman Doctrine was to keep communism from spreading. That Cold War policy was known as "containment."

Two signs sat on President Truman's desk. The first sign quoted a man from Truman's home state of Missouri. It said, ALWAYS DO RIGHT. THIS WILL GRATIFY SOME PEOPLE & ASTONISH THE REST. They were the words of Mark Twain.

The second sign said THE BUCK STOPS HERE.

Which means: the president has the final word and can't blame anyone else for his decisions.

Harry Truman had some big decisions to make. Those decisions would profoundly affect Americans and people around the world. In one of the most important of his decisions, he persuaded the American people to act generously to the defeated nations. What Harry Truman had in mind had never been done before in the history of the world.

Truman knew how defeated people feel after a war. He knew that his Confederate ancestors carried hate in

The Marshall Plan was named for Secretary of State George C. Marshall, who introduced the idea in a speech at Harvard College. General Marshall was the U.S. Army's chief of staff during World War II. The Marshall Plan was a team effort, developed by General Marshall and by Undersecretary of State Dean Acheson, Minister to Russia George F. Kennan, Presi-dent Truman, and others in his administration.

A Soviet cartoon portrayed an imperialistic Uncle Sam towed along by the European nations hungry for dollars—they would never get them, said the cartoon.

their hearts all their lives. He knew that Germany's anger after World War I had helped bring about a second world war.

So he supported a plan that would send billions of dollars in aid and assistance to our allies and to our former enemies. It was called the Marshall Plan, but it reflected President Truman's thoughts. After a terrible war, he was asking the winning nation to help everyone recover—including the losers. The president said:

> *You can't be vindictive after a war. You have to be generous. You have to help people get back on their feet....People were starving, and they were cold because there wasn't enough coal, and tuberculosis was breaking out. There had been food riots in France and Italy....We were in a position to keep people from starving and help them preserve their freedom and build up their countries, and that's what we did.*

Marshall Plan aid was offered to all of Europe's nations—including the Soviet Union and those countries under Soviet control. The Soviet nations refused the aid. Sixteen nations accepted with enthusiasm. It was very expensive. It was very unselfish. The plan encouraged Europeans to use American aid and add their own brains and know-how. It worked. Prosperity began returning to the free nations of Europe. It also helped us. Those newly prosperous European nations now had money to buy American goods. And they did.

Marshall Plan aid: (left) a U.S.-made Caterpillar bulldozer arrives to help rebuild France's electric power system; (right) a German construction worker in Berlin. The German poster says: *Berlin Relief Program—with Marshall Plan Aid.*

A person who is ***vindictive*** wants to have revenge.

Marshall Plan aid was very concrete (that's a pun). U.S. money rebuilt steel mills in Belgium, ceramics factories in France, railroads in Germany, and bridges

It was 1948, the Soviets were blockading Berlin, and fear of a third world war panicked many in Washington. Secretary of State George C. Marshall stayed calm. A young aide asked him, "How in the world can you remain so calm during this appalling crisis?" Marshall, who knew his history, said, "I've seen worse."

❓ *The Diet is the name of Japan's congress. What is the name of Great Britain's congress?*

Discrimination means choosing for unfair reasons. (The word has other meanings, too. Look it up.)

In East Asia, General Douglas MacArthur was sent to defeated Japan as head of an occupation army determined to rid Japan of its war leaders and bring democracy, freedom, and prosperity to that nation. The Japanese wrote a new constitution; it made Japan a democracy. Land was redistributed so that more people could have it. (Before, there had been a few huge landowners and many poor farmers; now there was a better balance. Soon there would be great prosperity.) Women were allowed to vote (39 were elected to the Diet). Secret political societies were prohibited. And religious discrimination was ended. The United States poured aid into Japan—food, clothing, medicines, and other supplies. Ancient temples and museums were restored. We were very generous. No nation had ever done that kind of thing for a defeated foe.

Another Truman plan, called "Point Four," gave aid to developing nations. Developing nations (another name for them is the Third World) are countries that are less wealthy and less modern than the industrial nations—many of those developing nations are in Africa, Asia, and Latin America.

Did everyone approve of these generous policies? Not at all. Some people in Europe and Asia said they didn't want to take aid from America. They thought we wanted something in return. Some people in Congress yelled about all the money it was costing. "Why should we help others?" they asked. "Why should we help our former enemies?" they screamed.

Their screams were nothing compared to those heard when President Truman decided to do something to help people in the United States. He decided it was time to do something about civil rights for all citizens. He decided to do something about lynchings and segregation. The army, navy, and air force were all segregated. Blacks and whites served in separate units. Blacks got the worst jobs. That wasn't fair. Like other Americans, they were willing to fight for their country. Why should they be treated differently?

In Mississippi, when some black soldiers returned home, they were dumped from army trucks and then beaten. In Georgia, a black man was shot and killed because he had voted. When Truman heard of those outrages he was horrified. The president had been brought up on Confederate ideas, but he was also taught to know right from wrong. Maybe Mark

"We cannot wait another decade or another generation to remedy these ills," said Truman. "We must work, as never before, to cure them now."

CIO says "WIPE OUT DISCRIMINATION"

In January 1946, the first General Assembly of the United Nations meets in London, England. Secretary of State James F. Byrnes heads the U.S. delegation, which includes Eleanor Roosevelt, widow of the former president. In October, the General Assembly accepts a gift of $8.5 million from John D. Rockefeller, Jr., to pay for a U.N. headquarters site. That site is in New York City.

Truman's 1947 speech denouncing racial discrimination and pledging to fight it was the first ever made by a president to the NAACP (the National Association for the Advancement of Colored People).

A *lynching* is an outside-the-law execution.

Twain's words on his desk helped inspire him. He sent proposals to Congress to stop lynchings, to outlaw the poll tax that kept some people (mostly blacks) from voting, and to end segregation in the armed services. He created a commission on civil rights.

Remember the villains of prejudice and hate? People infected with those viruses began to howl. A Florida county commission said the president's program was "obnoxious, repugnant, odious, detestable, loathsome, repulsive, revolting and humiliating." A Mississippi congressman said Truman had "run a political dagger into our backs and now he is trying to drink our blood." Read on, and you'll see what happened next.

(?) *Obnoxious, repugnant, odious, detestable, loathsome, repulsive, revolting, humiliating? Strong words — what do they mean?*

33

Israel and an American Peacemaker

Harry Truman recognized the state of Israel 11 minutes after its creation on May 14, 1948. It had been a hard birth. Coming after the horrors of the Holocaust, and after almost 2,000 years of Jewish longing to return to their homeland, and after promises of a Jewish state by the victors of World War I—well, you might think it wouldn't be difficult to achieve. But the Jews weren't the only people who laid claim to that hauntingly beautiful land. The Arabs, who lived there, claimed it, too—and didn't want to share it. The story is complicated. Here is some of it.

About 4,000 years ago, in the time of Abraham and Moses, Israel (or Palestine, as it came to be called) became the home of the Jews. Two thousand years later, in the year 70 c.e., the Romans drove many of the Jews from their country. They settled throughout the Roman Empire, living in a diaspora (die-ASS-por-uh), or exile. But wherever they lived, every Passover, Jews prayed for a return to the holy city of Jerusalem.

Then, at the end of the 19th century, Hungarian-born Theodore Herzl, reacting to fierce European anti-Semitism, founded the *Zionist* movement. Its aim was to re-create a Jewish nation in Israel. Zionist Jews began moving to Palestine. At the same time, a Russian Jew, Eliezer Ben-Yehuda, called for a revival of biblical Hebrew, the original language of the Jews. It had become a dead language, used only for prayers. Astonishingly, his idea caught on. By the time of the First World War (1914), 90,000 Jews were living in Palestine and speaking Hebrew. Palestine was part of the southern region of Syria, under the control of Turkey.

Turkey sided with Germany in that first World War, and lost its empire. The Allies (who won) gave Great Britain the job of ruling Palestine. In 1917, the British Foreign Office issued a proclamation, the Balfour Declaration (written by the Foreign Secretary, Arthur James Balfour), which said: "His Majesty's government views with favour the establishment in Palestine of a National Home for the Jewish People." President Woodrow Wilson cabled his support of the Declaration.

Jews set out for their ancient homeland. Those who didn't go put coin boxes in their homes to raise money for the Promised Land. Those who did go often faced dreadful conditions on land that was dry desert or malarial swamp. They drained and irrigated land, planted trees, built the new city of Tel Aviv, and made schools and homes. Some Arabs protested their presence. Some attacked and killed Jews, but persecution was nothing new to them. The Jews toughed it out.

By 1939, more than 30 percent of Palestine's population was Jewish. But that year (just when Hitler was making things awful in Europe), the British, bowing to Arab pressure, limited immigration into Palestine to 1,500 Jews a month. Jews were desperate to escape from Europe. The alternative was the death camps. But they had nowhere to go. The U.S. had immigration quotas that kept most Jews out. So did many other nations. Six million European Jews were murdered.

After World War II, about 250,000 survivors of the camps remained in Europe. Their homes had been taken, their families killed. President Truman urged that 100,000 be allowed to enter Palestine. But the British stuck to their monthly quotas. When boatloads of survivors arrived on their shores, they were turned away. The British announced that they would leave the region on May 15, 1948.

It was then, in 1947, that the United Nations got involved. The U.N. recommended that the land be divided into separate Jewish and Arab states—largely determined by population. It was called "partition." Jerusalem, a city sacred to three religions, would be held under international control.

Both sides wanted to control all of what was a tiny bit of land (about the size of Vermont). But the Jewish Agency agreed to the U.N.'s partition. Arab organizations were all against it.

Jews and Arabs were soon fighting a civil war. At first the Arabs seemed to be winning, but the Jews fought back and stunned everyone with their victories. The day before the British left Palestine, the Jews announced the birth of a new nation. They called it Israel. It was founded on democratic principles. The Arabs kept fighting.

Would anyone recognize Israel? Most Americans were sympathetic to Jewish hopes for a homeland. But the State Department was not. Arabs controlled vast quantities of oil. There were fears of Russian influence. The president was advised not to recognize a Jewish nation.

But an old friend had been to visit Harry Truman. They had both fought in World War I and then gone home to Kansas City to open a haberdashery (a men's clothing store). Eddie Jacobson was someone Truman knew he could trust. He had never asked Truman for a favor, but now he wanted one. He asked the president to meet with Chaim Weizmann, a scientist who was Israel's first president. It was Dr. Weizmann who had persuaded Lord Balfour to issue his famous Declaration. But Truman wasn't going to be pressured by anyone. He wrote later in his autobiography:

I told him that I respected Dr. Weizmann, but if I saw him, it would only result in more wrong interpretations. Eddie waved toward a small replica of an Andrew Jackson statue in my office. "He's been your hero all your life, hasn't he?" he said....I did not know what he was leading up to, but he went on.

"I have never met the man who has been my hero all my life," he continued. "But I have studied his past as you have studied Jackson's. He is the greatest Jew alive...I am talking about Dr. Chaim Weizmann. He is an old man and a very sick man. He has traveled thousands of miles to see you, and now you are putting off seeing him. That isn't like you."

When Eddie left I gave instructions to have Dr. Weizmann come to the White House.

After the United States recognized Israel on May 14, the Soviet Union did, too. But the Jewish celebrations didn't last long. On May 15, Lebanon, Syria, Transjordan, Iraq, and Egypt joined together to send armies to crush the young nation. Most of the Arabs in Israel fled, for reasons that would be disputed in years to come. The war created two refugee populations—equal numbers of Arabs from Israel and Jews from Arab lands.

In the months that followed, thousands of Jews and Arabs

Chaim Weizmann

Ralph Bunche

died. Neither side won, but the Jews controlled most major cities, and the Arab forces realized they faced real fighters.

That was when the U.N. got involved again. Count Folke Bernadotte, head of the Swedish Red Cross, was named as a special mediator. Bernadotte made plans to redo the partition arrangement, adding the huge Negev desert region to the Arab state. The Israelis, who had held off Arab armies, felt betrayed. A sniper from a Jewish underground group shot and killed Bernadotte.

Then an American peacemaker stepped onto that very dangerous stage. He was Bernadotte's aide, and he took over as the U.N. mediator. He was a man who had known prejudice himself. As a boy, he had been turned away from swimming pools. As a teenager, he achieved academic excellence that went unrewarded. He had learned the value of persistence.

This peacemaker had no special interest in the region. But he cared about justice. He was hardworking, and wise, and low-key. His name was Ralph Bunche, and he was the grandson of a slave.

Bunche was the first black to earn a Ph.D. in political science from Harvard. He had been a professor at Howard University in Washington, D.C. He set the boundaries of today's Israeli state. It took incredible determination and patience. At first the Israelis and Arabs wouldn't talk to each other. He vowed, "I'll never adjourn this meeting. I'll stay for 10 years if necessary." Actually it took him only 81 days.

When the final papers were signed, ending the hostilities (on February 24, 1949), Bunche hosted a party. Everyone played billiards together. Then Bunche gave all the participants beautiful pieces of pottery that he had had specially made for them. "What if we hadn't agreed?" asked one. "I'd have smashed the pottery over your heads," said Bunche.

Ralph Bunche was awarded the Nobel Peace Prize in 1950. He continued to work for world peace, taking U.N. assignments in Egypt and Africa. "When such men as Dr. Bunche...become 'great heroes' in the eyes of millions of Americans, we will be approaching maturity as a nation," an article in *Progressive* magazine stated, adding, "Until the world's peacemakers become our heroes, too, we will not have achieved that maturity."

6 A "Lost" Election

Ben Shahn's poster "A Good Man is Hard to Find" from 1948 satirizes a popular 1945 photograph of Harry Truman playing a piano adorned by actress Lauren Bacall (see page 17). Shahn, known for his socialist views, probably didn't think either Truman or Dewey was the right man for the presidency.

In 1948:

In London, American athletes won 38 medals at the first Olympic Games held since the Berlin Olympics in 1936.

Test pilot Chuck Yeager broke the sound barrier in the Bell X-1 rocket plane.

At Mount Palomar, California, the world's largest telescope, 200 inches in diameter, was unveiled.

In India, Mahatma Gandhi, who led his countrymen to emancipation from British rule, was assassinated.

Democrats could count on winning in the South. No southern state had voted for a Republican for president since before the Civil War. The South was known as "the solid South." It was solidly Democratic.

Now, because of Truman's civil rights proposals, many southern politicians were furious with their party. They weren't quite ready to turn Republican, but they were certainly against Harry. So some formed another party. It was called the Dixiecrat Party.

Other Democrats were unhappy with the president for different reasons. Some thought Truman was too hard on communism. They wanted the United States to try to get along with Joseph Stalin and the Soviet-controlled countries. Some wanted more domestic reforms. Those people formed another party. It was a new Progressive Party.

When a candidate splits his own party in three—well, he is in trouble. In 1948, Harry Truman and the Democrats were in trouble. Besides, the Democratic Party had been in power since 1932, so most people said they were ready for a change.

Truman was nice enough. But after that giant of the war years, Franklin Roosevelt, Harry Truman seemed almost embarrassing. Sometimes he just popped off and said whatever was on his mind. He wasn't dignified. He wasn't meant to be president, some people said.

So everyone knew that Harry Truman didn't have a chance to get elected in 1948. Some Democrats tried to dump him. They wanted someone else as their candidate. But Harry S. Truman was stubborn. He was head of the party and he was going to run for election.

The Republicans chose Thomas E. Dewey as their candidate for president. Dewey was governor of New York. He was much younger than Truman, but he acted old and wise. He had a trim, compact build, dark hair, and a small dark mustache. He was dignified. He didn't say much. He didn't campaign hard. He just began to act as if he were president, because everyone knew he would be soon. (Congresswoman Clare Boothe Luce said that Harry Truman was a "gone goose.")

Franklin Roosevelt had used radio to talk to the American people. Truman wasn't a good speaker on the radio. But he was pretty good in person, especially when he spoke without a prepared speech and just said what he thought. So Harry Truman got on a train and began his campaign. (In those days most people traveled long distances by train. There weren't many big highways, and air travel was still a novelty, and expensive.)

The president's train had bedrooms, a dining room, a car for newspaper reporters, a car for presidential aides, office space, and a wood-paneled sitting room for the president and his family—16 cars in all. The train crossed the nation—twice. When it pulled into a city, or town, or hamlet, the president stood on the back platform and spoke to anyone who came to the railroad station to hear him. Lots of people came. Wouldn't you go to hear a president?

Sometimes Harry Truman gave his first speech before six in the morning. He was a farm boy, and used to getting up early. He gave speeches all day long—10 or 15 a day. Sometimes he got off the train for an outdoor rally. Usually there were flags and bunting and local politicians to share the plat-

(?) *The presidential train was named the Ferdinand Magellan. Who was Magellan?*

If you can't stand the heat, get out of the kitchen.

—favorite Truman saying

Harry Truman had a hard time with Congress. That body approved his foreign-aid plans but turned down many of his domestic (home) proposals. Some of those proposals—for civil rights, national health insurance, and urban planning—were farsighted. But Congress did pass some important bills. One was called the G.I. Bill of Rights. It gave military veterans a chance for a free college education. It educated a generation of Americans (mostly men), and that helped create a broader and stronger middle class.

Bess—or "Boss"?

Truman liked to introduce his wife, Bess, and his daughter, Margaret, to those who appeared at the whistle stops. "Would you like to meet the Boss?" he'd say before Bess appeared. "He's the president," one editor wrote, "[yet] he's just an ordinary family man, proud of his wife and daughter. He has something in common with many who hear him." (Bess told her husband that if he called her "the Boss" one more time, she'd get off the train.) But the editor was right: Harry was a family man and *very* devoted to his wife and daughter.

Bess Truman (waving) said that the essential attributes for a first lady were good health and a well-developed sense of humor.

Black people gathered in huge numbers wherever Truman campaigned; these voters are in Harlem, New York. For the first time, black delegates were present in force for Truman's nomination at the Democratic National Convention.

The Hotel Roosevelt was named for Theodore Roosevelt (a Republican), not for Democrat FDR.

Truman was a good mimic. After the election, he liked to imitate H.V.Kaltenborn saying that Dewey would win.

form. Sometimes high-school bands played and marched, and the president gave a luncheon or dinner speech in a big city hall. It was exhausting to everyone except Harry Truman, who seemed to get more energetic and feisty as the campaign continued. His speeches were fighting speeches. He lashed out at the Republican Congress (which wasn't passing the laws he wanted), and he attacked those who asked for special government favors: he called them "power lobbies" and "high hats." People cheered his spirit (even if they didn't seem impressed with him otherwise). "Give 'em hell, Harry," they said.

Tom Dewey had a train, too. But he didn't get up early, and he didn't give many speeches. He didn't need to. It was clear that he was going to win. *Everyone said so.*

Newsweek magazine asked 50 leading journalists—people whose business it is to know politics—who would win. *All 50 said that Truman would lose.* One of Truman's aides bought *Newsweek* and read it on the train. Not even one reporter gave the president a chance to win. The aide tried to hide the magazine, but Truman spotted it and read the article. "Don't worry," he said, "I know every one of those 50 fellows, and not one of them has enough sense to pound sand into a rat hole."

The sensible *New York Times* conducted a survey. It sent reporters around the country for a whole month. The reporters concluded that 29 states would go to Dewey, 11 to Truman, and four to the Dixiecrats. The others were undecided.

Every leading poll showed a Dewey landslide.

On November 2, 1948, the American people voted.

That evening, Dewey's supporters crowded into the ballroom of New York's Hotel Roosevelt. They were there to celebrate. Men wore black tuxedos and women wore evening gowns. Each Republican woman was presented with an orchid as a victory corsage. Waiters carried trays of elegant food.

In Washington, the Democrats hadn't even rented their usual hotel ballroom. They were short of money and there was no point in wasting it—they had nothing to celebrate.

Newspaper reporters wrote articles congratulating the new president on his victory—that way they could go to bed as soon as the returns came in. At the *Chicago Tribune,* the morning's headline announcing Dewey's victory was set in type.

As night arrived, the counting began. (In this time before computers, vote counting was slower than it is today.) Maybe it was habit, but many people stayed up to listen to their radios. They expected a quick decision. Election results were being broadcast on television, for the first time. But most people didn't have television sets. Harry Truman didn't have one. He was staying at a small hotel. He ate a ham sandwich, drank a glass of buttermilk, and went to bed early. When it was announced that he had won in Massachusetts, one of his Secret Service men woke him with the news. "Stop worrying," said Truman, and went back to sleep.

At midnight he woke up, turned on the radio, and listened as a deep-voiced radio commentator named H. V. Kaltenborn announced that although Truman was a million votes ahead, they were just early votes: Dewey was sure to win.

At 1:30 A.M. the Republican National Chairman stood on a chair in the Roosevelt Hotel ballroom and said that it looked as if Dewey would win in New York State and would soon be president of the United States. The guests cheered.

At 4 A.M. the Secret Service agents received a call from Democratic headquarters. Illinois had been put in Truman's win column. They couldn't resist waking their boss. "That's it," he said. "Now, let's get back to sleep."

At dawn, Truman got up. Deep-voiced Kaltenborn was still on the radio. Now he was saying that it was a very close election—but Dewey would win. By mid-morning it was clear: all the experts were wrong! Truman was no accidental president. He had won the job on his own.

Left: President Truman relished the chance to laugh at the eagerness of the press to finish him off in advance. The crowd that gathered outside the White House (below) after his election was the biggest in history.

7 Spies

Hollywood producers, terrified of being accused of sympathy to communism, tried to prove their loyalty with strings of movies "exposing" red "conspiracies."

The times were prosperous, but not content. There was fear in the air.

Some Americans were afraid there might be a communist revolution in the United States. They believed that our nation was filled with communists.

Some thought that President Roosevelt's New Deal laws were inspired by communists. That legislation had changed America with strong child labor regulations, minimum wage standards, Social Security, and new taxes. All that had put some limits on capitalism. More people shared the wealth. The gap between rich and poor had been narrowed. There was a newly prosperous middle class (as there was when the nation was founded). That strong new middle class was challenging the old guard and its ways. Now Harry Truman wanted to change society even more, with his civil rights ideas and with a program of liberal reform called the Fair Deal. "Suppose he gets his national health insurance—who will pay for it?" some people asked. "Those who have the most money will pay most of the bills," they said. To many, it sounded like communism.

Then communist spies were discovered in the United States. They had stolen atom-bomb secrets and sold them to Russia. As if that weren't bad enough, shocking news came from England—some top British intelligence officials turned out to be Soviet spies. And

Left: These girls, all under four years old, march in New York in 1949 to protest the jailing of three supposed communists. Right: Ethel and Julius Rosenberg were convicted in 1951 of selling atomic secrets to the Soviets. Their case caused a wave of anti-communist hysteria, though some people remained convinced of their innocence. (Historians are now certain that Julius, at least, really was guilty.) They were executed by electrocution.

[South Korea's Syngman Rhee] was one of the early postwar, anti-Communist dictators, with an instinctive tendency to arrest almost anyone who did not agree with him. Only by comparison with his counterpart in the North, Kim Il Sung, did he gain: Sung not only arrested his enemies; he frequently had them summarily executed....[Sung] held the Order of Lenin, awarded by Stalin himself....At first he was a popular figure, for it was widely known that he had devoted his life to fighting the hated Japanese. That popularity would diminish as the harshness and cruelty of his rule became apparent.

—David Halberstam,
The Fifties

that wasn't all: in a case that filled newspaper headlines day after day, a former State Department adviser and president of an international peace organization—a man named Alger Hiss, whom everyone trusted—was convicted of lying about his involvement with an admitted communist. A young congressman, Richard Nixon, captured the attention of the whole nation with his hard questioning of Alger Hiss. When Hiss was found guilty of *perjury* ("lying under oath") Americans were dismayed. It really did seem that the State Department might be full of spies and traitors. Alger Hiss spent four years in jail. (Hiss was guilty of lying, but was he a spy? People still argue about that.) Of course, everyone knew that Russia had spies in the United States and that we had spies in Russia. Nations spied on each other then. They still do.

No question about it, these were confusing and frightening times. The United States had believed it was alone in having atomic power. Then, soon after the war's end, Russia tested an atom bomb. The thought of Joseph Stalin, a coldblooded tyrant, with an atom bomb was terrifying. (It became still more terrifying when both nations developed hydrogen bombs.)

And there was China. For centuries, China was under the rule of an emperor. In 1911 he was overthrown. So, even before World War II, the Chinese people looked to new leaders. That led to a civil war, with two groups fighting for control of the huge country. One group, led by Chiang Kai-shek, was known as the Nationalists. The others were the communists, led by Mao Zedong.

During the Second World War, most Chinese fought

Congressman Richard Nixon shows off some microfilm, part of the evidence used to convict Alger Hiss (right) of perjury in 1950.

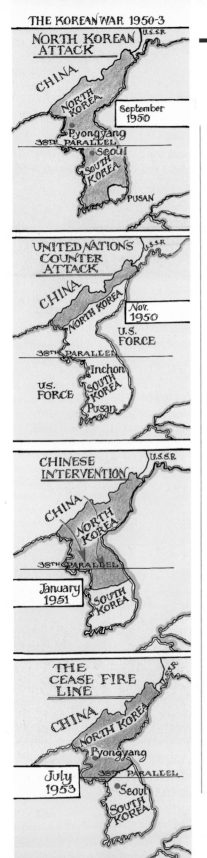

NORTH KOREAN ATTACK

CHINA

NORTH KOREA

September 1950

Pyongyang
38TH PARALLEL
Seoul
SOUTH KOREA

PUSAN

U.S.S.R.

UNITED NATIONS COUNTER ATTACK

CHINA

NORTH KOREA

Nov. 1950

U.S. FORCE

38TH PARALLEL

Inchon
SOUTH KOREA

U.S. FORCE

Pusan

U.S.S.R.

CHINESE INTERVENTION

CHINA

NORTH KOREA

38TH PARALLEL

January 1951

SOUTH KOREA

U.S.S.R.

THE CEASE FIRE LINE

CHINA

NORTH KOREA

Pyongyang

July 1953

38TH PARALLEL

Seoul

SOUTH KOREA

U.S.S.R.

together against their common enemy—Japan. But as soon as the war was over, they were fighting among themselves again. Finally, the communists won. But things didn't work out as most people expected. China's communists brought land reform and some stability to the country, but they also brought unfree totalitarian government. In America, people with loud voices said that Harry Truman was to blame for China's new communist government. (This may not seem to make sense now. Well, it didn't then, either, but some people listened.) Newspapers carried angry letters about China and how "we" lost it.

We had had some unusually well trained China experts attached to our State Department. When those experts predicted that China would fall to the communists, the anti-communists in America didn't want to hear that news. America's China experts were accused of being communists themselves. They were fired, and replaced by others who were strangers to the region. That left us with almost no experts in the difficult years that were to come. Because of poor advice, we would make some bad mistakes in East Asia, especially in a place called Vietnam.

In 1950, however, we acted boldly. Most people think we did the right thing when the ruler of North Korea sent a powerful army into South Korea. Look at the maps and you'll see Korea, the big peninsula that juts out into the sea between China and Japan. Korea was an ancient, independent country. It was divided in two at the end of World

The United States, trying to stop the Chinese Civil War, arranged peace talks with communist leader Mao Zedong (center), American Ambassador Patrick Hurley (behind Mao), and Nationalist leader Chiang Kai-shek in Chongqing in August 1945. The talks failed; the war continued.

War II. It was divided at latitude 38° north, also known as the *38th parallel*. Korea was supposed to be brought back together with free elections. The communists—who controlled the north—never allowed those elections.

The Russian-educated North Korean leader, Kim Il Sung, intended to make all of Korea communist. His army had the latest Russian tanks and equipment.

The leader of South Korea, Syngman Rhee, had been educated in America. His army was poorly trained and badly equipped.

When North Korea's army entered South Korea, it was a test for the world community, and for Truman and his policy of *containing* communism. Led by the United States, the United Nations acted quickly and sent troops. Russia could have vetoed the action but they were boycotting the UN. The Truman administration termed it "police action" and a "confict" rather than a war, setting a precedent that got around the Constituional requirement that Congress authorize war.

To the general public, and those who fought, it was a war, and not an easy one. At first the North Korean army drove the combined forces (South Korean, United Nations, U.S.) all the way to the southern tip of the peninsula. Then General MacArthur's army made a daring landing at Inchon Harbor and the North Koreans were driven back to the North. MacArthur then convinced Truman, who had his doubts, that the UN troops should advance into North Korea but when the soldiers drove almost to the northern border of North Korea and China, that brought communist China into the war. The Chinese sent highly trained, well-equipped troops. The war turned again. It was a terrible situation. We were no longer just at war with Korea. Truman and his advisers feared that this might be the start of World War III. The fighting kept zigzagging back and forth. Everyone had expected a quick war, but now it seemed as if the Korean War would never end.

The American people were jittery and worried. We were fearful that communism would dominate the world. Because of those fears, we did some foolish things at home. We lost faith in ourselves. Some people thought that communists were about to take over the United States. There was no good reason to believe that, but fear often isn't reasonable. So we Americans took part in (or kept quiet during) a communist hunt in the United States. We persecuted some of our own citizens. It was a time of panic—as bad as, or maybe worse than, the "red scare" of 1919 and 1920.

Early in the war, U.N. forces were pushed out of Pyongyang, North Korea's capital, back over the 38th parallel into South Korea.

In 1949, the United States and 10 European nations formed the North Atlantic Treaty Organization (NATO). It was to be an instrument of defense against the threat that they felt the Soviet Union and its eastern European satellite countries posed to the West.

General MacArthur visits the front. Truman eventually fired him for disobeying orders.

McCarthyism, says one dictionary, is "public accusation of disloyalty…unsupported by proof."

8 Tail Gunner Joe

A cannibal McCarthy plans tomorrow's menu: his enemies, the press.

Recently our understanding of the Cold War has changed a lot. When the Soviet Union broke up around 1990, its archives opened to western scholars for the first time. And in 1995 the U.S. government declassified its files on intercepted Soviet spy cables, too. Because of this new information, historians now know that, while McCarthy's "list of 205 names" was a fake, there really *was* a list: a Soviet list of hundreds of paid American spies in the U.S. government in the '30s and '40s. Some scholars believe that Soviet agents exaggerated the number of American spies to impress their bosses in Moscow, and that McCarthy's wave of terror harmed the country much more than any spying. Others say that, though McCarthy was wrong in every detail, he still came close to the truth. By 1950, the Soviets knew the Americans were on to them. Ironically, by the time McCarthy's witch-hunts began, most of the Soviet agents were gone.

He was a liar. Not your ordinary small-time fibber. No, Senator Joseph McCarthy was an enormous, outrageous, beyond-belief liar. Trouble was, some people believed him. After all, no one thought a United States senator would lie.

Of course, most people didn't realize he had lied to become a senator. He said he was a big war hero, a tail gunner who had shot down lots of enemy planes. Actually, he had spent most of the war at a desk job. And he made up stories about his opponent, Wisconsin senator Robert M. La Follette, Jr. Those stories helped him beat La Follette. Washington's newspaper reporters had voted Robert La Follette the best of all the senators; they soon voted Senator Joe McCarthy the worst.

Joseph McCarthy was a man who liked attention. He wanted people to notice him; he needed an issue. What was an issue that would capture headlines? Communism. Some people were afraid that America might become a communist nation. Joe McCarthy would tell them the danger was real. He would scare them. At a speech in Wheeling, West Virginia, he waved a piece of paper and said it contained the names of 205 communists who worked in the U.S. State Department (the State Department runs our foreign policy! Alger Hiss had been in the State Department!).

McCarthy was lying about the list, but many Americans believed him. That was the beginning of McCarthy's witch-hunt. Before he was finished he had accused hundreds of people of communist activity.

He never proved a single case against even one person. But it didn't seem to matter. He was a master of publicity. McCarthy was an exciting speaker. His accusations captured people's attention. Whatever he said got printed in bold headlines. And he knew how to use that new medi-

McCarthy's "list of 205 names" was not the only document he waved in public to scare people. Here he holds up a "report" on Democratic presidential candidate Adlai Stevenson in 1952. McCarthy charged that Stevenson associated with "subversive groups" and supported "the suicidal Kremlin-shaped policies of this nation."

um—television. He was almost like a circus performer putting on a show.

Joe McCarthy wasn't entertaining to the people he accused. They lost their jobs. Some lost their homes. Often their friends deserted them. Their lives were ruined.

The nation was infected with a bad case of anti-communist hysteria. It was sick. What about free speech and the guarantees of the 1st Amendment? Those rights were in trouble. During the McCarthy era, most people were afraid to speak out. It was a time of great fear.

McCarthy wasn't the only one who ignored the Bill of Rights and its protections. The House of Representatives had a committee called the House Un-American Activities Committee. It ruined lives, too. HUAC decided to investigate the movie industry; many people had the idea that artists and actors were likely to be communist sympathizers.

Anyone questioned by the committee might be put on a list, called a "blacklist." People on the blacklist—actors, producers, writers, cameramen—were unable to get jobs in the film industry. Some filmmakers had been members of the Communist Party; some had attended communist meetings, often out of curiosity, or out of Depression-time fear that capitalism was doomed. People called before the congressional committee were asked to name others who had attended those meetings. Anyone named would probably be put on the blacklist. Some writers and actors refused to answer HUAC's questions; many were sent to jail.

To repeat: it was a time of great fear. Ordinary people in America were afraid to buy books, subscribe to magazines, or join organizations that might have the slightest left-wing leanings. Lots of people believed McCarthy's baseless lies. Fear of communism muddied their thinking. But in a free country it is not a crime to hold any kind of belief—and that includes communist beliefs.

The anti-communist extremists wanted to prevent people from reading about communism. They wanted to make it a crime to be a communist. McCarthy made a list of 418 American authors who he said had disloyal ideas. His list included great writers like Ernest

Communism is a philosophy of the extreme left; HUAC and McCarthy represented the extreme right. Sound thinking is usually in the middle.

Hysteria is an exaggerated emotional reaction to fear, horror, or disgust.

When McCarthy's campaign began, the U.S. Communist Party was a legal organization—as it is today. That didn't stop some people from calling communists (and socialists, or anyone politically left-wing) insulting names like "reds" or "pinkos." Some Americans disliked and feared communists because communists do not believe in God. Thomas Jefferson would have defended their right to believe as they did. Writing about religious freedom, he said, "The legitimate powers of government extend to such acts only as they are injurious to others. But it does me no injury for my neighbor to say there are twenty gods or no god. It neither picks my pocket nor breaks my leg."

Anti-communism wasn't limited to the movies. In 1950, Chrysler autoworkers in Los Angeles beat up a fellow worker for refusing to say if he belonged to the Communist Party.

Detest means to loathe or hate.

The real scandal in all this [the McCarthy era] was the behavior of the members of the Washington press corps, who, more often than not, knew better. They were delighted to be a part of his traveling road show, chronicling each charge and then moving on to the next town, instead of bothering to stay behind to follow up. They had little interest in reporting how careless he was or how little it all meant to him. It was news and he was news; that was all that mattered.

—David Halberstam, *The Fifties*

Hemingway, John Dos Passos, and Henry David Thoreau. The State Department removed their books from overseas libraries (which were the only libraries it controlled).

Thirty-nine states passed anti-communist laws. Texas made membership in the Communist Party a crime punishable by 20 years in prison. A Connecticut law made it illegal to criticize the U.S. government or flag. Loyalty oaths were demanded of government workers, including many teachers! The oaths varied—generally the jobholders had to say that they supported the government or were not communists. (Ask your teachers what they think about this.)

If HUAC's members had read the Bill of Rights, they had forgotten what it says. They didn't seem to understand that our Founders had challenged us to do something very difficult: to provide free speech to all, including those whose ideas we detest. Thomas Jefferson and James Madison and the other Founders thought America's citizens should be free to examine any idea, including ideas most people find loathsome. Now that isn't easy at all. You can only do that if you really believe in Jefferson's words that "truth is great and will prevail if left to herself."

Many of our government officials turned cowardly during this time of great fear. Some hated communism so much that they didn't seem to care if people's lives were destroyed. Many really did think the government was full of communists. Others were scared. They had reason to be scared. Two senators who opposed McCarthy were defeated. Eight senators whom McCarthy supported were elected.

But some Americans had courage. Senator Margaret Chase Smith of Maine spoke out in Congress.

> *I think it is high time that we remembered that the Constitution speaks not only of the freedom of speech but also of trial by jury instead of trial by accusation....I am not proud of the way we smear outsiders from the floor of the Senate and...place ourselves beyond criticism.*

Edward R. Murrow, a television newsman (who had broadcast on the radio to America every night from London when it was being bombed during the Second World War), was another with courage and integrity, too. He decided to give the American people a clear picture of Joe McCarthy. Murrow made a TV film that showed the senator yelling

At the Army–McCarthy hearings, McCarthy points to a map purporting to show the location of communists. Joseph Welch (left), the army's lawyer, said later: "Until this moment, Senator, I think I have never gauged your cruelty or recklessness," he said. "Have you no sense of decency?"

at witnesses, belching, picking his nose, and making contradictory statements. Murrow knew he might get blacklisted himself, but that didn't stop him. He said, "This is no time for men who oppose Senator McCarthy's methods to keep silent." Then he added, "We must always remember that accusation is not proof."

McCarthy kept attacking. He accused the U.S. Army and many of its officers and soldiers of being communist sympathizers. But he produced only an army dentist who may, at one time, have been a communist sympathizer. Television (which was a new addition in many American homes) let people see the Army–McCarthy hearings and the senator's shouting, sneering manners.

Most people were disturbed by what they saw. But that didn't stop Joe McCarthy. He went on smearing innocent people.

Then a quiet, elderly man, who was well respected in his home state of Vermont but little known elsewhere, spoke out in the Sen-

Margaret Chase Smith

I Will Not Cut My Conscience to Fit This Year's Fashion

Playwright Lillian Hellman was called before the House Un-American Activities Committee. It was 1952, and she sent this letter to the committee chairman:

Lillian Hellman

Dear Mr. Wood:

…I am most willing to answer all questions about myself. I have nothing to hide from your Committee and there is nothing in my life of which I am ashamed.…But I am advised by counsel [lawyers] that if I answer the Committee's questions about myself, I must also answer questions about other people.…This is very difficult for a layman to understand. But there is one principle that I do understand: I am not willing, now or in the future, to bring bad trouble to people who, in my past association with them, were completely innocent of any talk or any action that was disloyal.…I do not like…disloyalty in any form, and if I had ever seen any, I would have considered it my duty to have reported it to the proper authorities. But to hurt innocent people whom I knew many years ago in order to save myself is, to me, inhuman and indecent and dishonorable. I cannot and will not cut my conscience to fit this year's fashions.…I was raised in an old-fashioned American tradition and there were certain homely things that were taught to me: to try to tell the truth, not to bear false witness, not to harm my neighbor, to be loyal to my country, and so on.…It is my belief that you will agree with these simple rules of human decency and will not expect me to violate the good American tradition from which they spring.…I am prepared…to tell you everything you wish to know about my views or actions if your Committee will agree to refrain from asking me to name other people.…

Sincerely yours,
Lillian Hellman

(?) *Lillian Hellman wrote a book about the McCarthy era and called it* Scoundrel Time. *Who do you think Hellman thought were the scoundrels? Do you agree with her? Do you think there are any scoundrels in politics today? It isn't enough to come up with names—you have to have a good reason for calling someone a scoundrel.*

ate. His name was Ralph Flanders, and he said of Joe McCarthy:

> He dons his war paint. He goes into his war dance. He emits war whoops. He goes forth to battle and proudly returns with the scalp of a pink dentist.

Flanders asked the Senate to vote to censure (condemn) Joseph McCarthy. One senator immediately said that Flanders must be on the same side as the communists.

But by this time most Americans had had enough of Joe McCarthy. Murrow's film had shocked them. Senators began hearing from the voters; most of them were tired of the witch-hunts. The Senate voted on Ralph Flanders's measure: Joseph McCarthy was censured for outrageous behavior. The man who had ruined lives and terrorized much of the nation was disgraced. However, he remained in the Senate. (McCarthy died a few years later from a liver ailment caused by too much drinking.)

Neither the executive branch, nor the legislative branch, nor the judicial branch of our government acted boldly during the time of the communist fear. Later, most Americans were ashamed of the McCarthy witch-hunts. Joseph McCarthy and HUAC made us aware of the preciousness and fragility of our right to free speech.

Freedom of speech is guaranteed by the Bill of Rights. It is your constitutional right as an American citizen. But that freedom to speak out is easy to attack in times of crisis. It takes citizens who appreciate its importance to make sure we keep it as a basic right. And don't forget, the right of free speech also belongs to those whose ideas you hate.

9 Liking Ike

Eisenhower was nominated as Republican presidential candidate at the first national convention covered on TV.

Some people called them "the nifty fifties" and said it was a glorious time. After all, there was a singer named Elvis Presley, the beginning of rock and roll, two new states (Hawaii and Alaska), hula hoops, a movie star named Marilyn Monroe, the Salk vaccine (which prevented polio), and television. TV wasn't new. It had been invented in the '30s. Back then, a Harvard expert said it would never make an impact like radio, because "it must take place in a semi-darkened room, and it demands constant attention."

By 1946, a few people were willing to pay attention. That year 7,000 small, black-and-white TV sets were sold in the United States, and regular programming was under way. By the mid-'50s, more than 5 million TV sets were sold each year. In 1956, videotape was developed. That meant shows could be taped, edited, and rerun. Before videotape, all TV was "live." If an actor made a mistake, everyone saw and heard it.

It took about 30 years for video cameras to be produced cheaply enough for ordinary people to be able to afford them. Until then, people made home movies with small movie cameras.

Two Californians made a plastic version of a bamboo toy that was popular in Australia. By 1958, they'd sold 25 million hula hoops.

By 1949, Americans were buying 100,000 TV sets a week; quiz shows and soap operas were popular. The most watched program by kids under 13 was the cowboy show *Hopalong Cassidy.* Television brought a new audience to professional sports such as baseball, boxing, and football.

49

In 1954, Dr. Jonas Salk prepares to inject a little girl with his polio vaccine. Polio and diphtheria vaccinations almost eliminated those crippling diseases.

Joseph Stalin died in March 1953, two months after Eisenhower took office as president. Many Russians—who didn't know about all the terrible things Stalin had done and all the innocent people he had killed—wept as though their own father had died.

In 1950, 90 percent of America's homes did *not* have TV. By 1960, 90 percent of America's homes did have it. That magic box brought the whole world into living rooms from Honolulu to St. Paul to Miami. TV wasn't just a luxury for the rich; it was very democratic. Everyone had TV: rich and poor, city folks and country cousins. Everyone saw the same events and laughed at the same comedians. It gave us a common culture. But some people asked: what kind of culture is it?

About a third of the children's programs featured crime and violence (although 1950s violence seems tame today). TV became a baby-sitter—it kept the kids quiet—and fewer parents took time to read to their children. Families ate their dinners in front of the TV set, and talked to each other less. Television changed the way politicians campaigned: there were no more Harry Truman whistle-stop train trips. Before long, the candidates—packaged by makeup artists and TV coaches—were coming right into the living room.

But all that was just beginning in 1952, when we elected a new president, our 34th. His name was Dwight D. Eisenhower, and he was immensely popular. People called him "Ike." Eisenhower, an army general, had been Supreme Allied Commander (which means he was head man) in Europe during World War II. He had light blue eyes, a balding head, a grandfatherly manner, and the friendliest grin you can imagine. His campaign buttons said I LIKE IKE—and most people did.

He was so popular that Democrat Harry Truman asked him to run for president. But Eisenhower was a Republican, so he ran against Truman's party. After 20 years of Democratic leadership, Americans were ready for a change. The Democrats had been the party of active government. Franklin Delano Roosevelt was a strong, dynamic president who gathered idea people around him; he brought college professors into government. Harry Truman was naturally combative; he liked to confront problems and make decisions.

Eisenhower's style was very different. He was a conservative,

Marilyn Monroe sometimes played a dizzy, dumb blonde—but she was neither dizzy nor blonde. She was glamorous, her movies were very funny, and Americans loved both.

and most of his advisers were businessmen. He believed the president should be a strong moral leader. But he didn't think he should take sides.

Ike believed in persuasion and patience. He thought the president should act quietly. Eisenhower put a sign on his desk. It was in Latin but, translated, it said: *gentle in manner, strong in deed.* Which was exactly how he tried to be. Eisenhower promised stability, and as little government action as possible. He played golf and always seemed relaxed. His critics called him the "stand-still" president. They thought he was lazy. They were wrong.

Eisenhower worked hard and held the reins of the presidency tightly. But he tried to give the appearance of being above the political battle. He believed in behind-the-scenes leadership. Eisenhower didn't think the president should be controversial. So he didn't speak out against Joseph McCarthy, even when McCarthy outrageously criticized his friend General Marshall. But he did fly to Korea, as he'd promised when he campaigned for the presidency.

Eisenhower wanted to end the Korean War. Sometimes it takes strength to quit a fight. Eisenhower had that strength. He didn't want any more deaths; he didn't want to risk war with China.

President Eisenhower knew the waste of war. He had seen

N NATIONAL CONVENTION

World War II British general Bernard Montgomery said of Ike, "He merely has to smile at you and you trust him at once."

The Latin motto that Eisenhower kept on his desk was *suaviter in modo, fortiter in re.*

Ike balanced the budget, kept America peaceful, and initiated a network of multi-lane interstate highways linking cities.

About 54,000 Americans died in the Korean War. We never officially declared war on Korea and there was no peace treaty.

Blustering Khrushchev

Khrushchev was a boisterous miner's son who once took off his shoe at a United Nations session and banged it on the table to make a point.

Nikita Khrushchev became the first secretary of the Soviet Communist Party in 1953 (we say KROOSH-chev, but the Russian pronunciation is more like hroosh-CHOFF. The *kh* sound is like the *ch* in *chutzpah*—pronounced HOODZ-pah—which Khrushchev had a lot of). He didn't really say "We will bury you" (*see page 53*). The translator got it wrong. Khrushchev actually said something like "We will leave you in the dust." But with all the Cold War hysteria, those wrong words got repeated. Fear was in the air; the arms race took off.

51

As Eisenhower viewed the situation…the possible menace of the Soviet Union took two forms. One was the external threat of Soviet military might. The other was internal—in the sense that the existence of this power…might drive the United States into weakening and eventually destroying its own economy through the indefinite expense of preparedness. What he proposed, therefore, was that the United States should strive for a middle road.

—Robert J. Donovan,
Eisenhower, the Inside Story

it with his own eyes. "Every gun that is made, every warship launched," said Eisenhower, "is a theft from those who hunger and are not fed, from those who are cold and are not clothed."

The Korean War came to an end with a truce. Korea was left divided as it had been when the war began. But the United States and the United Nations had proved what they had set out to prove: they would stand up to communist aggression.

Eisenhower saw a danger ahead for the nation. It was something he was an expert on: military power. In his farewell address he warned of a phenomenon "new in the American experience…an immense

Many liberals felt that Eisenhower didn't seem to care about social problems at home—especially the problems of civil rights, which were becoming hard to ignore. More about that later in this book.

The King

Elvis was called the King of Rock 'n' Roll, and that is exactly what he was. He was a white boy who sang black music with tremendous natural talent and energy. He made it acceptable to white listeners. Elvis said, "The colored folk been singin' it and playin' it just the way I'm doin' now, man, for more years than I know." In terms of popular success, no American musician could touch him. Elvis was polite and lonely; he didn't smoke or drink, but many adults found his performances dangerous. It was the way he danced that upset them most—they'd never seen anything like it. But America's youth fell in love with him. Elvis liked making money and he made a lot of it. But he didn't know how to handle celebrity. All the money and pressure gradually changed the clean-cut young man beyond recognition. Elvis began drinking, overeating, and taking prescription drugs doctors gave him. He died of a drug overdose in 1977 after years of stress.

From 1956 to 1958, Elvis made 14 consecutive million-selling records, starting with "Heartbreak Hotel"—and broke hearts wherever he went.

In 1953 American James Watson (left) and Francis Crick of Britain announced their discovery of the molecular structure of DNA (deoxyribonucleic acid)—the genetic code inside every living cell. The discovery was one of the greatest breakthroughs in the history of science. Here they pose in their Cambridge lab with their model of the DNA molecule.

military establishment and a large arms industry." He called those two groups (the military and the weapons makers) the "military-industrial complex." He was prescient (PRESH-unt or PRESH-ee-unt), which means he was seeing the future.

As soon as Eisenhower was out of office, an arms race began in earnest. It was a contest with Russia to see who could build the most weapons. And Republicans and Democrats jumped on the arms wagon. Both our nation and the Soviet Union spent—and went on spending—vast amounts of capital to build guns, bombs, and missiles. It was a theft from those who hungered and were not fed.

Stalin was dead, and no one in the United States knew quite what to make of the new Soviet leaders. But when Premier Nikita Khrushchev said, "We will bury you," it didn't sound friendly. So most Americans supported the arms race—which meant more and more weapons, more and more military, for more and more money, which put us further and further in debt. We didn't listen to President Eisenhower. He, a former general, had reduced military spending.

Good Times?

The Eisenhower years were prosperous. Jobs were plentiful. People had money to spend. During World War II, there had been shortages of consumer goods. Now you could buy bikes, vacuum cleaners, television sets, dishwashers, ballpoint pens, nylon stockings—almost anything you wanted. For three cents you could mail a letter; for five cents you could buy a Coke or a candy bar. There were no big fast-food chains, although they would come soon enough. (Five cents for a Coke wasn't quite as inexpensive as it sounds. Salaries were a whole lot lower then.)

These were good times.

But not for everybody. Some citizens were kept out of the good times. In the South, blacks couldn't eat in the same restaurants as whites, shop in the same stores, use the same bathrooms, drink from the same water fountains, or go to the same schools. It was humiliating—and unfair. But it was the law. It was all because of a Supreme Court decision, back in 1896, called *Plessy v. Ferguson.* That decision said that as long as facilities were equal, they could be separate. It made segregation legal. But the segregated schools, restaurants, and shops weren't equal; anyone could see that. Even if they were, who wants to be separated? Americans were supposed to be free. How can you be free when you can't go where you want to go?

10 Houses, Kids, Cars, and Fast Food

Thirty million "war babies" were born between 1942 and 1950—and that was just the beginning of the baby boom. These ones were competing in a "Diaper Derby."

What were people watching on their new television sets in the 1950s? The A. C. Nielsen company, which measures TV watching, says that the number-one show for most of the decade was *I Love Lucy* (more about Lucy in chapter 29). Other big shows were *Gunsmoke,* the *Ed Sullivan Show, Dragnet,* the *Jackie Gleason Show, Wagon Train, You Bet Your Life,* and *General Electric Theater.* The host of *GE Theater* was an actor named Ronald Reagan.

Couples had put off having children during the war years—and now they were making up for that. We were having a "baby boom." The war veterans had gone to college under the G.I. Bill of Rights, and the government paid for their tuition. By the '50s, most of those veterans were out of school, married, and having children. Their college degrees helped them find good jobs, usually better jobs than their fathers had ever had (most

Right: Levittown from the air. Every lot measured 60 by 100 feet; every house had 720 square feet.

women—at least middle-class women—didn't work).

Those new families needed places to live, and, in America, every family dreamed of a home of its own. But there was a big housing shortage. What to do? Use some American ingenuity.

William Levitt had it. Before the war, an average builder might build two or three or, at most, five houses a year. Bill Levitt was soon finishing 36 houses a day, which added up to 180 in every five-day week! How did he do it? By analyzing the building process, dividing it into 27 steps, and putting teams of people to work on each step. It was Henry Ford's mass-production idea applied to housing. A team did the same task, over and over, moving from house to house. There were framers and roofers, tile men and floor men, painters who did all the white painting and others who painted all the green. If anyone slowed down, it fouled up the whole production process. Bill Levitt made sure that didn't happen. He began producing his own nails and making his own cement. He even bought timberland in Oregon and cut his own lumber. By doing all that, he kept his house prices very low.

He had thought all this out while he was in the navy, where he was assigned to the Seabees. (They were the navy's builders.) Levitt was commissioned to build airfields, practically overnight. Lives depended on his speed. He analyzed, planned, brainstormed with other Seabees, and built the airfields. Later, he said the navy gave him a chance to experiment and learn how to get things done.

Levitt knew that a lot of veterans like himself would be looking for homes after the war. So he bought a huge tract of land on Long Island (near New York City). It was mainly potato fields. Those fields soon became a community called Levittown. Most of Levitt's houses had four and a half rooms and were exactly alike. They were sturdy, available, and a great value—like Ford's Model T. When the first advertisement for the first Levittown ran in the *New York Times,* people began lining up. In one day alone, Levitt sold more than 1,400 houses. Bill Levitt's ideas were soon copied by other builders. The communities they built were part of something that was about to boom: *suburbia.* Suburbs—on the outskirts of the cities—were springing up around the country. Some had low-cost houses, but others were for the affluent. As people moved out of cities, new people—often poor people—moved in. Cities began losing some of their most productive taxpayers just when they needed rebuilding.

In the new suburbs, where there was no mass transportation, something became essential: a car (or two). Well, General Motors (and the

Hula hoop and Frisbee fads were followed by a rage for 3-D comics that you read with special glasses.

There were suburbs before World War II. But they were mostly pretty communities for the very wealthy. The exodus from the city to modern suburbia was a mass movement.

Hanging out, 1950s style, at the record store (this one was in Webster Groves, Missouri). More listening went on than buying. The uniform (for girls) was pleated skirt, sweater, bobby socks, and saddle shoes.

Two monster symbols for the '50s: a 1957 Chevy Bel Air—whose engine could propel the car at least twice as fast as any speed limit allowed it to go—and an outdoor drive-in movie theater, where you and your sweetheart sat in your car to watch the show.

other auto companies) saw to that. Detroit (the home of the auto industry) began building big, fancy cars. They were status symbols with shiny chrome trim, shark-like tail fins, and seductive shapes. The advertising industry geared up to convince consumers that last year's car, like the hem length on last year's dress, was out of date. Styling changes, not engineering excellence, determined the big sellers. Raymond Loewy, a famous industrial designer, said the showy '50s cars looked like "jukeboxes on wheels."

But American consumers didn't care; they liked jukeboxes. To most people, bigger seemed better. And bigger and fancier seemed best of all. These young '50s families didn't seem to have a problem paying for the new houses and the big cars. We were becoming an affluent nation. In the old days, most workers had toiled for low wages to enrich factory owners. Now, new union contracts were giving auto workers and others a share of their own productivity. They became some of the best customers for the cars and appliances that were rolling out of the factories. And they set the standards for worker pay in other fields, too.

During this same time, oil was replacing coal as our major source of energy. In 1949, Americans used 5.8 million barrels of oil a day; by 1979 we were using 16.4 million barrels. Oil is much more efficient than coal. Getting it doesn't demand exhausting, killing work. (How would you like to dig coal in a coal mine?) And oil was very cheap. (That changed a few decades later.) Oil began driving the economy. It allowed Americans to get into their big new cars and not worry about how much gas they guzzled.

With a family and a car, chances are you'd want to take a trip. Kemmons Wilson, who was a house builder in Memphis, Tennessee, did just that. It was 1951, and he decided to take his family to Washington, D.C., to see the sights.

You know how kids sometimes behave in the car, don't you? Well, the Wilsons' children were no different from anyone else's. Kemmons and his wife couldn't wait each night to get to a motel and relax. But the motels they found were mostly either disappointing or awful—and they charged extra for each child in the room, even though the Wilsons' kids had brought their own sleeping bags!

Kemmons Wilson thought about those motels while he was in Washington, and then he couldn't wait to get back to Memphis. He had an idea

buzzing in his brain. He was going to build motels for families. The motels would all be similar, so people would know what they were getting. They would be clean and attractive. "And," said Wilson, "if I never do anything else worth remembering in my life, children are going to stay free at my motels."

Popular singer Bing Crosby had made a movie called *Holiday Inn.* Wilson thought it a great name for a motel. In 1956, when Congress passed a huge $76 billion federal highway program, Kemmons Wilson and his Holiday Inns were ready for all the traffic those new highways brought.

Cars, suburbs, and TV watching were changing American habits. But some things hadn't changed much. Most American families never went out to dinner. It was too expensive to eat out with the kids—unless it was a very special occasion. Restaurants were apt to be costly, or sleazy. Mothers—especially those suburban moms—were expected to stay home and cook meals.

A lot of working people didn't go out either. They packed lunch in a sandwich bag and brought it to work. Two California brothers were going to change that. They were going to build a restaurant that was fast, clean, and very inexpensive. It was a place where you could feed the whole family and your wallet wouldn't be wiped out.

Dick and Mac (Maurice) McDonald had come to California in the Depression '30s. They wanted to be movie producers. But it didn't happen. So they opened a small movie theater. That folded. Then, in 1940, they built a drive-in restaurant. People stayed in their cars at the drive-in and waiters, called "carhops," came out and served them. The restaurant appealed to families, especially during the war years, when lots of women went to work and didn't have time to cook.

But the McDonald brothers had a passion for efficiency, and cars were lining up. People were waiting to get service. How could they

Kemmons Wilson's first Holiday Inn, in his hometown of Memphis, Tennessee. It opened in 1952; by 1978, Memphis *alone* had 15 Holiday Inns.

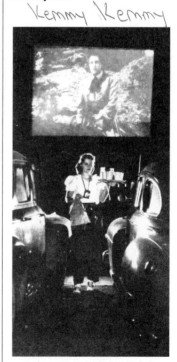

A carhop serves moviegoers at one of the 2,000 drive-ins built between 1947 and 1950.

Dick and Mac's original Mc-Donald's, in San Bernardino, California, in 1955. "We have sold over 1 million," the sign said. What do the McDonald's signs say today?

Suburbia has become the quintessential physical achievement of the U.S.: it is perhaps more representative of its culture than big cars, tall buildings, or professional football.

—Kenneth T. Jackson, *Crabgrass Frontier*

speed things up?

Well, the carhops would have to go. Then the McDonalds looked at their menu. There was too much choice—that slowed things down. And it took time for the customers to put ketchup and relish on their hamburgers. Besides, the condiment stand was always messy. The McDonalds hated mess. They decided to put pickles, mustard, ketchup, and onions right on the hamburgers. That really saved time. Instead of regular dishes and silver they changed to paper plates and plastic forks. That was faster. But what was most important was the way the kitchen was organized. They set up a production line. They even invented and adapted their own kitchen equipment. It was the Henry Ford idea again, this time applied to hamburgers. Grill men cooked the burgers, milkshake men made shakes, dressers wrapped the burgers, and countermen took orders. By the middle '50s, people were lined up to eat burgers at the one Mc-Donald's restaurant; it was in San Bernardino, California. The brothers were rich, and happy. They didn't need any more money than they had.

But some people wanted to open McDonald's restaurants in other places. They wanted to buy franchises (that means they were willing to pay for the McDonald's name and expertise). The brothers didn't want the bother.

One day, Ray Kroc came by. He sold milkshake makers, and he wanted to see why the McDonalds were buying so many of them. He was astounded by what he saw: long lines of people waiting to buy hamburgers. The place was spotlessly clean, the hamburgers were good, and they cost 15 cents. Dick and Mac McDonald were looking for someone to handle their franchising. Kroc was eager. A few years later, he bought the McDonald's name and idea outright. He was on his own and ready to make business history. Kroc was 52 and he had health problems, but that didn't stop him. He was a workaholic and a perfectionist. The McDonald brothers were amazing; Ray Kroc was more so.

He began opening McDonald's hamburger stores one after another. Soon they were ubiquitous (yoo-BIK-wit-us), which means they were everywhere. He wanted the hamburgers he sold in Des Plaines, Illinois, to be exactly like the hamburgers he sold in Willmar, Minnesota, or Kalamazoo, Michigan. He wanted every restaurant to be immaculate and to maintain high standards. He made rules, lots of rules. McDonald's workers couldn't have beards or mustaches, and they couldn't chew gum. He made sure their fingernails were clean. He didn't like to hire women; he thought they would flirt with the customers. He worked very, very hard. Even when he became enormously successful he never put on airs. When the company grew to be huge, with a McDonald's in almost every town and village, and his worth in the hundreds of millions, he still insisted that his executives answer their own phones. No high hats for him, he said. It wasn't money that interested him. "I worked for pride and accomplishment," he said. "Money can be a nuisance. It's a hell of a lot more fun chasin' it than gettin' it. The fun is in the race."

His success was related to the new way of life in America. McDonald's were suburban restaurants, they took advantage of locations on the new highways, and, as more and more women began to get jobs, dinner at McDonald's—or at one of the other fast-food chains that followed—became a regular thing.

Suburbs are small, controlled communities where for the most part everyone has the same living standards, the same weeds, the same number of garbage cans, the same house plans, and the same level in the septic tank.

—Erma Bombeck, humorist

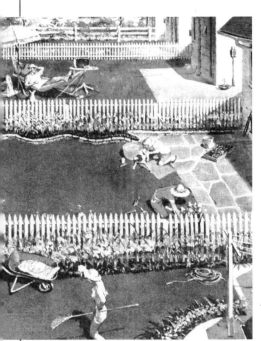

Families lined up to buy identical suburban houses; then they tried hard to make each one as different from the others as possible.

Ah, Suburbia, Happy Suburbia

Nineteen-fifties suburbia—or its image, anyway—was part Hollywood movie, part TV comedy series, and part slick magazine ad. There was Mom (who was pretty), Dad (who was handsome), two kids (who were cute), and Rover (who barked appealingly). A station wagon sat in the driveway. (The garage held a lawnmower, bikes, Dad's workbench, roller skates, the family camping gear, and had a basketball hoop above the door.)

Everyone was white. (Black people couldn't buy houses in Levittown, or most of the other early suburbs. That changed later.) Everyone was young. (Grandma and Grandpa were back in their small hometown, which was getting smaller as young couples moved to suburbia.) All the families earned about the same income. (If they began earning more, they usually sold the house and moved to a fancier suburb.)

Always before, communities had people of all ages to balance each other. In suburbia, children missed having grandparents nearby. And separating the races (blacks in the cities, whites in the suburbs) was not going to lead to harmony between them. Those picture-pretty suburban families were expected to conform; any who didn't felt out of place. Mothers weren't supposed to work—it spoiled the picture. But some women were bored; there wasn't a whole lot to do in the suburbs—except drive the kids here and there. And Dad got to hate the commuting and the highway traffic. Suburbia wasn't perfect, even though the magazine ads made you think it must be.

11 French Indochina

The French first captured Saigon, the capital of Indochina, in 1859. Catholic missionaries had come earlier and converted many Vietnamese to Christianity. The Catholics were persecuted. That was the reason the French gave for invading the country.

Ho Chi Minh's name means "enlightened leader of the Vietminh." He changed his name (from Nguyen Sinh Cung) to reflect his total, lifelong devotion to his country.

There was a beautiful country to the south of China. A country that had been ruled by France for about 100 years. The French called the land *Indochina*. The people who lived there called it *Vietnam* and *Laos* and *Cambodia*. Does that sound unusual, for a Western nation to rule an Asian nation? It wasn't unusual at all in the days before World War II. Britain ruled India. The Netherlands ruled Indonesia. The United States ruled the Philippine Islands. That kind of foreign rule is called "colonialism," or "imperialism."

Imperialism is the policy of expanding a nation by taking other lands. We were imperialists in the 19th century when we grabbed the Philippine Islands.

Women in Vietnam also fought for their country. Here Nguyen Thi Dinh (standing, hatless), a veteran leader, inspects a women's guerrilla unit in 1960.

Most people knew that colonialism wasn't fair. (We had once been an English colony and we hadn't liked it a bit.) Franklin Delano Roosevelt said that nations should determine their own form of government. As soon as World War II ended, we granted independence to the Philippines, but some Asian countries had to fight to become free. India's leaders fought with hunger strikes and nonviolent protests. In Vietnam they fought with weapons.

Vietnam had a leader named Ho Chi Minh. As a young man, he had visited in England, the United States, and France. He knew Western ways. He'd been a poet and a photographer, and he spoke many languages. Back in 1919, he had tried to get President Woodrow Wilson to help the people of southeast Asia gain their freedom. Wilson didn't respond.

When Ho learned of Philippine independence he was encouraged. He wrote eight letters to President Truman asking for help in making Vietnam free. Those letters were never answered. Perhaps Truman never saw them. We don't know about that, but we do know that in 1945 Ho Chi Minh founded the Democratic Republic of Vietnam. Some American military men were present at the independence ceremonies. "The Star-Spangled Banner" was played by a Vietnamese band, and Ho Chi Minh spoke words from the Declaration of Independence. When American planes unexpectedly flew overhead, everyone cheered.

But the French didn't want Vietnam to be independent. France had lost the country when Japanese soldiers invaded during World War II. Now that the war was over, the French wanted their old empire back. Ho Chi Minh stood in the way. Ho was a hero to his countrymen. He had fought against the French and then the Japanese; now he wanted to keep France from controlling Vietnam again.

The French asked the United States to help them fight Ho and his forces (called *Vietminh*). They said Ho was a communist, and he was. He had gone to Russia and studied communism there. He believed in freedom for his country (which didn't necessarily mean freedom for the individuals inside the country).

By the end of 1952, French casualties in Vietnam—dead, wounded, missing, and captured—totaled more than 90,000. The French kept throwing more soldiers against the Vietminh guerrillas. But the war was now unpopular at home in France and couldn't last much longer. Here, French troops flush Vietminh snipers from a jungle thicket in 1953.

Confucius

Traditionally, the Vietnamese were followers of the ideas of Confucius. It is hard for most Western peoples to understand that Confucianism is not a religion in the same sense as Judaism or Christianity or Islam. Confucius said, "I am simply one who loves the past and is diligent in investigating it." Confucius was a teacher who taught *morality,* or the way to a good life. That good way is called Tao (DOW). He found its guidelines by studying the wisdom of the past. Americans and other Westerners do much thinking of the future: about invention and progress. Confucians try to perfect systems that have been tried over time. These are very different ways of looking at the world.

61

ASIANS WIN BACK THEIR INDEPENDENCE

U.S.S.R.

CHINA

NORTH KOREA 1948

SOUTH KOREA 1948

JAPAN

PACIFIC OCEAN

AFGHANISTAN

PAKISTAN 1947

TIBET 1911

NEPAL

TAIWAN

LEGEND:
DATES SHOW YEAR of INDEPENDENCE

FORMERLY

BRITISH

AMERICAN

FRENCH

DUTCH

BANGLADESH 1971

NORTH VIETNAM 1954

INDIA 1947

MYANMAR 1948 (BURMA)

LAOS 1949

THAILAND

PHILIPPINES 1946

Bay of Bengal

SOUTH VIETNAM 1954

CAMBODIA 1953

BRUNEI 1984

NEW GUINEA 1963

SRI LANKA 1948

MALAYSIA 1963

BORNEO

CELEBES

INDIAN OCEAN

INDONESIA 1949

AUSTRALIA

Unlike the other
countries of southeast Asia, Vietnam has always lived in the orbit of China," writes Frances Fitzgerald. For much of its early history, Vietnam was ruled by Chinese warlords. When Vietnam rejected Chinese rule, it kept much Chinese culture. Both China and Vietnam were Confucian countries. In the 20th century, China turned to communism; so did Vietnam.

Ho was an independent kind of communist. His goal was to free Vietnam from all outsiders. He needed help. When the Chinese communists began sending supplies to Ho he was happy to have their aid.

Perhaps if Ho Chi Minh had not been a communist we would have stayed out of the affair, but we soon sent military advisers to help the French. Then we gave France $10 million a year to fight Ho and the Vietminh. That was when Harry Truman was president.

By 1953 (when Eisenhower was president), we were spending $400 million a year to help the French in Vietnam, and before long almost twice that amount. It wasn't enough. The Vietminh kept winning. Vice President Richard Nixon and our top military leaders urged the president to send American bombers to Vietnam. Eisenhower refused.

The French prepared for a major battle. They were confident. They shouldn't have been. Their army was beaten and trapped, and most of the surviving soldiers died in a terrible jungle march. That was more than enough for the French people. They

French motorboats on patrol shortly before final defeat in 1954. At one point the French debated dropping an atom bomb on Vietnam.

showed in elections that they were ready to get out of southeast Asia. And, since France is a democracy, the people prevailed. A peace conference was held in Geneva, in Switzerland. Vietnam was divided into two sections: north and south. The division was meant to be temporary (most of the food-growing regions were in the south).

Ho Chi Minh was the leader of North Vietnam. He was now a great popular hero. After all, he had driven the French out of the country. South Vietnam's leaders were chosen by France. According to the Geneva agreement, elections were to be held within two years to reunite the country.

The elections were never held. The South Vietnamese leaders wouldn't allow them. They knew Ho Chi Minh would win. Soon there was civil war between the communist North and the pro-Western South. (Remember the situation in Korea? Was this the same?)

We were now out of Korea, and many of our nation's anti-communists believed that Vietnam was the place to take another stand against world communism. Those who wanted to send bombers and fighting troops were called "hawks"; those who didn't want to get involved were called "doves."

President Eisenhower said that if we let Vietnam become communist, it would be like watching a row of dominoes fall. The first domino would set off the others. Soon all of Asia would be communist. Eisenhower's advisers were hawks; they urged him to fight. But none of them really understood southeast Asia. Hardly anyone in America did. We'd fired our China experts, who might have helped. Eisenhower was wary. "I'm convinced that no military victory is possible [there]," he said. (Remember that statement. You will read more about Vietnam.)

At Dienbienphu in 1954, the French were trapped in mountain jungles. The Vietminh brought up weapons and supplies along narrow roads, in columns of bicycles like these.

Hidden from sight behind their high hedges of bamboos, the villages stood like nuclei within their surrounding circle of rice fields. Within the village as within the nation the amount of arable land was absolutely inelastic. The population of the village remained stable, and so to accumulate wealth meant to deprive the rest of the community of land, to fatten while one's neighbor starved. Vietnam is no longer a closed economic system, but the idea remains with the Vietnamese that great wealth is anti-social, not a sign of success but a sign of selfishness.

—Frances Fitzgerald,
Fire in the Lake

12 Separate but *Un*equal

"A lawyer's either a social engineer," said Howard University's law-school dean Charles Houston in 1935, "or he's a parasite on society."

Back near the end of the 19th century, Homer Plessy was arrested for sitting in a whites-only railroad car. Was it legal for the railroads to separate the races? What does the Constitution say?

The 14th Amendment says:

No State shall…abridge the privileges…of citizens of the United States…; nor deny to any person within its jurisdiction the equal protection of the laws.

Abridge the privileges—that means take away or limit the rights of citizens. *Equal protection of the laws.* That seems clear. Does keeping people separate on a train abridge privileges? Does it deny anyone equal protection of the laws?

Some Americans weren't sure about that, and they looked to the Supreme Court for guidance. Finally, in 1896, the Supreme Court gave them an answer when it decided Homer Plessy's case. It was an answer that would cause a lot of people a lot of grief. Justice Henry Billings Brown wrote the decision for the majority of the justices. He said that the 14th Amendment called for

the absolute equality of the two races before the law, but…it could not have been intended to abolish distinctions based upon color, or to enforce social…equality, or a commingling of the two races.

Do you understand that? The races were equal before the law, but laws could prevent them from mingling.

Justice John Marshall Harlan disagreed with the majority decision. Supreme Court justices often disagree with each other. The majority rules, but those who don't agree can write their *dissenting opinions*. In that famous 1896 decision, Justice Harlan wrote:

In view of the Constitution, in the eye of the law, there is…no superior,

Black lawyers like Charlie Houston couldn't join the American Bar Association. Does that mean they couldn't get a drink? No, it doesn't. A bar association is a lawyer's organization. *Bar* is another word for the law. The word comes from the railing that encloses the part of the courtroom where the judges and lawyers sit and witnesses are heard.

dominant ruling class of citizens.... Our Constitution is color-blind, *and neither knows nor tolerates classes among citizens.*

But the majority opinion was the one that counted. The Supreme Court said that if facilities were equal they could be separate. The *Plessy* v. *Ferguson* decision made segregation legal in schools, restaurants, hotels, and public places in the southern states. Jim Crow had won the approval of the highest court. Separate but equal was the law.

Some people thought the Supreme Court had made a mistake. Some people thought the decision showed that the justices didn't understand the law of the Constitution. They agreed with Justice Harlan that "our Constitution is color-blind." One of those people was Charles Hamilton Houston. Houston graduated from Amherst College in 1915. He was an officer in World War I. After that, he went to Harvard Law School and got a law degree. Then he got still another college degree: a Ph.D. Even with all those degrees, Charlie Houston knew he had no chance of getting a job with a big law firm. His skin color would be held against him.

But Houston had no intention of working in a big law firm. He had studied law because he wanted to help his people. He believed Jim Crow should be tried, sentenced, convicted, and hanged—and that the courts should do it. So Houston decided that he would become an expert in the law of the Constitution and then train other black lawyers to be experts, too. And that is exactly what he did. He became dean of Howard University's law school. He was a very tough dean.

"He was so tough we used to call him 'Iron Shoes' and 'Cement Pants' and a few other names that don't bear repeating," said a student. "But he was a sweet man once you saw what he was up to."

What he was up to was making sure that his law students were as good as any lawyers anywhere.

"In all our classes," said another of Houston's students, "stress was placed on learning what our rights were under the Constitution...our rights as worded and regardless of how they had been interpreted to that time. Charlie's view was that we had to get the courts to change."

"He made it clear to all of us that when we were done we were expected to go out and do something with our lives," said Thurgood Marshall. Marshall was one of Charlie Houston's best students. He did something with his life—something important.

In 1963, more than 40 percent of Washington, D.C.'s families were African Americans living within sight of the Capitol—and below the poverty line.

"Like an eating cancer," said Thurgood Marshall, "segregation destroys the morale of our citizens and disfigures our country throughout the world."

Jim Crow in the Far North

This restaurant in Juneau didn't just prevent Native Alaskans and Eskimos from eating within its precincts. It made sure they didn't work there, either.

Jim Crow, who stands for legal segregation, had a big residence in the South, but that miserable weasel (who kept a smile on his face to fool people) managed to settle in lots of other places, too.

Alaska was one of them. Alaska? Yes. It was Jim who helped post signs there that said NO NATIVES ALLOWED on restaurants and hotels. And it was Jim who saw that schools were segregated. Whites sent their children to whites-only schools. Eskimos, Native Alaskans (Indians), and Aleuts went to other schools (although sometimes there were no other schools). Lots of nonwhite children just didn't get educated. They were illiterate, which means they couldn't read or write.

And then, because they couldn't read or write, the bigots said they were ignorant, "not civilized," and not fit to be with whites. You can see how frustrating this was for all decent people.

Back in 1905, an Aleut girl, a Miss Jones, wanted to go to the American public school in Sitka. Her father was white. But, since she went fishing with her Aleut grandmother, the judge said Miss Jones was "not civilized," and couldn't go to school.

Congress granted citizenship to all Native Americans in 1924, but that didn't integrate schools or end prejudice in Alaska. Then, during World War II, Americans everywhere began to look at prejudice with opening eyes. It was hard to condemn Hitler's racist policies and accept racism at home. A reporter who visited Alaska in 1943 said that the social position of Indians and Eskimos was "equivalent to that of a Negro in Georgia or Mississippi."

In Nome, the Dream movie theater was segregated. Whites sat in one section, Native Alaskans and Eskimos in another. Alberta Schenck was an usher at the Dream. Her mother was Inupiaq, her father was white, and she hated the idea of segregation. But when she said something about it she was fired from her job. Alberta wrote a school essay about her feelings. She said:

I believe we Americans and also our Allies are fighting for the purpose of freedom. I myself am part Eskimo and Irish and so are many others. I only truthfully know that I am one of God's children regardless of race, color, or creed.... What has hurt us constantly is that we are not able to go to

Despite the cold, foggy weather some Aleut children go barefoot, even to school.

a public theater and sit where we wish, yet we pay the same price as anyone else and our money is gladly received.

"That," said Alberta, was "following the steps of Hitlerism."

A few weeks later, Alberta had a date with a white sergeant from a nearby army base. They went to the movies. They sat in the whites-only section. The manager ordered her to move. "Get over there with the Eskimos!" he yelled.

Native Alaskan and civil rights fighter Elizabeth Peratrovich

"Don't move," the sergeant said. "You're my guest." The manager called the Nome chief of police. The chief grabbed Alberta, pulled her down the aisle, and took her to jail. Alberta Schenck spent the night in the Nome city jail.

Then she wrote Governor Ernest Gruening. She said, "My father was a soldier in World War I. I have two brothers in the army in this war." And she told him what had happened to her at the Dream theater.

The governor (a New Deal appointee) was furious. He said, "I consider it un-American... I deem it contrary to the spirit of our country and directly in conflict with the issues on which this great war is being fought."

Some Alaskans had been working hard to see segregation outlawed. Elizabeth Wanamaker Pera-

trovich and her husband, Roy, were two of those people. They moved to Juneau in the early 1940s, and found they could not buy a house in the part of town where they wanted to live. They were turned away because they were Alaskan natives. Elizabeth, a Tlingit, was president of the Alaska Native Sisterhood. She was determined to get an anti-discrimination act passed. It would make segregation illegal. The bill was defeated when it first came before the legislature in 1943. In 1944, it was defeated again. That was the year that Alberta Schenck spent a night in jail.

Governor Gruening wrote to Alberta and said he would work to see that the anti-discrimination bill was passed in the next legislative session. "If it becomes law, you may be certain that the unpleasant experience which has been yours will not happen again to anyone in Alaska."

But some people were opposed to the bill. Senator Allen Shattuck of Juneau spoke out in the Senate and said:

Far from being brought closer together, which will result from this bill, the races should be kept apart. Who are these

Allen Shattuck, the senator with 5,000 years of civilization behind him

people, barely out of savagery, who want to associate with us whites with 5,000 years of recorded civilization behind us?

Elizabeth Peratrovich was sitting in the Senate gallery. She rose and, in firm tones, answered the senator:

I would not have expected that I, who am barely out of savagery, would have to remind the gentleman with 5,000 years of recorded civilization behind him of the Bill of Rights.

The bill passed the Senate and the governor signed it on February 16, 1945. In Alaska today, that date is celebrated as Elizabeth Peratrovich Day.

Governor Gruening signs Alaska's Anti-Discrimination Act in 1945; Elizabeth Peratrovich is on his right.

13 Linda Brown— and Others

In 1954, segregation was legal if the facilities provided to blacks and whites were equal. This one-room North Carolina schoolhouse (for seven classes) contains a "library," "running water," and "central heating." See if you can find those things in the picture.

Linda Carol Brown—who was seven years old and lived in Topeka, Kansas—had to walk across railroad tracks and take an old bus to get to school, though there was a better school five blocks from her house. Linda couldn't go to that school because she was black and the schools in Topeka were segregated. Linda's father, the Reverend Oliver Brown, didn't think that was right. He went to court to try to do something about it. Their case became known as *Brown* v. *Board of Education.*

South Carolina's Clarendon County spent $43 a year on each of its black students. It spent $179 a year on each white student. The white children all had school desks; in two of the black schools there were no desks at all. Harry and Liza Briggs and 20 other black parents sued the Clarendon County school board. They wanted equal funding for the black schools. They sued in the name of 10-year-old Harry Briggs, Jr., and 66 other children. Right away, Liza Briggs was fired from her job. So were most of the other adults who signed the lawsuit that was titled *Briggs* v. *Clarendon County.*

Barbara Rose Johns, a junior at Moton High School in Farmville, Virginia, was angry about conditions in her school: it had been built for 200 students, but held 450. There was no cafeteria and no gym. The highest-paid teachers at Moton received less than the lowest-paid teachers at Farmville's white schools. A committee of black parents had petitioned the county for a new school and been turned down.

Racism wasn't (and isn't) just a problem of blacks in the South. It is a human problem, and it is found across the land (and across the world too). Racism is the irrational hatred of those who are different from you. Almost every minority group has, at one time or another, suffered the pain of irrational hatred.

Johns decided to act. She had a friend telephone the school principal and tell him he was needed at the bus terminal—at once. Then she called a meeting of all the students. She told the teachers they were planning a surprise event.

She was right; they were surprised. Barbara Johns talked the students at Moton into going on strike for a better school. They walked out of their classes. A member of the National Association for the Advancement of Colored People (NAACP) came to Farmville. He intended to tell the students that Farmville was not the place to fight segregation. But he was so impressed with their determination that he helped 117 Moton High School students sue the state of Virginia. They demanded that the state abolish segregated schools. Their case was called *Davis* v. *County School Board of Prince Edward County* because the first of the students listed was 14-year-old Dorothy E. Davis.

Each of those three cases was defeated in court, but that didn't stop the plaintiffs (those who were suing). They appealed the cases. They appealed them all the way to the United States Supreme Court. There they were grouped with two other cases dealing with school segregation: one from Delaware, and one from Washington, D.C. Together the five suits were called by the name of the first of them: *Brown* v. *Board of Education.*

That case would directly affect all the schools in the 21 states with segregated schools. It would indirectly affect almost every school in the United States. *Brown* v. *Board of Education* was to become one of the most important cases ever brought before the Supreme Court.

Supreme Court cases are not handled like the cases you see on television. The people involved—the schoolchildren, in this case—don't come before the court. There are no witnesses. Lawyers do all the talking. They often spend months—or years—preparing their cases. Then they present their argument to the nine justices. The Supreme Court justices usually ask questions. Sometimes those questions can be answered at once. Sometimes the lawyers have to come back and re-argue the case.

Anyone can attend a Supreme Court session if he or she is willing to stand in line. The court is in Washington, D.C., right near

What does *appealing* a law case mean? Our legal system begins with city and county courts, goes on to state courts and then to federal courts, and, finally, to the Supreme Court. Suppose you go to court and you don't think your trial was fair. You can appeal your case to a higher court. The higher court may reverse the lower court's decision. If it doesn't, you may, in some cases, appeal the case still further, and further, until finally you get to the Supreme Court.

Thurgood Marshall (center) with the lawyers working on the *Brown* case. They practiced their arguments on the students and faculty of Howard Law School.

In 1963, Ben Shahn painted the 1954 Supreme Court justices who handed down the historic *Brown* ruling.

the U.S. Capitol (which is where Congress meets). On December 9, 1952, all the seats were filled in the Supreme Court chamber and 400 people were turned away. That is unusual, but this was an unusual day. The court was ready to consider *Brown* v. *Board of Education*.

The NAACP was representing the children. Charlie Houston was dead, but his star pupil, Thurgood Marshall, the great-grandson of a slave, argued their case. Marshall, a hard worker, was a meticulous lawyer with a good sense of humor. He had argued 15 cases before the Supreme Court—and won 13.

The lawyer Marshall faced was John W. Davis. Some people said that Davis was the best lawyer in America. He had argued more cases before the Supreme Court than any living attorney. Davis had run for president against Calvin Coolidge, and everyone seemed to like him (though he lost the election). King George V of England said John Davis was "the most perfect gentleman" he had ever met. Even Thurgood Marshall liked Davis; they often ate lunch together.

Supreme Court justices do not decide questions of right and wrong. That can sometimes be a matter of opinion. We live in a society based on law. The Constitution is our highest law. The job of the justices is to decide the meaning of the Constitution. Does the Constitution permit segregation? Or does segregation break the rules laid out in the Constitution? That was the question the justices had to decide.

Marshall and the NAACP lawyers presented two arguments: first they argued that the 14th Amendment—which says *No State shall...abridge the privileges...of citizens of the United States...; nor deny to any person within its jurisdiction the equal protection of the laws*—made the doctrine of "separate but equal" unconstitutional. Then they argued that segregated schools can never be truly equal—separating people, of itself, makes them feel unequal and inferior. The *Plessy* decision was wrong, they said.

John Davis looked at the 14th Amendment and the rest of the Constitution. He said that nothing in it prevented separation, as long as equal facilities were provided. Each state, said Davis, has the right to make its own decisions on social matters such as segregation. He believed the *Plessy* decision was right.

In some places integration of schools was very slow; in some places it didn't seem to happen at all. In others, like Louisville, Kentucky, where these children attended school, superintendents made the changeover quite smooth.

This was a very difficult case. The justices asked questions. They took their time. A year passed. It looked as if the court might be split, with some justices saying segregated schools were unconstitutional and some saying they were not. This issue was dividing the country. If the court were to split, it would make those divisions worse. Then something unexpected happened: the Supreme Court's chief justice died. President Dwight Eisenhower named California's former governor Earl Warren as the new chief justice. Warren was a mild-mannered man who was not expected to be a dynamic chief justice. But a few people who knew him well understood that he had a gift for leadership. They also knew that he had a strong moral sense: he believed in justice and fairness.

Finally, the waiting was over. On May 17, 1954, Earl Warren read the decision in *Brown* v. *Board of Education.* Here is part of what he read:

It is doubtful that any child may reasonably be expected to succeed in life if he is denied the opportunity of an education. Such an opportunity…is a right which must be available to all on equal terms.…Does segregation of children in public schools solely on the basis of race…deprive children of the minority group of equal educational opportunities? We believe that it does.…We conclude, unanimously, that in the field of public education the doctrine of "separate but equal" has no place. Separate educational facilities are inherently unequal.

UNANIMOUSLY! The new chief justice had convinced all the justices that, because of the importance of this decision, it should be unanimous (which means they should all agree). It was, as the *Washington Post* said the next day in an editorial, "a new birth of freedom." *Plessy* v. *Ferguson,* a case about a railroad car, had made segregation a fact in almost all phases of daily life in the South.

Speaking Out

Thirteen-year-old Mary Beth Tinker came to school wearing a black armband to protest the Vietnam War. The principal told her to remove it. Mary Beth thought the armband was a form of speech—symbolic speech. She refused to take it off, was suspended from school, and went to court. Her case, *Tinker* v. *Des Moines Independent School District,* went to the Supreme Court. Here is what the court said in its 1969 decision:

School officials do not possess absolute authority over their students. Students in school as well as out of school are "persons" under the Constitution. They are possessed of fundamental rights which the State must respect, just as they…must respect their obligations to the State.

For more on the *Tinker* case, and others involving young people, read Nat Hentoff's *American Heroes: In and Out of School.*

Mary Beth & John Tinker

Third-graders in Wilmington, Delaware, in 1961, seven years after *Brown* v. *Board of Education* was handed down.

(?) **How did** Brown *v.* **Board of Education** *affect schools in your district?*

Brown v. *Board of Education*, a case about schoolchildren, would provide a way to attack segregation—and not just in the classroom.

But the battle wasn't over. Laws have to be enforced, and some people were determined not to enforce this one. Virginia's Prince Edward County closed all its public schools—for *five years*—rather than integrate the schools. White children were educated in "private" white academies funded with tax money (paid by white and black taxpayers). Black children were denied any schooling at all. Prince Edward County wasn't alone in its mean-spiritedness. Most southern communities refused to integrate schools. In Norfolk, Virginia, all public schools were closed for a year. Most children—black and white—didn't have any schools to go to.

It was a difficult time for moderate southern whites. They had always lived with segregation. Strong voices were shouting that the southern world they knew and loved would end if they agreed to integrate their schools. (It was the same message that had been used to defend slavery 100 years earlier.) Those who spoke out against segregation often lost their jobs and friends. Some white people were scared.

Where were the voices of reason? The moderate southern leaders seemed to have gone into hiding. But, remember, these were conforming times. All over the nation, people were keeping silent while others were abused.

In a few areas—especially in the states bordering the North—integration proceeded, usually without incident. White children had no trouble going to school with black children. It was the adults who were creating problems. They were dragging out all the old, tired arguments.

In some places, when black children marched into integrated schools, grownups insulted them, or threw rocks. Because of that new medium—television—everyone, all over the world, could see the rocks and the taunting faces. Decent folks hid their heads in shame. *Brown* v. *Board of Education* may have been a new birth of freedom, but the baby was having a hard time breathing on its own.

Nettie Hunt explains to her daughter Nikie the meaning of the Supreme Court's *Brown* decision, about which the *New York Times* said: *The highest court in the land, the guardian of our national conscience, has reaffirmed its faith and the underlying American faith in the equality of all men and all children before the law.*

Getting Integrated: Two Southern Experiences

In the tiny mountain town of Piedmont, West Virginia, school commissioners integrated schools soon after the Supreme Court's decision. Henry Louis Gates, Jr., who is black, describes how that affected his life:

Less than four years after my birth, something happened that would indelibly mark me and my peers for life—something that would open up another world to us, a world our parents could never have known. Brown v. Board was decided in 1954.

I entered the Davis Free Elementary School in 1956, just one year after it was integrated. There are many places where the integration of the schools lagged behind that of other social institutions. The opposite was true of Piedmont. What made the Supreme Court decision so determining for us was that school was for many years after 1955 virtually the only integrated arena in Piedmont....

We were the pioneers, people my age, in cross-race relations, able to get to know each other across cultures and classes in a way that was unthinkable in our parents' generation. Honest hatreds, genuine friendships, rivalries bred from contiguity rather than from the imagination. Love and competition. In school, I had been raised with white kids, from first grade. To speak to white people was just to speak. Period....

Only later did I come to realize that for many colored people in Piedmont...integration was experienced as a loss. The warmth and nurturance of the womblike colored world was slowly and inevitably disappearing, in a process that really began on the day they closed the door for the last time at Howard School, back in 1956.

Kathryn Harris Morton, who is white, was a schoolgirl in 1958 in Norfolk, Virginia, when her school, like many in Virginia, was closed to all students to prevent integration. This is what she says of that time of "massive resistance":

I was one of the students locked out of classes and one of the 17 children who together successfully sued the governor, the attorney general, and Norfolk's school superintendent, thus ending the lockout.

I remember the Norfolk Committee for the Public Schools...the public rally...the newspaper coverage, the petition we took from door to door asking people to say they favored public education. I remember neighbors saying they would be afraid for their jobs if they put their signatures on such a request....I remember the resounding public silence of Norfolk's business leaders during all the months of the school closing.

November 1958 we had our day before the special three-judge federal court. Our lawyers charged that we were being denied due process and equal protection under the law. There had been a struggle to find a lawyer willing to risk his career by taking so unpopular a case. I remember the threatening phone calls late at night, the eggs thrown at our house, our Halloween pumpkin blown up on our porch, our picture in Life magazine. Neighbor children said, "Why do you bother? Don't you know they'll take care of it?"

And when [the judges] came down with their decision on a point of law, ending massive resistance and opening the schools, the same children said, "See, they took care of it." I remember laughing the next morning to see that the business "leaders" of Norfolk finally had something to say. Now that the battle was decided, they took a full-page ad supporting public education. Leading from the rear is safer than risking those midnight phone threats.

Now, as the story is retold and retold, the "leaders" of Norfolk are airbrushed into the picture of what happened that fall and winter. Doubtless many of those high-minded men wanted to do something when their actions would have made a difference....

Still, I hope the next reporter or historian who plans to write again about the school closing will go look at the [newspaper] coverage at the time. Readers should not be misled into thinking when a public problem arises that individuals don't need to fret themselves, under the delusion that "the leaders" can be counted on to take care of it.

14 MLKs, Senior and Junior

Martin Luther King, Sr., born in Stockbridge, Georgia, became pastor of Ebenezer Baptist Church in Atlanta. Here, in 1975, at age 75, he delivers the last sermon of his 44-year ministry there.

Mike King was a Georgia sharecropper's son who was teased when he went to school because he smelled of the barnyard. "I may smell like a mule," he said, "but I don't think like one." He could handle the teasing—but he couldn't handle his father. The man drank too much and was violent when he was drunk. Mike's mother had saved some money, so she bought him an old car—a Model T Ford—and he headed off to the big city: Atlanta. As he drove away from home, he passed a two-story brick house that belonged to a banker. "I'm going to have a house like that," he said, "and I'm going to be a bank director, too."

King was muscular, energetic, and ambitious, with a zest that attracted people. In Atlanta he worked on the railroad and discovered that what he really wanted to do was preach. So he did that, on Sundays, in small Baptist country churches. Then he learned of a girl, Alberta Williams, who was the daughter

What's in a Name?

Negro, black, colored, Afro-American, and African American are all words used to describe those who are descended, in whole or in part, from people of African origin. Words, like other things, have fashions. Negro was the preferred term for many generations. Today, African American—or black— is most people's choice.

Martin Luther King, Jr., met Coretta Scott in Boston, where she was studying singing. This photo shows them with three of their four children in 1963, the day after an Atlanta school refused to admit their son Martin Luther III (left).

of the leading Negro preacher in Atlanta. She was a student at Spelman College and a talented organist. Before they even met, he decided he would marry her.

In the segregated South, the church was the center of the black world. It was the place where you took your troubles and your heart and found friends and support in an often unkind world. The minister was apt to be the most respected and best-educated man in the black community.

There was no way a rough country boy could marry the daughter of the Reverend A. D. Williams. Why, both her mother and her father had college degrees. Young King couldn't even speak properly. Well, Mike King decided, if it was necessary, he would get an education. So he went to a public school and said he wanted to learn. They tested him and found he was barely ready for fifth-grade work. King was 20. They brought a big desk into the fifth grade and he sat there with the 10-year-olds and did his lessons and worked at night. A few years later he was finished with high school, but that wasn't enough. To be accepted in the Williams family he needed a college degree. So he went to Morehouse College—where the Reverend Williams had studied—took the entrance tests, failed them, and was turned away. But there was no stopping Michael Luther King. He marched into the college president's office, right past an exasperated secretary, told the president he wanted to go to college and that he would work hard and do well, which is exactly what he did. He got a college degree; and he got the girl he wanted; and, eventually, he got his father-in-law's church, and a two-story brick house—and he even became a bank director.

But what he was proudest of was his family. He and Alberta, who was church organist, took their three children everywhere and beamed with pride at their accomplishments. His older son, named for him and called M.L., was a small, wiry, athletic kid who loved to play ball and had lots of friends. When M.L. was five, his father changed their names. Each became Martin Luther King, after the German priest, Martin Luther, who had founded Protestantism.

Martin Sr. and Alberta made sure their son had a good education. They sent him to a laboratory school at Atlanta University, to segregated Booker T. Washington High School, and, at age 15, to Morehouse College. Martin intended to be a doctor. During the summers—they were World War II years—he went off to Connecticut and picked tobacco. There he changed his mind: he would become a minister. His father told the church members that young Martin had been "called by God to the pulpit." But Martin's friends joked

After he grew up and became famous, Martin Luther King, Jr., wasn't often seen laughing in public. But he had a great sense of humor and loved to tell jokes with friends.

King with a portrait of Gandhi, who, he said, taught him that "there is more power in socially organized masses on the march than there is in guns in the hands of a few desperate men."

Captain Charles Boycott was a 19th-century Irish land agent and owner whose tenants got mad when they thought his rents were too high in a time of poor crops. They refused to cooperate with him. Without workers, his land, crops, and animals were useless. Local merchants wouldn't supply him. Eventually Boycott was forced off his land, but his name passed into the English language. To *boycott* something is to refuse to use it or have anything to do with it.

that it was the hot sun of the tobacco field that had something to do with his decision.

Martin Luther King, Jr., chose Crozer Seminary, in Pennsylvania, to study theology—about religion—and he chose well. That small, elite school had white and black students from North and South, some Asian Americans, several American Indians, and students from other lands. It was an astounding mix—unique in its time. For a privileged boy from a protective family, living with all those people was an education in itself.

Martin Luther King, Jr., who had been a cut-up at Morehouse, became the valedictorian—the top student—in his class at Crozer. Books were piled high on his bedroom floor; sometimes he read all night. There he discovered that he had a passion for words and ideas and a talent for public speaking.

At Morehouse, King had read a book by Henry David Thoreau called *Civil Disobedience*. Thoreau believed in the power of nonviolence. He believed in the power of even "one honest man" to create great change in the world.

At Crozer, King learned about India's great leader Mohandas (Mahatma) Gandhi, and that Gandhi had been inspired by Thoreau. Gandhi, a small, skinny lawyer with a squeaky voice, was the honest man Thoreau believed in. He led millions of people in nonviolent boycotts and marches to protest British rule in India. When British soldiers taunted and beat and jailed Gandhi and his followers, they didn't fight back with fists or guns; they just kept peacefully marching and protesting. Gandhi's reasoned courage and calm dignity turned away the guns and cannons of a mighty empire. Gandhi showed the world the power of goodness and right action. India became free. Martin Luther King was fascinated to discover that Gandhi had been full of rage when he was young and had learned to control his anger. King was often angry. Could he teach himself self-control? Could he teach others?

Martin Luther King, Jr.'s new learning seemed to expand his ideas on Christianity and Christian love. In his father's world, Christianity was simple and sure; at Crozer, King found a Christianity that was questioning.

He still wasn't finished with school. After Crozer he went to Boston University for more study and reading and for a Ph.D. (that made him the Reverend *Dr.* Martin Luther King, Jr.). His professors wanted him to become one of them: a teacher and a scholar. But Martin wanted to be a preacher. He had an idea that a minister could do things to make the world better. He wanted to fight injustice. He wanted to lead his people—the black people—because he thought they had a message for all people. Segregation and racial hatred were wrong. Injustice and unfairness were wrong. Social cruelties and meanness hurt everyone (like a worm that turns a good apple rotten).

The more Martin Luther King, Jr., thought about Thoreau, and Gandhi, and about Christian ideas on loving your enemies, the more he began to believe in the power of peaceful protest. When he thought about America's founding idea, that "all men are created equal," he wondered if nonviolent action could be used to actually bring that equality to all people. Could nonviolence overcome the evil of segregation? He knew it wouldn't be easy.

How *do* you face evil?

You can turn away from it, which is the easiest thing to do.

You can fight it with weapons or fists—which is harder, and may hurt or kill people.

The hardest way of all is nonviolence. It means standing up to evil without weapons. It means taking punches and not returning them. Now that takes courage.

Martin had a lot to think about. He wasn't sure how he would lead his people—he just knew that was what he wanted to do. In the meantime, his father was getting impatient. He wanted his son as assistant pastor at his fine big church in Atlanta, Georgia. But Martin Jr. decided he would start his career at a small church in a quiet city. He had no idea that an explosion—called the "civil rights movement"—was about to begin in that quiet city.

It was Montgomery, Alabama, and soon everyone in America would know about it.

"I went to bed many nights scared to death by threats against myself and my family," said Dr. King to his Montgomery congregation. "Then in my kitchen...I heard a voice say, 'Preach the gospel, stand up for the truth, stand up for righteousness.' Since that morning I can stand up without fear." Here, Dr. King delivers a sermon from the pulpit of an Atlanta church in 1967.

To **taunt** is to jeer, tease, and goad with words.

15 Rosa Parks Was Tired

"I handle and work on clothing that white people wear," said Rosa Parks. "This is what I wanted to know: when and how would we ever determine our rights as human beings?"

In America, people accused of a crime do not have to stay in jail before their trial because, according to our laws, people are considered innocent until proved guilty. A judge sets an amount of money, called "bail," that an accused person must pay to get out of jail. Bail is a way of guaranteeing that they will appear in court. The amount of the bail usually varies with the severity of the crime, and whether the accused seems likely to run away. Bail, also called "bond money, is returned at the time of the trial.

The Civil War was fought over an idea. It was property rights *vs.* human rights. Human rights won. But it was only a partial victory. This was another battle in the same war for human rights.

Rosa Parks, who worked as a tailor's assistant in a department store in Montgomery, Alabama, was a small, soft-voiced 43-year-old woman who wore rimless glasses and pulled her brown hair back in a bun. Parks had been secretary of the Montgomery chapter of the NAACP, so she was well known to Montgomery's black leaders. She was also well respected. Rosa Parks was refined and reliable.

But on the evening of the first day of December in 1955, Mrs. Parks was mostly just plain tired. She had put in a full day at her job. She didn't feel well, and her neck and back hurt. She got on a bus and headed home.

In 1955, buses in all the southern states were segregated. Laws said that the seats in the front were for whites, those in the back for blacks. Parks sat down in the section for blacks. Then, when all the seats filled up, the driver asked Parks to stand and give her seat to a white man (that was customary in Jim Crow Alabama). Rosa Parks wouldn't budge. She knew she might get in trouble, she might even go to jail, but suddenly she found herself filled with determination. She stayed in her seat.

The bus driver was filled with rage. He called the police. Rosa Parks was soon arrested and on her way to jail. She knew that blacks were beaten and abused in Montgomery's jail. It didn't seem to matter to her. She was tired of riding on segregated buses. She was tired of being pushed around. She was even ready to go to jail.

When the ministers and black citizens of Montgomery heard of her

Artist Marshall Rumbaugh commemorated Rosa Parks's determination in this painted wood sculpture. "I feel sure we will win in the end," said Parks. "It might take plenty of sacrifice, but I don't think we'll ever again take such humiliating treatment as dished out by bus drivers in this city."

arrest, they were stunned. Of all people—mild-mannered, dignified Mrs. Parks in jail? E. D. Nixon, who had been president of the local NAACP chapter, raised bond money to get her out of jail. But she would have to go on trial for breaking the law—the segregation law.

Rosa Parks knew that some of Montgomery's black leaders (members of the NAACP, and a group of professional women) were trying to find a way to do something about segregation on the city's buses. E. D. Nixon asked her if the NAACP could use her case to fight segregation. They both knew that might put her life in danger. Blacks who stood up for their rights were sometimes lynched (hanged). Parks talked to her husband and her mother. Then she thought a while and said quietly, "I'll go along with you, Mr. Nixon."

As soon as Jo Ann Robinson heard that Rosa Parks had been arrested, she began organizing a boycott of the buses. Robinson felt humiliated and angry each time she had to sit in the back of a bus. She had longed to do something about Jim Crow buses. Now she was ready to act. She decided to ask all Montgomery's blacks to stay off the buses for one whole day as a protest. Robinson and some friends stayed up most of the night (it was a Thursday). They printed leaflets—35,000 of them—telling the black community to keep off the buses the next Monday, the day of Rosa Parks's trial.

Montgomery's leading Negro ministers agreed to support the one-day boycott. In their sermons on Sunday they urged everyone

How she sat there,
the time right inside a place
so wrong it was ready.

That trim name with
its dream on a bench
to rest on. Her sensible coat.

Doing nothing was the doing:
the clean flame of her gaze
carved by a camera flash.

How she stood up
when they bent down to
    retrieve her purse.
That courtesy.

—from "Rosa"
by Rita Dove, 1999

When E. D. Nixon went to get Rosa Parks out of jail, two white friends went with him. They were Virginia and Clifford Durr. Durr, a lawyer, helped the boycott movement, and because of that lost many white clients. The Durrs were not the only whites who sided with the marchers. White minister Robert Graetz's house was bombed. Others lost their businesses or had to put up with insults and threats.

to stay off the buses on Monday. They knew that wouldn't be easy. Those who rode the buses were mostly the poorer citizens. They were people who needed to get to work. Some were elderly. It was December, and cold. Some could find rides, but many would have to walk miles. And they all feared white violence. It was customary to intimidate blacks who tried to stand up for their rights. It was fear that made segregation work.

But something unexpected happened in Montgomery. Like Rosa

Montgomery, 1955: Dr. and Mrs. King are arrested for organizing the bus boycott. "Where segregation exists we must be willing to rise up en masse and protest courageously against it," said Martin Luther King. "I realize that this type of courage means suffering and sacrifice. It might mean going to jail. If such is the case we must honorably fill up the jails of the South."

Parks, most black people no longer seemed afraid. They had had enough. They stayed off the buses on Monday. And also on Tuesday. And then all week. And all month. And on and on, in rain and cold and sleet and through the heat of summer. They stayed off the buses. They shared rides; they worked out elaborate carpools; they walked. Houses were burned, churches were bombed, and shots were fired, but Montgomery's black people stayed off the buses. The jails filled with people whose only crime was riding in a carpool; still the boycott continued.

Rosa Parks is fingerprinted after her arrest. Four days later, she was convicted of violating Montgomery's segregation laws and fined $14. On the same day, the bus boycott began, and all over town black citizens organized carpools to get themselves to work.

Montgomery's black citizens had always thought of themselves as ordinary folk, but they were proof that ordinary people can do extraordinary things. They were lucky: what they were doing was important, and they knew it. They were doubly lucky: they had remarkable leadership. The community had several strong leaders, but one was outstanding.

That leader was a 26-year-old minister, newly arrived in Montgomery, with a pretty, musically gifted wife named Coretta and a two-week-old daughter. He was Martin Luther King, Jr.

When King was asked to lead the boycott, he accepted. He was a beginner—as a minister and a leader—and he didn't know what he would have to do. But he and others found out that when it came to strength and vision and courage, Martin Luther King, Jr., had what was needed.

And so a great leader, a just cause, and an inspiring idea came together at the same time, and made history.

The cause began with Rosa Parks. It was the cause of fairness. Segregation is unfair. Segregation is humiliating. Segregation is wrong.

The idea was nonviolence. King had been considering that idea, and he wasn't the only one. A number of others—black and white—believed Gandhi's methods would work in America. It was King who took the idea, spoke it in powerful words, and inspired others to act on it.

"We are not here advocating violence," he said in Montgomery. "The only weapon that we have...is the weapon of protest...[and] the great glory of American democracy is the right to protest for right." And so, while the segregationists screamed bad words and kicked cars and set off bombs, Montgomery's black community protested with calm, unflinching courage. They didn't scream back. They maintained their dignity. Newspaper reporters began to come

The amazing thing about our movement is that it is a protest of the people. It is not a one-man show. It is not the preachers' show. It's the people. The masses of this town, who are tired of being trampled on, are responsible.

—Jo Ann Robinson, 1955

Ralph Abernathy (left) greets Dr. and Mrs. King just after Dr. King's 1956 conviction for leading the boycott. Nine months later, the boycott over, they boarded the bus together to sit up front. "We are glad to have you this morning," said the bus driver.

They'll find that all they've won in their year of praying and boycotting is the same lousy service I've been getting every day.

—White Montgomery bus rider, December 1956

The boycott over, Rosa Parks rides the bus again—at the front. Why wasn't she riding on that first desegregated bus with the male leaders? Could it be that women weren't taken seriously by most men—white or black? More on that later.

to Montgomery to see what was happening. Television crews came too. Soon people around the nation, and in other nations as well, were watching the people of Montgomery marching. They marched to work; they marched to well-organized carpool centers. When they were arrested, they marched to jail. TV watchers also saw and heard the screamers and rock throwers. And they listened to Martin Luther King, Jr.'s eloquent words:

> There are those who would try to make of this a hate campaign. This is not a war between the white and the Negro but a conflict between justice and injustice. If we are arrested every day, if we are exploited every day, if we are trampled over every day, don't ever let anyone pull you so low as to hate them. We must use the weapon of love.

The weapon of love won the battle. Thirteen months after Rosa Parks's arrest, the Supreme Court ruled that segregation on Alabama buses was unconstitutional. The boycott was ended! Martin Luther King, Jr., E. D. Nixon, Ralph Abernathy (a black minister and boycott leader), and George Smiley (a Texas-born white minister) rode the first integrated bus—and they all sat up front together.

The people of Montgomery not only changed their world, they changed their times.

16 Three Boys and Six Girls

Some white children in segregated schools wanted to try integration. "They don't want you to think for yourself," said one Central High student. "Let us try it. Make the parents go home." But others, like those above, needed to learn about fairness—and about spelling, too.

The fight to see that all Americans—black, white, Hispanic, Asian, female—would be treated fairly was called the **"civil rights movement."** Some of its most important battles were fought by school students.

After the Supreme Court announced its decision in *Brown* v. *Board of Education* in 1954, the court said integration should take place with "all deliberate speed." What does that mean? The southern states decided that it meant with the speed of a snail. So, in the Deep South in 1957, there were still no classrooms where black boys and girls and white boys and girls sat together. Then a federal judge ordered schools in Little Rock, Arkansas, integrated.

Little Rock's Central High School was built in 1928. Some people, then, called it the finest public high school in the nation. Twenty-nine years later, it was still a good school. It had generous playing fields, modern facilities, and more than 2,000 students. But not one black child had ever gone to Central High. In Arkansas, as in all the southern states, laws said that blacks could not go to public schools with whites.

Melba Pattillo wanted to go to Central High. "They had more equipment, they had five floors of opportunities. I understood edu-

> You just realize that survival is day to day and you start to grasp the depth of the human spirit, and you start to understand your own ability to cope no matter what. That is the greatest lesson I ever learned.
>
> —Melba Pattillo

1957 was the year Dr. Seuss published *The Cat In The Hat*, Althea Gibson became the first black athlete to win a tennis championship at Wimbledon, Smith Corona introduced a portable electric typewriter, teenage girls were wearing poodle skirts and teased hair, Dick Clark helped make rock 'n' roll respectable on TV, and nine black students integrated Little Rock High School.

Nine Brave Kids

In 1987, 30 years after they entered Central High, the Little Rock Nine came together for a reunion. Elizabeth Eckford, now a social worker, was the only one who had stayed in Little Rock. Thelma Mothershed was a teacher in Illinois, Terry Roberts a professor at UCLA, Minnijean Brown a writer and mother of six, Jeff Thomas a Defense Department accountant in California, Ernie Green a vice president of a New York investment firm, Carlotta Walls a Denver realtor, Gloria Ray a magazine publisher living in the Netherlands, and Melba Pattillo a communications consultant and author living in San Francisco. Do you think they might have been strengthened by their struggle? The *Chicago Defender* said: "The Supreme Court ruling would have been meaningless had these Negro boys and girls failed to follow the course mapped out for them by the law....They should be applauded by all of us."

The Little Rock Nine pose with Daisy Bates, president of the Arkansas chapter of the NAACP, during their high school years.

When Melba Pattillo got to her English class on her first day of school, "One boy jumped up to his feet and began to talk. He told the others to walk out with him because a 'nigger' was in their class. The teacher told him to leave the room." Melba went on, "The boy started for the door and shouted: 'Who's going with me?' No one did. So he said in disgust, 'Chicken!' and left. I had a real nice day."

cation before I understood anything else. From the time I was two, my mother said, 'You will go to college. Education is your key to survival,' and I understood that." Otherwise, Melba said, she had no "overwhelming desire to go to this school and integrate this school and change history."

But 15-year-old Melba would change history. She was one of nine black children to integrate Central High. At first, she didn't expect problems. Neither did most other people. Little Rock's citizens thought their city had good race relations. But some people in Little Rock decided to fight integration. They used threats, rocks, and nasty words.

Others, who might have shown some courage, kept quiet. Arkansas's governor, Orval Faubus, announced that he would call in the National Guard. Most people thought the guardsmen would protect the black students, but Faubus meant to use them to keep the nine out of Central High. He knew that aiding integration would make him lose white votes. (And blacks weren't able to vote, so they didn't matter to him.)

Later, Melba remembered:

The first day I was able to enter Central High School, what I felt inside was terrible, wrenching, awful fear. On the car radio I could hear that there was a mob. I knew what a mob meant and I knew that the sounds that came from the crowd were very angry. So we entered the side of the building, very, very fast. Even as we entered there were people running after us, people tripping other people....There has never been in my life any stark terror or any fear akin to that.

Melba Pattillo had reason to be afraid. The mob was threatening to hurt her and the other black students. Slim, shy Elizabeth Eckford faced the mob alone. Elizabeth was wearing a starched new black-and-white cotton dress for her first day at school. She had not gotten the message that the black students were to enter school together. So she was by herself, at the opposite end of the building from the others. Elizabeth must have been scared, but she held her head high and tried to walk up to the school door. The guardsmen stared at her. Adults screamed awful words. A woman spat. Some boys threatened to lynch her. Elizabeth ran back to the curb, and a *New York Times* reporter put his arm around her. "Don't let them see you cry," he whispered. A white woman (who was on her side) took Elizabeth home.

Three black reporters weren't as lucky. They were beaten by enraged whites. One of them, Alex Wilson, was a former marine and more than six feet tall. He was hit with a brick and "went down like a tree."

In the nation's capital, President Eisenhower said he didn't want to take sides. He believed in persuasion. But there was no persuading the lawbreakers who stood outside Central High that day and the next.

Finally, the president acted. "Mob rule cannot be allowed to override the deci-

(The story continues on page 87.)

Elizabeth Eckford (below) goes to school. "Around the massive brick schoolhouse," wrote Daisy Bates, "350 paratroopers stood grimly at attention. Within minutes a world that had been holding its breath learned that the nine pupils, protected by the might of the U.S. military, had finally entered the 'never-never land.'" The black students had to leave school under guard, too (above).

Warriors Don't Cry

Many of the words in this chapter were said by Melba Pattillo when she was a teenager. But long after she left Central High, after she had a graduate degree from Columbia University, and after she had worked as a reporter for NBC, Melba Pattillo (who was now Melba Pattillo Beals) wrote a book called Warriors Don't Cry. It is a detailed telling of her extraordinary, and harrowing, experiences.

I arrived at school Tuesday morning, fully expecting that I would be greeted by the 101st soldiers and escorted to the top of the stairs. Instead, we were left at the curb to fend for ourselves....

"Where are your pretty little soldier boys today?" someone cried out.

"You niggers ready to die just to be in this school?" asked another....

I wanted to turn and run away, but I thought about what Danny [a soldier in the 101st Airborne] had said: "Warriors survive." I tried to remember his stance, his attitude, and the courage of the 101st on the battlefield....Early that morning a boy began to taunt me as though

he had been assigned that task. First he greeted me in the hall outside my shorthand class and began pelting me with bottlecap openers, the kind with the sharp claw at the end. He was also a master at walking on my heels. He hurt me until I wanted to scream for help.

By lunchtime, I was nearly hysterical and ready to call it quits, until I thought of having to face Grandma when I arrived home. During the afternoon, when I went to the principal's office several times to report being sprayed with ink, kicked in the shin, and heel-walked until the backs of my feet bled...the clerk asked me why I was reporting petty stuff....

I thought a lot about how to appear as strong as I could as I walked the halls: how not to wince or frown when somebody hit me or kicked me in the shin. I practiced quieting fear as quickly as I could. When a passerby called me nigger, or lashed out at me using nasty words, I worked at not letting my heart feel sad because they didn't like me. I began to see that to allow their words to pierce my soul was to do exactly what they wanted.

Left: September 5, 1957: waiting for the Little Rock Nine. They don't get to register until September 25. "At 9:45 A.M. the Negroes crossed the threshold of school," wrote one magazine that day. But the conflict was not over. Day after day, troops had to enforce the president's orders. "It is time," said one senator, "for the South to face up to the fact that it belongs to the Union and comply with the Constitution."

sions of our courts," he said. Reluctantly, he ordered federal troops sent to Little Rock.

"The troops were wonderful," said Melba Pattillo. "I went in not through the side doors but up the front stairs, and there was a feeling of pride and hope that yes, this is the United States; yes, there is a reason I salute the flag; and it's going to be okay."

Ernest Green remembered the convoy that took him to school. There was a jeep in front and a jeep behind.

They both had machine gun mounts...the whole school was ringed with paratroopers and helicopters hovering around. We marched up the steps...with this circle of soldiers with bayonets drawn....Walking up the steps that day was probably one of the biggest feelings I've ever had.

At the end of that year, Ernest became the first black person to graduate from Central High. "I figured I was making a statement and helping black people's existence in Little Rock," he said. "I kept telling myself, I just can't trip with all those cameras watching me. But I knew that once I got as far as that principal and received that diploma, I had cracked the wall." He was right.

The NAACP lawyers who won *Brown* v. *Board of Education* congratulate each other: George E. C. Hayes, Thurgood Marshall (center), and James Nabrit. Said Marshall: "In some states—where people wanted to integrate but were afraid...they may go ahead now that they see they really have the backing of the federal government."

Knowing Your Place

The TV was the ritual arena for the drama of race. In our family, it was located in the living room, where it functioned like a fireplace in the proverbial New England winter. I'd sit in the water in the galvanized tub in the middle of our kitchen, watching the TV in the next room while Mama did the laundry or some other chore as she waited for Daddy to come home from his second job. We watched people getting hosed and cracked over their heads, people being spat upon and arrested, rednecks siccing fierce dogs on women and children, our people responding by singing and marching and staying strong....Whatever tumult our small screen revealed, though, the dawn of the civil rights era could be no more than a spectator sport in Piedmont. It was almost like a war being fought overseas. And all things considered, white and colored Piedmont got along pretty well in those years, the fifties and early sixties. At least as long as colored people didn't try to sit down in the Cut-Rate or at the Rendezvous Bar, or eat pizza at Eddie's, or buy property, or move into the white neighborhoods, or dance with, date, or dilate upon white people. Not to mention try to get a job in the craft unions at the paper mill. Or have a drink at the white VFW, or join the white American Legion, or get loans at the bank, or just generally get out of line. Other than that, colored and white got on pretty well.

—Henry Louis Gates, Jr., *Colored People*

17 Passing the Torch

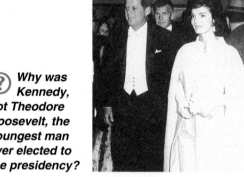

President Kennedy and his wife, Jackie, on their way to the inaugural ball. Her glamour nearly stole the show.

Why was Kennedy, not Theodore Roosevelt, the youngest man ever elected to the presidency?

It had been cold all week in Washington, D.C., and Thursday night—January 19, 1961—snow fell thick and heavy. Washington, southern in its graciousness and geography, handles snow poorly. Everywhere cars stalled and people shivered.

That evening the army and navy were called. Three thousand servicemen, using 700 snowplows and trucks, worked through the night. The next day the wind was mean and the temperature stayed below freezing, but the streets were clear. Wooden bleachers were set up outdoors in front of the Capitol. At noon, when some 20,000 invited guests filled those bleachers, the winter sun reflecting off the banks of new snow seemed unusually bright. It was Inauguration Day.

Most of the presidential party wore scarves and mittens with their top hats and formal clothes. But the president-elect seemed to generate his own warmth—a quality he had in abundance. He took off his overcoat before he spoke. Then John Fitzgerald Kennedy put his hand on his grandfather's Bible and swore to uphold his mighty responsibilities. At 43, he was the youngest president since Theodore Roosevelt and the youngest man ever

The United States is today the country that assumes the destiny of man....For the first time, a country has become the world's leader without achieving this through conquest, and it is strange to think that for thousands of years one single country has found power while seeking only justice.

—André Malraux, French politician and Man of Letters, on a visit to President Kennedy, 1962

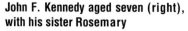

John F. Kennedy aged seven (right), with his sister Rosemary

elected president. Next to him stood 70-year-old Dwight D. Eisenhower, at the time the oldest man ever to be president.

The contrast between the two was as strong as the winter sun. Genial, likable Ike was the son of a poor midwestern creamery worker. But his easy manner was an outside face; inside was a core of steel. Eisenhower had worked his way through an army career to the nation's top job.

Harvard-educated JFK, the patrician son of a wealthy businessman, had been given every advantage our society has to give. But the silver spoons that fed him had not made him lazy. Quite the opposite. He, and the other members of the large Kennedy family, were trained to serve their country, to achieve, and to do their best.

The wind blew as Robert Frost, America's favorite poet, read part of a poem he had written for this occasion:

Summoning artists to participate
In the august occasions of the state
Seems something for us all to celebrate.

And then came lines about *a Golden Age of poetry and power, of which this noonday's the beginning hour.*

A "Golden Age of poetry and power." Would this handsome young president bring it about? There were many who believed he could. Not since the first days of Franklin Roosevelt's New Deal had so many eager people clamored to join the political process. The new cabinet (the president's top advisers) was going to be bipartisan. That meant it would include people from both political parties. Some of Kennedy's college professors were leaving their classrooms to become government officials. Thousands of Americans wanted to be part of the excitement that seemed to be building. It was amazing, the number of people who hoped to work to help their nation. John Kennedy

A Chip Off Old Blocks

John F. Fitzgerald and Patrick J. Kennedy (both sons of 19th-century Irish immigrants) became politicians. Fitzgerald, known as "Honey Fitz," was Boston's mayor. Kennedy, a saloon keeper (that means he owned a bar), was a senator in the Massachusetts legislature. But when he ran for the U.S. Senate, Henry Cabot Lodge, Sr. (an old-guard Bostonian) defeated him. (Lodge had also defeated Woodrow Wilson's dream of an American-supported League of Nations.) Years later, a grandson of Honey Fitz and P. J. Kennedy ran for the Senate against Henry Cabot Lodge, Jr.—and beat him. The new senator was John Fitzgerald Kennedy.

P. J. Kennedy

Honey Fitz

To *clamor* means to agitate noisily for something.

President Kennedy with all the children of the Kennedy clan at the family's summer house in Hyannisport, on Cape Cod. John F. Kennedy, Jr., heads off on his own in the foreground.

A Peace Corps worker teaches English to a group of children in Katmandu, the capital city of Nepal. By 1963, about 5,000 volunteers were doing two-year stints in more than 40 Third World countries.

In 1961 the nuclear submarine *Triton* surfaced after making the first underwater around-the-world trip. *Triton* was named for a god of the sea in ancient Greek mythology. It had taken the sub 83½ days to complete its trip. (That was three days longer than Jules Verne's fictional hero Phileas Fogg took in what adventure book?)

had already suggested a "peace corps," a volunteer agency that would let Americans unselfishly share their experience and knowledge with less fortunate nations.

The young president, with his intense blue eyes, his thick head of hair, and his engaging smile, stepped up to the lectern and began to speak. "We observe today not a victory of party but a celebration of freedom," he said in strong, self-confident New England tones.

Let the word go forth from this time and place, to friend and foe alike, that the torch has been passed to a new generation of Americans, born in this century, tempered by war, disciplined by a hard and bitter peace, proud of our ancient heritage, and unwilling to witness or permit the slow undoing of those human rights to which this nation has always been committed....Let every nation know, whether it wishes us well or ill, that we shall pay any price, bear any burden, meet any hardship, support any friend, oppose any foe to assure the survival and the success of liberty....Let us begin anew... remembering on both sides that civility is not a sign of weakness.

Then he challenged his listeners:

If a free society cannot help the many who are poor, it cannot save the few who are rich.... And so, my fellow Americans, ask not what your country can do for you, ask what you can do for your country.

A Solitary Child

Ecology—which comes from the Greek word meaning habitation—is the scientific study of our home: the earth. Here are some words about a famous ecologist named Rachel Carson.

Rachel Carson was, in her own words, "a solitary child." Brought up in Springdale, Pennsylvania, she spent "a great deal of time in woods and beside streams, learning the birds and the insects and flowers." When she was young, Rachel loved to read and thought she would become a writer. Then she decided to be a scientist, and at first believed that meant giving up writing. But of course it didn't have to mean that at all. She wrote of science and the natural world, and she did it so well that all who read her books gained a new awareness of their environment. Although, at first, no one paid much attention to what she wrote.

Then, in July of 1951, Oxford University Press (see the name on the spine of this book) published Rachel Carson's book *The Sea Around Us*. Oxford didn't expect much in the way of sales. What would you think if you were publishing a book about the ocean? There were hardly any humans in the book; it was all about reefs and islands and sea creatures and coral and sea plants. Would you think many people would read it? Oxford printed a modest number of copies.

The publisher was quickly astonished (and out of books). *The Sea Around Us* became a best-seller—a huge best-seller.

The *New York Times* called it "the outstanding book of the year." Eventually it was translated into 32 languages. It introduced the ideas of ecology and conservation to large numbers of people. It was enormously influential.

By the end of the '60s, at least five state legislatures, alarmed by Rachel Carson's picture of a poisoned world, had banned or limited the use of DDT.

"We live in a scientific age; yet we assume that knowledge of science is the prerogative of only a small number of human beings, isolated and priestlike in their laboratories. This is not true. The materials of science are the materials of life itself. Science is part of the reality of living; it is the what, the how, and the why of everything in our experience," said Rachel Carson.

"It is impossible to understand man without understanding his environment and the forces that have molded him physically and mentally," she wrote. Then she attempted to explain that environment. Here is an excerpt from *The Sea Around Us*:

The Hawaiian islands, which have lost their native plants and animals faster than almost any other area in the world, are a classic example of the results of interfering with natural balances. Certain relations of animal to plant, and of plant to soil, had grown up through the centuries. When man came in and rudely disturbed this balance, he set off a whole series of chain reactions.

Vancouver brought cattle and goats to the Hawaiian Islands, and the resulting damage to forests and other vegetation was enormous. Many plant introductions were as bad. A plant known as the pamakani was brought in many years ago, according to report, by a Captain Makee for his beautiful gardens on the island of Maui. The pamakani, which has light, wind-borne seeds, quickly escaped from the captain's gardens, ruined the pasture lands on Maui, and proceeded to hop from island to island....

There was once a society in Hawaii for the special purpose of introducing exotic birds. Today when you go to the islands, you see, instead of the exquisite native birds that greeted Captain Cook, mynas from India, cardinals from the U.S. or Brazil, doves from Asia, weavers from Australia, skylarks from Europe, and titmice from Japan. Most of the original bird life has been wiped out.

The *Sea Around Us* made Rachel Carson famous; the last book she wrote, *Silent Spring*, brought her enemies (among some powerful interest groups). It took courage to write that book. It was a look at a grim subject—pesticides—and how they were poisoning the earth and its inhabitants. In *Silent Spring*, Carson attacked the chemical and food-processing industries, and the Department of Agriculture.

They lost no time in fighting back. Rachel Carson was mocked and ridiculed as a "hysterical woman." Her editor wrote, "Her opponents must have realized... that she was questioning not only the indiscriminate use of poisons but the basic irresponsibility of an industrialized, technological society toward the natural world."

But the fury and fervor of the attacks only brought her more readers. President Kennedy asked for a special report on pesticides from his Science Advisory Committee. The report confirmed what Carson had written, and it made important recommendations for curtailing and controlling the use of pesticides.

The public, which had been generally unaware of the danger of the poisons sprayed on plants, was now aware. Modestly, Rachel Carson said that one book couldn't change things, but on that she may have been wrong.

Above: John F. Kennedy, Sr., and Jr., in the Oval Office. Below: The new president delivers his inaugural speech, hatless and coatless. His dislike of hats did serious damage to the hat industry.

After the applause, which was long and strong, the new president joined his wife, Jacqueline. "Oh, Jack, what a day," she whispered. And it was. On that bright January afternoon, hope vibrated in the air. Our president was intelligent and graceful and knew how to laugh, especially at himself. He had big dreams that everyone could share. He intended that the nation reach for greatness within itself. He was surrounding himself with men and women who would be called "the best and the brightest." He expected to get things done.

And so, when he noticed in the inaugural parade that there were no black cadets among the Coast Guard marchers, his first act as president was to call an aide and ask him to do something about that. The next September there was a black professor and several black cadets at the Coast Guard Academy.

This man, John F. Kennedy, was determined to be an active president, a good president, a president who would inspire the nation. That wouldn't be difficult for him. Everyone talked of his *charisma* (kuh-RIZ-muh), which the dictionary says is *a rare power given to those persons with an exceptional ability for leadership and for securing the devotion of large numbers of people.*

18 Being President Isn't Easy

When Fidel Castro took over in Cuba, many Americans felt that democracy had a chance. But Castro soon embraced (literally) the Soviet leader Khrushchev.

The small island of Cuba, near Florida, had terrible problems. Its government was corrupt, criminals were making fortunes on the island, and most Cubans were very poor. So when Fidel Castro came along and took charge, in 1959, many Cubans and Americans were hopeful. But when they learned that Castro was a communist—a Marxist-Leninist-Soviet communist—most stopped cheering. Castro did clean up much of the corruption in Cuba, improve the schools, and better race relations. But he was a dictator. The Cuban people were not free to oppose him or his ideas.

Many Cubans fled Cuba for the United States. They didn't intend to stay here. They wanted to go back to their own country and overthrow Castro. Most Americans would have liked that. The idea of a communist nation with ties to Russia sitting 90 miles off the coast of the United States made people in this country very nervous.

As soon as John F. Kennedy became president, he learned that the CIA—the Central Intelligence Agency—had been secretly training Cuban refugees as warriors and planning to land them on the island. The CIA experts said that the Cuban people would then rise up, join the invaders, and throw out dictator Castro. President Kennedy didn't want to seem soft on communism. After Joseph McCarthy, no one did. He told the CIA to go ahead.

The invasion, at a place called the Bay of Pigs, was a fiasco (fee-ASS-ko), which means it was a flop, fizzle, bomb, washout, dud, botch,

The CIA (Central Intelligence Agency) was established by Congress in 1947 and is America's foreign sleuthing operation. CIA agents are apt to be spies, or foreign-intelligence gatherers. During the Cold War, the CIA became very influential, employing thousands of agents overseas and many others at its headquarters in Langley, Virginia (near Washington, D.C.). It spent its large budget without congressional scrutiny. (See what you can find out about what the CIA does today. Do you think we still need a spying organization?)

Can you find out why the Bay of Pigs is so named?

THE CUBAN MISSILE CRISIS, 1962

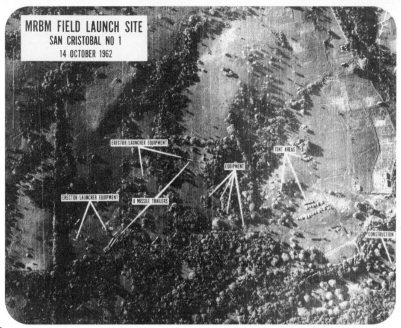

ERECTOR/LAUNCHER EQUIPMENT

TENT AREAS

EQUIPMENT

ERECTOR/LAUNCHER EQUIPMENT

8 MISSILE TRAILERS

CONSTRUCTION

bungle, failure. Nothing worked right. The invaders were captured; the Cuban people didn't rise up; America—and Kennedy—looked foolish.

The young president took all the blame himself. "There is an old saying that victory has 100 fathers and defeat is an orphan," he said. "I am the responsible officer in this government," he added. The American people admired his honesty. His ratings in the popularity polls soared.

But around the world people wondered, "Is he strong enough to be president?" Russia's leader, Nikita Khrushchev, was sure he wasn't. It seemed a good time to bully the United States. Premier Khrushchev decided to do something bold. He decided to put nuclear missiles in Cuba. They would be aimed right at America's most important cities and military targets. Some missiles were already in place when spy planes flying over Cuba brought news that missile sites were being prepared. Then Russian ships were sighted carrying more missiles.

What should the president do? The wrong move could start World War III. Both Russia and the United States had weapons that could destroy the world as we know it.

What would you do? The joint chiefs of staff (our top military leaders) wanted to bomb Cuba. Kennedy said no to his experts. He would not drop the first bomb, but he did announce that American troops were ready to invade the island if the missiles were not removed.

Khrushchev was in a tough spot, too. Castro wanted the Russians to launch a missile at the United States. Khrushchev said no to that. But he did tell the Russian military experts in Cuba that they could use nuclear weapons if there was an invasion.

Kennedy was firm. He said the missiles had to be removed. He gave Khrushchev time to make a decision. Secretly, Kennedy agreed to remove U.S. missiles from Turkey. (Missiles there were a threat to Russia.) For 13 days the world held its breath, wondering if there would be a nuclear war. Then the missile-carrying Russian ships turned around and sailed home. The Cuban missiles were removed. The crisis was over.

But everyone knew that no one could win a nuclear war. Kennedy wanted both Russia and the United States to sign a treaty to stop testing nuclear bombs. We began talking with Russia about disarmament (reducing or doing away with weapons). Then, suddenly, Russia announced

A U.S. U-2 spy plane took this aerial photograph of a medium-range nuclear missile site that was built by the Soviets in Cuba.

The Cuban Missile Crisis began on October 22, 1962, when President Kennedy said ships carrying arms to Cuba would be turned away.

95

The president and his closest adviser, his brother Bobby, during the missile crisis.

A **lobby** is a group that tries to persuade politicians to do what it wants. Some people think lobbies are a danger (most give congressmen money for campaign expenses). Others say that lobbying for your own interests is what democracy is all about.

A left-handed pitcher from Havana University tried out for the Washington Senators (now the Minnesota Twins), but the club turned him down. His name? Fidel Castro. (History is full of "what ifs." What if Castro had become a ballplayer?)

that bomb tests would begin again. Those tests put radioactive particles into the atmosphere—and that poisoned the air. Kennedy appealed to the United Nations. But Russia's tests continued. Finally, Kennedy said that the United States would have to begin testing again. Then he made a great speech at American University in Washington. The president said:

> *Let us reexamine our attitude toward the Soviet Union....The wave of the future is not the conquest of the world by a single...creed but the liberation of the diverse energies of free nations and free men.*

He was telling the Russian people that we needed to work together, not continue as enemies. Some Americans couldn't imagine getting along with Russia. Kennedy spoke to them:

> *Some say it is useless to speak of world peace. I realize that the pursuit of peace is not as dramatic as pursuit of war...but we have no more urgent task....we all inhabit this small planet. We all breathe the same air. We all cherish our children's future. And we all are mortal.*

A few weeks later, Khrushchev accepted the U.S. proposal for a test-ban treaty. "This treaty...is particularly for our children and grandchildren," said Kennedy, "and they have no lobby in Washington."

Meanwhile, things were still a mess in Vietnam. Remember, governments in the north and south were fighting for power. North Vietnam was backed by communist China and communist Russia; we were sending aid to South Vietnam. The North seemed to be winning. President Eisenhower had told Kennedy of the situation, "This is one of the problems I'm leaving you that I'm not happy about. We may have to fight."

President Kennedy wanted to know what was going on. He sent his vice president, Lyndon Johnson, on a fact-finding trip. When Johnson returned, he said the same thing that almost all our military and State Department experts were saying: if we wanted to see the communists defeated we would have to send more money and more supplies and more experts to train the South Vietnamese. So JFK sent the first American troops (called "advisers") to Vietnam. Except for a few lonely dissenters, no one asked if it was right to fight communists in Vietnam. Just about everyone in the early 1960s seemed to think we had to. By 1963 we had 11,000 military advisers in Vietnam; we were spending a million and a half dollars a day supporting that war.

Meanwhile, the struggle for civil rights continued in the American South.

On August 5, 1963, the Soviet premier, Nikita Khrushchev, toasted the signing of the Test Ban Treaty between the United States, the Soviet Union, and Britain.

19 Some Brave Children Meet a Roaring Bull

In 1960, a *New York Times* reporter wrote of Birmingham, Alabama: "Whites and blacks still walk the same streets. But the streets, the water supply, and the sewer system are about the only public facilities they share."

WHITE CUSTOMERS WARNING THIS STORE IS INTEGRATED

Many southern whites felt threatened by integration.

It was hot, very hot, in the summer of 1962 in Birmingham, Alabama. But that didn't seem to make any difference to the city's white leaders. They closed all the city's public recreational facilities because they didn't want to see them integrated. That meant 68 parks, 38 playgrounds, 6 swimming pools, and 4 golf courses were locked up, and no one in Birmingham—kindhearted or mean-spirited, young or old—could enter the parks or swim in the city pools. For the wealthy, there were private pools and clubs, but for most people, there was no escaping the heat.

Birmingham, Alabama's largest city, had plenty of moderate, clear-headed citizens, but the South's moderates were used to keeping quiet. Perhaps they feared mob action, or the disapproval of some of their friends, or the violence of the Ku Klux Klan. The Klan had helped elect Eugene "Bull" Connor as Birmingham's commissioner of public safety (police chief). Connor was about as big a bully as the South has ever produced. Besides that, he wasn't very smart. Bull Connor helped the civil rights movement a whole lot, although that wasn't what he intended to do.

Above: On Good Friday, April 12, 1963, peaceful marchers led by Dr. King gather to conduct an outdoor prayer vigil, in direct violation of a court order. "Freedom has come to Birmingham," they sing. King and 52 others are jailed by "Bull" Connor's police. Below: Armed patrol officers stand by near Birmingham's 16th Street Baptist Church.

Students and a professor stage a sit-in at a segregated Woolworth's lunch counter in Mississippi's state capital, Jackson, in 1963, while white youths drench them with soda, ketchup, and mustard.

When Henry Louis Gates, Jr., applied for admission to Yale University, he wrote: "My grandfather was colored, my father was Negro, and I am black." What did he mean by that? Later, after he'd grown up and become a Harvard professor, Gates wrote in a letter to his daughters, "In your lifetimes, I suspect, you will go from being African Americans, to 'people of color,' to being, once again, 'colored people.'...I don't mind any of the names myself. But I have to confess that I like 'colored' best, maybe because when I hear the word, I hear it in my mother's voice and in the sepia tones of my childhood."

This is what happened: Birmingham's black citizens were marching, protesting, and demonstrating. They wanted the same rights as everyone else. They wanted to be able to eat in any restaurant. They wanted an end to segregation. They wanted to vote. Those were all their civil rights. They were demonstrating peacefully and nonviolently, but Bull Connor threw them in jail.

Martin Luther King, Jr., came to Birmingham, joined the marchers, and he was thrown in jail. Around the nation, people began to be concerned. A southern jail was a dangerous place for a black civil rights leader. King decided to write a letter from Birmingham jail and explain the reasons behind the civil rights movement. He didn't have any writing paper so he wrote on the margins of a newspaper and on toilet paper. He chose his words carefully. His powerful and persuasive letter explained what the marches were all about. He said it was unjust laws.

But Dr. King and the other leaders knew something dramatic was needed to capture the nation's attention. Demonstrators were being sent to jail every day, yet no one was doing anything

Firemen turn high-pressure hoses on Birmingham civil rights demonstrators. "Every channel of communication," said a reporter, "has been fragmented by the emotional dynamite of racism, reinforced by the whip, the razor, the gun, the bomb, the torch, the club, the knife, the mob, the police."

"All you gotta do is tell them you're going to bring the dogs," Birmingham police chief Bull Connor told the press in May. "Look at 'em run....I want to see the dogs work."

about it. Thousands of demonstrators were needed. Most blacks knew they would lose their jobs if they marched. Where could they find thousands of people who would march and not worry about losing their jobs?

In the schools.

"We started organizing the prom queens of the high schools, the basketball stars, the football stars," said Reverend James Bevel. Those student leaders got others interested. "The first response was among the young women, about 13 to 18. They're probably more responsive in terms of courage, confidence, and the ability to follow reasoning and logic. Nonviolence to them is logical....Then [came] the elementary students. The last to get involved were the high-school guys, because the brunt of violence in the South was directed toward the black male."

Bevel had already helped organize a demonstration in Nashville, Tennessee. College students there sat down at lunch counters and politely asked for items on the menu. When they weren't served, because of the color of their skin, they stayed in their seats—until the police took them off to jail. Across the South, black and

The Highest Respect for Law

Martin Luther King, Jr., wrote a letter from the Birmingham jail. He addressed it to eight clergymen—Christian ministers and a Jewish rabbi—who had criticized the civil rights demonstrations and wondered why Dr. King had come to Birmingham. Here is part of what King said.

I am in Birmingham because injustice is here....I cannot sit idly by in Atlanta and not be concerned about what happens in Birmingham. Injustice anywhere is a threat to justice everywhere....What affects one directly affects all indirectly. There are two types of laws: just and unjust. I would be the first to advocate obeying just laws....

One who breaks an unjust law must do so openly, lovingly, and with a willingness to accept the penalty. I submit that an individual who breaks a law that conscience tells him is unjust, and who willingly accepts the penalty of imprisonment in order to arouse the conscience of the community over its injustice, is in reality expressing the highest respect for law.

On Sunday, September 15, 1963, a bomb exploded with the force of 12 sticks of dynamite during Sunday school at Birmingham's 16th Street Baptist Church. On May 22, 2002, a jury found 71-year-old Bobby Frank Cherry—a former Ku Klux Klansman and the last living defendant—guilty of that horrible crime. *Above:* relatives at the funeral of one of the four girls killed by the blast.

white students took part in *sit-ins* at lunch counters. Some people poured ketchup on the students' heads; others hit and kicked them. President Kennedy said, "The new way for Americans to stand up for their rights is to sit down." (But privately, JFK was urging Dr. King to ease up on the confrontations. He didn't want trouble.)

In Birmingham, boys and girls from the high schools, junior highs, and elementary schools wanted to march. "We held workshops to help them overcome the crippling fear of dogs and jails, and to help them start thinking on their feet," said Bevel, who taught the children the ways of nonviolence.

In Montgomery, when a woman was asked why she got involved in the bus boycott, she had said, "I'm doing it for my children and grandchildren." In Birmingham, Martin Luther King, Jr., said, "The children and grandchildren are doing it for themselves."

Some 600 children there marched out of church singing, and Bull Connor arrested them all. The next day another 1,000 children began a peaceful march. Connor called out his police dogs. Firemen turned on high-pressure hoses. The fire hoses were so strong they ripped bark off trees. When the water hit the children they were thrown on the ground and rolled screaming down the street. Television cameras hummed and people, worldwide, saw what was happening to Birmingham's children. Police dogs bit three teenagers so badly they had to be taken to the hospital. A small girl and her mother who knelt to pray on the steps of City Hall were arrested and taken to jail. Seventy-five children were squeezed into a cell built for eight prisoners. They sang freedom songs.

Patricia King was one of the children. She said:

> Some of the times that we marched, some people would be out there and they would throw rocks and cans and different things at us. I was afraid of getting hurt, but still I was willing to march to see justice done.

The Reverend Shuttlesworth was thrown against a wall by the powerful hoses; he had to be taken to a hospital in an ambulance. Bull Connor laughed when he heard that, and said he was sorry it wasn't a hearse.

Can you see why Connor helped the civil rights movement? Decent people were outraged. Most hadn't realized how bad things were for blacks in the segregated South. Now they could see for themselves on TV. In Washington, President Kennedy remembered stories his grandfather Honey Fitz had told him about anti-Catholic mobs who burned Catholic houses in 19th-century Boston. Kennedy knew that racial and religious hatred had no place in America. He asked his brother, Attorney General Robert "Bobby" Kennedy, to work to bring justice to all Americans. Bobby Kennedy would devote much of his energy to that cause.

20 Standing with Lincoln

"We are not going to stop until the walls of segregation are crushed," said King. "We've gone too far to turn back now."

Former Brooklyn Dodger Jackie Robinson with his son at the March on Washington.

The civil rights leaders were human, and so there were rivalries and jealousies. They disagreed among themselves. Those from older organizations, like the NAACP (National Association for the Advancement of Colored People), were at their best working through the courts and trying to change the laws. That was a slow process; it took skilled leadership. The lawyer Thurgood Marshall and the labor chief A. Philip Randolph were that kind of leader.

NAACP

Martin Luther King, Jr., had helped organize the SCLC (the Southern Christian Leadership Conference). Its appeal was to the mass of moderate churchgoing blacks; most of its leaders were ministers. But many young people were impatient with both of these approaches, which seemed too slow-moving. They formed the Student Nonviolent Coordinating Committee (SNCC), known as SNICK. SNCC and the Congress for Racial Equality (CORE) organized many of the sit-ins in college communities.

SCLC

CORE

SNCC

Some black groups wanted to fight with fists, weapons, and anger. Everyone knew that if they

You will never know how easy it was for me because of Jackie Robinson," said Martin Luther King, Jr., to Dodger pitcher Don Newcombe as the two of them ate dinner together one evening. "I never forgot those words," Newcombe remembered later. "It's a shame today when I ask a young ballplayer, or a young black kid I'm counseling on drug and alcohol abuse, who Jackie Robinson was and he can't tell me. It was Jackie and then it was me and Campy [Roy Campanella]....I make sure I talk about Jackie wherever I go. He was my idol, my mentor, my hero."

101

A. Philip Randolph, one of the main organizers of the March on Washington, at the Lincoln Memorial.

"We Shall Overcome" became the anthem of the civil rights movement. The song is said to have originated in the 1940s at Tennessee's Highlander Folk School, where black textile workers gathered together.

We shall overcome,
We shall overcome,
We shall overcome someday.
Oh, deep in my heart,
I do believe.
We shall overcome someday.

A group organized by CORE for the March on Washington gets ready to board the buses. "If I ever had any doubts before, they're gone now," said one marcher. "When I get back tomorrow I'm going to do whatever needs to be done."

got their way, much of the high purpose of the civil rights movement would be lost. Leaders like Martin Luther King, Jr., had made civil rights a cause for all Americans. It was about equality. It was about justice and freedom for all. It wasn't just for blacks—although most of the leadership was black.

For years, A. Philip Randolph had talked of a freedom rally in the nation's capital. Perhaps it would bring the diverse black leaders together. Perhaps it would bring black and white people together. Perhaps it would influence Congress.

President Kennedy had sent a civil rights bill to Congress. Would it be passed? No one was sure. A march would show Congress and the president the importance of the civil rights movement. Many thought that Kennedy was paying more attention to affairs in Cuba and Vietnam than to the problem of unfairness at home. When President Kennedy gave a speech in West Berlin, Germany, about political freedom, it inspired cheers from people around the world. But some Americans weren't enthusiastic. They knew there was a kind of freedom that was missing right here in America—it went straight to the soul and spirit of an individual. The black leaders understood that soul freedom.

Exactly 100 years had passed since Abraham Lincoln signed the Emancipation Proclamation. Some white people were still telling black people to be patient. Martin Luther King, Jr., said, "We can't wait any longer. Now is the time."

Philip Randolph was 74. If ever he was to have his march, it had to be soon. And so it was decided: on August 28, 1963, there would be a march for freedom in Washington, D.C. Black leaders hoped that 100,000 people would participate. The marchers were going to demand four things: passage of the civil rights bill; integration of schools by year's end; an end to job discrimination; and a program of

Bayard Rustin addresses a group of march marshals in New York as they prepare for the march on Washington.

job training. Bayard Rustin, who was a whiz at organizing, was in charge.

Rustin got to work. He had 21 drinking fountains, 24 first-aid stations, and lots of portable toilets set up on Washington's grassy Mall. Workers made 80,000 cheese sandwiches. Movie stars, singers, high-school bands, preachers, and politicians practiced speeches and songs. The speakers and entertainers were to stand on the steps of the Lincoln Memorial and look toward the tall, slender Washington Monument and, beyond that, to the nation's Capitol.

Rustin worried about every detail. He got a big hook and put it on the end of a long stick. Then he gave careful instructions to a helper he called the "hook man." Anyone who spoke too long was to be pulled from the microphones by the hook man.

Two thousand buses headed for Washington, and 21 chartered trains. A man with a freedom banner roller-skated from Chicago. An 82-year-old man bicycled from Ohio. Another, who was younger, came by bike from South Dakota. Sixty thousand whites came. Television crews, high in the Washington Monument, guessed that there were 250,000 people altogether.

It was a day filled with song, and hope, and good will. Finally, in the late afternoon, the last of the speakers stood on the steps of the Lincoln Memorial. It was Martin Luther King, Jr. He began with a prepared speech, which was formal and dignified, as was his nature. Then something happened inside him. Perhaps he responded to the crowd. Perhaps his training as a preacher took over. Whatever it was, he left his written speech and began talking from his heart. *"I have a dream,"* he said.

> *I have a dream that one day down in Alabama...little black boys and black girls will be able to join hands with little white boys and white girls as sisters and brothers. I have a dream today!*

Then he challenged the whole nation, not just those who were marching.

> *So let freedom ring from the prodigious hilltops of New Hampshire, let freedom ring from the mighty mountains of New York, let freedom ring from the heightening Alleghenies of Pennsylvania, let*

W. E. B.

Someone was missing on August 28. He had gone to Africa, discouraged, feeling that nothing like the march could ever take place in America. And yet it was he and his ideas that had helped make the march possible. He was W. E. B. DuBois, one of the best-educated men—of any background—that this country has produced. He was a writer, a thinker, and a spokesman for his people whose masterwork, a book called Souls of Black Folk, had inspired new scholarship in black history. As marchers gathered around the Lincoln Memorial, a whisper went through the sweltering crowd. Minutes before Dr. Martin Luther King, Jr., carried them away with his passionate words, people told each other the news they had just heard: W. E. B. DuBois was dead. Perhaps he was there with them after all.

Less than a year after the march, groups of volunteer workers, black and white, most of them students,

arrived by the busload in Mississippi on the Freedom Summer project. Their mission: to encourage blacks to register to vote. Three of them—James Chaney, a black Mississippian, Jewish New Yorkers Michael Schwerner and Andrew Goodman—disappeared, murdered by the Ku Klux Klan of Philadelphia, Mississippi. The killers were never convicted.

"I have a dream," said Dr. Martin Luther King, Jr. "I have a dream that my four little children will one day live in a nation where they will not be judged by the color of their skin, but by the content of their character. I have a dream today!"

What made King the most powerful and extraordinary black leader of this century was not his race but his morality.

—Shelby Steele

freedom ring from the snow-capped Rockies of Colorado; let freedom ring from the curvaceous slopes of California. But not only that. Let freedom ring from Stone Mountain of Georgia; let freedom ring from Lookout Mountain of Tennessee; let freedom ring from every hill and molehill of Mississippi. From every mountainside, let freedom ring.

And when this happens and when we allow freedom to ring, when we let it ring from every village and every hamlet, from every state and every city, we will be able to speed up that day when all God's children, black men and white men, Jews and gentiles, Protestants and Catholics, will be able to join hands and sing in the words of the old Negro spiritual: "Free at last. Free at last. Thank God Almighty, we are free at last."

21 The President's Number

"Kennedy could grasp an idea as fast as he could deal with figures," said an adviser. "He absorbed ideas voraciously—and...permanently."

The president didn't have much interest in arithmetic, said an aide, although he spent "most of his time counting." What President Kennedy was counting was votes in Congress, and the numbers never seemed to add up. Congress was controlled by an alliance of northern Republicans and southern Democrats. They voted as a bloc—against change. Kennedy, a liberal Democrat, wanted to take the country in new directions. The conservative Congress stood in his way. "When I was a congressman, I never realized how important Congress was. But now I do," moaned the president, with wry humor.

The nation had enjoyed quiet calm during the Eisenhower years. Now Kennedy had action in mind. Besides, after recessions in the later Eisenhower years, the economy needed a shove. And there was that continuing problem of unfairness. Most people thought that the American dream meant that everyone should have a chance to get a good education, to have decent housing, and a job. Some people weren't getting that chance. The president spoke to the American people of a "New Frontier" that would go beyond FDR's New Deal.

Kennedy had legislation that he wanted passed: civil rights bills, tax-cut bills, and health-care bills. There were also bills on equal pay for women, aid to the cities, aid to poor rural areas, manpower training, and a minimum wage. At first, the president was frustrated. Some people called his ideas "socialist." Fear of change, especially in the field of civil rights, caused his popularity to drop way down.

Zipping Around

What does ZIP stand for? Zone Improvement Program. ZIP codes weren't around when Benjamin Franklin was the first postmaster general. The five-digit numbers that tell the post office where your house is began under JFK's postmaster general, J. Edward Day. "The U.S. Post Office was handling more than half the world's mail in 1963," said Day. "Anybody could see that a machine could comprehend the meaning of 70631 easier than it could locate and direct a letter to Anaktuvuk Pass, Alaska." To get people to start using the codes, the singer Ethel Merman recorded a special version of the song "Zip-A-Dee Doo-Dah" from the movie *Song of the South*. It seems to have worked.

Voraciously (vo RAY shus lee) means "hungrily."

A *recession* is a period of decline in economic activity. It is not as bad as a *depression*.

"Dallas is a very dangerous place," Arkansas senator J. William Fulbright told Kennedy before the president left on his Texas trip. "I wouldn't go there." But the crowds greeting the president in Fort Worth were enthusiastic.

Rational means "reasonable" or "sensible."

Bobby Kennedy used these words from Shakespeare's *Romeo and Juliet* to pay tribute to his brother:

When he shall die,
Take him and cut him
    out into little stars,
And he shall make the
    face of heaven so fine,
That all the world will
    be in love with night,
And pay no worship to
    the garish sun.

He seemed, in his own person, to embody all the hopes and aspirations of this new world that is struggling to emerge.
—Harold MacMillan,
Prime Minister
of Britain in 1963

But by 1963, the president saw signs that his ideas were being heard. John F. Kennedy seemed to know how to inspire people. He was optimistic, funny, intelligent, and forceful. Remember that charisma? It was working, and not just with Americans. Premier Khrushchev was blustering around and making loud statements, but later he wrote, "It quickly became clear that he [Kennedy] understood...that an improvement in relations [with Russia] was the only rational course."

In Congress, the numbers seemed finally to be adding up. The president was beginning to count enough votes to pass his bills. And Kennedy believed that the next election might bring him a Congress with even bigger favorable numbers. He expected to win a second term in the presidential elections in 1964. He hoped Congress would support his New Frontier. Except for that situation in Vietnam, things were looking good.

But there was trouble in Texas—political trouble—and Texas's votes would be important in the coming election. The Texas Democratic leaders couldn't seem to get along with each other. So when Vice President Lyndon B. Johnson, a Texan, asked Kennedy to go on a peacemaking mission, the president felt it his job to go.

Kennedy's press secretary got a letter. DON'T LET THE PRESIDENT COME TO DALLAS, it said. TEXAS IS TOO DANGEROUS, the letter writer added. The secretary put the letter aside. Everyone knew there was a group of noisy hatemongers in Dallas, but this president didn't seem to worry. And so, on a day filled with sunshine, he and Jackie waved goodbye to their two children and flew off to the Lone Star State.

Things started wonderfully well. The crowds in San Antonio and Houston and Fort Worth were unusually warm and encouraging. At

Fort Worth, unexpectedly, Kennedy went out into a parking lot and shook as many hands as he could. It bothered the Secret Service men, who were there to protect him, but the president liked contact with people.

Later in the day, when *Air Force One*, the presidential plane, touched down at Love Field in Dallas, thousands of people were waiting to cheer the president and First Lady. Mrs. Kennedy was handed a big bouquet of roses and asters. The weather was so fine and the crowds so enthusiastic that the plastic bubble top was taken off the presidential limousine. The bulletproof side windows were rolled down. Texas's governor, John Connally, and his wife sat in the front seat of the big car; the Kennedys sat behind. They were on their way to a luncheon, and they took the busiest route through the city, so they could see the most people. Crowds lined the streets: a few among them were protesting, but most were cheering. When the car passed an old, seven-story schoolbook warehouse, Mrs. Connally

One witness recalled, "The movements in the president's car were not normal. Kennedy seemed to be falling to his left....There were two more explosions...only seconds after the first....People along the street were scattering in panic."

Jackie, her stockings bloodstained, gets into the ambulance carrying her husband's body away from *Air Force One* after landing in Washington. "I don't think I ever saw anyone so much alone in my life," said Lady Bird Johnson, the vice president's wife.

Above: Mrs. Kennedy with her children and Robert Kennedy during the funeral. It was John-John's third birthday. "I could actually hear people crying above the sound of the drums," said a member of the funeral drum corps. "There was nothing but the muffled drums and the tears."

turned around and said to the president, "You can't say that Dallas isn't friendly to you today!"

But President Kennedy never answered. Two bullets had pierced his head.

For the rest of their lives, most Americans would remember exactly where they were on November 22, 1963, when they heard the news. Again and again, they would stare at their TV screens and see the motorcade, the president falling into his wife's lap, the press at Parkland Hospital, and Jacqueline in her blood-stained suit.

At 1 P.M., John F. Kennedy was pronounced dead. At 2:30 P.M., Lyndon B. Johnson was sworn in as chief executive on *Air Force One*. That plane carried him, and the martyred president, back to the nation's capital. And the world wept.

Lyndon Johnson is sworn in as 36th president of the United States. "He was extraordinary; he did everything he could to be magnanimous, to be kind," said Jackie. "I almost felt sorry for him, because I knew he felt sorry for me."

Ruby's Revenge

Millions were watching on TV as Jack Ruby (right) shot Lee Harvey Oswald (center) on his way to the county jail.

Dallas police capture Lee Harvey Oswald in a movie theater after he shoots a policeman who notices his suspicious behavior. Oswald, who has lived in Russia and Cuba, is charged with the shooting of President Kennedy and Governor Connally (who was wounded). Two days later, going through a jail passageway, Oswald is shot and killed by Jack Ruby, a Dallas nightclub owner. The debate about whether others were involved in JFK's assassination continues to this day.

22 LBJ

LBJ's Texas ranch, near Johnson City, where he grew up, became the "Western White House"; the president would pretend to rope cattle for the cameras.

The new president was big. Taller than six feet three inches, he had big bones, big ears, a big nose, big hands, and big feet. His voice was big, his ego was big, and when it came to his ambition—it was bigger than big. His ambition was colossal.

He wanted to be a great president, right up there with Washington and Lincoln. No, he wanted more than that. He said he wanted to be "the greatest of them all, the whole bunch of them."

Johnson's vice president, Hubert Humphrey, said later:

He was an all-American president. He was really the history of this country with all of the turmoil, the bombast, the sentiments, the passions. It was all there, all in one man, and if you liked politics, it was like being at the feet of a giant.

Johnson's dream was to wipe out poverty in America. He wanted to see blacks, whites, Hispanics—all people—treated as equal citizens. He wanted old people to be cared for. He wanted no barriers to hinder the handicapped. He wanted every child in the country to get a good education. He wanted to see an America where *all men [and women] are created equal.* And he worked for those goals with more energy and political savvy than any president before or since. He understood, as few have, that helping the poor and the disadvantaged would enrich the whole nation.

Lyndon Baines Johnson came from Texas, from the scruffy Hill

Ego (EE-go) is a person's sense of self.

Those LBJ initials were a family thing. The First Lady was Lady Bird Johnson and the president's daughters were Lynda Bird and Lucy Baines.

Turmoil is chaos.
Bombast is big, loud, bragging talk.
Sentiments are thoughts.

LBJ, aged about five

Lyndon's father, Sam Ealy Johnson, in the state legislature in Austin. Father and son's best times together were spent campaigning for Sam's reelection. "We drove in the Model T Ford from farm to farm, up and down the valley, stopping at every door," LBJ recalled.

Country near Austin, a region so isolated when he was a boy that no one had electricity at home, and almost no one had running water indoors, or an indoor toilet. If you wanted to take a bath, or do the dishes, or wash clothes, you had to pump water from a well in the yard, carry it inside the house, and heat it over a fire. At the first school Lyndon went to, all the grades were in one room, with just one teacher. Most of the children didn't wear shoes. But the Hill Country people didn't think of themselves as poor. They had food to eat and roofs over their heads—and they knew and cared about each other.

Lyndon was bright—everyone could see that—but he was a rebellious student. Sometimes he did well; often he didn't. A tutor who was called to help him remembered that he was "Mischievous! That boy was terrible." A cousin said, "Lyndon would always have to be the leader."

From the time he was a little boy it was politics that fascinated him. That wasn't surprising. His mother was the daughter of a Texas secretary of state. His father, Sam Ealy Johnson, served in the Texas legislature.

Lyndon Johnson (middle row, center) with the Mexican-American children of Cotulla, Texas. As teacher he taught the kids to play ball games; he made them speak English in school, and recite and debate and compete in spelling bees. He was very popular with both children and parents. "It was like a blessing from a clear sky," said one pupil later on.

Everyone knew Sam Ealy. He wore a six-shooter on his hip, a cowboy hat on his head, and he tucked his pants into high boots. He was tall, loud, boastful, and sometimes mean. He could also be very loving. His son both feared and adored him.

By the time Lyndon was six he was attending political rallies and handing out pamphlets. When he was 10 he would go with his father to the legislature and "sit in the gallery for hours watching all the activity on the floor." He knew what he wanted to do with his life. "I want to wind up just like my daddy, gettin' pensions for old people," he told a friend.

But when he was ready to go to college, his father was in debt. The family farm had failed. Lyndon borrowed $75 to help pay his expenses. After a year he had to drop out and teach in order to earn money to finish. He taught Mexican-American children that year and saw real poverty—worse than anything he knew. He never forgot those children.

Back at college, he got a job carrying trash and sweeping floors. "He made speeches to the walls he wiped down, he told tales of the ancients to the doormats he was shaking the dust out of," a friend said. Others remembered that he was "always in high gallop," or "clamoring for recognition." It was his energy everyone talked about. He never seemed to stop. If he was asked to do a job, he did double the job. "It pained him to loaf," said another friend. He ended up working as an assistant to the college president, who later laughed and told him, "You hadn't been in my office a month before I could hardly tell who was president of the school—you or me."

When Lyndon Johnson graduated, the college president said, "I predict for him great things in the years ahead." But he had no idea he was talking to a future president of the United States.

When young LBJ first arrived in Washington (right, as a congressional assistant, outside the Capitol), said an observer, he was "tall as a plow horse and slim as a lodgepole; he boasted a slick of black curly hair and a smile as wide as the Pedernales [River]—a very attractive guy so cocksure of himself that he never stopped talking."

When we say, "One Nation under God, with liberty and justice for all," we are talking about all people. We either ought to believe it or quit saying it.

—Hubert H. Humphrey

A ***pension*** is retirement pay or old-age insurance.

111

23 The Biggest Vote in History

FDR and LBJ meet in Galveston, Texas. In the center is Texas governor James Allred; later on he was often airbrushed out of this picture to enhance Johnson's importance.

Some people are born to be preachers and some to be teachers and some to be ball-players. Lyndon Johnson was born to be a politician. He was 29 when he was first elected to Congress, and he set out like a sprinter in a running race. Right away, he arranged to meet President Franklin Roosevelt. Afterward, FDR called an assistant and said, "I've just met a most remarkable young man...this boy could well be the first southern president [in a century]."

As a congressman, Johnson worked 16-hour days and sometimes longer; he expected his aides to work right along with him. That was nothing new for him, but one of his assistants had a nervous breakdown. Naturally, Johnson got a lot done, and impressed some Washington old-timers. One of them recalled, "There was this first-term congressman who was so on his toes and so active and overwhelming that he was up and down our corridors all the time." An-

Andrew Johnson, who was president right after the Civil War, and who also succeeded a martyred leader, was the last southern president until Lyndon Johnson.

[Johnson] said the only power he had was the power to persuade. That's like saying the only wind we have is a hurricane.

—Ralph Huitt, a Senate Committee assistant

Lyndon and Lady Bird. Their Alabaman friend Virginia Durr (see page 80) said: "Bird was a sweet-looking, dark-haired, dark-eyed girl who seemed to adore her husband....She talked very little and let him do all the talking."

other remembered, "This fellow was a great operator....Besides the drive and the energy and the doing favors, which he did for everybody, there was a great deal of charm in this man." All that energy meant benefits for his district. He got the government to help finance slum-clearance projects and low-cost housing in Austin, the state capital. And he insisted that Mexican Americans and blacks have a fair share of the new houses. Money he got for the region helped farmers go from back-breaking horse-and-plow farming to 20th-century farm machinery. He brought electricity to the Texas Hill Country.

Farming wives soon had washing machines. Farming families could turn on the lights. "Of all the things I have ever done," said Johnson 20 years later, "nothing has ever given me as much satisfaction as bringing power to the Hill Country of Texas."

A congressman represents one district in a state. Some states have many congressmen; the number depends on the state's population. But each state has only two senators; each senator represents the whole state. Twelve years after entering Congress, Lyndon Johnson was elected to the Senate. Four years after that, he was elected leader of the Democratic Party in the Senate. A cyclone in the Senate chamber might have been less noticed. When Lyndon Johnson let loose with his never-stop Texas energy, he usually got whatever it was he wanted. But he wasn't all bluster. He knew how to compromise. During the Eisenhower presidency he worked closely with the Republicans. He helped them get bills passed; they helped him get favors for Texas.

President Kennedy's programs had been stalled in the Republican Congress. President Johnson knew how to trade and maneuver and twist arms. He soon began to get Kennedy's programs passed, and then he added his own vision—it extended the New Frontier and the New Deal. He called it the "Great Society." It was a vision of a place where there was no poverty; where all children were well schooled; where health care was a birthright; where jobs and job training were attainable by all. If he could make all that happen—well, he would be the greatest president.

The American people didn't know quite what to make of Lyndon Johnson. Sometimes he just seemed like a big, crude country boy

Johnson (left) at Austin's Santa Rita Housing Project. He fought for federal money to build these apartments, and he won; Austin was one of the first five cities in the country to get FHA (Federal Housing Authority) approval for a new kind of loan issued through the Public Works Administration.

The Great Society is not a safe harbor, a resting place, a final objective, a finished work. It is a challenge constantly renewed, beckoning us toward a destiny where the meaning of our lives matches the marvelous products of our labor.

—Lyndon Johnson, 1965

113

Psychiatrist, scholar, and writer Robert Coles, describing Lyndon Johnson, said that he was "a restless, extravagantly self-centered, brutishly expansive, manipulative, teasing and sly man, but he was also genuinely, passionately interested in making life easier and more honorable for millions of hard-pressed working-class men and women. His almost manic vitality was purposefully, intelligently, compassionately used. He could turn mean and sour, but...he had a lot more than himself and his place in history on his mind."

who had stumbled into the presidency. Some people made fun of him. The Kennedys had served gourmet meals to Harvard professors, artists, and Nobel prize winners in the White House dining room. The Johnsons seemed to be serving Texas chili to politicians.

Johnson was hurt. He wanted everyone to admire and love him. He didn't want to be an accidental president. He wanted to be elected president himself. He soon had that chance. In 1964 he took his ideas to the American people. He ran for the presidency

Johnson worked for years to get the 278-foot-high Mansfield Dam (also called the Marshall Ford Dam) approved. Built between 1937 and 1942, it controls floods on the Lower Colorado River (in Texas) and supplies hydroelectric power, too. The Hill Country, where Johnson came from, was one of the poorest, most isolated parts of Texas. Before the dam, it had no effective electricity. That didn't just mean no lights or refrigerators; it meant no running water, because you needed electricity to pump water. When Johnson got the government to electrify the Hill Country, he changed its farmers' lives.

on his own. He didn't just want to be elected; he wanted the biggest popular vote in the history of the country.

Well, he got what he wanted: the biggest popular vote ever! And he also got a Congress that was Democratic; it would support his programs. Now he had an opportunity few presidents have had. He had that grand vision of a Great Society. He had support from the people to get things done. And he had the ability and energy to make it happen.

The American people had elected him so overwhelmingly that he could be himself. He decided he would wear a gray business suit to his inauguration instead of the traditional top hat, tails, and striped pants. He even danced at his inaugural ball. According to the record books, only two presidents had done that: George Washington and William Henry Harrison. Isaac Stern (a great American violinist) and Van Cliburn (a great American pianist who happened to be from Texas) performed with the National Symphony Orchestra at an inaugural party. At a State Department reception, composers, writers, and dancers were honored. The president was triumphant.

But he had already done something that would tear down much of what he had carefully constructed. He had told the American people and Congress that the North Vietnamese had attacked an innocent American ship in the Gulf of Tonkin. That wasn't quite true, and he knew it. (If you keep reading, you'll hear more about the Gulf of Tonkin—and that untruth.)

"All the way with LBJ" was Johnson's election slogan. He shook so many hands on his 1964 campaign that he had to be bandaged to protect his own bruised, bleeding hand.

January 8, 1964.

President Johnson tells Congress that he is declaring a war on poverty. He outlines a plan that includes aid to Appalachia, youth employment programs, improved unemployment insurance, a domestic Peace Corps, and expansion of the area redevelopment program. Later, his budget puts the cost of the war on poverty at $1 billion. Actual expenditures in fiscal 1964–1965 are slightly more than $600 million. The deficit for that year is the lowest in five years. (A government has a *deficit* when it spends more money than it brings in—from taxes, import duties, etc. What is a fiscal year?)

This administration, here and now, declares unconditional war on poverty in America....It will not be a short or easy struggle, no single weapon or strategy will suffice, but we shall not rest until that war is won.

—Lyndon Johnson, 1964

115

24 Salt and Pepper the Kids

Often, a president's hardest job is making Congress pass the laws and programs he wants. This cartoon portrayed Johnson as a brilliant dealmaker who could get Congress to play any tune he desired.

As new discoveries are made, new truths disclosed…institutions must advance also, and keep pace with the times.

—Thomas Jefferson

Hi-fi is short for high fidelity—meaning true sound reproduction. It was what everybody called stereo systems when they first became popular in the late '50s and early '60s.

In 1721, an English writer named Jonathan Swift wrote a satire. (Swift is the author of *Gulliver's Travels,* and if you haven't read that book, try it. You will like it.) *Satire* is literature that uses wit, humor, and irony to expose wickedness. Benjamin Franklin loved satire, and wrote it, too.

In case you are wondering why an 18th-century English satirist is in a book about 20th-century America, here is the explanation.

England was prosperous in the 18th century. Most Englishmen and women thought they were living in good times. But they couldn't understand why there were so many poor people in England and Ireland. They decided that the poor must be to blame for their own problems.

The same kind of thing happened in 20th-century America. The United States was thriving. We were called an "affluent society." That means we were rich. Many Americans had cars, bikes, television sets, hi-fi sets, and nice houses. But some people were left out. Some people went hungry. They didn't get a fair chance to go to a good school or to get a good job. Were they to blame for that?

What should be done about poverty? That problem was as old as society, and not easy to solve. In 18th-century England and Ireland, many poor families and children struggled and starved. Some, who were convicts, were just shipped off to America. Jonathan Swift suggested something else in his satire, which was called *A Modest Pro-*

posal for Preventing the Children of Ireland From Being a Burden to Their Parents or Country.

What did Swift propose to do to keep poor children from being burdensome? His solution was simple: eat them!

> *A Child will make two Dishes at an Entertainment for Friends, and when the Family dines alone, the fore or hind Quarter will make a reasonable Dish and seasoned with a little Pepper or Salt will be very good Boiled on the fourth Day, especially in Winter.*

Does that sound grisly? Remember, this was satire. Swift wanted to make people think. He wanted them to see how silly some of their ideas were. Jonathan Swift thought something real could be done about poverty, and he wanted to shock people into thinking about it.

Lyndon Johnson also thought something could be done about poverty, and he meant to do it. He intended to build his Great Society. It would take money, the talent to get bills passed in Congress, and the leadership to make Americans understand that ending poverty would make everyone richer.

Johnson revved up his jet-engine personality and blasted away.

It is part of the American character to consider nothing as desperate; to surmount every difficulty by resolution and contrivance.

—Thomas Jefferson

According to the Census Bureau, between 1960 and 1990, poverty was reduced by 39 percent—from 22.2 percent of the nation's population to 13.5 percent. That was still too many poor people, but many fewer than there would have been without anti-poverty programs.

President and Mrs. Johnson tour poor areas of Kentucky during his election campaign. (His own roots were in a poverty-stricken part of Texas.) "Our aim is not only to relieve the symptoms of poverty," he said, "but to cure it, and above all, to prevent it."

In 1964, the 24th Amendment outlawed poll taxes as a requirement for voting in federal elections. Some feared—as this cartoon shows—that the amendment would make it harder to get the Voting Rights Act passed, but in 1965 it was done.

? See if you can find out which of Lyndon Johnson's agencies and programs still exist. You could start on the Internet.

Rosemary Bray

grew up in Chicago on welfare. But her mother made her children study and she helped them do well in school. Rosemary got a scholarship to Yale University, graduated in 1976, and became a writer. She says that her mother, and the anti-poverty programs started by LBJ, saved her from a life of penury, which is exactly what they were supposed to do.

The Civil Rights Act of 1964 was passed—it outlawed most discrimination, helping women as well as minorities. *Headstart* helped little children prepare for kindergarten. The *Job Corps* found work for school dropouts. *Upward Bound* helped needy children go to college. The *Neighborhood Youth Corps* trained unemployed teenagers. The *Teacher Corps* trained schoolteachers. *Medicare* helped old people pay their hospital bills. *Medicaid* helped those without much money afford a doctor.

Johnson went to the Statue of Liberty to sign a bill that ended narrow, racist immigration quotas. Because of an immigration bill passed early in the century, only people from some privileged regions, like western Europe, were able to come to the United States in large numbers. Just a few from other regions—Asia, for instance—were allowed to enter and become citizens. Johnson's new law let new groups of immigrants (especially Asians and Latinos) broaden the American family.

The president began beautification programs and environmental-protection programs. Congress and the president worked together. FDR had accomplished a lot during his first 100 days in the presidency; Johnson got even more laws passed.

All the new programs cost money. But we had the money. We were a rich nation. Johnson knew that. We could afford the Great Society. We could afford the war on poverty—until something else began taking most of our money. That was the war in southeast Asia.

American soldiers were now fighting in Vietnam. But things weren't going the way we hoped they would go. North Vietnam was fighting back. That little nation didn't seem to be frightened by America's power.

Being president had turned out to be harder than Lyndon Johnson expected it to be. His

Johnson had a great sense of drama. He signed his immigration bill beneath the Statue of Liberty; he signed an education bill in the one-room schoolhouse he had attended; he signed the Voting Rights Act in the Rotunda of the Capitol in Washington.

"I do not find it easy to send our finest young men into battle," said LBJ about Vietnam. But he sent them anyway. Meanwhile, more and more people were turning against the war, and the war's ever increasing cost was making it hard to pay for Johnson's domestic reforms.

military and political advisers kept telling him to send more men and more weapons to Vietnam. But some of America's citizens were saying that the war was a mistake. They thought we needed to quit the war. Johnson didn't like that advice at all; he didn't want to be a quitter.

And then there was the black community. President Johnson thought that African-American people, and other minorities, would be thrilled with the Great Society programs. They were pleased. But they weren't satisfied; they wanted more. They wanted what everyone else had. They wanted to be equal partners in America. Why, they even wanted to vote!

When it came to voting, Lyndon Johnson asked the black leaders to be patient. He explained that it wouldn't be easy to get a voting act through Congress. Change would have to come one step at a time, he said. But some people were fed up with being patient.

Hey, hey, LBJ,
how many kids
did you kill today?

—anti-war chant

By 1967, the Vietnam War was costing the country $70 million a day.

LBJ's presidency began with the support of civil rights leaders such as Martin Luther King, Jr. (right), who said, "We're on our way to a Great Society." But the war eventually drove them apart.

25 A King Gets a Prize and Goes to Jail

Nobel Prizes are awarded each year in Sweden for outstanding achievement in physics, chemistry, physiology, medicine, economics, and literature. But the prize that usually gets the most attention is the peace prize, given for work promoting international peace. Many consider the Nobels the most prestigious prizes that there are. They include a gold medal and a substantial sum of money as well as great acclaim.

Here are the names of a few Nobel winners. Can you find out who they are and what their awards were for?

Rabindranath Tagore, Rudyard Kipling, Albert Einstein, Max Planck, Thomas Mann, Sinclair Lewis, Luigi Pirandello, Eugene O'Neill, Harold Urey, Pearl Buck, William Faulkner, Par Lagerkvist, Boris Pasternak, Ernest Hemingway, Juan Ramón Jimenez, Albert Schweitzer, Linus Pauling, Isaac Bashevis Singer, the Dalai Lama, Paul Samuelson, Andrei Sakharov, James Watson, Francis Crick, Joseph Brodsky, Mother Teresa, S. A. Waksman, Elie Wiesel, Gabriel Garcia Marquéz, Steven Weinberg, Nelson Mandela, Saul Bellow, Derek Walcott, Mikhail Gorbachev, Toni Morrison.

(see page 281 for more on Alfred Nobel and his prizes)

"Nonviolence is the answer to the crucial political and moral questions of our time," said Martin Luther King, Jr., in his Nobel acceptance speech.

Martin Luther King, Jr., was in the hospital. He wasn't seriously ill; it was a case of exhaustion. It was Tuesday, and he'd given three speeches on Sunday and two on Monday, and then there were all those trips to jail, and the marches, and the pressures. But when the phone rang he felt a whole lot better. Matter of fact, he felt great.

His wife, Coretta, had big news: Martin had been awarded the Nobel Peace Prize. That prize is given each year to the person, from anywhere in the world, who has contributed most to peace. Along with the great honor, there is a sizable cash award. Theodore Roosevelt had won the Nobel Peace Prize, and so had Woodrow Wilson and Jane Addams. Martin Luther King, Jr., at 35, was the youngest person ever to receive it.

Some Americans were furious, and they wrote to the Nobel committee in Sweden and told them so. Bull Connor said, "They're scraping the bottom of the barrel." Some racists called it a communist plot. But most Americans were proud. Newspaper columnist Ralph McGill, writing in the *Atlanta Constitution*, said Europeans understood King better than most Americans; they saw in him "the American promise," with its message for the whole world.

King flew to Europe to receive the Peace Prize. He invited his parents and his wife and Bayard Rustin and Ralph Abernathy—25 friends in all—to go with him. In England, he gave a sermon at London's most famous church, 291-year-old St. Paul's Cathedral. He was the first non-Anglican to preach there. The chairman of the Norwegian parliament said he was "the first person in the Western world to have shown us that a struggle can be waged without violence." (Gandhi was part of the Eastern world.) When Norwegian students sang, "We Shall Overcome," King realized that his message had become part of a universal language of freedom.

King was soon back in the United States—and in jail again. He was in Selma, Alabama, trying to help black citizens vote.

President Johnson's Civil Rights Act didn't solve the voting problem. It did allow black people to check into any hotel they desired, sit on buses wherever they wished, and eat in any restaurant. But in much of the rural South, blacks still couldn't vote. In 1964, when blacks tried to register to vote in Alabama or Mississippi or some other southern states, they were likely to be beaten, or to lose their jobs—even though the 15th Amendment to the Constitution says that every citizen has the right to vote. Those who kept trying to register were given impossible questions to answer, or asked to pay a poll tax they couldn't afford.

Selma was the seat of Dallas County, Alabama. The county offices were located in its courthouse. It was a town of 30,000 people; more than half were black. Selma was Bull Connor's birthplace. It was an Old South cotton town on the banks of the Alabama River. Mule-drawn carts still clattered down Selma's dusty streets, hauling cotton.

Before the Civil War one of the town's buildings had been used to hold slaves—sometimes 500 of them—as they waited to be auctioned off. During the Civil War, Selma was a Confederate military depot. In the 1960s, the streets in the black section of town were made of red dirt; those in the white section were paved.

The leaders of Selma's black community asked Dr. King (and his organization, the SCLC) to come to town. In 1965, when King and the SCLC arrived, SNCC workers had already been in Selma for more than a year. They had worked hard to

A demonstrator campaigns for the vote and equal employment outside the Florida state capitol in Tallahassee.

We are a great nation, I think, largely because of our protection of the right to criticize, to dissent, to oppose, and to join with others in mass opposition—and to do these things powerfully and effectively.

—Abe Fortas, Associate Justice, U.S. Supreme Court

Martin Luther King gave his Nobel prize money to the civil rights movement.

I have sworn upon the altar of God eternal hostility against every form of tyranny over the mind of man.

—Thomas Jefferson

In 1964 only two-fifths of the South's eligible black population was registered to vote.

Marchers on their way to Mont-gomery, Alabama

The 24th Amendment, outlawing the poll tax as a device to prevent citizens from voting, is ratified by South Dakota on January 23, 1964, completing approval by three-quarters of the states.

In the Selma jail, King discovered a man who had been locked up for more than two years—and still hadn't been told why he'd been arrested. That was against the Constitution. It was not unusual in some areas of the South. Check Article 1, Section 9 of the Constitution. If you don't know what it means, see book 3 of *A History of US.*

try to get blacks signed on the voting rolls. SNCC had doubled the number of registered black voters to 333 (out of 15,000 of voting age).

A few SNCC members weren't happy that King was asked to come to Selma. They wanted to stay in charge. But John Lewis, SNCC chairman, was not one of them. He was thrilled that Dr. Martin Luther King, Jr., was coming to town. So were the majority of Selma's citizens.

Dallas County Sheriff Jim Clark wasn't thrilled—he was angry. Clark was a big, crude, blustery white guy who wore a military jacket, carried a nightstick, hated Negroes, and said so. Clark was an embarrassment to Selma's leading white families, but he'd been elected sheriff anyway. (If the county's black citizens had been voters it wouldn't have happened.)

Martin Luther King, Jr., spoke out at Brown's Chapel (an old, sturdy, red-brick church with two steeples and an outside balcony). "Give us the ballot," he cried. A group of Selma's black citizens marched to the courthouse to try to register. They weren't allowed inside. Sheriff Clark made them stand in an alley. When SNCC workers tried to bring them sandwiches and water, the workers were hit with billy clubs. That just made Selma's black citizens more determined.

More than 100 black teachers marched. Teachers usually steer clear of controversy, but this time they didn't. They wanted to vote. The teachers' march was the real turning point, said the Reverend Frederick Reese. "The undertakers got a group, and they marched. The beauticians got a group; they marched. Everybody marched after the teachers marched," said Reese.

Martin Luther King, Jr., marched with 250 citizens who wanted to register to vote. They were all thrown in jail. King, too. When they heard of Dr. King's arrest, 500 schoolchildren marched to the courthouse. They were arrested. Two days later 300 more schoolchildren were arrested. The evening television news covered it all. King wrote a letter from jail. He said, "This is Selma, Alabama. There are more Negroes in jail with me than there are on the voting rolls." Fifteen congressmen came to Selma. They announced that "new legislation is going to be necessary." President Johnson held a press conference and said, "All Americans should be indignant when one American is denied the right to vote."

Coretta Scott King went to the jail to visit her husband. She brought a message from Malcolm X, who was in Selma. Malcolm, a black leader who was electrifying urban audiences with hard facts and a spirit of militancy, had been invited to Selma by SNCC's leaders. His ideas were different from King's. Malcolm had never recognized the power and force of nonviolent action. But Malcolm seemed to be heading in a new direction. He told Coretta, "I want Dr. King to know that I didn't come to Selma to make his job difficult." Then he added, "If the white people realize what the alternative is, perhaps they will be more willing to hear Dr. King."

The alternative was violence. Speaking to a big crowd in Brown's Chapel, Malcolm said, "White people should thank Dr. King for holding people in check, for there are others who do not believe in these [nonviolent] measures."

Malcolm had broken with the Black Muslims who believed in the separation of blacks and whites. He'd gone to Mecca in Saudi Arabia—the center of the Muslim world—where he converted to orthodox Islam. That experience moved him deeply. It caused him to change some of his ideas—especially ideas that called for hate and violence. He told a journalist about that change in himself.

> *The sickness and madness of those [early] days. I'm glad to be free of them. It is a time for martyrs now. And if I'm to be one, it will be in the cause of brotherhood. That's the only thing that can save this country. I've learned it the hard way—but I've learned it.*

Two and a half weeks after his trip to Selma, Malcolm X was martyred—killed by Black Muslims—a victim of the violence that he had once tolerated. Malcolm's new belief in brotherhood made the loss of this brilliant Muslim especially tragic.

Malcolm X (above) urged black people to be proud of their blackness and their African roots. He had been a leader of the Nation of Islam, or Black Muslims, but broke with the movement over the advocacy of violence by some members. Below: Women at a Nation of Islam meeting that proclaimed them property to be protected from contamination by whites.

Muslims are followers of Islam and its prophet, Mohammed. Islam, like Judaism and Christianity, is based on belief in one God. Mecca, in Saudi Arabia, is Mohammed's birthplace. It is considered Islam's holiest city and its religious center.

A ***martyr*** is someone sacrificed to a cause.

26 From Selma to Montgomery

Selma police, Alabama State patrolmen, and Dallas County deputies block the road out of Selma. The marchers hoped that the President would call in the army to protect them.

Ain't going to let no
    posse turn me 'round,
Keep on walkin', keep
    on talkin',
Marching up to
    Freedom Land.

—hymn sung by Selma-to-
    Montgomery marchers

To live anywhere in the world today and be against equality because of race or color is like living in Alaska and being against snow.

—William Faulkner, novelist,
    in *Essays*, 1965

The tension in Selma was awful. Marchers, and even reporters covering the marches, were being roughed up and beaten. Where could they go for protection? Not to the police. The police, the state troopers, and Sheriff Clark were doing most of the beating. When 82-year-old Cager Lee marched, a state trooper went for him and whipped him until he was bloody. Jimmy Lee Jackson, Cager's grandson, carried his grandfather into a café. But the troopers weren't finished; they stormed right into the café. One trooper hit Jimmy's mother, another shot Jimmy Lee Jackson in the stomach. He died seven days later.

That murder did it. It was too much for the civil rights workers to bear. They felt responsible. There was no stopping them now. "We had decided that we were going to get killed or we were going to be free," said one leader. The murder was also too much for some of Selma's white citizens. Seventy of them marched in sympathy to the courthouse. One white minister said:

> We consider it a shocking injustice that there are still counties in Alabama where there are no Negroes registered to vote....We are horrified at the brutal way in which the police at times have attempted to break up peaceful assemblies and demonstrations by American citizens.

Six hundred people—men, women, and children—gathered at Brown's Chapel. They were prepared to march the 58 miles from Selma to Alabama's capital, Montgomery. They intended to face

Governor George Wallace and demand that all of Alabama's citizens be protected in their right to vote.

Most of the 600 were black, although some were white. Hosea Williams, a young firebrand, was in charge. (Martin Luther King was in Washington consulting with the president.) First they prayed, and then they began their march, singing as they went. They marched six blocks from Brown's Chapel to the Edmund Pettus Bridge. No one stopped them; all was quiet except for their voices. They knew that once they crossed the bridge they would be on the road to Montgomery.

When they mounted the sloping crest of the bridge they were stunned by what they saw: Alabama state troopers were lined up, gas masks in place, bullwhips and billy clubs raised. The troopers didn't give anyone time to decide what to do. They moved forward; some were on horseback, some on foot. Then they released tear-gas bombs. Eight-year-old Sheyann Webb said:

> *I saw people being beaten and I tried to run home as fast as I could....I saw horses behind me....Hosea Williams picked me up and I told him to put me down, he wasn't running fast enough.*

But something new had come to this out-of-the-way southern town. That something was television coverage. Camera crews were filming the action. Sheriff Clark's bullying was not just Selma's problem; it was national news. Television stations across the nation interrupted their regular programs to show scenes of policemen on

March 9, "Turnaround Tuesday" (below): Two days after "Bloody Sunday" (March 7), King led the marchers across Selma's Edmund Pettus Bridge a second time. State troopers blocked the highway; King turned around, and marched back to Selma, avoiding confrontation. March 10: After seeing "Bloody Sunday" on TV, thousands of people began to pour into Selma to join the march. Mounting tension erupted in violence as police officers attacked groups of protestors, gassing, clubbing, and kicking them.

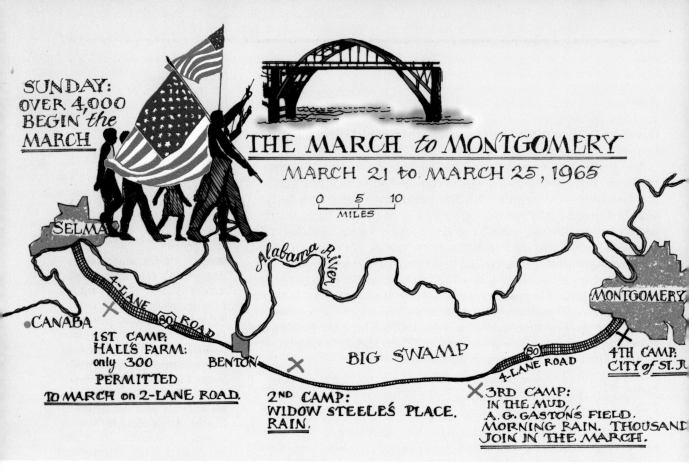

SUNDAY: OVER 4,000 BEGIN 'the MARCH

THE MARCH to MONTGOMERY
MARCH 21 to MARCH 25, 1965

0   5   10
MILES

SELMA

Alabama River

•CANABA

4-LANE (80) ROAD

1ST CAMP:
HALL'S FARM:
only 300
PERMITTED
TO MARCH on 2-LANE ROAD.

BENTON

BIG SWAMP

MONTGOMERY

(80) 4-LANE ROAD

4TH CAMP:
CITY of ST. J.

2ND CAMP:
WIDOW STEELE'S PLACE.
RAIN.

3RD CAMP:
IN THE MUD,
A. G. GASTON'S FIELD.
MORNING RAIN. THOUSAND
JOIN IN THE MARCH.

Rob a people of their sense of history and you take away hope.

—Rev. Wyatt T. Walker,
Aide to Dr. Martin Luther King, Jr.

Truth is great and will prevail if left to herself.

—Thomas Jefferson

? *Where are Lexington and Concord? Why are they famous? What about Appomattox?*

horseback clubbing peaceful marchers. "It looked like war," said Selma's mayor. "The wrath of the nation came down on us."

How would you feel if you watched all that on television? Most good people were sickened. So, when Martin Luther King, Jr., sent telegrams to prominent clergymen saying "Join me for a ministers' march to Montgomery," ministers came from many places and many faiths. White-bearded Rabbi Abraham Heschel came from the Jewish Theological Seminary, world leader Ralph Bunche came from the United Nations (he, too, had won a Nobel Peace Prize), and Unitarian minister James Reeb came from Boston.

Reeb did not go back to Boston. The nightmare of brutality wasn't quite finished in Selma. Reeb and some other white ministers made the mistake of eating in a black café. For Reeb it was a fatal mistake. He was clubbed to death when he came out of the restaurant.

President Johnson was shocked, and said:

> *What happened in Selma was an American tragedy. At times, history and fate meet in a single place to shape a turning point in man's unending search for freedom. So it was at Lexington and Concord. So it was a century ago at Appomattox. So it was last week in Selma, Alabama.*

The president announced that he was sending a voting rights bill to Congress. Then he spoke to the 70 million people who listened on television. *It's not just Negroes,* he said. *It's really all of us who must overcome the crippling legacy of bigotry and injustice. And,* he finished with these words from the civil rights theme song, WE SHALL OVERCOME.

"We were all sitting together," said a black leader who heard the president speak. "And Martin was very quietly sitting in the chair, and a tear ran down his cheek. It was a victory like none other."

Six days later, 4,000 people—black and white—marched from the Pettus Bridge in Selma to Montgomery, camping out at night and singing songs of freedom. This time National Guardsmen protected them. By the time they reached the capital, 25,000 people had joined the march.

Rosa Parks was there, and so were many of those who, 10 years earlier, had walked through winter's bluster and summer's heat rather than ride Montgomery's segregated buses. Martin Luther King, Jr., had been an unknown preacher then. Now he was world famous.

March 26: Martin Luther King (center) leads thousands of demonstraters on the last leg of their 54-mile, five-day march to Montgomery. Also in the front row are SNCC leader John Davis (in white vest), Rev. Ralph Abernathy (3rd from left), Dr. Ralph Bunche, (5th from left), Coretta Scott King, and Rev. Hosea Williams (carrying a little girl, right). "We are on the move now," said Dr. King. "Let us therefore continue our triumph and march...on ballot boxes until the Wallaces of our nation tremble away in silence."

27 War in South-east Asia

By 1971—when this cartoonist drew "The Blind Leading the Blind"—four presidents had found themselves entangled in Vietnam. Can you name them all?

Henry David Thoreau had protested during the Mexican War. He had even gone to jail rather than pay taxes that would support the war. A few people protested with him. But not enough to make a difference. Besides, we won that war, and quickly, too, which made it popular. Vietnam was different. It went on and on and on. And we didn't win.

The war in Vietnam was costing billions of dollars a year. Someone said we had to make a choice between *guns* and *butter.* (Guns symbolized war and butter stood for goods and helping programs.) At first, President Johnson thought we could have both. But the guns got more and more expensive. Soon we were spending more in Vietnam than on all the welfare programs combined. Funds for the Great Society had to be cut. Many of its programs were eliminated.

The Vietnam War turned out to be a terrible mistake. We blundered into it without knowing much about southeast Asia. We never took time to learn.

It was a civil war. We made it our war. It became a battle between the most powerful nation in the world and a small country of farmers. It was bombers, helicopters, and rockets in a nation with water buffalo and barefoot runners. What were we fighting for? It was supposed to be for freedom and democracy. But since we hadn't done our homework and didn't know much about the country we were fighting in, we backed corrupt leaders in South Vietnam who robbed the treasury and bossed everyone around.

It is easy to see mistakes after you've made them; that is called "hindsight." No nation wants to make mistakes. We didn't enter the Vietnam War in order to do wrong. It was that issue of communism that caught us. The North Vietnamese were getting money and supplies from communist China and from the Soviets, too. Many Americans feared that the Chinese communists would control a united Vietnam. Because we hadn't studied much Vietnamese history, we didn't know that the Chinese and the Vietnamese didn't get along very well.

Most of the advisers to Presidents Eisenhower, Kennedy, and Johnson believed we should fight in Vietnam. They believed it was

America's role to stand up to any communist nation, anywhere. They believed that all communist nations were part of a large conspiracy. If Vietnam was allowed to become communist, everyone seemed sure that all of southeast Asia would soon follow.

Actually, the Vietnamese could have used our help. They were faced with a poor choice: between a miserable dictator and a repressive communist government. We might have given them some guidance. Uncle Sam could have sent teachers and business advisers and our democratic ideas. But many of our 20th-century leaders talked about freedom and democracy, yet sometimes acted as if they didn't really believe in them. We didn't back free elections in Vietnam. Instead, we spent vast sums of money on weapons and we tried to solve problems the unthinking way—by fighting.

We got into the war in Vietnam one step at a time. It wasn't the fault of the Republicans or the Democrats. It was bipartisan. In the early 1960s, war hawks in both parties were screaming that we needed to fight. Our presidents didn't want to be called soft on communism. Besides, they remembered Hitler, the terrible tyrant who started World War II. If Hitler had been stopped early, that war might not have happened. But the leader of North Vietnam, Ho Chi Minh, was no Hitler (though he wasn't a democratic leader, either).

Our leaders didn't ask the right questions, and so we sent more than half a million Americans to do battle in a faraway land.

We got deeper and deeper into the Vietnamese jungle—and then we didn't seem to know how to get out. First there was that little step of Truman's. Then Eisenhower invested more money and sent more advisers. And Kennedy sent much more money and lots of advisers.

President Johnson didn't know what to do. His advisers were pushing him to enter the war in a big way. Barry Goldwater, who was the Republican candidate for president in 1964, ran a get-into-the-war campaign and even talked about using nuclear weapons. Johnson ran as the peace candidate. You remember Lyndon Johnson's big ego, though. He didn't want to look like a coward. Then something happened soon after he was elected that gave him an excuse to become a warrior.

The U.S. military forces destroyed Vietnamese villages, turning peasants into refugees and making them flee to the cities. The Americans believed this would make it harder for Viet Cong soldiers to find food and support in the countryside. Here, U.S. Marine Corporal Dave Taylor guards Vietnamese women and children at Qui Nhon in 1965. Most of the villagers had fled. The marines rounded up the few who remained, fearing that they had been armed by the Viet Cong for sniper attacks against the Americans.

South Vietnam's chief of police executes a man suspected of being a Viet Cong guerrilla on a street in Saigon. This scene was later watched on TV by millions of Americans.

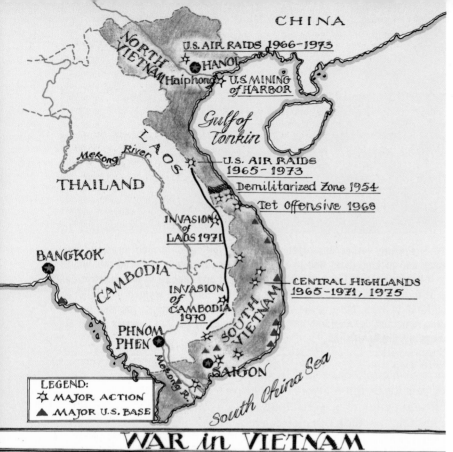

Map labels:
CHINA

U.S. AIR RAIDS 1966-1973
★ HANOI
Haiphong ✕ U.S. MINING of HARBOR
NORTH VIETNAM

Gulf of Tonkin

Mekong River
LAOS

THAILAND

U.S. AIR RAIDS 1965-1973
Demilitarized Zone 1954
Tet Offensive 1968

INVASION of LAOS 1971

BANGKOK

CAMBODIA

INVASION of CAMBODIA 1970

CENTRAL HIGHLANDS 1965-1971, 1975

PHNOM PHEN

Mekong R.

SAIGON

SOUTH VIETNAM

South China Sea

LEGEND:
✕ MAJOR ACTION
▲ MAJOR U.S. BASE

WAR in VIETNAM

An American ship was on a secret mission in the Gulf of Tonkin. It wasn't supposed to be there. A torpedo was fired at the ship. Two days later there was a second report of torpedoes. It turned out to be untrue. Maybe a sailor saw a flying fish. President Johnson said an American ship had been attacked. He got Congress to pass a resolution that let him go to war. It was called the Gulf of Tonkin resolution. The Vietnam War went into high gear.

We began bombing North Vietnam. Before we finished we dropped more bombs on that small country than we had on both Germany and Japan during all of World War II. And that wasn't the worst of it. We sent soldiers. Lots of them. Most of our soldiers were decent and many were heroic. Many helped the people of Vietnam. But some didn't. Imagine trying to fight in a hot jungle where you can't even see the enemy. Some soldiers were angry and violent. Many were introduced to drugs in Vietnam. They had killing weapons and they used them on innocent villagers as well as on enemy soldiers. The war became a national nightmare. It went on and on and on. We killed and were killed.

The Pentagon (which is the name for our military control center) just couldn't understand how guerrilla (say it like GORILLA) fighters who had their ammunition carried over jungle trails on the backs of old men and women could beat a modern army supplied

"Only Thing We're Sure Of—There Is a Tonkin Gulf!"

Arkansas senator J. William Fulbright—pointing at map, left—opposed the war policies of LBJ and his advisers, such as Robert McNamara (pointing, right). Once friendly colleagues, Fulbright and Johnson stopped speaking to each other.

An Unwilling Guest at the Hanoi Hilton

It was July 18, 1965, and U.S. Navy Commander Jeremiah A. Denton, Jr., was sitting in the cockpit of a bomb-loaded A6 airplane on the carrier *Independence*, located in the Gulf of Tonkin. The deck of an aircraft carrier seems huge, but its runway isn't long enough for a normal takeoff. So the plane was catapulted—like an arrow from a bow—off the deck.

Denton was on his way to North Vietnam. As he dropped his bombs over the target, near Hanoi, he felt a jolt. His plane had been hit. The controls were dead. "My heart pounded. It was over. I was very frightened," he wrote later. Jeremiah Denton descended into the Ma River, was picked up by Vietnamese soldiers, and became a POW: a prisoner of war.

At home in Virginia, Denton's wife, Jane, and his seven children learned that he had been captured (other pilots had seen him eject from the plane). They didn't know that he was put in solitary confinement—which means he was all alone in a tiny cell with only a concrete bed, wooden stocks that held his legs, and a bucket for a toilet. They didn't know other things, either. That he was physically tortured, mentally tortured, starved, and taken on a march through Hanoi where people hit him and spat on him. Or that he sometimes lost all sense of who he was. Imagine if it were you. Could you handle it? For Denton, 1965 became 1966, and '67, and '68, and on, and on.

He was one of the first POWS, but eventually some 700 Americans were captured and held in several prisons near Hanoi. They gave the prisons names like the Hanoi Hilton, Dogpatch, Heartbreak, Alcatraz, and Briarpath. The prisoners kept their sanity and their pride in themselves and their country by defying their

Jeremiah Denton as a hostage of war, in a Vietnamese film designed to show that hostages were well treated by their captors

captors. They maintained military discipline. As a high-ranking officer, Denton was often in command. How could he do that?

The POWS talked to each other by tapping on the walls of their cells with a special code. When the jailers stopped the tapping, they whistled or coughed the code. The tap code was based on this chart:

	1	2	3	4	5
1	A	B	C	D	E
2	F	G	H	I	J (K)
3	L	M	N	O	P
4	Q	R	S	T	U
5	V	W	X	Y	Z

Try it. To tap *A* you go 1-1. *B* is 1-2, *R* is 4-2, and *X* is 5-3. The letter *K* is 2-6.

The American people disagreed about the war—its purpose and necessity—but everyone was in agreement when it came to the POWS. We wanted them home. The Vietnamese soon realized that they had important hostages. They filmed some of the POWS, intending to show that they were being well treated. Commander Denton kept blinking his eyes. Most people thought it was the bright camera lights, but Denton was blinking the word *torture* in Morse code.

International law sets standards for the treatment of prisoners. Torture is forbidden. Four people who saw the film recognized the code and called government officials.

The North Vietnamese were not the only ones who tortured prisoners. The South Vietnamese army also committed terrible atrocities.

What happened to the POWS? How long were they guests at the Hanoi Hilton? Read on and you'll find out.

131

Children from Trang Ban, South Vietnam, flee after their school was burned with napalm during an American raid.

by helicopters. The military chiefs kept telling the president that if we just sent a few thousand more soldiers and dropped a few more bombs it would all be over. But the old men and women and the guerrilla fighters, who seemed to know how to vanish into the jungle, finally made the great and mighty United States give up and go home.

We thought we were doing the right thing when we began. We really were unselfish. We weren't imperialists. We didn't want to make Vietnam a colony. And we left much of our national wealth in that nation halfway around the world. So why did we make such a terrible mistake?

We didn't understand what the war was all about.

It was about freedom. The Vietnamese wanted to be free of foreign rule. They wanted to choose their own leaders. They wanted freedom even to make the wrong decisions. This was a nasty civil war. We soon made it much worse. We made it a high-tech war. We brought in grenades, rocket launchers, jellied-gasoline explosives (called "napalm"), and chemicals (called "defoliants") that took all the leaves off the jungle trees—and we still couldn't beat the Vietnamese.

We should have known that could happen. After all, we ourselves started out as a little pipsqueak nation that defeated the great and mighty British empire. Didn't we remember that people fighting for their own freedom are apt to be unbeatable? What had happened to us?

Going to Jail to Fight War

Dorothy Day (right) protests the war at a draft card–burning ceremony.

Dorothy Day was in her sixties when she stood outside a missile base and tried to block its entrance. She was protesting against an industry that built weapons of destruction. At the same time, she urged Americans not to pay their income taxes, because tax money supported the war in Vietnam. (Henry David Thoreau had done the same thing at the time of the Mexican War.) Day was willing to go to jail for her beliefs—and she did.

She believed that war was wrong. She thought that capitalism led people to concentrate on getting and spending money, and she didn't think that brought happiness. She thought that nationalism—love of country—often led to war and misery. So what did she believe in? The power of God's love. She believed that God could be found among the poor, and that helping the poor was a way to change society and find meaning in life.

Abbie Hoffman, a fiery young 1960s radical, called her "the first hippie," and Dorothy Day was proud of the label. She was the founder of the *Catholic Worker,* a newspaper devoted to educating the public about the plight of the poor and uneducated. The *Catholic Worker* sponsored soup kitchens and hospitality houses for the poor.

But how do you treat someone who breaks rules? Dorothy Day was a problem to some Catholic church members. They wanted to take official action against her; others found her inspiring. *Time* magazine didn't see a problem. It called her "a living saint," and put her on its cover.

28 Lyndon in Trouble

By 1967, Vietnam was a raw scar on the president's body. "I feel like a hitchhiker caught in a hailstorm on a Texas highway," said LBJ. "I can't run. I can't hide. And I can't make it stop."

Lyndon Johnson was miserable. He knew he was losing his dream of a Great Society. But he didn't know how to stop the war in Vietnam. He didn't seem able to admit that he had made a mistake. He had started with that fib about an attack in the Gulf of Tonkin. But you know how those things go: one lie usually leads to another, and sometimes another, and another.

That's what happened to President Johnson. He said, "We are not going to send American boys nine or ten thousand miles away from home to do what Asian boys ought to be doing for themselves." But he was already planning to do just that. He said all the bombing was "aimed at military targets." But newspaper reporters told of houses, schools, and stores flattened by bombs. President Johnson kept saying that we were winning the war and it would soon be over. TV made people realize he wasn't telling the truth. For the first time in history, ordinary people could see exactly what war was like. The TV screen showed dead American soldiers and dead Vietnamese.

At first, it was mostly students on college campuses who began demonstrating against the war. Then more and more American people began to join them. Martin Luther King, Jr., was now leading anti-war protests, as well as civil rights marches. Ministers of many faiths were doing the

Nineteen sixty-seven was the height of the hippie era—the "summer of love." That year, even all-American *Life* magazine published an editorial that said the Vietnam War was no longer worth winning—and was too much "to ask young Americans to die for." All over the country, students protested the war. In one famous demonstration outside the Pentagon, some young Americans planted flowers in the barrels of the military policemen's rifles. Below: Protesting the Vietnam War in Wichita, Kansas.

In 1966, race riots in some cities, like Cleveland, Ohio, escalated into looting. *Above:* Looters walk off with clothing and an electric fan as policemen look on. Store owners and the police both gave up trying to protect the shops.

A year later, in 1967, violence on Detroit's west side lasted a week, leaving 43 dead and 2,000 wounded. After hidden snipers drove city police from a square-mile area of town, Michigan National Guard tank crews had to use heavy machine guns to blast the snipers out. *Above:* Michigan National Guardsmen push rioters away from a burning building with fixed bayonets.

Above: Militant Black Power leader Stokely Carmichael speaks to college students—"We been saying freedom for six years, and we ain't got nothing." *Inset:* Playwright LeRoi Jones, who led a voter registration campaign that put blacks in control of Newark, New Jersey.

same thing. The college protests began to get ugly and violent.

And then the cities, especially those in the North, started exploding. America's cities had been neglected. In many, schools were terrible, transportation was terrible, crime made life frightening, and there weren't enough jobs for those who wanted to work. City people were fed up. That was a bad break for the president. He was trying to do something to improve the cities. But not everyone was willing to wait for his programs to work. Things had been too bad for too long. In 1965, riots in the Watts section of Los Angeles lasted six days and left 34 dead. Newark, Chicago, Cleveland, and other cities erupted with riots of their own. America's cities were like volcanoes filled with frustration and pain. The riots may have eased the frustration; they didn't do much to help the pain. Johnson asked Illinois governor Otto Kerner to head a commission to investigate the riots. The governor said they could be traced to "white racism." The Kerner Commission warned, "Our nation is moving toward two societies, one black, one white—separate and unequal."

Black protests began changing direction. New leaders appeared; many were angry young people. They had no patience with nonviolence. The new leaders didn't talk about brotherhood and love; they talked of power, separation, and sometimes hate. Martin Luther King said of one militant group, "In advocating violence it is imitating the worst, the most brutal, and the most uncivilized value of American life." Anti-Vietnam protests grew louder and more strident. Many who had supported the war were now changing their minds.

Black Power voices were followed by Brown Power, or Mexican-American, voices. These were people who wanted their full rights as citizens. So did the female half of the population. Women had been demanding equal pay for equal work and not getting it. Women's rights leaders joined the protest fray. Some were just angry; others had clear ideas and programs.

Would you like to have been president in the '60s? By 1968, the country seemed to be coming apart.

By the end of 1967, only 26 percent of Americans approved of Johnson's handling of the Vietnam War.

Conscience of the Court

Thurgood Marshall (left) calls his wife from the Oval Office with the news that the president has appointed him to the Supreme Court.

Lyndon Johnson and Thurgood Marshall were friends. They were both energetic men, and talkers, and they understood each other. Each of them wanted to make the world better than it was. But there was one thing Lyndon Johnson told Thurgood Marshall he wasn't going to do. He wasn't going to make Marshall a Supreme Court justice. If Thurgood Marshall were a justice, he wouldn't be free to talk politics with the president. They couldn't be friends anymore.

So, in 1967, Marshall didn't know what Lyndon John-son had in mind when he was invited into the Oval Office of the White House. The president was sitting at his desk. They chatted a bit, and then, according to Marshall, Presi-dent Johnson said, "You know something, Thurgood?"

"No, sir," said Marshall. "What's that?"

"I'm going to put you on the Supreme Court."

And Marshall said, "Oh, yipe!" and "What did you say?"

But he had heard right. President Johnson had changed his mind. Thurgood Marshall was to be the first black justice ever appointed to the Supreme Court. After a while, after they talked some more, Marshall called his wife and told her to sit down because the president had something to tell her. After that, Johnson said, "I guess this is the end of our friendship."

"Yep," said the justice-to-be. "Be no more of that." Then the president recalled when a justice that Harry Truman had appointed made a decision that Truman opposed.

"You wouldn't do like that to me?" he said to Marshall, who answered: "No sooner than," which meant he certainly would do like that if he thought it the right thing to do. To which Johnson replied, "Well, that's the way I want it." And that is the way it was. Thurgood Marshall was an independent-minded justice, a great justice, a justice one lawyer described as the "conscience of the court."

A Farming Village in Vietnam

On the map, My Lai (me-LY) was a pinprick of a place on the northeast coast of South Vietnam, near the South China Sea. Early on the morning of March 16, 1968, when the men of Charlie Company of the 11th Brigade of the Americal Division entered the village, My Lai entered the annals of history. The American soldiers shot, at point-blank range, everyone they could find: old men, pregnant women, children, babies—504 civilians in all.

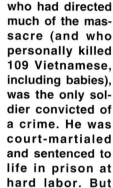
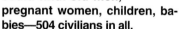
Lieutenant Calley

Then the soldiers ate lunch, went back, shot all the domestic animals—water buffaloes, pigs, chickens—threw the carcasses into the village wells (to poison the water), and burned the place down. Their officers didn't seem to think they had done anything wrong.

But a few of the soldiers had refused to participate, and Hugh Thompson, Jr., who was in a helicopter overhead, threatened to shoot the G.I.s if he saw them "kill one more woman or child." He landed between the G.I.s and the villagers.

A few miles away, soldiers in Bravo Company (of the same army division) wiped out a hamlet called My Khe in a similar bloodbath. Later, officers and men lied about what they had done. Only after a newspaper reporter (Seymour Hersh) wrote the truth (and won a Pulitzer prize) did Americans at home understand what their soldiers had done.

Lieutenant William Calley, Jr., who had directed much of the massacre (and who personally killed 109 Vietnamese, including babies), was the only soldier convicted of a crime. He was court-martialed and sentenced to life in prison at hard labor. But President Nixon intervened (to his and America's shame), and Calley was released after three years of house arrest in his own apartment.

If Americans had any illusions about the war, My Lai shattered them. Writer Neil Sheehan said:

Had they killed just as many over a larger area in a longer period of time and killed impersonally with bombs, shells, rockets, white phosphorus, and napalm, they would have been following the normal pattern of American military conduct. The soldier and junior officer observed the lack of regard his superiors had for the Vietnamese....The military leaders of the United States, and the civilian leaders who permitted the generals to wage war as they did, made the massacre inevitable.

A long time ago, war was a gentleman's pursuit. It was often heroic. There were things in war to boast of, and tell your grandchildren about. But even then—in the days of knights and valor—there had always been the other side, which was brutal, gruesome, and disgusting. After Vietnam, and especially after My Lai, there was almost nothing left in war but the shame of it.

After massacring the villagers at My Khe—men, women, and children—the G.I.s used ordinary cigarette lighters to burn their houses to the ground.

29 Friedan, Schlafly, and Friends

"For the first time in their history," wrote Betty Friedan, "women are becoming aware of an identity crisis in their lives, a crisis which began generations ago."

Television programs (and newspaper and magazine articles) can tell you a lot about a time—or at least the way people of that time saw themselves. And in the '50s, the number-one TV program was *I Love Lucy*. Lucy was a dippy dame—a white, middle-class wife and mother—who didn't work, was kind of bored, and was always getting into mischief with her neighbor Ethel. One day, Lucy and Ethel decided to get jobs on the production line at a candy factory. As the chocolates passed by—zip-zip fast—Lucy and Ethel got farther and farther behind. So they began stuffing chocolates in their mouths and then in their dresses—and it was all a big laugh.

There were mixed messages in that *Lucy* show. Did women belong in the candy factory, or at home? Lucy and Ethel always seemed to be trying to break away from the household routine. But they usually goofed up. And behind the show was

Helmer: *Before all else, you are a wife and mother.*

Nora: *That I no longer believe. I believe that before else, I am a human being, just as much as you are—or at least that I should try to become one.*

—Henrik Ibsen, *A Doll's House* (1879)

Right, a typical day at home with Lucy and Ethel. In January 1953, more people saw *I Love Lucy* on Monday nights than watched President Eisenhower's inauguration in the same month.

137

"The suburban housewife," wrote Betty Friedan, "was the dream image of young American women and the envy, it was said, of women all over the world." Top: The '50s ideal: Mom and daughter look on admiringly as their lord and master mans the barbecue. Bottom: A young mother deals with reality. Right: Two of TV's blissfully happy families: *Ozzie and Harriet* (top) and *Father Knows Best* (bottom).

the real Lucille Ball, who was not only one of the most gifted comedians this country has produced but a powerful businesswoman as well.

The reality of the '50s was that most middle-class white women—like it or not—did stay home. A lot of them lived in the new suburbs, in new houses, with new washing machines and a kind of life that seemed idyllic. Most TV programs told you that as long as Mom didn't venture out into the big world, her life was close to perfect. The shows were all full of happy suburban couples and cute kids: *Ozzie and Harriet, Leave It to Beaver,* and *Father Knows Best* (note that title) were three very popular shows that portrayed terrific, happy households.

Yet when writer Betty Friedan decided to do an article about suburban women, she found that many of them were not happy—and they didn't know why. She called it the "problem that has no name." Then she investigated, and said that women weren't being given a chance to develop their talents. They were taught to "keep their place." If a woman had the potential to be a brain surgeon, if she wanted to be a veterinarian, if she thought being an architect would fill her life with pleasure—well, too bad. Those, and most professions, were for males only. Women had a separate—and unequal—role in society. They were expected to stay in the kitchen and the nursery, perhaps get involved with community volunteer work, or maybe just putter around, look pretty, and be frustrated.

Friedan knew something about frustration. She had lost a reporting job when she got pregnant. And she couldn't get that article on discontented women published—magazines only seemed to want to tell about domestic bliss. So Betty Friedan decided to turn her research into a book. She called it *The Feminine Mystique.*

That book, published in 1963, put in words what a lot of women had been thinking. More than a million copies were sold. It made people think—some men as

well as women. It carried an idea—that all people, including women, have the natural right to develop their potential. It told how the media (advertising, TV, radio, newspapers, and magazines) were manipulating women in order to keep them at home where they could be sold vacuum cleaners and dishwashers. Friedan's book came along at the same time that other things were happening to make women reconsider their role in society.

Suburban women may not have been working, but many other women were at work. It had begun during World War II (from 1941 to 1945), when about 6.5 million women who had not worked before got jobs. It was patriotic. Men were fighting; women were needed on production lines. Many women found they liked working. Some had no choice: they had to work.

After the war, many of those women kept working. Others began to work too. "By 1960," writes William H. Chafe, an expert in the field, "both the husband and the wife worked in over 10 million homes (an increase of 333 percent over 1940)." But attitudes didn't change. Working women were paid less than men. And they hardly ever got prestige jobs. Many were teachers, but women were not superintendents of schools. Many were nurses, but very few were doctors.

And those who worked had to put up with prejudice against working women. An article in the *Atlantic Monthly* was typical of the times. It said, "What modern woman has to recapture is the wisdom that just being a woman is her central task and her greatest honor."

But what the magazines and TV shows were saying was in conflict with what more and more women were beginning to believe: that they had minds and talents equal to men's.

In 1969, some California women held an Anti-Bra Day to protest the pressure that society put on women to wear constricting, "feminine" garments. "I ask college students not born in 1963, 'How many of you have ever worn a girdle?' They laugh," wrote Betty Friedan. "So then I say: 'Well, it used to be, not so long ago, that every woman from about the age of 12 to 92 who left her house in the morning encased her flesh in rigid plastic casing.'"

Then, when the civil rights movement erupted in the '60s, women became some of its hardest workers. And they often found that the men in the movement expected them to make coffee, do the cleaning up, and not make major decisions. That was infuriating. The civil rights movement was all about equal rights. So some women took the activism they learned as civil rights workers and brought it to the women's liberation movement.

Many of those women, and others who called themselves radical feminists, didn't think Betty Friedan went far enough. Friedan wanted women to

Portrait of Herself

Margaret Bourke-White was one of America's great photo-journalists and a groundbreaker for women in the field. A photographer for both Life *and the U.S. Air Force during World War II, she later went on assignments in India and Korea. In her autobiography,* Portrait of Myself, *published in 1963, Bourke-White wrote:*

My father was an abnormally silent man. He was so absorbed in his own engineering work that he seldom talked to his children at all, but he would become communicative in the world of out-of-doors....If Father had been money-minded, he might have become quite wealthy, but he paid no attention to money, was essentially the inventor and researcher, and made some unsound investments. ...Just how unsound they were came out only when he died. I was 17 then, just starting college, and I know now that if we had been wealthy, and I hadn't had to work my way through college as I did after his death, I would never have been a photographer....It is odd that photography was never one of my childhood hobbies when Father was so fond of it....Everything that had to do with the transmission and control of light interested my father, and I like to think that this keen attention to what light could do has influenced me....That, and the love of the truth, which is requisite No. 1 for a photographer.

Margaret Bourke-White

be equal partners in American society. Some of the radical feminists wanted to overthrow society. They saw male-dominated institutions as hopeless. Robin Morgan wrote:

> *I call myself a radical feminist....I believe that sexism is the root oppression, the one which, until and unless we uproot it, will continue to put forth the branches of racism, war, class hatred, ageism, competition, ecological disaster, and economic exploitation.*

The radical feminists developed feminist publishing houses, health organizations, child-care centers, food cooperatives, and other women-run institutions. Some said they hated all men. Some wanted to integrate everything—even bathrooms. Although they were few in number, their extreme ideas got a lot of publicity.

By 1970, seven years after the publication of *The Feminine Mystique*, women activists were picketing and demonstrating for equal job opportunities and equal access to all-male clubs, restaurants, and schools. Feminists were making daily headlines in the newspaper—competing with the civil rights movement and the war in Vietnam.

The demonstrations made good newspaper copy, and they reflected a whole new attitude on the part of women. When one feminist leader was told, at a national political convention, to "calm down, *little girl*," she was anything but calm. All the brouhaha (BREW-ha-ha—it means "uproar" or

In 1966, 30 women, including Betty Friedan, founded the National Organization for Women (NOW), "to take action to bring American women into full participation in the mainstream of American society." In 1970, these women marched for equal rights up New York's Fifth Avenue.

"hubbub") was making a difference. Some women began to get good jobs in banking, law, engineering, and other previously male-only fields. Women were now newspaper editors and TV anchors.

But that news was only part of the picture. Things did not go well for all women—especially poor, black, or Hispanic women. According to Chafe:

> From 1955 to 1981, women's actual earnings fell from 64 percent of men's to 59 percent, and even in the late 1980s their earnings had climbed back only to 62 percent—still below the figure thirty years earlier....Eighty percent of all women workers were employed in just 5 percent of all jobs—the lowest-paying 5 percent....By the end of the 1980s, one in every four children in America was poor, and women comprised almost 70 percent of the adult poor....Middle and upper-class white women might be experiencing a new freedom, but almost none of the benefits they derived from women's new opportunities trickled down to the poor. For these women, race, class, and gender represented a triple whammy.

The women's rights movement had hit a class and race wall. It was unintended. Betty Friedan and others had worked for racial as well as female equality. But it was the women who were educated and talented who were going places. If you were poor, it was difficult to get a really good education. (For those who did, no matter their race, there were jobs aplenty.) Women without training or skills—who made up a majority—were usually stuck in dead-end, low-paying jobs, and still suffering from sex discrimination. (Actually, the same thing was happening to men. Education was becoming more and more important for all as the 21st century approached.)

In 1977, thousands of women took part in a 2,610-mile marathon from Seneca Falls, New York—where Susan B. Anthony and Elizabeth Cady Stanton had drawn up a declaration that said "All men and women are created equal"—to Houston, Texas, to publicize the first National Women's Conference in support of an equal rights amendment to the Constitution. They were joined for the last lap by tennis star Billie Jean King (second from left), Susan B. Anthony (great-niece of the first Susan, third from left), politician Bella Abzug (fourth from left), and Betty Friedan (far right).

Milestones of the Women's Movement

In 1920, Carrie Chapman Catt campaigned hard for the 19th Amendment to the Constitution.

In 1791, English-woman Mary Wollstonecraft wrote: "It is time to restore women to their lost dignity and to make them part of the human race."

In 1821, Emma Willard founded the Troy Female Seminary in Troy, New York, to give girls the kind of education that was available to boys.

Women who wear pants can thank Amelia Jenks Bloomer, who had the courage to get out of her hoopskirt—in the 1840s—and wear "bloomers." New York Herald editor James Gordon Bennett wrote, "If women mean to wear the pants, then they must also be ready in case of war to buckle on the sword!"

In 1848, Elizabeth Cady Stanton led a Women's Rights Convention in Seneca Falls, New York, and issued a female Declaration of Independence that said "all men and women are created equal."

In 1857, when no hospital would let her practice, Dr. Elizabeth Blackwell opened the New York Infirmary with an all-woman staff. Dr. Blackwell had never let adversity stop her. She was turned down by 29 medical schools before finally being accepted as a medical student.

In 1873, Susan B. Anthony was tried and convicted (by a court in Rochester, New York) of the crime of having voted!

In 1920, women finally got the right to vote when enough states ratified the 19th Amendment. Women suffragists had demonstrated (and suffered) to get it passed. *Carrie Chapman Catt,* a leader of the movement, then founded the National League of Women Voters.

There was something else, besides class and race. Women weren't all alike. They had different political ideas. Many women were *traditionalists:* they thought that a woman's primary role *was* as a wife and mother, and that a career detracted (took away) from that role. The traditionalists were conservative, but, like the radical feminists (who were not conservative), they emphasized the differences between men and women. Phyllis Schlafly (SHLAFF-lee) was the spokeswoman for the traditionalists. She wrote of the "Positive Woman" who "understands that men and women are different, and that those very differences provide the key to her success as a person and fulfillment as a woman." She attacked the women's liberation movement.

Schlafly was part of a powerful political force, the conservative "New Right," which developed in response to the turmoil of the times (the Vietnam war, growing rates of drug use, crime, and divorce, and new sexual ideas). The ideas of the New Right reached many Americans through something new: television church programs. TV preachers like Jerry Falwell, Pat Robertson, and Tammy and Jim Bakker were speaking to millions of Americans.

Phyllis Schlafly, national leader of the "Stop the Equal Rights Amendment" movement, talks to reporters at a rally in Springfield, Illinois, in 1975.

It was a Supreme Court decision that gave the New Right a focus. In 1973, in the case of *Roe* v. *Wade*, the Supreme Court said that a woman, in consultation with her doctor, could decide to end her pregnancy. That means she could choose to have an abortion. That decision gratified some Americans and outraged others.

Feminists said that women were finally in control of their own bodies. Anti-feminists said that abortion was murder and at odds with traditional religious values.

Does all this sound confusing? Well, change is rarely orderly. Women were sorting out new ideas. Men were, too. Fathers were enjoying their children and participating in home activities in ways that other generations had not done. And some of the statistics carried good news for women.

In the '50s and '60s, women had made up between 5 and 8 percent of the students in medical, law, and business schools. By the mid-'80s, they were at 40 percent, and heading upward. Educated women could now make choices. They could work as veterinarians or as housewives. They could be Supreme Court justices, brain surgeons, or, like that pioneer Lucille Ball, television producers. For women—of all races and backgrounds—there was now a hard question to consider: just how do you manage a job, marriage, children, a home, friends, and community involvement?

A Great Professional

In the 1950s, tennis was a country-club game. Mostly, it was a sport for the wealthy. Billie Jean Moffitt (who became Billie Jean King when she married) didn't belong to a country club. She learned to play tennis on public courts in California. When she entered her first tournaments, in 1955, she ran into some snobbish treatment. But King was a fighter. She fought her way to the top of the tennis world, she fought against elitism in tennis, she fought for equality for women in sports, and she fought for professionalism in tennis.

Billie Jean King

The big tournaments—for men and women—were open only to amateurs. That meant that champions played for the love of the game—not for money. (If you accepted money, you were thrown out of the tournament.) That was fine for those who were rich, but very hard on everybody else. By the 1960s, the U.S. Lawn Tennis Association was paying the top men and women players "under the table." King blasted that practice. She said it kept tennis from becoming professional. She called it "shamateurism." She said it wasn't fair. She wasn't alone.

In 1968, tennis became an open sport. Amateurism was finished. Anyone who qualified could compete for money prizes.

Now women players faced another problem. The prizes for the winners of men's tennis tournaments were as much as 12 times higher than the women's. The USLTA and most male tennis players said that women's tennis wasn't as good as men's tennis. They said that spectators weren't interested in watching women.

Billie Jean King said they were wrong. She and eight other top women players quit the USLTA–sponsored tournaments. They formed their own tour. They took a chance. They proved that women's tennis did attract a following. Crowds cheered the women on. Finally, the USLTA began to change its sexist practices.

In 1972, *Sports Illustrated* named Billie Jean King its first Sportswoman of the Year. When she retired, in 1984, King had won nine U.S. championships and a shelf full of other trophies. She'd helped bring respect and professionalism to women's athletics. (For a good book on the history of women's tennis, read *We Have Come a Long Way*, by Billie Jean King.)

30 As Important as the Cotton Gin

Long after Reconstruction, many southern blacks still lived in houses hardly better than slave cabins—even in 1936, when Walker Evans took this picture in Atlanta.

Everyone knows about Eli Whitney's cotton gin, and that it made growing cotton profitable, and that cotton demands lots of fieldworkers, and how that led to the creation of an enormous slave society in the cotton-growing South.

But most people don't know what ended that cotton-growing society. It wasn't the Civil War. When slavery ended, most of the former slaves kept on picking cotton. Now they were sharecroppers, or tenant farmers, instead of slaves. Some of them could hardly tell the difference. They didn't own land, they lived in plantation-owned cabins, they picked for a plantation owner, they had almost no schooling, and they didn't have much control of their lives.

So what ended that cotton-picking life? A machine. The mechanical cotton picker. That machine could do the work of 50 people. When the mechanical cotton picker was demonstrated on a Mississippi farm in 1944, cotton sharecropping was on its way to extinction. Cotton workers were no longer needed—or wanted. If their cabins were torn down, cotton could be planted where they stood. The cotton pickers had to go.

In the old sharecropping days, blacks had sometimes been pulled off buses heading north. They were needed in the cotton fields. After 1945, some Mississippi communities began passing out free bus tickets for Chicago. Back in the 16th century, something like that had happened in England. Tenant farmers were thrown off the land because it was more profitable to graze sheep where they had farmed. The roads to London and Edinburgh became crowded with displaced

While the modern civil rights movement had a momentum of its own, the activism that characterizes the Afro-American community... was directly influenced by the generation of Afro-Americans who moved north during the Great Migration....After the Great Migration, American society was never again the same.

—Spencer Crew,
Field to Factory

144

farm workers and, when those cities couldn't absorb them all, many kept going—right on to America.

Well, now the United States was seeing the same kind of exodus: from field to factory, from rural to urban, from South to North. This was an *internal*—inside the country—migration, but it was larger than that of any ethnic group to America from outside.

Between 1910 and 1970, 6.5 million blacks moved from the South to the North. Of that number, 5 million moved after 1940. They moved to Chicago, New York, Detroit, and Los Angeles. Others, who didn't go north, moved to the South's urban centers: Atlanta, Norfolk, Little Rock, Memphis, and Houston. A people with a tradition and culture based on farming became city folk. By 1970, more than three-fourths of black Americans lived in cities.

What was astonishing about all this was that hardly anyone in the rest of the country seemed to notice. Black people themselves didn't quite understand what was happening. Most Americans thought segregation was a southern problem. Its historical roots were southern. It was the legacy of slavery. The civil rights movement was something happening in the South, wasn't it? Why should anyone worry about racial problems in the North? They didn't exist, did they? Segregation in the North? Urban ghettoes? Poor schools? Poor jobs? The problems of the big cities? What problems?

You know about ostriches, don't you? They are the long-necked birds that supposedly hide their heads in the sand (they don't, really). Well, something big was happening in America—and the nation's leaders had their heads buried. All those people were moving into cities that were already crowded. They

Emmett Till

As Good as a White Man

Emmett Louis Till was 14 when he was found, brutally beaten, shot in the head, wired to a heavy weight, and dumped into Mississippi's Tallahatchie River.

Why? Because he had dared to say a flirtatious word to a white woman.

It was 1955, and the Chicago boy didn't understand the ways of the white-dominated South. His mother had warned him when she put him on a train heading for Mississippi and his southern cousins. "If you have to get down on your knees and bow when a white person goes past, do it," said Mrs. Till.

But that wasn't Emmett's way. He did just the opposite. Some boys dared him, and he went into a store, bought some candy, and then turned to the wife of the owner, Roy Bryant (who wasn't there), and said, "Bye, baby."

Within hours, two white men—Bryant and his brother-in-law, J. W. Milam—took Emmett away. Later, Milam told a writer exactly what had happened—how they beat and murdered him. Why did they do it? "Well, what else could I do?" said Milam. "He thought he was as good as any white man."

Bryant and Milam were found not guilty by an all-white jury (no blacks were registered to vote in the whole county, so there were no black jurors, either). Across the nation, all people of decency were outraged. "The murder of Emmett Till was the spark that set the civil rights movement on fire," wrote Sara Bullard in her book *Free at Last.*

Myrlie Evers, widow of civil rights leader Medgar Evers (another murder victim), said that the Emmett Till killing showed that "even a child was not safe from racism and bigotry and death."

A War in Our Emotions

Timidly, we get off the train. We hug our suitcases, fearful of pickpockets, looking with unrestrained curiosity at the great big brick buildings. We are very reserved, for we have been warned not to act "green," that the city people can spot a "sucker" a mile away. Then we board our first Yankee street car....We pay the conductor our fare and look about apprehensively for a seat. We have been told that we can sit where we please, but we are still scared. We cannot shake off three hundred years of fear in three hours....Sometimes five or six of us live in a one-room kitchenette, a place where simple folk such as we should never be held captive. A war sets up in our emotions: one part of our feelings tells us that it is good to be in the city, that we have a chance at life here...that we no longer need bow and dodge at the sight of the Lords of the Land. Another part of our feelings tell us that, in terms of worry and strain, the cost of living in the kitchenettes is too high, that the city heaps too much responsibility upon us and gives too little security in return.

—Richard Wright and
Edwin Rosskam,
12 Million Black Voices

were being squeezed into places that weren't prepared. They needed good schools, they needed opportunity, they needed all the things America does so well—and it wasn't happening. The president, the Congress, the government experts, and the college professors weren't paying attention.

There were some exceptions. A few people noticed. One of them was a Mississippi lawyer, businessman, and writer named David Cohn. In 1947, he wrote:

The country is upon the brink of a process of change as great as any that has occurred since the Industrial Revolution.... Five million people will be removed from the land within the next few years. They must go somewhere. But where? They must do something. But what? They must be housed. But where is the housing?...If tens of thousands of Southern Negroes descend upon communities totally unprepared for them psychologically and industrially, what will the effect be upon race relations in the United States?...Will the victims of farm mechanization become the victims of race conflict?

There is an enormous tragedy in the making unless the United States acts, and acts promptly.

But the United States did not act. Most Americans remained unaware. All those people were soon packed into cities like powder in a firecracker. In the '60s, the fuses on the firecrackers were lit and the cities began to explode.

In South Carolina in the 1960s, living conditions for poor folks differed little from those of a century earlier. This is Annie Chaplin of Beaufort.

31 Picking and Picketing

Picking cotton in California. "We need Mexicans for their labor, for the same reason you need a mule," said one farmer.

Lucía and María Mendoza, 18 and 17, stumbled out of bed at 2 A.M., dressed in the dark, went into the kitchen of their adobe house, made a lunch of tacos and soda pop, and filled a thermos with hot soup. Then they woke their dad and their younger brother. Soon the four of them were heading north, toward the border between Mexico and the United States. They were on their way to pick lettuce in California. Each of them expected to make $16 that Tuesday. It wasn't much, but it was more than they could earn at home. They would use short-handled hoes that kept them bent over all day. It was hot, dusty, back-breaking work. The Mendozas were soon part of a line of cars making for the picking fields.

These Mexican farm workers were entering the United States legally. They were wanted to help harvest crops to feed people across the nation. But some of them would stay in the United States illegally. Hundreds of thousands of them had already done it. Most of those il-

Mexico is sinking
California is on Fire
& we all are getting burned
    aren't we?
But what if suddenly the continent
    turned upside down?
what if the U.S. was Mexico?
what if 200,000 Anglo-Saxicans
were to cross the border
    each month
to work as gardeners, waiters,
3rd chair musicians, movie extras,
bouncers, babysitters, chauffeurs,
syndicated cartoonists, feather-
    weight boxers, fruit-pickers &
    anonymous poets?
what if they were called waspanos
waspitos, wasperos or waspbacks?
what if we were the top dogs?
what if yo were you
& tú fueras I, Mister?

—Guillermo Gomez-Peña,
"Mexico Is Sinking"

Yo means "I," and **tú fueras** means "you were."

147

Migrant children (left) pick oranges; others play marbles as their parents work. These pictures are from the 1970s. In 2000, The General Accounting Office estimated that 300,000 children were working in agriculture. The United Farm Workers Union said it was 800,000 and they averaged 30 hours of work per week, even during the school year. More than half never graduate from high school.

Resent means to feel annoyed or angry at someone. If you're resentful you are apt to be bitter, aggravated, incensed, indignant, irate, livid, mad, sore, burned up—or, if you live in Britain, cross and waxy.

legal immigrants had little schooling and few marketable skills. They were crowded in cities in poor districts *(barrios)*. Their children needed to go to school. They needed job training and help. All that cost taxpayer money. Some Americans resented them.

Many said the Mexicans took jobs from American citizens, especially from Mexican Americans. It wasn't their fault that they took those jobs. The growers wanted them instead of Americans because they would work for less money. They could live on less. Life in Mexico was cheaper than life in the United States.

Once they were across the border, the Mendozas parked their car and walked to a place where workers were hired for agricultural jobs. By 3:30 A.M. they were settled just behind the driver in an old, rattletrap bus heading north toward lettuce fields. Most of the 46 passengers tried to sleep. They knew they had a long ride ahead of them, and it was still dark. Later, one passenger would remember that they had been going very fast when the driver missed a curve and the bus became airborne—crashing into the bank of a canal, bouncing off that bank to the other bank, and settling in a shallow waterway. All the seats in the old bus flew out of their sockets in a mess of arms, legs, twisted metal, and broken glass. Nineteen passengers were trapped in the bottom of the bus; they drowned in two and a half feet of water. The four Mendozas were among them.

César Chávez wept for Lucía and María and the others who lay in silent caskets. Chávez was an American of Mexican heritage. Like most of the 2,000 mourners at a special funeral mass for the victims, he was a devout Roman Catholic. Everyone knew Chávez. He was the leader of the Farm Workers Association, and famous. They knew he cared about people, especially farm workers. They wanted to hear what he had to say. Speaking in Spanish, Chávez told them:

Caskets are coffins.

> *This tragedy happened because of the greed of the big growers who do not care about the safety of the workers and who expose them to grave dangers when they transport them in wheeled coffins to the field.*
>
> *The workers learned long ago that growers and labor contractors have too little regard for the value of any individual worker's life. The trucks and buses are old and unsafe. The fields are sprayed with poisons. The laws that do exist are not enforced. How long will it be before we take seriously the importance of the workers who harvest the food we eat?*

Chávez knew all about harvesting food. He had been a migrant worker himself, traveling from bean fields to walnut groves to grape arbors, following the harvest of the seasons. That meant living in a tent, or whatever room could be found. When he was a boy, it meant changing schools as often as he changed picking fields. It meant sometimes not having shoes or a bathroom to use. By the time César graduated from eighth grade he had attended 38 different schools.

There was something special about Chávez, although it was hard to decide quite what it was. He had a pleasant, round face with brown skin and dark straight hair—there was nothing out of the ordinary about that. He was a gentle man, and he didn't boast or call attention to himself. But when he had a job to do he did it carefully

(*The story continues on page 151.*)

This is the beginning of a social movement in fact and not in pronouncements. We seek our basic God-given rights as human beings. Because we have suffered—and are not afraid to suffer—in order to survive, we are ready to give up everything, even our lives, in our fight for social justice. We shall do it without violence because that is our destiny. To the ranchers, and to all those who oppose us, we say, in the words of Benito Juárez, "El respecto al derecho ajeno es la paz." [which means respect for human rights is peace].

—César Chávez and others,
The Plan of Delano

César Chávez speaks to migrant workers. They trusted him because he was one of them; he had lived their life and understood its hardships.

149

The MORENO FAMILY'S LONG ROAD to WORK

Picking starts in March
Home of the Moreno Family.
Donna

CROPS PICKED by the MORENO FAMILY.

Strawberries

Lettuce, Cucumber Peas and Beans

Tomatoes, Squash

Wheat and Alfalfa

Potatoes

Corn

Cotton

Onions & Carrots

Kale & Cabbage

Cherries

Graciela Moreno grew up in Donna, Texas, near the Gulf of Mexico, in the 1950s. Until she was about 10 years old, says Graciela, "In winter and spring I went to school. In the summer the whole family piled into a big flatbed truck and set off on a long, long trip." But it wasn't a vacation trip. The Morenos picked fruit and vegetables, starting with strawberries at home in March and moving slowly north as crops ripened. The kids picked alongside the grown-ups. "Sitting in the truck while we drove was boring," says Graciela. "But the camps where we ate and slept were kind of fun." They picked lettuces and cucumbers and peas and beans in Texas and Oklahoma and Kansas, and tomatoes and squash and potatoes in Iowa and Wisconsin. They picked cherries in Michigan and onions and carrots in Kansas again. They picked cotton in Arkansas. Back in Texas, they picked citrus fruit in October. It felt very good to come home again.

and well. He could be trusted; he was honest, thoroughly honest. So when people needed help, they often turned to him.

Fred Ross, an organizer who came to California to try to help the farm workers, heard about César Chávez and gave him a job with the Community Service Organization, which helped poor people deal with many kinds of problems.

Chávez was soon helping those people find housing, medical care, food, and, if they needed legal aid, a lawyer. He got them to register to vote, and he made them realize the power of the vote. Then he began to think about starting a labor union for farm workers. A labor union is an organization of people, usually all doing the same kind of work, who get together to try to make life better for themselves. Factory unions are easy to organize—most of the workers are together in one place—but getting agricultural workers organized isn't easy at all. In California, farm workers labored on thousands of farms that stretched the length of the state. Chávez knew that many growers took advantage of workers. They paid them little, they ignored unsafe conditions, they got their children to work even though that was against the law, and sometimes they cheated them on their pay. By themselves the workers had no power, but if Chávez could organize them into a union, they could demand fair wages and safe conditions.

César Chávez had a wife, eight children, and that steady job with the CSO. When he told his wife he wanted to quit his job to try to start a union, what do you think she said? She knew the family might go hungry if he had no regular work. What would you say? Helen Chávez said okay. She understood that if *La Causa*—the cause—were successful, it would help millions of people. And, knowing César, Helen Chávez thought there was a good chance it would be successful.

It was 1962, and César Chávez started going from farm to farm, talking to workers. Three years later, his Farm Workers Association voted to join Filipino farm workers in a strike against the grape growers. The workers refused to pick grapes until they got better pay and better working conditions. Then the growers hired other pickers. Union members marched near the grape fields with signs that said *Huelga!*, which means *strike* in Spanish. Chávez convinced some of the new pickers to stop work and strike with them.

Retired teacher Alice Barnes, CSO leader Fred Ross, and Chávez (left). Barnes, like many other ordinary citizens, marched again and again with the field workers.

Farm workers struck for the right to unemployment and health insurance as well as decent wages.

California's biggest industry is agriculture, and grapes are the biggest money crop. Before *La Causa*, those who picked the crops got little benefit from the riches they helped create.

151

California migrant workers have to camp in their automobile in the 1930s. Things had hardly changed when César Chávez began working for better conditions for grape pickers. (The photo is by a great photographer, Dorothea Lange. For more of her work, see book 9 of *A History of US*.)

Your **conscience** tells you what is right and wrong (if you listen to it).

Grapes began rotting because no one was picking them. The growers were furious; union members were attacked and beaten. The police helped the growers.

César Chávez had been inspired by Gandhi, Martin Luther King, Jr., and his own religious beliefs. He insisted that the farm workers fight with peaceful marches and prayers. Nonviolence, he told them, took more courage than violence. He also believed that it achieved more. It appealed to the conscience of good people everywhere.

Chávez needed to draw attention to *La Causa*. He decided that a 300-mile march across much of California might just do it. He got university students and religious leaders to agree to march with the farm workers. Look at a map and find someplace that is 300 miles from your home. Now imagine walking that far. Chávez's feet became blistered and his legs swollen. He could hardly walk—but he kept going. Television cameras whirred. Suddenly everyone knew about *La Causa*.

Some farm owners called César Chávez a communist (he wasn't), but most people believed he was on the side of justice and fairness. Finally, a few growers signed contracts with the union—but most still would not. (About this time, the Farm Workers Association was renamed the United Farm Workers; it became part of a national union—the AFL-CIO.)

Chávez announced a boycott. He was going to ask people across the United States not to buy grapes grown in California. But boycotts work slowly, and some of his union members were impatient. They wanted to use violent methods.

Chávez had to do something to control them and to make the growers pay fair wages. He did what Gandhi did. He went on a fast. For 25 days he ate no food. Finally, 26 growers signed contracts with the union.

César Chávez started eating again.

32 "These Are the Times that Try Men's Souls"

Poor People's Campaign 1968

"We will place the problems of the poor at the seat of the government of the wealthiest nation in the history of mankind," said Dr. Martin Luther King, Jr.

That astonishing idea—that all people are created equal and are equally entitled to pursue happiness—still seemed revolutionary in the 1960s, almost 200 years after the days of Thomas Jefferson and Tom Paine. All men and women did *not* have equal opportunity in the United States in the 20th century: some were privileged and some were disadvantaged. The American Revolution was unfinished.

Yet there had been enormous changes in the two decades since the end of World War II. Martin Luther King, Jr., could look at the South with some satisfaction. Where segregation had once flourished, blacks and whites now worked together, voted together, went to school together, ate in restaurants together, and rode on buses together. The changes were amazing to those who knew the old South. The new racial harmony had helped bring industry and a progressive spirit to the South. The region was thriving.

But when King decided to take his movement north—into big-city ghettoes—he discovered problems that were tougher than any he had faced before. He had believed that the methods that worked in the South would work in other regions, too. But the situation was different in America's northern cities.

In the South, the problem had been Jim Crow laws and police-enforced segregation. The solution was to get the laws changed and to get the police to enforce those laws. The job wasn't finished—but the laws were in place and the direction was clear.

There were no Jim Crow laws in the North or West. The urban nightmare had nothing to do with laws. The problem there was economic.

"These are the times that try men's souls," wrote firebrand Tom Paine of the violent revolutionary days of 1776.

? *How many years in a decade?*

Flourish means to grow and thrive.

A ***ghetto*** is a city neighborhood where poor people live crowded together, usually in bad conditions. It comes from an Italian word used to describe a walled section of a city where Jews were required to live, apart from the rest of the townspeople.

153

The Bones of Their Ancestors

The old woman was wheeled into the Senate. No one knew how old she was; even she didn't know. Maybe in her eighties. She had come a long way, flying inside a steel bird across a land that had once belonged exclusively to birds and fish and animals, and then to her ancestors (who had intruded from Asia). Now it was called home by a rainbow of humans (and by robins and salmon and grizzly bears, too). Mary Jim Chapman came from the state of Washington (which was lapped by the waters of the Pacific) to the city of Washington (which got some of its breezes from the Atlantic). She came from the Yakima Indian Reservation (with boundaries that fenced in once-nomadic Indians) to a place where the great chiefs of the land sat in buildings of marble and granite.

Her daughter Carrie pushed her chair into the Senate hearing room, and Senator Daniel Inouye asked her to speak. Mary Jim cleared her throat, and in high, trembling tones, sang out: *Ayyyaaaaaaaaaaaaa*. It was the wail of a people. It got attention.

She had come for what belonged to her and the other Palouse: the bones of their ancestors. They had been wrested from their graves on Fishhook Island by archaeologists who claimed scientific rights. That was in 1959. It was now 1988; Mary Jim had spent all those years obsessed, haunted, miserable, feeling incomplete.

Sociologists explained this. They said the Native American cultures were different from the other culture—the one called "Western," or "dominant." For Native Americans, life was a woven ribbon that was centered in community and continuity, they explained. One generation was responsible for both those who came before and those who were to come. To disrupt that pattern was to tear the fabric.

But perhaps the differences weren't as great as the sociologists believed. How would those sociologists feel if the bones of their mothers and fathers were ripped from the earth and put in museums for strangers to touch and chuckle over?

Mary Jim Chapman and her daughter went to the Smithsonian Institution's National Museum of Natural History. There were Indian bones there. They were not Palouse bones from Fishhook Island. So they went home, still haunted by their obligation to their ancestors.

And then in 1991, Roderick Sprague, an archaeologist from the University of Idaho, pulled into their driveway. He had dug Indian bones when he was younger. Now he, too, was obsessed with returning the bones to their homes. Finally, 34 skeletons were found and reburied on Fishhook Island. But the skeletons did not include Chapman's grandfather, Chow-wah-what-yuk, who had been buried in his canoe. The search for his remains continues.

The cities were filled with poor people—black, white, brown—who weren't being given a chance to rise out of poverty. Usually they went to schools that were tattered and poor, where they didn't get good training for the new kinds of jobs that technology was bringing. But there were hardly any jobs in the inner cities, anyway. Many city people were almost without hope. Young blacks in cities were full of frustration and rage.

And urban whites? When King marched in the Chicago area he was met with white hatred more vicious than anything he had encountered in Mississippi or Alabama. Many of the city's whites were poor, too. They were competing with blacks for jobs—and there weren't enough jobs to go around. Instead of coming together, black people and white people seemed to be growing farther and farther apart. Some leaders, on both sides, were encouraging hatred.

The war in Vietnam wasn't helping. The soldiers who came home had been trained to be violent and wield weapons. Many had learned to use drugs in southeast Asia. They were like lighted matches in those packed cities.

President Johnson still hadn't found a way to get out of Vietnam. He was

putting pressure on those, like Martin Luther King, Jr., who protested against the war.

It was a tough time for King. John Kennedy's brother, Robert (Bobby) Kennedy, was telling him he needed to bring his battle for justice north. Kennedy said the same thing to the ministers and the others who had gone south. To the thousands who had marched from Selma to Montgomery, he said:

Coretta Scott King (outside the gate, center) demonstrates against the war in Vietnam.

> *But the brutalities of the North receive no such attention. I have been in tenements in Harlem in the past several weeks where the smell of rats was so strong that it was difficult to stay there for five minutes, and where children slept with lights turned on their feet to discourage [rat] attacks. Thousands do not flock to Harlem to protest these conditions.*

Martin Luther King, Jr., decided to begin a new campaign. It would be a campaign against poverty. King's program was aimed at "all the poor, including the two-thirds of them who are white." Poverty was not just a black problem, or just a white problem—it was a national disgrace. King planned to bring poor people to Washington. This would not be a one-day march. They would stay; they would camp in the city; the government leaders would have to pay attention.

King believed that eliminating poverty made economic sense, as well as being the right thing to do. If you turn the poor into purchasers, King said, they will solve many of their own problems. The vast amounts of money that the nation spent on military goods could be used to make life better for all people. "Poverty has no justification in our age," he said. "War is obsolete." He believed that nonviolence was the way nations must learn to solve their differences. But time was running out for King and his nonviolent ideas. "The only time that I have been booed," said Dr. King, "was one night in a Chicago mass meeting by some young members of the Black Power movement."

King talked over his problems with Bobby Kennedy. So did César Chávez. Kennedy really seemed to care about poor people. Few other politicians did. The senator was now on the campaign trail, attempting to win the Democratic nomination for president. It looked as if he might do it.

Bobby Kennedy campaigns for the Senate in New York. "All of us ... have a great lesson to learn," he said. "The importance of getting a dialogue going between people in the North and South."

In 1968 the first major rock musical, *Hair*, opened on Broadway; Robert Moog introduced an electronic synthesizer which gave musicians a new tool for making music; comedians Dan Rowan and Dick Martin created "Laugh-In," a TV variety show; Peggy Fleming won the figure-skating championship at the Winter Oympics in France; and University of California graduate student Carlos Castaneda encountered a Yaqui Indian shaman and published *The Teachings of Don Juan*, which inspired New Age thinking.

155

Civil Rights for Native Americans

The civil rights movement inspired Indian leaders. They, too, had faced discrimination and persecution. They knew that many who were Indian pretended to be otherwise because they were ashamed of their heritage. But that was changing.

In the state of Washington (Mary Jim Chapman's home), tribes held "fish-ins" to protest restrictions on their treaty-given

The Indians occupying Alcatraz offered to pay $24 in beads and cloth for it, the price paid for Manhattan 300 years earlier.

right to harvest salmon. In Minneapolis, urban Indians created AIM (the American Indian Movement) and shouted of Red Power. In San Francisco, like-minded Indians formed Indians Of All Tribes, and when the Bureau of Indian Affairs refused to listen to their grievances, they seized an abandoned federal prison on Alcatraz Island in San Francisco Bay and held it for a year and a half (much of it spent under the glow of TV klieg lights).

Traditionally, Indians had focused on their tribal identity. Alcatraz was a *pan-Indian* action. That means that Indians from tribes that had sometimes been one another's enemy were now banding together—although it didn't happen easily. Many tribes, especially those on reservations, were still determined to go their own way.

The militant activists went from Alcatraz to the Bureau of Indian Affairs in Washington, where they staged a protest occupation in 1972. Next they took over a trading post at Wounded Knee, South Dakota, where there had been a terrible massacre of Indians in 1890.

Those very dramatic takeovers accomplished what was intended. They made non-Indians aware of Indian grievances. And they made some Indians rediscover and take new pride in their heritage. Mohawk Richard Oakes said that Alcatraz was not "a movement to liberate the island, but to liberate ourselves."

The most tangible successes came to Native Americans through the courts. Again and again the courts decided in their favor in disputes over rights granted in treaties (many signed 100 or more years earlier).

In 1971, Aleuts, Eskimos, and other native Alaskans won 40 million acres of land and nearly $1 billion in settlements of long-standing claims. In Maine, Penobscots received $81 million for claims based on a law passed in 1790. Several other tribes received similar awards.

Overall, however, things were still not good for many Native Americans. Alcoholism devastated whole peoples. Unemployment was high on reservations and among urban Indians.

But some Indian entrepreneurs were taking a new look at Indian reservations, which were nations within a nation and thus not subject to most state requirements. Indian business people realized that the status of reservations allowed for activities that were often illegal outside, like gambling. In the 1980s and '90s, casinos began to bring enormous wealth—which meant jobs, good schools, and nice homes (along with controversy and power)—to some Indian reservations.

Other things were happening: in Washington, D.C., the Smithsonian Institution returned Indian skeletal remains and funeral objects to their rightful owners. In Colorado, voters elected an American Indian, Ben Nighthorse Campbell, as a representative to the U.S. Congress (and as a senator in 1992). And in Oklahoma, Wilma Mankiller, the first female chief of the Cherokee Nation, spoke of her "firm belief that 500 years from now there will be strong tribal communities of native people in the Americas where ancient languages, ceremonies, and songs will be heard." If so, all the peoples of the land will be richer for it.

33 Up to the Mountain

Memphis's black garbage workers formed a union and went on strike. They struck because some black workers—but no white workers—had been sent home one day when it rained. When the rain stopped, the whites went back to work and were paid a full day's wages; but the blacks, because they had been sent home, were paid for only a few hours.

Martin Luther King, Jr., was preparing for the Poor People's Campaign in Washington when the garbage workers in Memphis, Tennessee, went on strike. They needed help, and King agreed to lead a march on their behalf. That march had hardly begun— King was in the front row—when teenagers at the back of the line began smashing windows and looting stores.

King was furious. "I will never lead a violent march," he said. "Call it off." A staff member urged the marchers to turn around and return to the church where they had begun. Dr. King left. But the police and the rock-throwing youths weren't finished. By the time they were, 155 stores were damaged, 60 people were hurt, and a 16-year-old boy had been killed by police gunfire. It was the first time that anyone had been killed in a march led by Martin Luther King, Jr. He felt sick that a boy had died. He was horrified by the violence. He couldn't sleep. What should he do? He asked a friend. "It may be that those of us who [believe in] nonviolence should just step aside and let the violent forces run their course, which will be…very brief, because you can't conduct a violent campaign in this country."

But King couldn't step aside. He decided that he had to lead a

In a speech after the Selma march, Dr. King said, "I know you are asking, 'How long will it take?' I come to say to you…it will not be long, because truth pressed to earth will rise again."

157

"Tonight I want to speak to you of peace in Vietnam and southeast Asia," said LBJ in the speech with which he announced that he would not run for president again. "In the hope that this action will lead to early talks, I am taking the first step to de-escalate the conflict. We are reducing the present level of hostilities. And we are doing so unilaterally, and at once."

(?) **What does de-escalate mean? Hostilities? Unilaterally?**

peaceful march in Memphis. "We must come back," he said, "Nonviolence…is now on trial." Some of Dr. King's aides didn't agree. They thought Memphis was too dangerous. J. Edgar Hoover, the head of the FBI (the country's federal law-enforcement agency), hated Dr. King. He was using illegal methods to tap King's phone, and he was starting rumors and planting false articles in newspapers. Later, the truth came out about Hoover, but right now Dr. King was receiving death threats in the mail. That didn't stop him. He was going to go back to Memphis.

The night before his trip, King turned on the television. President Johnson was making an announcement. First Johnson said that he was cutting back on the bombing of North Vietnam and would try to get a settlement of the war. That was a surprise—and a relief. Then Lyndon Johnson stunned the nation. "I shall not seek and I will not accept the nomination of my party for a second term as your president," he said. The big man who wanted to be the greatest of all presidents, who wanted to end poverty, who wanted to do his best for America, had failed. The war had claimed another victim.

The very next evening, in Memphis, Dr. King spoke before a huge crowd at a church rally. He didn't have a written speech; he just spoke from his heart. He pretended that he was at the beginning of time and God was asking him, "Martin Luther King, which age would you like to live in?" He thought about being there when Moses led the children of Israel out of slavery in Egypt. Then he wondered about the time when the gods of the ancient Greeks were believed to live on Mount Olympus. He imagined what it would be like to see Martin Luther nail his 95 arguments to the church door in 16th-century Germany. He thought about being with Lincoln in 1863, when the president signed the Emancipation Proclamation. He even considered the time of Franklin Roosevelt and the problems of worldwide war. But King decided that none of those was the time he would choose. "Strangely enough," he said, "I would turn to the Almighty and say if you allow me to live just a few years in the second half of the 20th century, I will be happy."

Now that did seem a strange choice, but King said, "Only when it is dark enough can you see the stars." He understood that he and others in the 20th century had been given a great opportunity. They were grappling with problems of the first order: war and peace and human rights. Everywhere, people were rising up, saying, "We want to be free." But Dr. King knew that some people and nations thought freedom gave them the right to do anything they wanted—even to act violently.

Throughout all of history, violence had marred human life. No one is really free in a violent society. Martin Luther King, Jr., had dedicated his life to a protest against violence and hatred and unfairness. He understood that freedom brings responsibility. That understanding had helped enlarge the quest for life, liberty, and the pursuit of happiness. King had shown the power of a decent individual. Was he right to be happy to have lived in the tumultuous 20th century?

Those who heard him that day would always remember his next words:

> *I would like to live a long life. But I'm not concerned about that now. I just want to do God's will. And He's allowed me to go up to the mountain. And I've looked over. And I've seen the Promised Land. And I may not get there with you. But I want you to know tonight that we as a people will get to the Promised Land....I have a dream this afternoon that the brotherhood of man will become a reality.*

The next evening, after making plans for the Memphis march, Martin Luther King, Jr., went out onto the balcony off his room at the Lorraine Motel to breathe some fresh air before dinner. His friend Ralph Abernathy heard something that sounded like a firecracker. But it was no firecracker. Martin Luther King, Jr., had been shot dead.

Robert Kennedy heard the news in Indianapolis, just before he was to speak to a black crowd in a troubled section of the city. The people on the street had not heard the awful news. "Cancel the talk," the mayor of Indianapolis urged. The police refused to protect the senator. But Kennedy would not leave. He climbed onto the flat back of a truck under some oak trees and told the crowd of the

(?) *Someone in the Hebrew Bible (the Old Testament) led his people to the mountaintop and looked over into the Promised Land. Who was it?*

Senator Robert Kennedy said he supported a "massive effort to create new jobs—an effort that we know is the only real solution." A friend said that he "would have torn the country apart to provide jobs for everybody."

It is April 4, 1968, and on the balcony at Memphis's Lorraine Motel, Martin Luther King's companions point to the source of the shots from the high-powered rifle that killed the civil rights leader. King was 39 years old. The assassin, James Earl Ray, a white escaped convict, was captured two months later at London Airport, in England.

Some think that Martin Luther King, Jr.'s last speech, the night before he was killed, showed that he had a premonition that he would die. "So I'm happy tonight," he said. "I'm not worried about anything. I'm not fearing any man. 'Mine eyes have seen the glory of the coming of the Lord.'" Left: Coretta Scott King and her children view their father as he lies in state at Ebenezer Baptist Church.

tragedy in Memphis. Then he said:

> Martin Luther King dedicated his life to love and to justice for his fellow human beings, and he died because of that effort. In this difficult day, in this difficult time for the United States, it is perhaps well to ask what kind of a nation we are and what direction we want to move in. For those of you who are black—considering the evidence there evidently is that there were white people who were responsible—you can be filled with bitterness, with hatred, and a desire for revenge. We can move in that direction as a country…black people amongst black, white people amongst white, filled with hatred toward one another.
>
> Or we can make an effort, as Martin Luther King did, to understand and to comprehend, and to replace that violence, that stain of bloodshed that has spread across our land, with an effort to understand with compassion and love.

He told his listeners that he understood their anguish because he had lost a brother to an assassin's bullet.

> What we need in the United States is not division; what we need in the United States is not hatred; what we need in the United States is not violence or lawlessness, but love and wisdom, and compassion toward one another, and a feeling of justice towards those who still suffer within our country, whether they be white or they be black….The vast majority of white people and the vast majority of black people in this country want to live together, want to improve the quality of our life, and want justice for all human beings who abide in our land.
>
> Let us dedicate ourselves to what the Greeks wrote so many years ago: to tame the savageness of man and to make gentle the life of this world.
>
> Let us dedicate ourselves to that, and say a prayer for our country and for our people.

The crowd was hushed; people wept; and there was no violence.

The night Martin Luther King, Jr., died Robert Kennedy spoke these lines from the ancient Greek drama *Agamemnon*. The play was written by Aeschylus (who is known as the father of tragedy) about 2,500 years earlier.

In our sleep, pain which cannot forget falls drop by drop upon the heart until, in our own despair, against our will, comes wisdom through the awful grace of God.

Kennedy didn't have the quote quite right. Aeschylus said "despite," not "despair." But Kennedy's misquote seems more appropriate than the original. Did he do it on purpose? Scholars still wonder about that.

34 A New Kind of Power

Martin Luther King, Jr.'s final journey to Atlanta, in a mule-drawn farm cart, was broadcast by satellite to millions all over the world.

Martin Luther King, Jr., was carried to his grave in a casket of polished African mahogany on a plain farm cart pulled by two mules. The cart and the mules reminded people that King's ancestors had farmed America's land with courage and dignity. The mahogany symbolized his African heritage. Weeping at the graveside were leaders from around the world, who had come to pay tribute to the man who had earned a Nobel Peace Prize with his message of love and brotherhood and peace.

But, at the very time King was being lowered into the ground, 130 cities around the nation were burning. Rioters—looting and shooting—were killing people and destroying homes and businesses; 65,000 troops had to be called in to put down the riots. Almost all the victims were black. It didn't make sense. "We are living in an era when the lunatics, not the leaders, are writing history," wrote columnist Mary McGrory in the *Washington Star*.

When the fires cooled, 39 people were dead. The rioters said they

Each time a man stands up for an ideal, or acts to improve the lot of others, or strikes out against injustice, he sends a tiny ripple of hope, and crossing each other from a million different centers of energy and daring, these ripples will build a current which can sweep down the mightiest walls of oppression and resistance.

—Robert Kennedy, speaking in South Africa

161

This picture looks like a scene from World War II. It's actually a picture taken after a riot in Washington, D.C., that followed Martin Luther King's assassination. Seven people were killed and more than 1,000 wounded. Decades later, black neighborhoods in many cities had still not recovered economically from such riots. At the same time, students and Black Panther activists staged antiwar protests and took over buildings at many of the nation's colleges (below: at Cornell University).

History will say that my voice—which disturbed the white man's smugness, his arrogance, and his complacency—that my voice helped to save America from a grave, possibly fatal catastrophe.

—Malcolm X

were responding to the murder of Martin Luther King, Jr. But was that the right thing to do in memory of a man who had dedicated his life to nonviolence? Hadn't they heard his message?

Most black people had. Every poll showed that the majority of African Americans approved of the ideas of Martin Luther King, Jr., and disapproved of violence. But a black minority—a strong, active minority—was listening to other voices. Mostly those voices were young, male, urban, and angry. They were Black Power leaders; they wanted to change their world, and it certainly needed changing.

Some of them seemed to want power so they could get even for the terrible oppression of slavery and segregation. Some, disgusted by all oppression, wanted to separate themselves from whites. But some others wanted to bring respect and power to a black community that could then act on equal terms with whites.

That first idea didn't go far. Most black people had no intention of being oppressors. A few did want to separate themselves from the rest of America's citizens, which, after the sacrifices of the civil rights time, was difficult for many to understand. But that idea of power through respect—now that was appealing. Soon blacks—and whites, too—were studying African-American history. They were also learning about Africa and its history. They were wearing African-inspired clothes. They were telling stories of slavery from the slaves' point of view. They were taking pride in an inheritance full of stories of achievement. They were voting and electing blacks as sheriffs and mayors and congresspeople.

Black writers were bringing new sensitivities to readers. They were not just writing for African Americans; they were writing for all people. In 1940, Richard Wright published *Native Son;* five years later, his *Black Boy* was a main selection of the Book of the Month Club (both are books I recommend). Ralph Ellison had much of America tied up in his genes.

162

Richard Wright

His ancestry was black, white, and Native American. In *Invisible Man* (1952), he wrote of the ways in which society ignores the ordinary person and makes him feel invisible and powerless and sometimes less than whole. In a stunning first novel titled *Go Tell It on the Mountain* (1953), James Baldwin wrote about the religious awakening of a boy living in Harlem.

Black women were among the best writers of the time. Zora Neale Hurston (who was part of the before–World War II Harlem Renaissance) was rediscovered and celebrated. Hurston's great novel *Their Eyes Were Watching God*—which is both funny and profound—inspired many other writers. Toni Morrison was one of them. She won the Nobel prize for literature—there is no higher honor. Alice Walker, Maya Angelou, and Paule Marshall, too, found power in words and ideas.

Malcolm X

Malcolm X found power as a speechmaker. Malcolm had quit school, become a thief and a drug peddler, and landed in jail. He was frustrated; he wanted to turn his life around. But he couldn't express himself because he didn't have control of the English language. He decided to do something about that. He got a dictionary from the prison school and carefully copied every word onto a tablet. "With every succeeding page, I also learned of people and places and events from history." As his vocabulary grew, so did his sense of power and confidence. He began to read:

Anyone who has read a great deal can imagine the new world that opened up. Let me tell you something: from then until I left that prison, in every free moment I had, if I was not reading in the library, I was reading in my bunk. You couldn't have gotten me out of books with a wedge....Months passed without my even thinking about being imprisoned. In fact, up to then, I had never been so truly free in my life.

To create one nation has proved to be a hideously difficult task; there is certainly no need now to create two, one black and one white.

—James Baldwin

Alice Walker   Toni Morrison   Maya Angelou

My dearest friends have come to include all kinds—some Christians, Jews, Buddhists, Hindus, agnostics, and even atheists! I have friends who are called capitalists, socialists, and communists! Some of my friends are moderates, conservatives, extremists—some are even Uncle Toms! My friends today are black, brown, red, yellow, and white!

—Malcolm X

The total number of white people who were poor at the end of the 1960s was larger than the *total number* of poor black or Hispanic people—but the *percentage* of blacks, other minorities, and especially women who were poor was higher.

At the 1968 Olympic Games in Mexico City, Tommy Smith and John Carlos—the gold- and bronze-medal winners in the 200-meter race—raised fists in the Black Power salute as the American national anthem was played, and refused to look at the flag. They were suspended from the games.

In 1960 blacks had very little political power. In that year there were only a few more than 100 black elected officials in the whole United States; by 1993 there were more than 8,000, including 40 members of Congress. Thurgood Marshall and Clarence Thomas had been appointed justices to the Supreme Court.

Between 1950 and 1990, the number of African Americans in white-collar jobs—which means those who work in offices—leapt from 10 percent to 40 percent of all black workers. Black men and women were engineers, doctors, lawyers, politicians, ballplayers, government workers, and artists. Many lived in beautiful houses and belonged to fancy clubs. As to entertainment and sports, Bill Cosby and Earvin "Magic" Johnson were hard to top (until Oprah Winfrey, Michael Jordan, and Tiger Woods came along).

Although most people still seemed to think in racial terms, that concern was just obscuring (which means "hiding") the real problem. It was poverty in this prosperous land. Martin Luther King, Jr., had seen that. Bobby Kennedy understood that America would never truly be a land of the free if some people were trapped in poverty and inequality. "Today, in America," he said, "we are two worlds." They were the worlds of rich and poor. He said he hoped to build a bridge between those worlds.

Kennedy decided he would run for president; there were many who believed he would win that prize. And so he set out, giving speeches across the country. Young people flocked to his side. "It was an uproarious campaign, filled with enthusiasm and fun," his biographer wrote. Yet some, who had hated his brother, hated Bobby, too. Wherever he went, along with the cheers there were also hate pamphlets. But in California, two months after Dr. King's funeral, there was cause for celebration. Bobby had won the Democratic primaries in California and South Dakota. "Here is [California], the most urban state of any of the states of our Union, South Dakota the most rural of any of the states of our Union. We were able to win them both. I think that we can end the divisions within the United States." On June 5, 1968, in front of a cheering crowd, he thanked some of those who had helped him: his staff, his friends, his wife, and César Chávez.

Then Robert Kennedy, heading for a press conference, took a short cut through the hotel kitchen. A shot rang out—and the man who might have been president was no more. It was the end of an era.

Later, a historian wrote, "Born the son of wealth, he died a champion of outcasts of the world."

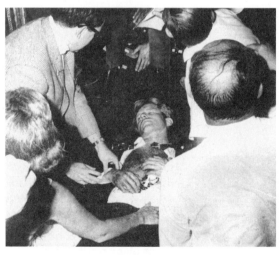

Two months after Dr. King's death, Robert Kennedy was killed by Sirhan Sirhan, who was born in Jerusalem and hated Kennedy for his support of Israel.

35 The Counter-Culture Rocks

Giving the peace sign at an anti-war protest. "Peace, man," became a way of saying hello.

In the '60s, a group of young people—mostly college age and middle class—started living differently from most Americans. They wore different clothes; they marched; they demanded power in their schools and colleges; sometimes they went off to live in their own little communities, called "communes"; and some refused to serve in the army because they didn't believe in fighting.

They were part of something that was called the "counterculture." It had nothing to do with counters, and a few people (who felt threatened by those who weren't in the mainstream) said it had nothing to do with culture, either. But according to the dictionary, culture is *behavior patterns, arts, beliefs, institutions, and all other products of human work and thought characteristic of a population.* And that was what the counterculture was all about: behavior patterns. People in the counterculture just didn't behave as most other people did in the 1960s.

One meaning of the word *counter* is "against," and those in the counterculture stood against many of the ideas that guided the Vietnam era. Some people called them "hippies"; some people called them strange.

Mostly, they were energetic and idealistic. They were Jewish and Catholic and Protestant and Muslim and Buddhist. They had skin tones that were chocolate and honey and peach and mustard. They were male and female. None of that seemed to matter. What did matter was music and protest and ideas.

They thought the Vietnam War was wrong and immoral.

Someone who won't serve with the military because of deep religious convictions (his conscience tells him or her that it is wrong to fight) is called a "conscientious objector."

Many Americans saw communes only as havens for drugs and free love, but they were part of a long American tradition: the utopian community that tries to realize ideals of sharing and cooperation.

165

A national scandal erupted in 1970 when students at Ohio's Kent State University protested against our invasion of Cambodia. The National Guard was called in, and the nervous guards opened fire. When it was over, four students were dead and ten hurt.

They were civil rights marchers and they helped register new voters. Many wore their hair long and their clothes loose and colorful. Many lived in California, and they made other Americans realize that much of the nation's population had shifted west—and that maybe its ideas had shifted, too. They had big dreams: they wanted to make America live up to its ideals, and they might have achieved more, if it hadn't been for some of their experiments, like drugs, which turned to disaster.

But they did change things. They questioned everything, refused to conform, and made their favorite music—rock music—a national passion. Rock was a throbbing, pulsing, new kind of sound that took advantage of the electronic wizardry that was just being developed. It was urban music. It merged sounds from the music of blacks and whites. It was speeded up, and loud, and had a beat that was repeated and repeated so you couldn't get it out of your head. Some of it was political music. Some of it was disturbing music.

Rock wouldn't have happened, at least not quite the way it did, if it hadn't been for an unusual man—a very rich white man—who was a descendant of the 19th-century railroad tycoon Cornelius Vanderbilt. His name was John Henry Hammond, Sr., and he was born in 1910; but he might have been a child of the '60s, he was so far ahead of his times. Hammond grew up in a New York mansion on East 92nd Street with two elevators, a ballroom that could seat 200 people, and 16 servants. The African-American servants had a phonograph—an early

Drugs and the Sixties

The drug culture was one part of the counterculture, and it did untold harm to many—those who experimented with drugs at the time, and thousands who came after them. The '60s produced the first generation in America to make taking drugs fashionable among a large group in society. But drugs take a terrible toll. Among the well-known musicians, actors, and entertainers of the '60s, '70s, and early '80s who died of drug overdoses (or related effects) were:

JOHN BELUSHI, actor

JOHN BONHAM, musician (Led Zeppelin)

LENNY BRUCE, comedian

TIM BUCKLEY, singer

JUDY GARLAND, actress and singer

ANDY GIBB, singer

TIM HARDIN, singer

Jimi Hendrix

JIMI HENDRIX, musician

BRIAN JONES, musician (the Rolling Stones)

JANIS JOPLIN, singer

FRANKIE LYMON, singer (the Teenagers)

KEITH MOON, musician (the Who)

JIM MORRISON, musician (the Doors)

RICKY NELSON, singer

PIGPEN, musician (the Grateful Dead)

ELVIS PRESLEY, singer

SID VICIOUS, musician (the Sex Pistols)

Janis Joplin

record player—and John learned to love the music they played.

He had so much money that he could do whatever he wanted, and what he wanted was to listen to black music (especially jazz), and learn about black culture, and make recordings of the music that was now becoming his, too. He dropped out of Yale College and drove around the country in a convertible in search of black musical talent, and he put that talent on record. Because of John Hammond, a whole young generation could turn on the radio and hear music that had African ancestry.

Billie Holiday

One of Hammond's first great discoveries was a jazz singer named Billie Holiday. Billie Holiday was a woman, and black. Hammond convinced white bandleader Benny Goodman to make records with her. Goodman was doubtful; blacks and whites didn't perform together in the well-known bands. But when Goodman heard Billie Holiday, he forgot his doubts. Then Teddy Wilson joined the Benny Goodman Trio and became the first black musician in a big-time white American jazz band.

That bringing together of black and white musicians led to a mixing of white folk and country music with black rhythm and blues, jazz, and gospel (church) music. (All this happened at about the same time that radio and records became really popular, which was before World War II.)

Hammond made lots of other discoveries, and, in the late '30s, he staged a concert where an integrated New York audience listened to black music—from spirituals to jazz. Most of the audience had never heard music like that before; the concert was a sensation. Hammond not only liked black music; he also liked the people who made it. He wrote about black issues for magazines and served as a vice president of the NAACP (the National Association for the Advancement of Colored People). But he understood that talent has no color, and he discovered some terrific white musicians, too.

In 1961 he found a 20-year-old songwriter and performer in Minnesota who called himself Bob Dylan (although his real name was Robert Allen Zimmerman). Hammond got a big record company to sign Dylan to a contract. Dylan became the most influential musician of the Viet-

With rock and pop came discothèques, miniskirts, and dances: the twist, the mashed potato, the shake, the swim, the locomotion.

The importance of John Hammond to jazz history cannot be overestimated....Fortunately, his taste in jazz was impeccable. One after another, he brought forward young musicians who turned out to be important players; he recorded them, got them signed to good managers, and found them work. Among the people whose careers he furthered are Bessie Smith (he produced her last record session and paid the musicians out of his own pocket), Billie Holiday, Count Basie, and Charlie Christian.

—James Lincoln Collier,
The Making of Jazz:
A Comprehensive History

Above: Joan Baez and Bob Dylan singing at the March on Washington in 1963. "How many ears must one man have / Before he can hear people cry? / How many deaths will it take till he knows / That too many people have died?" sang Dylan. Right: The Beatles pose for a publicity photograph in the 1960s. When the Beatles sang, millions of teenage girls wept, screamed, and fainted.

John Hammond was an adventurous listener; he liked many kinds of music. He had courage, too. It took some courage when he signed folk singer Pete Seeger to a contract. Seeger had protested against the Vietnam War and was under indictment for contempt of Congress. Hammond also signed the Four Tops, a great Motown-sound group of the '60s—and in 1973 he signed a songwriter-guitarist named Bruce Springsteen (who went on to become one of rock's all-time superstars).

nam era. He was a poet who played a guitar and a harmonica and wrote music and lyrics about the worries of the times. He was against the war and for civil rights, and his songs "Blowin' in the Wind" and "The Times They Are A-Changin' " became theme songs for the counterculture.

Dylan was intense and intellectual and sad. He wrote his own words and music, and his lyrics had a message. Everyone sang Dylan's songs, including Elvis Presley. The Beatles said that Dylan was their hero. Those four English musicians weren't sad at all; they were charming and inventive and electric—full of energy and terrific tunes. And talk about making money—the money they brought to England reduced its foreign debt. The queen gave them all medals (later, John Lennon gave his back when he disapproved of things the British government was doing).

Some said there was a kind of rivalry between Dylan and the Beatles, but that wasn't true. Beatle Paul McCartney said, "It was really a question of everyone admiring Dylan—and we felt kind of honored that he admired us." But it was the Beatles who became the most important popular musicians of their time (maybe of all time).

The Beatles had listened to a lot of black music on the radio in Liverpool, England, the big industrial port city where they grew up. They loved its drum beat, its rhythm, and its energy and emotion. "It was

168

Aretha Franklin (above) began singing as a child in her father's church. At age eight, Gladys Knight (top right) won the grand prize on a radio amateur hour. Joined by the Pips (bottom right) and signed by Motown, she had a string of hugely popular hit songs.

the black music we dug," said Beatle John Lennon. They took that music and turned it into something that was all their own. "We didn't sound like the black musicians because we weren't black and because we were brought up on a different kind of music and atmosphere."

The Beatles were good; even people who didn't like rock were likely to agree about that. Even classical musicians were listening to them. It was hard for anyone to ignore the Beatles. But there were many other good musicians, too. Aretha Franklin, the daughter of a Detroit Baptist minister, was one of the superstars. Franklin was another Hammond find. She managed to take gospel and blues and merge them together into something that was sad and raw and cool all at the same time—it was called "soul." Franklin, like most of the rock stars, came from an ordinary background—it was her talent that was extraordinary.

Not everyone liked rock—in fact, some people hated it. The lyrics were often about sex or drugs, and the volume of the instruments—which were usually electrically amplified—could be ear-splitting. The great jazz artist Duke Ellington said rock "had nothing to do with music." But a lot of people didn't agree, especially young people, who had those amplifiers turned way up.

36 Nixon: Vietnam, China, and Watergate

The Nixons in Yorba Linda, California, where Richard (far right) was born in 1913. When he was nine, they moved to Whittier, where Richard's father ran a gas station and a grocery store.

Some years, like some people, stand out. Take 1492, or 1776, or 1860, or 1917, or 1945. You know what happened in each of those years, don't you? Well, find out if you don't, because each is noteworthy, significant, momentous, and consequential—which means they are not-to-be-forgotten years.

Now, 1968 doesn't rank up there with 1492—it wasn't *that* important. But, in the second half of the 20th century, it stood out as a pivotal year. And that means that things changed in 1968; they changed dramatically.

It was the year of those two awful assassinations. It was the year of the Tet offensive in Vietnam. *Tet* is the Vietnamese New Year. It is a big holiday—a kind of Christmas, New Year's, and Thanksgiving rolled into one. The North Vietnamese launched an attack during Tet; a lot of American soldiers were killed, and we realized we weren't winning that war (although our leaders had been telling us that we were).

Nineteen sixty-eight was also a year of urban riots and protests on college campuses. It was the year a computer named Hal starred in a movie and people gasped when they considered where technology might lead. It was an election year, and the end of a liberal era and the beginning of more conservative times. It was the year Republican Richard Milhous Nixon was elected president.

In 1962, Nixon lost the race for governor of California and told reporters, "You won't have Nixon to kick around anymore, gentlemen, because this is my last press conference." Six years later he ran for the presidency and won easily.

I have never thought much of the notion that the presidency makes a man presidential. What has given the American presidency its vitality is that each man remains distinctive. His abilities become more obvious, and his faults become more glaring. The presidency is not a finishing school. It is a magnifying glass.

—Richard Nixon, *Memoirs*

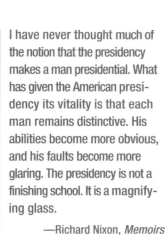

Richard Nixon played football in high school, but not in college. One observer said, "I've often thought with Nixon that if he'd made the football team, his life would have been different."

Words that Richard Nixon never learned:

When tempted to do anything in secret, ask yourself if you would do it in public; if you would not do it, be sure it is wrong.

—Thomas Jefferson

Nixon's story begins way back in the 18th century, when a family named Milhous arrived in William Penn's colony. They'd come from Ireland and were Quakers: hardworking, peace-loving folk. Eventually the Milhouses moved to Indiana, where there were also many Quakers, and, after that, some of them went to California and helped found a Quaker town named Whittier (named after a 19th-century American poet. Who was—?). When the 20th century began, Frank Milhous was running a nursery (the kind where you raise plants, not children) in Whittier. He was prosperous and said to be a bit snooty. He wasn't at all impressed with Frank Nixon, the man his daughter Hannah chose to wed.

The Nixons, too, had come to America in the 18th century. They first settled in Delaware, about 10 miles away from the Milhouses, across the border in Pennsylvania. But they probably didn't know each other.

Life was never easy for the Nixons. It certainly wasn't easy for Frank Nixon, who became an orphan when he was young and never got much love. People had mixed feelings about Frank Nixon: he could be thoughtful and kind, but he had a bad temper. Everyone agreed that Hannah was kindly; some called her a saint. Frank and Hannah had five sons and struggled to get by on Frank's modest earnings.

Their second son, Richard, a quiet, dark-eyed, serious boy, was the kind who never seemed to get his clothes dirty. Richard got good grades in school; in high school he learned to debate and to act. Then he went to Whittier College, was president of the student

Nixon went to China in 1972. Here are his words describing what happened:

Chou En-lai stood at the foot of the ramp, hatless in the cold. Even a heavy overcoat did not hide the thinness of his frail body....I knew that Chou had been deeply insulted by Foster Dulles's refusal to shake hands with him at the Geneva Conference in 1954. When I reached the bottom step, therefore, I made a point of extending my hand as I walked toward him. When our hands met, one era ended and another began.

In 1971, the 26th Amendment to the Constitution was ratified. It said that 18-year-olds could vote. Are you getting ready? The most important job in the nation is that of citizen. This is a people's government. The people are in charge. The president, the governors, and the other public officials all work for us citizens. They are called *servants of the people.* But if you don't know enough about your government to understand what your servants are doing, they may rob you and steal your power.

This boy was a soldier in the Cambodian army. U.S. policy in Cambodia ended in disaster for the people, whether they were communists or not.

council, and got a scholarship to Duke University Law School (across the country in North Carolina). He was graduated in time to serve in the U.S. Navy during World War II.

It was politics that always seemed to interest him. So, as a young lawyer, when he got chances to run for Congress and then for the Senate, he grabbed them. Some people would never forget the campaign methods he used. They were unsavory—which means "dirty." For one thing, he accused some of his opponents of being communists, when he knew they weren't. He ran against a woman senator and said she was pink right down to her underwear—because *red* and *pink* were words used to describe communists. That might have been amusing, but it was untrue. Someone on his campaign staff even forged a picture of the lady senator with a leading communist. Everyone was doing it, his supporters said of his mud-slinging and dirty tricks. Do you think that excused him?

No question, Dick Nixon was bright and capable. In Congress he became known as a tough anti-communist, a kind of well-behaved Joe McCarthy. On most other issues, he sided with the moderates. As to civil rights, he was usually for them; in foreign affairs, he supported the Marshall Plan. He impressed people: he was smart, industrious, serious, and ambitious. Dwight D. Eisenhower asked him to be his vice president, and he did a good job in that office. People began talking about the two Nixons. One was very capable. The other Nixon didn't seem to care about truth and honor.

When he became president, he brought those two personalities with him. Richard Nixon the statesman talked of "law and order," and, after months of riots in our cities, that was just what most Americans wanted to hear. But the other Richard Nixon had no respect for the law when it affected him.

He claimed he had a plan to end the war, but he never said what that plan was. Then he kept us fighting in Vietnam for almost five more years (he was re-elected in 1972). He took the war into neighboring Cambodia and Laos, without telling Congress that he planned to do it. He dropped more bombs than any president in our history, although he said he wanted

to be a peacemaker. The anti-war demonstrations had been bad when Lyndon Johnson was president; they were worse for President Nixon.

Nixon's intelligent, reasonable side helped him lead the nation in a new foreign-policy direction. Nixon was a pragmatist, which means a "practical thinker," and he understood that the world was changing and that it was time to try to work with the communist nations. So he went to China (and took along three cargo planes, with 50 tons of television equipment, so the whole world could watch him walk China's Great Wall). He improved relations with that enormous nation. Then he went to Moscow (Russia's capital), the first American president to do so, and once again showed concern for world harmony.

We got out of Vietnam much as we had gotten in—one step at a time. It was called "phased withdrawal." But, after Saigon, the capital of South Vietnam, fell to northern forces, we finally withdrew completely. We had lost a war—although we didn't quite admit it. We were confused and humbled and weary. We needed to feel good about ourselves again, but something was going on at home that left us even more upset and dismayed. The problem, again, was one of leadership.

Something happened to Richard Nixon that is important for you to understand. It happened because of that distrustful side of his nature. He imagined enemies. He did what he wanted, and didn't

Richard and Pat Nixon visit the Great Wall of China, along with Chairman Mao and his wife to the right. Nixon "recognized" China. He instituted diplomatic relations with its communist government. Asked for his thoughts on the wall, the president said, "I think you would have to conclude that this is a great wall."

Captain Denton Comes Home

Jeremiah Denton was the 13th American pilot to be shot down in the Vietnam War. That was back in 1965 (see page 131). Now it was seven years later, and a big C141 plane touched down at Gia Lam airport, outside Hanoi. The POWS were leaving the Hanoi Hilton, and Heartbreak, and Alcatraz. They were going home. (Some 50,000 Americans who had been in southeast Asia would not return home with them.) These men had endured great hardship and had survived. They didn't know it yet, but they were national heroes. (One of them, John McCain, would become Arizona's

Jeremiah Denton

senator and a spokesman for political change.) They flew east, to Clark Field in the Philippines. Jeremiah Denton—now Captain Denton—on the first plane to land was asked to speak. He stood straight and spoke clearly:

We are honored to have had the opportunity to serve our country under difficult circumstances. We are profoundly grateful to our commander in chief and to our nation for this day. God bless America!

They were words that made Americans proud.

WANTED

JAMES McCORD · DWIGHT CHAPIN · H. R. HALDEMAN · JOHN MITCHELL · JOHN ERLICHMAN

MAURICE STANS · EUGENIO MARTINEZ · G. GORDON LIDDY · CHARLES COLSON · HERBERT KALMBACH

JOHN DEAN · ROBERT MARDIAN · JEB MAGRUDER · RICHARD M. NIXON · BERNARD L. BARKER

VIRGILIO GONZALEZ · DONALD SEGRETTI · FRANK A. STURGIS · E. HOWARD HUNT JR. · HUGH SLOAN JR.

"This office is a sacred trust," said Nixon in 1973, the year he and dozens of others were investigated in connection with the Watergate break-in.

worry about breaking the law, or about hurting people. He seemed to think that because he was president, he was above the law. But he was missing the whole point of American democracy. No one is above the law—not even the president. As North Carolina's Senator Sam Ervin, Jr., said, "divine right went out with the American Revolution."

Anyone who understands our democracy knows that the president is a servant of the people. Richard Nixon forgot that. He allowed his staff to play dirty, illegal tricks on his opponents. Burglars broke into Democratic Party headquarters and stole documents. Burglars broke into a psychiatrist's office and stole the confidential records of someone Nixon disliked. People tapped telephone lines and listened to private conversations. Money was gathered and used in illegal ways. Lies were told about people Nixon disliked. The government's tax office was used against his enemies. All of those things were against the law.

When some of that wrongdoing became known, people in the Nixon White House did something even worse. They paid hush money to keep some people quiet and to have others lie in sworn testimony to judges and juries. It was disgraceful. It was the bottom moment in the history of the presidency. It was called "Watergate" because the Democratic Party headquarters were in Washington's fancy Watergate apartments. Nixon's dirty-tricks workers burglarized those Watergate headquarters. They rented a room in a nearby hotel so they could spy on Watergate. (Americans spying on each other? The president involved! Sad but true.)

Shameful as it was, there was something positive about Watergate: our democratic system worked. When two reporters (Bob Woodward and Carl Bernstein) found out about the burglaries and the dirty tricks, they told of them. It took great courage to accuse a president

It was after Tet
that American public opinion changed. After Tet, most Americans no longer supported the war.

174

and his aides. Their newspaper, the *Washington Post,* stood behind them. The press—the *fourth estate*—acted as it was meant to: as a responsible watchdog alerting the nation to danger.

Richard Nixon almost got away with criminal acts—but he didn't. The president was not above the law. Nor were other people in his administration. Vice President Spiro Agnew admitted to filing a "false and fraudulent" tax return. Agnew left office, was fined $10,000, and sentenced to three years' probation. Fifty-six men in the Nixon administration were convicted of Watergate-related crimes. Some went to jail. The Constitution writers had prepared

The story continues on page 178.

"I am not a crook," Nixon told reporters. His biographer Stephen Ambrose said of him, "Mr. Nixon wanted to become Richard the Great. He wanted nothing short of world peace and a prosperous, happy America. He was brought down by his own hubris, by his own actions, by his own character. This is tragedy." Below: By October 1973, Nixon's approval rating had hit a low of 17 percent. Ten months later, Republican senator Barry Goldwater informed him that he had lost almost all support in the Senate; Nixon resigned the next day.

Mercury, Gemini, and Apollo

Some 4 billion years ago, a small planet hurtled onto Earth and sent exploding pieces into the atmosphere. Those objects circled the earth, collided, collected, and became the moon. The earth and the moon eventually settled into a gravitational balance about 239,000 miles apart, with the moon orbiting Earth and its pull influencing the oceans' tides.

It was a long time before earthlings appeared; when they did, they watched the moon and the cycles of its appearance, and planted crops when the moon seemed to tell them to do it. They told stories of the moon, and dreamed by its bright, reflected light. So it was not surprising, when we actually pushed ourselves off the surface of the earth, that the moon was where we wanted to go.

It was an outrageous idea, to expect to leave the earth's atmosphere and make it to that distant globe, especially in the very century that people had first learned to fly.

We might not have tried it at all if it hadn't been for Russia. When the Russians sent a vehicle into space—called *Sputnik*—we couldn't quite believe it. We Amer-icans had the idea that we were better than others. It was a kind of national arrogance. We aren't better or smarter than other people. (What we have is a terrific idea—for free govern-ment—that is the envy of a lot of other nations and has helped most of us pursue happiness.)

But scientific achievement? We have to work as hard as anyone else to make and do things. Russia's *Sputnik* got us energized. We didn't want our communist foes to take over space.

Then, in April 1961, the Russians sent a man rocketing into space. His name was Yuri Gagarin (guh-GAR-in), and he had a boyish grin and a lot of courage. When he came back to earth he landed in a field where he startled a cow and two farm workers. "Have you come from outer space?" stammered Anya Takhtarova to the man in the orange flight suit. "Yes. Would you believe it, I certainly have," said cosmonaut Gagarin.

The United States had a space agency, NASA (the National Aeronautics and Space Administration), and a space program—but we were behind the Russians, and we couldn't stand that idea.

President John F. Kennedy made a speech announcing our intention to put a man on the moon "before the decade is out." We were off on a space race.

What would life be like in space? On the earth, it is the pull of gravity that keeps your legs on the ground. But when there is zero gravity—as in space—there is no pull. You float around. You have no weight. If you eat a cookie in space, the crumbs float. If you want to sleep in a bed, you have to be strapped down. Other things have to be considered. Normal breathing is impossible in the vacuum of

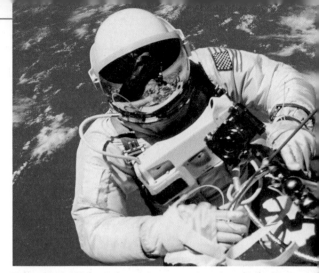

Edward H. White II floats in space in a specially designed spacesuit and helmet, which has a gold-plated visor to protect him against the sun's rays. In his hand is an HHSMU (a "hand-held self-maneuvering unit") with which he controls his movements in space.

space; a spacecraft or spacesuit has to be equipped with its own atmosphere.

A trip to the moon would be a voyage like the one that Columbus made. No one knew where it might lead. Would we create colonies in space? Would we mine the moon's resources? Would we put factories in space and re-turn the earth to its gardenlike heritage? Would we explore other galaxies? Would we meet other beings out there?

This moon trip became the will of a nation. It took the tal-ent of thousands of brains, it took the lives of some astro-nauts (who were killed in explosive misfires), and it cost $25.5 billion, which came from the earnings of America's citizens.

The first step toward the moon was a flight into space. Alan B. Shepard was squeezed into a spacesuit in a space capsule just big enough to hold him. This was the Mercury project, named for the swift messenger of the ancient Roman gods. (The craft was called *Freedom 7.*)

Some smart scientific brains worked on Project Mercury, but they forgot something important: astronauts have to go to the bathroom. Shepard had a big breakfast the day of his flight. Finally, he had to go in his spacesuit. Then he was off, blasted into space with a great roar and arched back to his home on earth with a mighty splash into the ocean. The flight lasted 15 minutes. (Today's space shuttles have toilets. Flowing air substitutes for gravity and draws wastes into storage containers. Astronauts now wear everyday clothing inside the space vehicle. Space-suits are needed only for activities outside the spaceship.)

The Mercury flights—there were six of them—were an important first step. One Mercury flight lasted 34 hours.

Next came *Gemini*, named for twin stars. They were two-man flights intended to test rendezvous (meeting) and docking techniques. Gemini met a target vehicle, named *Agena*; the spacecraft touched noses and clamped themselves together. The Gemini astronauts walked outside the capsule—into outer space—but with a cord that firmly tied them to their vehicle.

The Gemini spacecraft was a big improvement over Mercury. It was bigger and could be steered by the astronauts.

On the morning of July 16, 1969, five months before President Kennedy's deadline of the end of the decade (Richard Nixon was now president), the sun was bright and the skies were clear at Cape Canaveral on Florida's east coast. Some 8,000 people were packed into a special viewing area; others jammed nearby roads and beaches. Photographers in TV helicopters flew overhead taking pictures of the crowds and of the good-luck messages written in beach sand.

Nearby, three men sat strapped elbow to elbow inside a narrow capsule on top of a rocket that stood as tall as a 30-story building. Neil Armstrong, a civilian pilot, was in the left seat. Some said he was the nation's best jet test pilot. Armstrong had the personality of a cowboy-movie hero: cool. Edwin E. Aldrin sat in the middle. Everyone called him by his school nickname, Buzz. Buzz Aldrin was an air force colonel with a big brain. Some of his scientific ideas had gone into this mission. Michael Collins, another air force officer and test pilot, was to pilot the command ship, which would orbit the moon while the other two men descended to the lunar surface in the landing vehicle.

The rocket—named *Saturn*—belched fire and its own billowing clouds, lifted off, and seemed to rise slowly. But that was an illusion; after two and a half minutes *Saturn* was 41 miles above Earth. It was traveling at 5,400 mph (miles per hour) when its first stage fell away. (How fast can an automobile go? How about a commercial jet?)

The next stage took the astronauts 110 miles above Earth, carrying them at 14,000 mph, and was jettisoned (dropped away). The third stage got them to 17,400 mph; they were now weightless and orbiting the earth. It was 17 minutes after liftoff. After they had circled the globe twice, the third-stage engine fired the ship away from Earth's orbit. "It was beautiful," said Armstrong. He was cruising toward the moon. It would take three days to get there.

(Three days was the time it took Thomas Jefferson to make the 90-mile trip, in a horse-drawn carriage, from his plantation at Monticello to his plantation at Poplar Forest.)

Everyone on Earth went on this trip. Television took us into space and then put us on the rocky, craggy, pock-marked moon. When two men stepped out of the landing vehicle, we were there—all the peoples of the earth. It was an American spaceship, but it was a world event.

Neil Armstrong stepped onto the moon's crunchy soil and said, "One small step for man, one giant leap for mankind." It was an understatement. The man in the moon was now real, and we were standing with him.

The view from the moon was of one Earth—it was not one of small, separate nations. Perhaps the next bold journey would be one that the united nations of the earth would take together.

The fate of empires depends on the education of youth.

—Aristotle

Sputnik was a shock. It made us feel that we were falling behind Russia when it came to technology and science. It made us look hard at our schools. In 1958 Congress passed the National Defense Education Act to give federal aid to schools to increase instruction in science and math.

for this kind of emergency by giving Congress the power to impeach and try a president. (See book 7 of *A History of US* to read of the impeachment of Andrew Johnson.)

In the House of Representatives, articles of impeachment were prepared. President Nixon was charged with lying, obstructing justice, and using the Internal Revenue Service (the tax office) and other government agencies illegally. Nixon was going to be impeached. After that, he would face a trial in the Senate for "high crimes and misdemeanors." He chose to leave the presidency instead. He resigned as president of the United States (the only man ever to do so).

In England, an editor of the London *Spectator* wrote that the U.S. presidency had gone from George Washington, who could not tell a lie, to Richard Nixon, who could not tell the truth.

Barbara Jordan Examines the Constitution

Representative Jordan, a lawyer, and the first black woman elected to the Texas State Senate, was a member of the House Judiciary Committee that considered the impeachment of President Nixon for "high crimes and misdemeanors" (see Article II, Section 4, and Article I, Sections 2 and 3, of the U.S. Constitution). Here is an excerpt from her impassioned speech, which was carried on national television and earned her the role of keynote speaker at the 1976 Democratic National Convention.

Mr. Chairman...Earlier today we heard the beginning of the Preamble to the Constitution of the United States, "We, the people." It is a very eloquent beginning. But when the document was completed, on the 17th of September in 1787, I was not included in that "We, the people." I felt somehow for many years that George Washington and Alexander Hamilton just left me out by mistake. But through the process of amendment, interpretation, and court decision I have finally been included in "We, the people."

Today, I am an inquisitor....My faith in the Constitution is whole, it is complete, it is total. I am not going to sit here and be an idle spectator to the diminution, the subversion, the destruction of the Constitution.

"Who can so properly be the inquisitors for the na-

tion as the representatives of the nation themselves?" (The Federalist, no. 65). The subject of its jurisdiction are those offenses which proceed from the misconduct of public men. That is what we are talking about....It is wrong...to assert that for a member to vote for an article of impeachment means that that member must be convinced that the president should be removed from office. The Constitution doesn't say that....In establishing the division between the two branches of the legislature, the House and the Senate, assigning to the one the right to accuse and to the other the right to judge, the framers of this Constitution were very astute. They did not make the accusers and the judges the same person.

"If you're going to play the game [of politics] properly," said Barbara Jordan, *"you'd better know every rule."*

(?) **What is Barbara Jordan's point? Can you put her thoughts in your own words? What do these words mean: inquisitor, diminution, subversion, astute?**

37 A Congressman and a Peanut Farmer

"I am a Ford, not a Lincoln," said Gerald Ford when he was sworn in as vice president. He was a keen golfer and did push-ups and swam daily in the White House.

Gerald Ford was never elected president or vice president, and yet he became president of the United States. How did that happen?

This was the way: President Nixon chose him to replace Spiro Agnew when Agnew resigned as vice president. Then, when Nixon resigned, Ford became president.

Ford, a popular, pleasant man, was a congressman from Michigan and House minority leader. That means he was the Republican leader in the House of Representatives (where there was a Democratic majority). When he became president, he put his feet into two hornet's nests: the messes that were left from Watergate and Vietnam.

He said he would heal the "long national nightmare," and he was talking about the scandal of Watergate. He promptly granted Nixon an unconditional pardon for any wrongdoings against the United States. Some people howled in protest—they thought Nixon should be put on trial—but others believed the country was better off spared that agony; they were glad to forget the national nightmare. Then Ford pardoned draft protestors who had refused to fight in Vietnam, although there were some conditions attached to their pardons.

During Gerald Ford's presidency the last U.S. troops and support workers were evacuated from Vietnam. Vietnam

"To me," said Ford, seen here with his wife, Betty, waving goodbye to Nixon as he left the White House for good, "the presidency and the vice presidency were not prizes to be won but a duty to be done."

I believe that truth is the glue that holds government together, not only our government but civilization itself....As we bind up the internal wounds of Watergate, more painful and more poisonous than those of foreign wars, let us restore the golden rule to our political process, and let brotherly love purge our hearts of suspicion and of hate.

—Gerald Ford,
in his inaugural address

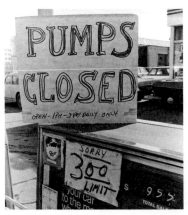

The Energy Crisis, 1974: oil shortages caused long lines and restrictions at gas stations around the country. In the '70s, with 6 percent of the world's population, the United States used 33 percent of the world's energy.

No president's child had gone to public school since the days of Theodore Roosevelt. But Amy Carter did. She walked to public school with a bookbag on her back. (The Secret Service followed her.) Amy roller-skated on the porch in front of the White House and played in a treehouse her father had built for her.

would take its place in history as America's worst foreign-policy defeat.

As president, Gerald Ford didn't break new ground or excite the imagination of most Americans. His wife, Betty Ford, did. She spoke out openly on controversial subjects, especially the rights of women. She talked of her own problems with cancer and alcoholism and discussed the pressures on young people to use drugs. But that wasn't enough to get her husband elected. In 1976, when Ford tried to win an election for president, he lost.

James Earl "Jimmy" Carter became the 39th president. A red-headed peanut farmer with a big, toothy grin, Carter had graduated from the U.S. Naval Academy at Annapolis and become governor of Georgia. When he decided to run for president he was hardly known outside his state. Most people laughed at the very idea; his own mother laughed. But Jimmy Carter was determined. Soft-spoken and deeply religious, Carter told the American people, "I will not lie to you." And, as far as we know, he never did.

Carter was a southern Democrat with progressive views on civil rights and moderate ideas on economics. But he was an outsider when it came to dealing with the government in Washington. He brought his friends from Georgia with him to the capital. They had some good ideas, and President Carter thought Congress would go along with those ideas. But Jimmy Carter hadn't learned the ways of Congress. He couldn't get things done. It was frustrating for him and for the country.

Besides, he was unlucky. While he was president, a worldwide energy crisis made prices—especially the price of oil and gas—in the United States zoom way up. (It was an inflationary time.) Then the ruler of Iran, the shah, was overthrown and replaced by a fundamentalist Muslim religious leader, the Ayatollah Khomeini, who preached hatred of the United States. The Iranians captured some

The Carter family— Rosalynn, Jimmy, and Amy—at the White House

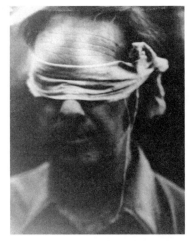

In 1978, militant Moslem students stormed the U.S. embassy in Teheran, the capital city of Iran, and took 52 of the embassy staff hostage. During their imprisonment, their captors frequently humiliated the hostages by parading them, bound and blindfolded, in front of Iranian photographers and TV cameras. When American TV networks rebroadcast scenes like this, American viewers were horrified and angry. It was the single worst disaster of Carter's presidency.

Americans and held them as hostages for 444 days. President Carter ordered a daring rescue mission, but it fizzled into an embarrassing mess of poor planning and failed equipment. As if that weren't bad enough, the Soviet Union invaded Afghanistan, another Muslim country in Central Asia, and, when we protested, relations with Soviet Russia became icy.

President Carter did serve as a peacemaker between Egypt and Israel. And he did get Congress to agree to turn the Panama Canal over to Panama at the end of the century (which was a new Good Neighbor policy). And he did support measures to help protect our natural environment.

But Jimmy Carter never seemed to capture the enthusiasm of most Americans. A highly intelligent, compassionate man, he was, nevertheless, a poor communicator. He tried to solve problems of national debt and energy conservation by asking people to make sacrifices. Maybe he didn't know how to ask—or maybe Americans weren't ready to make sacrifices. When Carter ran for reelection, he was defeated.

Why did Iran's Ayatollah Khomeini preach hatred of America? It's a complicated story, but here's a bit of it. When Eisenhower was president, Iran had a ruler, Mohammed Mossadegh, who was trying to exist independently—outside the influence of the Unite States. We wanted influence—especially since Iran is oil-rich. We helped return the Shah of Iran to power through secret—and illegal—activities of our CIA (Central Intelligence Agency). The shah was out of touch with his people; the CIA helped train and support his secret police (*Savak*); it tortured and murdered political opponents.

Then the shah was overthrown, to be replaced by the anti-American and repressive governent of the Ayatollah Khomeini. Khomeini took American citizens as hostages, defying the Carter administration. Later, the Reagan administration sold arms to Iran in the hope of getting other hostages released in Lebanon. This is a tangled tale.

In 1978, Carter invited the prime minister of Israel, Menachem Begin (left), and Egypt's president, Anwar Sadat (right), to a summit meeting at Camp David, the presidential retreat in Maryland. It was a big breakthrough, getting these angry neighbors to sit down and agree to a peace treaty.

181

38 Taking a Leading Role

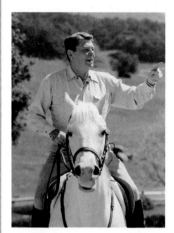

Ronald Reagan was an actor who became president. That training helped make him a brilliant and persuasive speaker.

Reagan believed in the magic of individual freedom. He believed that the appeal of free markets and personal freedoms ultimately would prove irresistible to all people everywhere. He believed in spreading the gospel of freedom. He believed in the attainability of world peace and in the eventual abolition of nuclear weapons. He believed in himself. "Over time, he converted much of the country to his own views and values," wrote David Gergen, who had served as communications director in the Reagan White House and cautioned against measuring the Reagan legacy merely by statistics. "His more important legacy is how much he changed our minds."

—Lou Cannon, *President Reagan: The Role of a Lifetime*

The next president was a great communicator—in fact, that was what people started calling him. His name was Ronald Reagan, and he was in his 70s during most of his presidential years.

Although he was old enough to be a grandfather, few people thought of Ronald Reagan as an old man. He was boyish, easygoing, likable, and friendly. He had a great sense of humor. And he knew how to use television as no president had before him.

After the turmoil of the '60s and '70s, and the unsettled presidencies of Ford and Carter, many Americans thought Ronald Reagan just right for the times. He called himself "Mr. Normal," and he didn't seem to take himself too seriously. As for ready wit, hardly anyone could touch him. But he didn't joke when it came to ideas. He knew exactly what he believed, and he explained those beliefs clearly and simply. In a complex world that was harder and harder to understand, he seemed reassuring and honest and old-fashioned.

It was 1981, and Reagan was about to bring about a radical change of direction in American politics—and be very popular doing it. Few presidents have been as effective.

This, in brief, is what happened. Many of the ideas of an era—begun 50 years earlier with the New Deal—were overturned. "Welfare state" was the term used to describe pro-

Nancy and Ronald Reagan at one of their inauguration parties, held in Washington's Air and Space Museum. A black-tie, mink, and diamond affair, it was the fanciest, most expensive inauguration in American history, costing five times more than Jimmy Carter's inaugural had.

grams designed to help the poor and needy. Although well intentioned, many welfare programs had become bureaucratic dead ends. Reagan not only attacked those New Deal/Great Society anti-poverty programs, he rejected the liberal philosophy that conceived them.

That liberal idea was this: government has a responsibility to help those at the bottom of the ladder. It can use tax money to direct that effort. It can tax the rich at a higher rate than the poor. Helping those who need help is in the interest of all.

This is a hot issue—perhaps the central issue of government in our time. So, consider it. Here it is in a different form:

Liberals think government can actively solve social problems and make our society more fair.

Conservatives believe that doesn't work, and that unrestricted capitalism leads to opportunity and prosperity, and that helps everyone.

Moderates are in between.

Calvin Coolidge was a conservative hero to Ronald Reagan. (Jefferson's picture came down from a wall in the White House when Reagan arrived; Coolidge's went up.) Coolidge economics was called "trickle-down" economics by its critics. It was based on the idea that economic freedom helps create wealth that naturally trickles down to all levels of society. If the rich get richer, everyone benefits. Reagan's economics had a similar goal. It was called "supply-side" economics.

He created a "Reagan revolution." Much of what the nation became at the century's end could be traced to that revolution. Did it make the nation stronger and healthier and more fair?

Well, there's disagreement on that, too. But one thing is sure: his administration changed things. The changes of the '80s were just as significant as those of the '60s (although a pendulum swing away). Now for a few details on our 40th president.

Ronald Reagan started life as a poor boy, the son of a pious mother and an alcoholic father. He didn't seem to have much going for him—except for unfailing optimism, a great memory, and belief

Ronald Reagan was born 11 years after the 20th century began, and his two-term presidency ended 11 years before the beginning of the 21st century.

183

Left: Ronald Reagan and his wife Nancy starred in the 1957 movie Hellcats of the Navy. For Reagan, the transition from acting to politics seemed natural. Right: A poster from Reagan's 1980 presidential campaign. Reagan's landslide victory won him the greatest role of his career: President of the United States.

Before *Brown v. Board of Education*, only .001 percent of black southern children attended integrated schools. In 1988, that figure had zoomed to 43.5 percent. But during the Reagan years, federal officials and the courts relaxed the enforcement of desegregation. By the 1990s, the trend was back toward segregation; 33 percent of Hispanic and African-American students attended schools with 90 percent or more minority enrollment.

in himself and his country. His family moved a lot when he was a boy, finally settling in Dixon, Illinois, a small town 90 miles from Chicago. After graduating from Eureka College near Peoria (run by the Disciples of Christ), Reagan got a job as a radio sportscaster—that was during the Depression, when hardly anyone could find a job. After that he went to Hollywood and became a movie actor, appearing in family films about cowboys, football, and wartime heroics.

But politics fascinated him, so he began with the politics of moviemaking and became a labor leader in the film-making community, and, eventually, governor of California.

His critics laughed at his background. For heaven's sake, they said, a movie star and the host of a TV series! What kind of training is that for a president? As it happened, it wasn't bad. The corporation that sponsored his TV show (General Electric) sent him around the nation speaking to groups of people—especially business people. That gave Reagan powerful friends, and knowledge of the hopes and worries of a lot of Americans.

Reagan was anti-tax, anti-union, and fiercely anti-communist. He wanted to reduce the size of the government. He wanted to cut spending on welfare programs, eliminate most government regulations on business, take the national government out of the field of education, and balance the budget. He also wanted to build up the armed forces and increase military spending.

How did things turn out? Well, some people think Ronald Reagan was one of our great presidents, and some think he was way down the list. By the end of the '80s, the United States was the world's greatest superpower, and very wealthy. But many inner-city schools, bridges, roads, and buildings were falling apart, much of our population was poorly educated, and access to good health care was not equal to that in many developed nations. Read some other

In his budgets, Reagan embraced defense spending and cut taxes for businesses and people with high incomes. He reduced federal money for welfare programs and aid to big cities.

books on this era before you form judgments. No question, the '80s were a seminal decade (which means they planted seeds for things to come).

Balancing the budget was one of his key goals: Reagan was strongly critical of the Carter deficits. A *balanced budget* means that your annual spending equals your annual revenues (taxes provide revenues for the government). If you spend more than you earn you have a *deficit* (DEF-uh-sit); if you spend less you have a *surplus*. A deficit means you have to borrow to pay the bills. That puts you in *debt*.

The national debt in 1979 (under Carter) was very high. Reagan said, "You and I, as individuals, can, by borrowing, live beyond our means, but for a limited period of time. Why then should we think that collectively, as a nation, we are not bound by that same limitation?"

Reagan believed that if his administration cut taxes and public welfare programs and eliminated as much government regulation of business as possible—as Calvin Coolidge and John F. Kennedy had done—it would stimulate the economy and tax revenues would increase. He thought that would pay for the huge increase in military spending that he believed necessary.

Congress enacted the largest single tax cut in our history, which did increase tax revenues, and did increase the total taxes paid by those in the higher income range. But it was not like the Coolidge tax reform. According to historian Sheldon M. Stern, "Ninety-eight percent of federal taxes were borne by the wealthiest Americans when Coolidge left office."

Assassination Attempt

Shots were fired, and a Secret Service man pushed President Reagan to the floor of the limousine. "Jerry, get off me. You're hurting my ribs," he said. But a bullet had gone through his lung and was three inches from his heart. That was why his ribs hurt. When he coughed, blood came up, and the limousine sped for the hospital. As the president was being wheeled to an operating room, he saw his wife, Nancy. "Honey, I forgot to duck," he said. When he saw the doctors who were removing the bullet he said, "I hope you fellas are Republicans." Ronald Reagan had spunk (and a sense of humor).

In the Reagan years, tax cuts let people earning $50,000 a year or more keep 35 percent of the revenue lost by the federal government. Of each dollar the government collected in taxes, 13 cents had come from corporations; after Reagan's tax reform, their share was only 8 cents.

Programs directed at the poor and the middle class were reduced by $41 billion (but the Democratic-controlled Congress refused to cut major welfare programs for mothers and children).

At the same time, Congress embarked on a $1.6 trillion military expansion. (See page 189 for some words on billions and trillions.) Both parties approved. Jimmy Carter's budget had called for bigger military outlays than Reagan's.

What happened to the national debt? It went from $383 billion in 1980 to $2.3 *trillion* in 1988. Reagan's deficits totaled more than the deficits of all the presidents before him combined. That wasn't his intention.

"Government is not the solution to our problem," Reagan said. "Government is the problem." Many agreed. Too often, Americans dealing with their government faced a frustrating, often arrogant, unresponsive bureaucracy. Bureaucracies—in big business, big schools, and big government—seemed to define the 20th century. What could be done about it? Was there a creative answer? How do you conduct public business wisely without oppressive regulations?

The Republican administration decided to cut or cut back the watchdog agencies that oversee business; it weakened already weak union power; where it could, it turned public lands and agencies over to private interests; it lifted restrictions on TV and the public airwaves. The intent was to actively encourage private interests. The theory was that if private interests and competition benefited they would pass some of those benefits on to the public.

But some companies were unprepared for the responsibilities that went with new freedom. Savings-and-loan associations, which were created to lend money to ordinary people to buy homes, began making speculative investments that they didn't understand, knowing that the government would guarantee their customers' deposits. When the value of their investments went down, many of the savings and loans became insolvent. That cost taxpayers an estimated $481 billion—more than the whole national debt under President Nixon. (In the 1980s we spent less than $2 billion a year on all

In 1986, the *Challenger* spacecraft exploded 73 seconds after liftoff. All seven crew members were killed, including teacher Christa McAuliffe.

A homeless man sleeps next to the shopping cart full of his belongings in Canton Alley, in Seattle's International District, in 1986. During the Reagan years, poverty and homelessness often went together. Some of the homeless had lived in hospitals for the mentally ill. When federal and state governments slashed funds for such hospitals, many of them closed their doors to patients who were not considered a danger to society. Unable to cope alone, some ended up on the streets.

schoolbooks for all grades. Imagine what $480 billion would do for our schools.)

"If men were angels, no government would be necessary," said James Madison. "In framing a government…the great difficulty is this: you must first enable the government to control the governed, and in the next place oblige it to control itself. A dependence on the people is, no doubt, the primary control on the government; but experience has taught mankind the necessity of auxiliary precautions."

Auxiliary precautions means government watchdogs. But there were almost none at the Department of Housing and Urban Affairs, where scandals cost the taxpayers billions of dollars. Reporter Haynes Johnson said, "The scandal here was not one of public corruption. It was of public negligence." One hundred and thirty-eight members of the administration were investigated for criminal misconduct (the most ever); many were convicted.

All the money spent on military procurement was just too tempting for those who couldn't resist temptation. (In 1985 alone, military contracts awarded to businesses totaled $163.7 billion.) Arkansas Senator David Pryor described "an eight-year feeding frenzy at the Department of Defense." A reporter called it "plunder in the name of patriotism." (For some details, find out about the Wedtech affair.)

At the same time, libraries, public radio and television, museums, national parks and other public institutions found themselves with less government aid. Spending on education dropped 15 percent in real dollars. ("Real dollars" is a phrase used when statistics take into account what happens in inflationary times. Dollars don't buy as much.)

With the federal government doing less, city and state government had to spend more. They grew enormously during the Reagan years.

It is often said that the rich became richer during the Reagan years while the poor became poorer, but this is not quite right. The real income of every strata increased during the 1980s after declining during the 1970s. What distinguished Reagan's America was that the very rich became much richer, while the difference between those who prospered and those who didn't…became demonstrably wider.

—Lou Cannon

Reagan in Russia

President Reagan and General Secretary Gorbachev sign the INF (intermediate-range nuclear forces) treaty at the White House in 1987. The treaty was mainly symbolic. It eliminated only a small number of weapons, mostly in East and West Germany. But it did encourage more substantial arms control agreements, which were still to come.

None of this seemed to affect Reagan's popularity. After Vietnam and some flawed presidencies, his optimism and vitality restored many citizens' confidence in themselves and in their country. Whatever the problems, he believed this nation would solve them.

Again and again, Reagan spoke out on the dangers of Russian communism. He called Russia an "evil empire." At the same time, he preached the virtues of democracy. Speaking in England to both houses of Parliament, he said:

> *Let us be shy no longer. Let us go to our strength. Let us offer hope. Let us tell the world that a new age is not only possible but probable...For the sake of peace and justice, let us move toward a world in which all people are at last free to determine their own destiny.*

And then something astonishing happened. President Ronald Reagan and Russian Premier Mikhail Gorbachev (gor-buh-CHOFF) began talking to each other. They met at Geneva, Switzerland, in 1985, and in Reykjavik, Iceland, in 1986. They talked about the dangers of nuclear war, and about grandchildren (surprising negotiating tools); and that led to historic arms-control agreements.

The following year, the president went to Berlin, Germany. That city was divided into two parts. In West Berlin, people were free to come and go and practice democracy. In East Berlin, a communist government had walled in its own people. There, a strong, well-guarded wall kept East Germans from visiting friends and neighbors in the West. The Berlin Wall was a bald example of communist repression. It imprisoned a whole people. President Reagan stood before the wall and said, "Mr. Gorbachev, tear down this wall!"

Although few people in the West realized it, forces were at work in the eastern-bloc nations that would cause that wall to tumble. Mikhail Gorbachev, who was a communist but also a pragmatic leader, was aware that Russia needed to change. Ronald Reagan, the Cold Warrior, was now anxious to become a peacemaker.

In 1988, Reagan went to Moscow, this time as a friend of the Russian premier. A beaming Gorbachev took his guest around Red Square, pointing out the sights. Smiles and handshakes replaced the Cold War chill. These two leaders surprised everyone when they realized they had a chance to change history. They could end the insane arms race that had been so costly for both nations and had affected the whole world. They found ways to do it. And history's direction did change. Keep reading. You'll see.

In democracies, nothing is greater or more brilliant than commerce: it attracts the attention of the public, and fills the imagination of the multitude; all energetic passions are directed toward it.

—Alexis de Tocqueville,
Democracy in America
(1835–1839)

One, Two, Wow!

Senator Everett Dirksen once said, "A billion here, a billion there, and pretty soon you're talking about real money." If you're like me, your eyes glaze over when you hear talk of the national debt. Not many people have a sense of big numbers or of what the difference between a billion and a trillion actually means. Author John Steele Gordon, writing in 1996, said, "Today, the American debt has grown, a dollar at a time, to a point where, at $5.1 trillion, it is incomprehensible to the average American. (For the record, laid out in silver dollars, it would be about 120 million miles long, wrapping around the equator 5,000 times.)"

What is the difference between a billion and a trillion? Try this to get a picture in your mind. Go to a blackboard (or imagine one). Write zero on one side, one trillion on the other, and put a line between. Now you have a number line that stretches from zero to a trillion. Where do you think the one billion mark will fall on that number line? Pick a spot.

Did you put it right over near the zero? One billion is just one-thousandth of a trillion. If you make one thousand marks on the board, the first of them will represent one billion. All the rest of the number line is the difference between one billion and one trillion. So when our national debt went from billions to the trillions, it was a big hike. It took a lot of Senator Dirksen's billions to get to the "real money" we spend today.

What do we do

about violence? Mahatma Gandhi, whose ideas on non-violence inspired many American thinkers, gave his grandson Arun a list of seven kinds of passive violence. He thought they were blunders that led to active violence. Here is Gandhi's list:
- Wealth without work
- Pleasure without conscience
- Knowledge without character
- Commerce without morality
- Science without humanity
- Worship without sacrifice
- Politics without principles

Arun added an eighth: Rights without responsibilities.

(?) *Was Gandhi realistic? Are these blunders? What is passive violence?*

189

Congress Shall Have the Power to Declare War

World War II was the last war declared by Congress. What about the Korean War, Vietnam War, the war in Grenada, and—still to come—the Persian Gulf War? The War in Afghanistan?

They were all begun by presidents who claimed special powers. Was that the intent of the Framers of the Constitution?

This is what Alexander Hamilton wrote in the Federalist Papers in 1788: "The President is to be Commander and Chief of the Army and Navy of the United States. In this respect his authority would be nominally the same as that of the King of Great Britain, but in substance much inferior to it. It would amount to nothing more than the supreme command and direction of the land and naval forces...while that of the British King extends to the declaring of war and to the raising and regulating of fleets and armies; all of which by the Constitution would appertain of the legislature."

When Pierce Butler of South Carolina urged that presidents be given the power to declare war, Elbridge Gerry of Massachusetts said he "never expected to hear in a republic a motion to empower the Executive to declare war." George Mason of Virginia said he was "against giving the power of war to the executive...[he] is not safely to be trusted with it."

The words of the Constitution are clear. Article 1, Section 8, says that "Congress shall have the power to declare war."

President Reagan ordered 2,000 Marines into Lebanon to help restore order to that war-ravaged country. But Muslim leaders made it clear they didn't want U.S. help. In October 1983, a terrorist drove a truck loaded with explosives into a U.S. Marine barracks, and 239 Marines died.

That same month, the United States invaded the small Caribbean island of Grenada, ousting an unfriendly government and responding to reports that Cuban communists were building an airfield there. Most Grenadians approved. Many Americans wondered if it was our business to be there.

"Almost everything went wrong, in the invasion of Grenada, that could have. The war was won because it could not be lost—the American invaders had a 10-to-1 superiority over the defenders, and all of the air and artillery weapons used in the "war." Two-thirds of American casualties were inflicted by other Americans or by accident. The exclusion of reporters from the scene helped suppress knowledge of these facts."

—Garry Wills, from *Reagan's America: Innocents at Home*

Grenadian prisoners of war captured during the U.S. invasion of Grenada in 1983. The poorly armed Grenadians had no chance against the U.S. forces.

39 Living on the Edge

In 1935, Tyson's Corner, Virginia, was just that: a corner where two country roads met. Today, it is a concrete, steel, and glass edge city.

Do you remember right after the war (at the end of the '40s), when Bill Levitt built Levittown, with its look-alike houses?

It was a long drive from that potato-field suburb to the big city, where most jobs were located. At first you didn't mind, because the highways weren't too crowded, but as more and more suburbs got built, the roads became turtle slow. The solution was to build more roads. But every time a new highway was built, there would be new suburbs—with everyone crowded onto those highways, heading for the city and the things the city held: jobs, shopping, and entertainment.

Then something began to happen. It was the well-off executives who lived in fancy suburbs near the big cities who seem to have started it. They didn't like that commute now that there were added cars on the road. So they moved their work out to where they lived—usually to pretty, green areas on the edge of the city.

All of this started happening at a good time to make changes. We had been a nation of industrial workers. But factories

More than anyplace else, California became the symbol of the postwar suburban culture. It pioneered the booms in sports cars, foreign cars, vans, and motor homes, and by 1984 its 26 million citizens owned almost 19 million motor vehicles and had access to the world's most extensive freeway system.

—Kenneth T. Jackson,
Crabgrass Frontier

For those who commuted from suburbs to city, the commuter train was a kind of office.

Zones for Clones

Alex Marshall, who writes on urban affairs, says:

As the suburbs become the norm, all the problems of the norm are becoming part of the suburbs. There have been some studies done that show income dropping and crime rising faster than in center cities.

Exclusionary zoning is a bedrock of suburbia and edge cities and people often overlook it. The suburbs have systematically kept the poor and lower working classes out of their cities by refusing to build high-density housing. You have to get to a certain income to afford suburbia. It's designed that way, to keep the "riffraff" out. Virginia Beach has few racial problems. Not because it doesn't allow black people in, but because it allows only middle-class black people in. That's the main reason its suburbs (a lot of them) have integrated so easily.

Zoning laws say what kinds of buildings can be built and where they can be built. (You can't turn your house into a restaurant if its zoning says your block is residential.)

Cities are always created around whatever the state-of-the-art transportation device is at the time. If the state of the art is sandal leather and donkeys, you get Jerusalem....When the state of the art is carriages and oceangoing sail, you get the compact, water-dominated East Coast cities of Paul Revere's Boston and George Washington's Alexandria....Canal barge and steamship give you Boss Tweed's New York....[Railroads yield] Chicago. The automobile results in...Los Angeles.

When, in 1958, you threw in the jet passenger plane, you got more Los Angeles in strange places—Atlanta, Denver, Houston, Dallas, and Phoenix.

The combination of the present is the automobile, the jet plane, and the computer. The result is Edge City.

—Joel Garreau, *Edge City*

were getting fewer, and the new work was likely to be thinking work.

In 1952, more than half of our workers held manufacturing jobs; by 1992, the figure was less than 18 percent. We were on our way from the Industrial Age (with its factories) to the Information Age (with offices).

We were still a great industrial nation—we just didn't need as many people to make things. Our steel industry had become so efficient it could make a ton of steel with fewer man-hours than in any other nation. Instead of getting a job on a production line, you were likely to find work as a computer specialist or as an engineer. People without a good education were having a hard time getting good jobs. Many of them were stuck in the old cities—and out of work.

Meanwhile, as the business leaders moved their offices and office workers to new headquarters and office parks on the city's edge, other jobs appeared in those same locations. After all, the office workers had to be fed, clothed, and have their children cared for. So lots of Americans began moving—to the edge, to new *edge cities*—where jobs, shopping, homes, and entertainment were all appearing.

By the mid-1980s there was more office space on the fringes of New York than in the big city itself. The same thing was happening across the country. Edge cities (some called them "superburbias") were a new phenomenon, and growing like dandelions after a rain.

How do you recognize an edge city? Joel Garreau, who wrote a book about them, says they are places where the population *increases* at 9 A.M. on workdays. Edge cities have a whole lot of office space (at least as much as downtown Seattle has); they are near a traditional city, and near an airport, too. They are almost always near an intersection of highways; they usually hold several giant shopping malls, and a variety of housing. But most edge cities seem to be designed more for cars than for people. The critics say that few of them have any kind of a soul—or the feel of community.

Do you live in an edge city? You can find them

all across the nation. Atlanta has edge cities at Midtown, Buckhead, Perimeter Center, and the Cumberland Mall–Galleria area. If you live near Phoenix, consider Scottsdale, Camelback–Biltmore, and Uptown–Central Avenue. Houston has the Galleria area, Westheimer–Westchase, Greenspoint–North Loop, the Rice University–Texas Medical Center area—and more.

New Jersey is filled with edge cities; they have larger populations than the old cities of Newark and Trenton. One New Jersey edge city, around the intersection of interstate highways 78 and 287, is headquarters to some big companies that make products—from telephones to toothpaste—that you use every day. Those headquarters are mighty swanky, with gyms, tennis courts, hanging gardens, and elegant dining rooms.

Our traditional cities with their downtowns—like Chicago, Kansas City, Duluth, Dallas, or Milwaukee—were all built before the 20th century began. Those big cities are granddaddies—and they are not reproducing. The edge cities are kids; most were born in the last quarter of the 20th century.

Are they the way of the future? Don't bet on it. Things are happening fast. Information-age technology keeps changing the way we work and live. Today, lots of people are taking their jobs home. Many are moving to rural areas, plugging in a fax, a computer, and a modem—and going to work. That trend is expected to continue.

But the edge cities aren't standing still. The newest ones are being planned with grassy malls, meeting rooms, gazebos for outdoor performances, and streets for walking—all intended to foster public activities and a sense of community.

And those old cities? Well, they're changing, too. In Denver, inner-city warehouses are being turned into apartment lofts. The city's core is vibrating with revamped shops, trolley cars, a sunny outdoor mall, and a big in-town amusement park. People are choosing to come back downtown to live.

Urban designer Todd Johnson says, "Balance is the key. A healthy city grows in all areas—it offers a wealth of choice—that's what makes great urban areas great. Seeking your own niche in the supermarket of choice is the fun of it all."

According to Joel Garreau, "Eighty-eight percent of Americans live outside what has traditionally been defined as a big city...a place ...with half a million population."

In Fort Worth, Texas, (as in many other cities), the old and the new stand side by side.

40 The End of the Cold War

In 1989, the Soviet Union—and its monuments, such as this statue of the founder of the Soviet secret police—finally came crashing down.

In 1994, two old men met in Vietnam. Admiral Elmo Zumwalt, Jr., who had commanded U.S. naval forces in southeast Asia, faced Vietnam's General Vo Nguyen Giap. Each was a legendary leader. Each had lost loved ones in that cruel war. They had been bitter enemies. Now, for the first time, the old warrior-foes looked into each other's eyes. They shook hands; then they embraced. Giap autographed his book *People's War, People's Army*, and gave a copy to the admiral. Zumwalt signed *On Watch*, his tale of his wartime experiences, "With respect to a former adversary and friend."

The 20th century came to an end—in 1989—before its years were finished. That's when the Soviet Union broke into pieces.

Yes, the Soviet Union, the U.S.S.R., the land we called Russia—a nation composed of many states—fell apart. The Soviet Union's military power didn't collapse. Communism did. As a political system, communism had failed. It had begun with high hopes as a visionary experiment. The experiment hadn't worked. It had turned Russia into an unfree, tyrannical, clumsy nation. Karl Marx's economic ideas hadn't worked either. Government ownership of land and products didn't bring efficiency and productivity. Finally, the burden of ever-growing military needs helped wreck Russia's economy. (Trying to keep up with Reagan-era military might have helped do it.)

When the Russian people had had enough, they just threw communism out. It was stunning; it was peaceful; it meant that everything had changed in the world's politics. The Cold War was over. The "evil empire" had turned nice. It was hard to believe. Now that Russia was a free nation, there was no giant to battle. At first we didn't seem to know what to do.

But it was becoming clear to most people that we are all passengers on the same global spaceship. The European nations had joined together to form a Common Market—called the European Union. They began acting—economically—as if they were one giant nation. Japan was a major economic power. Nations like Korea, China, India, and Indonesia were making big moves in business. The world's economies were all becoming linked, as nations that had once been communistic began to change to free-market economies.

All that demanded new thinking and new leadership, but it had nothing to do with our founding ideas about democracy and freedom. Those ideas seemed better than ever. People all over the world wanted freedom. When students in China rebelled against their corrupt government, they paraded around with a statue of the "Goddess of Democracy" modeled after our Statue of Liberty. The Chinese government sent troops, who opened fire on civilians in Beijing's Tiananmen Square. The Chinese students didn't get what they wanted: dialogue with the government, recognition of their student union, and political and economic reform. Instead, many were killed.

In 1989, thousands of Chinese students demonstrated in Tiananmen Square in the center of Beijing, the capital of China, demanding political and economic reform. The government cracked down, broke up the demonstrations, and persecuted and killed many of the rebels.

Shen Tong, a leader of the Tiananmen Square uprising, speaking to students at Brown University in 1995, said, "I feel that somehow, throughout all the tragedies, all the suffering, Chinese people will somehow rise up to the international norm of individual freedom and democracy."

The fall of Russian communism was giving oppressed peoples everywhere an awareness of possibilities. It gave us a new appreciation of our freedoms. Ronald Reagan championed those freedoms worldwide, but it was the 41st president, Republican George Bush, who was able to take us in a new direction. Bush was a practical fellow with a low-key manner and an ability to tackle details. The son of a Connecticut senator, Bush was the youngest pilot in the navy during World War II and a genuine war hero. After the war, he moved west to Texas, and became an oil man. But it was government that fascinated him, and he served in a series of important jobs—right up to the vice presidency under Ronald Reagan. In 1988, he became president himself.

He promised "no new taxes." (Reagan had, finally, raised taxes, calling them, in bureaucratic doublespeak, "revenue enhancements.") Bush pointed with pride to the low inflation and the 18.4 million new jobs created during the Reagan years.

But all those years of war preparation had been hard on us as well as on Russia. Bush became president at a time when cities were in decay, schools were behind those of many other nations, crime was epidemic, and the huge national debt was making many

Whether the communist rulers shift their policies of their own free will—or whether the change comes about in some other way—I have not a doubt in the world that a change will occur. I have a deep and abiding faith in the destiny of free men. With peace and courage, we shall someday move on into a new era.

—George Bush,
President of the United States,
1988–1992

President Bush rides in an armored jeep with General Norman Schwartzkopf, leader of U.S. forces in the Gulf War, in 1990. The United States and its allies succeeded in driving Iraqi forces out of Kuwait. Its monarchy returned.

Americans fearful of the future. Most experts were predicting that the annual deficits would get bigger and increase the debt (which is the total bill from all those deficits). The economy turned sour.

Then President Bush went back on his promise and worked out an agreement with Congress—which was controlled by a Democratic Party majority—to raise taxes. It may have helped restrain the debt and thus take a step toward the prosperity that was coming; it didn't help George Bush with the American people. But his foreign policy did win approval.

When Saddam Hussein, dictator of Iraq, sent troops into neighboring Kuwait and took over that nation, Bush led a forceful response. The United States, with the United Nations, stopped that aggression in the powerful, short Persian Gulf War.

President Bush led a military response (from August 1990 to February 1991) that would be known as the First Gulf War, or Operation Desert Storm. Working with the United Nations, the president put together a coalition of nations that quickly drove Iraq out of Kuwait. Air strikes on well-defined targets were coordinated with an effective ground force that raced through Kuwait and into southern Iraq. Then the American-led forces declared a unilateral cease-fire and began to negotiate a peace agreement. President Bush and his military advisors achieved their goal: an independent Kuwait. They resisted pressure to capture Baghdad and remove Saddam Hussein for two reasons: Iran, they thought, was an even more dangerous threat than Iraq and a strong Iraq was necessary to contain Iran. The second reason for holding back? They understood that occupation of a defeated Iraq would be costly and dangerous. Some criticized President Bush for that decision, it left Saddam Hussein in power in Iraq.

The next time President Bush called out American forces, it was to help starving people in Somalia. That nation, which elbows out into the Indian Ocean from the east coast of Africa, was in a state of crisis. Crops failed. Armed thugs were terrorizing and killing. There was no effective government. Our marines brought food and some help. We worked with the United Nations. Our aim was to make peace-keeping a whole-world venture.

But good intentions don't always

Environmental damage is part of war's cost: Oil fields aflame in Kuwait in March 1991.

matter. In the former eastern-European nation of Yugoslavia—now split into several different nations, some of them claiming the same land—Serbs and Croats and Muslims began killing each other, partly because their religions were different. That horrendous war, with "ethnic cleansing" or mass killings, finally ended with an agreement negotiated in Dayton, Ohio in 1995.

For decades we looked at turmoil—in places like Vietnam, Grenada, Nicaragua—and saw the menace of international communism. Now we were beginning to understand that much conflict is indigenous (in-DIDGE-ih-nus—it means "homegrown").

We started asking ourselves some hard questions: does the United States have a responsibility to try to solve the problems of other nations? Is it done best with armies or with negotiators? Or should we concentrate on creating a just society at home and hope that the rest of the world will take notice?

There are some 1,290 different practicing religions in the United States. In this country people of all faiths live together in relative harmony. *We have never fought a war over religion.* Most people agree that is because of our First Amendment—it separates church and state, which means that our government keeps its hands off when it comes to religion. That isn't true in most other countries. At the beginning of the 1990s, more than 30 religious wars were being fought around the globe.

Camouflaging Language

The National Council of Teachers of English gave an award to the Department of Defense. It was their Double-speak Award—for language meant to *befuddle, bamboozle, and obfuscate* (which means?). It was during the Gulf War, but the Defense Department didn't call it a war, they said it was an "armed situation." Bombing attacks were "efforts" and war planes were "weapons systems" or "force packages." Pilots sent out on missions were "visiting a site." Buildings were "hard targets"; people were "soft" ones.

Killing the enemy was "servicing the target."

George Orwell satirized government doublespeak in a satire of communism called *Animal Farm;* it's worth reading. He also wrote a famous essay, "Politics and the English Language," in which he showed how evil can ride on honeyed words. "Political language," said Orwell, "is designed to make lies sound truthful and murder respectable, and to give an appearance of solidity to pure wind." Orwell hated *obfuscation.* He hated *euphemisms.* I have his

rules for good writing tacked to the wall above my desk.
Here they are:
1. Never use a metaphor, simile or other figure of speech which you are used to seeing in print.
2. Never use a long word where a short one will do.
3. If it is possible to cut a word out, always cut it out.
4. Never use the passive where you can use the active.
5. Never use a foreign phrase, a scientific word or a jargon word if you can think of an everyday English equivalent.

41 A Quilt, Not a Blanket

The Perezes reunited (left to right): Victoria, Reyniel, and Lorenzo holding Alejandro.

Orestes Lorenzo Perez, a Cuban military pilot, stepped into his Soviet-built jet fighter plane and flew toward the United States. He was risking his life, but he believed the risk was worthwhile. He wanted to live in a land that was free.

Lorenzo kept his plane low, just over the water, so it would not be detected by radar. There was no way his wife, Victoria, and his sons, Reyniel and Alejandro, could go with him. "Don't worry," he told his wife. "I will come back for you."

As soon as he arrived in the United States, Orestes Lorenzo Perez tried to get his family out of Cuba. He tried all the legal means. He lobbied members of Congress; he founded an organization called Parents for Freedom—but nothing worked. His wife and children were hostages of Fidel Castro, Cuba's dictator. Castro would not let them out of the country.

In the meantime, Lorenzo became part of the flourishing Cuban-American

> America is not like a blanket—one piece of unbroken cloth, the same color, the same texture, the same size. America is more like a quilt—many pieces, many colors, many sizes, all woven and held together by a common thread.
>
> —Jesse Jackson,
> 20th-century political leader

In 1980, 100,000 Cubans, in boats big and small, made it to the U.S. across the Straits of Florida.

community. He learned to fly American planes and became a licensed American pilot. He came up with a plan, and he got a secret message to his wife. The message told of a spot on a highway near a beach. Then he borrowed a plane and called his wife on the telephone. They spoke of children's clothing, of his father, of the sunset. It was all a code. He said, "I'll send money to buy a TV."

"Already?" she asked, startled. Those code words meant he was coming the next day. He needed to know exactly when the sun set in Cuba. He asked about the children's shoe sizes. She said they were 5½ and 6½. The sun set between 5:30 and 6:30 P.M.

The next day, Victoria packed a lunch and she and the boys went to the beach. They spread out their towels and sat down. Two policemen were nearby. Victoria had brought a Bible. She read it. She tried to look like any other mother out for a day on the beach with her children. But Reyniel, who was 11, wanted to go home. He didn't want to swim. She hadn't told the boys of the plans. "Go swim," she whispered. "This is a matter of life and death." Reyniel knew something important was happening. He swam.

At five o'clock, casually, they got up to leave. At 5:45, they were standing beside the highway when they saw a plane landing two blocks away. "Run, run!" said Victoria. "It's Daddy!" The plane missed a car, a bus, a huge rock, and a traffic sign. It came to a stop about 10 yards from a truck. The startled driver managed to hit his brakes just in time. The plane's pilot, Orestes Lorenzo, stayed on the ground for about 40 seconds, which was enough time to pick up his wife and boys. Then he turned the plane around and took off. He had told his wife, in the secret message, not to talk or hug him; he would need all his powers of concentration. Twenty-one minutes and forty-three seconds later, he shouted out, "We did it!" They were in United States territory. They were free.

Bang Huy Le's mother shook his bed. He got up sleepily. Two strange men were in his house. Bang Huy, who was seven years old, was soon squeezed beside his 14-year-old sister in a small open boat with 50 other Vietnamese. Out at sea, they were attacked by pirates, who took their few possessions. But they were lucky; they made it to Indonesia, and, six months later, to the United States. Four years after that, when Bang Huy had almost forgotten the Vietnamese language, his parents, his grandmother, his younger sister, and his two brothers all joined him in America.

The Lorenzos and Les were part of a long im-

All this part of the Perez family's adventures happened in December 1992.

It remains true that nearly all of the world's richest countries are free (meaning, among other things, democratic) and nearly all of the poorest countries are not....Across the world, in other words, the correlation between political freedom and prosperity is a close one.

—*The Economist,* August 1994

Bang Huy Le

Bang Huy had a naming party in his American school. He is now called John Le.

As the U.S. pulled out of Vietnam in 1975 and the North Vietnamese closed in on Saigon, thousands of South Vietnamese fled. Many crossed the South China Sea in small boats like these—and some didn't make it; storms wrecked many of the boats, and others were hijacked by pirates.

In 1849, Kentucky senator Garrett Davis wrote of the dangers of immigration. "The German and Slavonic races are combining in the state of New York to elect candidates of their own blood to Congress. This is the beginning of the conflict of races on a large scale, and it must, in the nature of things, continue and increase....If it does not become a contest for bread and subsistence, wages will at least be brought down so low as to hold our native laborers and their families in hopeless poverty." Was Senator Davis right in his prediction?

migrant tradition in America. It began tens of thousands of years ago, when the first immigrants came from Asia—on foot or by dogsled or in small boats. The previous inhabitants of the land—the birds and animals—must have been surprised by the newcomers.

The people spread out over the two great American continents. Then, just 500 years ago—an eyeblink in the long view of time—new immigrants arrived from lands across the Atlantic Ocean. It was a meeting of two worlds; each had been unaware of the other.

At first, those who settled in the region that became the United States came mostly from Great Britain (England, Scotland, Wales, and Ireland), and from Africa. The Africans came unwillingly. They were forced to become workers in a society that needed them badly.

A new nation was founded—the United States of America. It was an unusual nation—a nation of free citizens (except, of course, for those who were slaves) in a world that was mostly unfree. It was born with the idea that people could govern themselves. It was a democracy.

Freedom, and the opportunities of a big, rich land, were like a magnet. People came. Lots of different people came. Many—like many of the English before them—were failures or outcasts in their old world. Comfortable people don't usually leave their homes.

Some of the English Americans became concerned about the newcomers. Benjamin Franklin worried that the many German immigrants weren't bothering to learn English. He feared that the United States might become a two-language nation. He needn't have worried; their children quickly learned English. They became Americans. Another large group of 19th-century immigrants came from Ireland. They were very poor, but they worked and studied hard and soon they, too, were Americans.

When gold was discovered in California in 1848, boatloads of people came from all over the world—some from China and other nations in East Asia, then called the "Far East" because of its geographic relationship to Europe.

It was astounding. No matter where they came from, everyone wanted all the freedoms and rights that were in the U.S. Constitution. They wanted to be Americans. But some of them, being human, became jealous of the next group of newly arriving immigrants.

So, when the 19th century began to turn into the 20th, and more new people came—this time speaking Italian and Polish and Russian and Greek and Turkish and Yiddish—the earlier immigrants worried. They said the newcomers would never learn

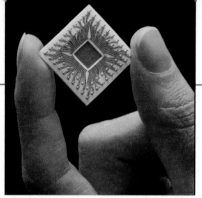

Power in a tiny space: the microchip

The New Technology

Indiana's Howard Hathaway Aiken was generous. Actually, he had the same notion that Benjamin Franklin had had. He thought scientific ideas should be shared. So he didn't patent his inventions—he let anyone who wanted use them. His biggest idea took shape as Mark I. Mark was really big: he was 8 feet high, 51 feet long, had 530 miles of wire in his insides, and was known as a "superbrain." Born in 1943—with IBM's money and Harvard's resources—Mark was the first completely automatic computer.

Mark used mechanical switches to do its calculations, something like those on the telephone switchboards of the day. They were reliable—and much faster than the brains of any team of human mathematicians—but still, they were slow. Electric switches would be much faster.

Eniac had them. It was the first all-electronic computer. Which, in 1946, meant that it had thousands of vacuum tubes. Eniac (*electronic numerical integrator and calculator*) was even bigger than Mark—it weighed 30 tons. And it was fast. J. P. Eckert and J. W. Mauchley designed it for the army.

Mark I attracted moths; a tiny moth could stop the behemoth in the middle of a calculation—its operators had to keep *debugging* it. Eniac's vacuum tubes got hot; it had to be cooled down regularly. Both were frightfully expensive. It didn't seem likely that computers and calculators would ever reach ordinary people.

Then William Shockley invented something that was mostly *silicon*. Silicon is sand. His may be the most important invention of our times.

Shockley grew up in Palo Alto, California. His father was an engineer,

his mother a surveyor. They taught him at home until he was eight. For Shockley, work and play were the same. He didn't waste time—until later in life, when he came up with some wacky, and despicable, racial theories. But that's another story.

After he got a Ph.D. at MIT, Shockley went to work at Bell Telephone's research laboratory. Bell was looking for something to replace its mechanical telephone switches; some kind of electric-circuit switch. Vacuum tubes could do it, but the tubes got hot and burned out. Bell wanted to find a way to improve the vacuum tube.

But Shockley started thinking about something different, called a "semiconductor." Semiconductors are materials that conduct electricity and insulate, too (which means they don't heat up). He found that electrical current flowing from a metal contact point, through a semiconductor to another contact point, and on to a metal base, gets strengthened in the process. Then Shockley and his colleagues came up with a device that didn't look like much—just a little piece of matter (*germanium*) with a few wires in it—but it could do everything the vacuum tube could, and more. It boosted electrical current, produced no heat, didn't burn out, eliminated miles of wiring, was very, very small, and very cheap to produce. A contest was held at Bell Labs to pick a name for the new device. The winning name was "transistor."

When computer designers got hold of transistors—well, those giants Eniac and Mark were dead ducks. Small is beautiful in

the world of modern technology. And transistors kept getting smaller. But one transistor had to be wired to another and that wire took up space. You just couldn't make computers or other electronic devices small. It was a big problem. Two American engineers, working separately, solved it. Jack Kilby, in Texas, and Robert Noyce, in California, figured out that you could etch transistors and their connections onto bits of silicon (a great semiconductor); out of that idea came the microchip and today's technology. You could call Kilby and Noyce the Edison and Ford of modern times. They made pocket-sized video games and hand-held and desktop computers and other electronic wonders possible. Noyce founded a company called Intel and made a whole lot of money. Kilby won the Nobel Prize in physics.

Are the transistor and the microchip the most important inventions of our times? I think so, but you can argue with me. When you use superlatives (the most, the best, the worst, etc.), it's easy to get on shaky ground. No question, though, one of the biggest stories of the last century was in technology. It is a magic show that keeps going on and on.

America is so vast that almost everything said about it is likely to be true, and the opposite is probably equally true.

—James T. Farrell (1904–1979), novelist

How are you going to remember all the presidents after World War II? They are Truman, Eisenhower, Kennedy, Johnson, Nixon, Ford, Carter, Reagan, Bush, Clinton, and Bush. Just use their initials to make a sentence. For example: *The Evil Kryptonite Just Nailed Foolish Clark— Real Big Catastrophe! Bam!*

English. They said they were poor people and uneducated. They said they were outcasts. All that had been said before, and much of it was true. But they had forgotten that in America something happened when people were given opportunity and freedom. The new immigrants worked hard. They invented. They built. They achieved. They learned. Soon those people from southern and eastern Europe were successful Americans, and old-timers themselves.

Then, near the end of the 20th century, another group of new immigrants began arriving. Many spoke Spanish. Some people worried that they wouldn't bother to learn English and that the United States would become a two-language nation. But it wasn't likely. Their children were like all the children before them—eager to learn.

It was the same with Asians, who now arrived in force. (Until 1965, laws restricted Asian immigration.) The Asians, like Bang Huy Le and his family, were searching for opportunity and freedom. They would find it.

People came from Africa now because they wanted to be Americans. And, like all the immigrants who had arrived before them, they brought talent and energy. Other African Americans—whose ancestors had been in America for a long, long time—were finally permitted to achieve success in large numbers. Civil rights laws had opened doors to schools and jobs that for too long had been shut.

All these peoples were changing the look of America. They were making us rich in imagination and achievement.

For we all benefit from the American magic that finds wonders in the world's outcasts. There is nothing secret about that magic. It is called respect for each person's inalienable rights. It is called "freedom."

Every year, students from all over the country participate in National History Day. In 2000, (left to right) Asona Lui, Becky Kopp, and Shruti Challa of Topeka, Kansas, won third place in the competition (held in College Park, Maryland) for their performance, "Breaking Down Barriers: *Brown* v. *Board of Education.*"

42 Is It Me or We?

In the '80s and '90s, many U.S. immigrants came from Asia. Like the Chinese and Vietnamese owners of the businesses at this shopping mall, they were often drawn by the freedoms the United States allows its entrepreneurs.

Reading history is like watching a tennis match. The ball keeps changing sides. To many observers, the 1960s and the 1980s seemed like opposite sides of a tennis court, or a coin, or a pendulum swing.

The 1960s was a time of high drama—of overalls and backpacks and peace symbols—with marches in the streets and sit-ins at lunch counters. People who had been kept out of power banged on opportunity's doors and pushed them open. It was messy, it was exhilarating, it was problem-filled. It was an attempt to do something about long-ignored injustices. Much was achieved, but the action of the '60s—its dreams and its drugs—got all mixed up.

The '80s were different. This time the drama was so quiet that sometimes hardly anyone noticed. Mostly the revolution took place in corporate headquarters, on Wall Street's money exchanges, in people's minds, and in Congress—but it was effective. Some called it a conservative reaction to the excesses of the liberal decades that preceded it. Goals changed. Most voters no longer thought government should be used to solve social problems. Labor unions lost power.

Business was the focus of the '80s (and the '90s, too). New jobs, new wealth, new financial practices, and astounding

> The ideas of economists and political philosophers, both when they are right and when they are wrong, are more powerful than is commonly understood. Indeed the world is ruled by little else.
>
> —John Maynard Keynes, British economist (1935)

> However appropriate it may be for the economy, the "market model" is a grossly inadequate model for the rest of society.
>
> —Howard Gardner, psychologist, Harvard University

 What does he mean?

Chairman Bill

Bill Gates was born in Seattle, and got interested in programming computers as a boy—he sold a traffic-light control system to his home town when he was only 14. As a student at Harvard, Gates had a vision: he imagined a computer on every desk in every office and every home, everywhere. He founded Microsoft Corporation with a boyhood friend, and dropped out of college. Microsoft licensed operating systems to IBM and to other computer makers. Those systems—MS-DOS (Microsoft Disc Operating System) and, later, Windows— soon dominated the market. They weren't completely original, but Gates marketed them with astonishing business savvy and perfect timing. Soon you almost had to have a Microsoft product in your computer in order to run some games and other programs.

Bill Gates became the world's richest man. By 2001, Gates had given away nearly $7.9 billion—more than any other living American philanthropist.

new technology began transforming the ways we live and work and think. New groups of business people got very rich, while many middle-class families found themselves working harder and longer for a smaller portion of the national pie.

More moms were going to work (at home, kids often had less supervision), but sometimes even two incomes weren't enough to keep up with the enticing new lifestyles.

The '80s were the heyday of the "yuppies" ("young urban professionals"), who traveled, experimented, set trends, spent money, influenced the media, and didn't feel bound by old ideas.

New peoples, arriving from Asia, Africa, and Latin America, quickly made an impact. They even got grocery stores to change. Instead of being a white-bread culture, we were suddenly eating pita, and tacos, and focaccia. You could find hummus and mangoes and cilantro and lemongrass on shelves where a few years earlier bananas and apples were as far as variety took you.

It may all have been too frantic for some Americans, who turned to meditation and inward-looking lifestyles. Some, who were outside the mainstream, joined gun-toting, defiantly independent groups.

The times demanded brains. In the late 1970s, Californians Steven Jobs and Stephen Wozniak, operating out of Jobs's garage, developed a small computer. By 1977, sales of that computer, the Apple II, had reached $118 million. The personal computer was just getting started. Bill Gates saw its future and started selling software for computers. By 1990, he was one of the world's richest men.

And computers were only part of the story. They were joined by fiber optics, cable TV, satellites, fax machines, copiers, scanners, cellular phones, the Internet, automatic teller machines (ATMs, or cash machines), and an array of imaginative services. The new technology quickly became inexpensive enough for ordinary people to have in their homes and businesses. All that increased choices. Some Americans began going to work in home offices. And some started educating their children at home, as part of a vigorous home-schooling movement.

Education was clearly a key to success in the Information Age, but, in international comparisons, our 12th-grade students' scores— especially in math and science—were at or near the bottom of the heap. Schools in many cities, like factory-age relics, seemed primarily oversized warehouses for young people. Tax rebellions on the state and local levels—begun in California and copied elsewhere— cut school spending at the very time we needed to increase it.

In the 20th century, we had believed that big was better, and had gone from small neighborhood schools to consolidated behemoths, where principals rarely knew each of their students by name. Many of those students could not identify the Bill of Rights, or Patrick Henry, or Sojourner Truth.

Apple Computer president John Sculley, with founders Steve Jobs (left) and Steve Wozniak (right), unveils the Apple IIc at a San Francisco trade show in 1984. The new model was a big success in its day.

(?) *If you want to run for Congress, where will you get money to pay for commercials? Do you see a problem if office-holders are beholden to money givers? Should equal TV time be set aside for candidates for public office? What is campaign finance reform all about?*

Some Americans looked at all this with puzzlement, but were too busy to get involved. TV took a whole lot of their time. By 1986, the average American was spending as many as 30 hours a week in front of the tube. There was now cable TV and the VCR (videocassette recorder), which made home viewing more flexible (although programming didn't seem to get more interesting).

TV viewing (along with the popularity of "talk" radio) had changed politics. Campaigning now took lots of money. If you couldn't buy TV time (which is very expensive) it was almost impossible to win. Where did candidates get all their money? They had to woo and win the support of the rich and powerful. So, in the years that closed the century, ordinary citizens, who were supposed to be the foundation of a democracy, became less and less important. Corporate insiders, who were funding candidates on all levels, expected payback legislation and favors. None of that was really new; it was the scale of it that was new. Everyone talked about campaign finance reform, but those who were in power, and knew how to play the game, did little more than talk.

More than a few people still thought of public service as an obligation or a noble calling, as the Founders believed it to be. But, for many others, politics was about power, and lots of groups wanted it.

The media didn't help. Reporters showed little restraint. The president could hardly blow his nose without someone reporting on it. When George Bush campaigned, he called for a "kinder, gentler America." People smiled, but no one seemed to take him seriously. "Somewhere, in the decades of upheaval, came a wrong turning," wrote Theodore White, a historian of the presidency. The President and Congress seemed to have shrunk.

Today ATMs (automatic teller machines) are found all over the world, but in 1976, it was a novelty to get your money out of a machine rather than from a human bank teller.

Picturing Ourselves

Taking a census is something like taking your picture. It's a way to see yourself—where you've gained and where you've lost—it can help you figure out what the future may bring. We do it every ten years.

In 1820, which was the first year the United States kept statistics on immigration, 8,395 foreigners entered the country with the intention of becoming citizens. Most were English, Scotch-Irish, or German, but they also included 20 Danes, 14 Russians, 6 Asians, 5 Poles, and 1 Mexican.

The 2000 census was the first in which Americans could list themselves as multiracial (but only if they wanted to). Nearly 7 million people took that option (that's 2.4 percent of the nation).

The Hispanic population grew 58 percent from 1990, to 35.3 million, making blacks and Hispanics about equal in numbers. (In 2001, Hispanics became the nation's largest minority.)

The 21st century's first census told us there were 281.4 million people in the United States. It showed the largest number growth in our history – we added 32.7 million between 1990 and 2000. (Many industrial nations had declining birthrates and populations in those same years.) We were adding one person every 14 seconds, or about 6,300 every day. Of that daily gain, about 4,400 came from the larger number of births than deaths in the U.S. (10,600 over 6,200). The rest of the increase came from immigration. We added one immigrant every 35 seconds (and one person left the country every three minutes). The population increased in every state—from a half-percent in North Dakota to 66 percent in Nevada.

Here are some of the things we learned from the 2000 census:

People are moving back to cities (a few years ago they were fleeing them).

Four out of five Americans live in cities or suburbs.

New York, Los Angeles, Chicago, Houston, Philadelphia, and Phoenix are our largest cities.

Eight of our ten largest cities gained population (only Philadelphia and Detroit shrank).

The population center of the nation shifted 40 miles southwest, from DeSoto, Missouri (in 1990) to Edgar Springs, Missouri (in 2000). If you imagine a flat map of the country and then have all 281.4 million Americans stand on it where they live (and assume that they all weigh exactly the same), the spot where the map balances is the population center. (In 1790, the population center was in Charlestown, Maryland. It has moved steadily westward.

Other things we learned: The West grew by 19.7 percent, the South by 17.3 percent, the Midwest by 7.9 percent, and the Northeast by 5.5 percent.

For the first time in our history, we are evenly divided into age groups. Earlier census graphs looked like pyramids with a big, young population on the bottom and a small peak of older folk on top. The 2000 census was more like a Santa Claus with a fat stomach: 32 percent of our population is under the age of 25; 54 percent is between 25 and 60; and 14 percent is over 60.

Each census is used to reapportion seats in Congress. Shifting populations can make a political difference. New York and Pennsylvania each lost two seats in the House of Representatives. Texas, Georgia, Florida, and Arizona each gained two House members.

How can this information be useful? What kinds of people and organizations might use census data?

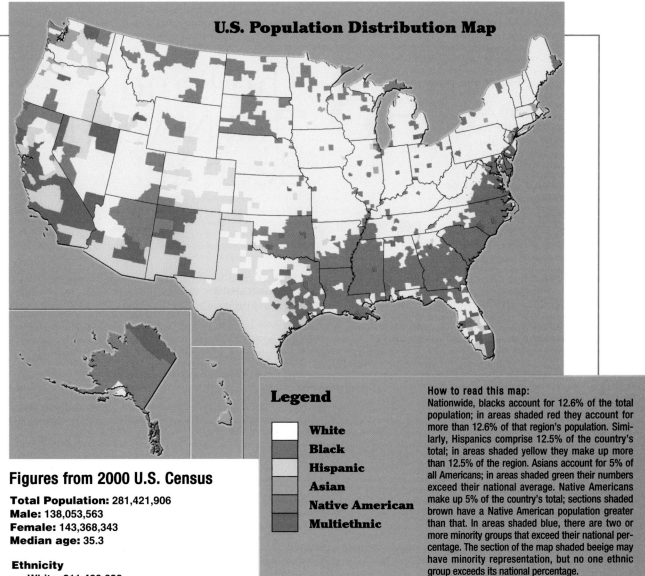

U.S. Population Distribution Map

Legend

- White
- Black
- Hispanic
- Asian
- Native American
- Multiethnic

How to read this map:
Nationwide, blacks account for 12.6% of the total population; in areas shaded red they account for more than 12.6% of that region's population. Similarly, Hispanics comprise 12.5% of the country's total; in areas shaded yellow they make up more than 12.5% of the region. Asians account for 5% of all Americans; in areas shaded green their numbers exceed their national average. Native Americans make up 5% of the country's total; sections shaded brown have a Native American population greater than that. In areas shaded blue, there are two or more minority groups that exceed their national percentage. The section of the map shaded beeige may have minority representation, but no one ethnic group exceeds its national percentage.

Figures from 2000 U.S. Census

Total Population: 281,421,906
Male: 138,053,563
Female: 143,368,343
Median age: 35.3

Ethnicity

White: 211,460,626
African American: 34,658,190
American Indian and Alaska Native: 2,475,956
Asian: 10,242,998
    People from India: 1,678,765
    Chinese: 2,432,585
    Filipino: 1,850,314
    Japanese : 796,700
    Korean: 1,076,672
    Vietnamese : 1,122,528
    Other Asian: 1,285,234

Native Hawaiian and
Other Pacific Islander: 874,414
Others: 18,521,486

Hispanic or Latino: 35,305,818
    Mexican: 20,640,711
    Puerto Rican: 3,406,178
    Cuban: 1,241,685
    Other Hispanic or Latino: 10,017,244

43 The Land That Never Has Been Yet

Until recent decades, most people worked with their hands—not their heads. Reading wasn't essential for most work. If you were a farmer, carpenter, or factory worker, you learned work skills on the job. But in the 21st century, to succeed, almost everyone—including the farmer—will need to be a thinker.

A poet who was farseeing (as poets are supposed to be) wrote in 1916: *Things fall apart; the center cannot hold; / Mere anarchy is loosed upon the world.* (His name was William Butler Yeats.) What did he mean?

Clue: one historian says that we are in the midst of a change—from an industrial society to an information society—that is as big as the Neolithic revolution, 10,000 years ago. That's when we went from being hunter-gatherers to being farmers and city dwellers who lived in smaller families and belonged to religious and political groups (city-states, nations, etc.).

Our families, religions, and cities are in the turmoil of change. Will things fall apart? Or will we make the most of the knowledge revolution?

Douglas Wilder (above) won a medal for bravery in the Korean War. The year he was elected governor of Virginia, David Dinkins became the first black mayor of New York City.

"As a boy, when I would read about an Abe Lincoln or a Thomas Jefferson...when I would read that all men are created equal and that they are endowed by their creator with certain inalienable rights...I knew it meant me," said Douglas Wilder, who in 1989 was elected governor of Virginia.

Virginia's capital, Richmond, had once been the capital of the Confederate States of America. The Confederate states were the slave states. Most of Wilder's ancestors were slaves. Do you think they ever imagined that their great-grandson would be sitting in the governor's mansion in Richmond?

Well, maybe they did, because that idea of freedom is so powerful—especially when you don't have it—that it sets you dreaming and planning and hoping. And it is the people with dreams and hopes who make things happen.

The United States was founded by dreamers—men like Thomas Jefferson, John Adams, and Ben Franklin—who had a vision of freedom and fairness that spoke to all people, rich and poor, all over the world.

But that vision was cloudy. Not everyone was to be treated fairly. Some of those in power weren't ready for a nation where every person was to be free and equal.

A poet named Langston Hughes had something to say about that:

Langston Hughes

208

Oh, let America be America again
The land that never has been yet—
And yet must be—the land where every man is free.
The land that's mine—the poor man's, Indian's, Negro's, ME—
Whose sweat and blood, whose faith and pain
Must bring back our mighty dream again.

"Must bring back our mighty dream again." Would it happen? Could America be what it was meant to be?

Oh yes,
I say it plain,
America never was America to me.
And yet, I swear this oath,
America will be!

The astonishing thing about the 20th century was that it was a time when we listened, at last, to dreamers and poets like Langston Hughes.

Yes, despite all the troubles of the 20th century, some great things happened. For the first time in our history, the United States began to be a nation for all its people. Segregation—and its terrible unfairness—was finally thrown out. Some extraordinary individuals extended those Founding Ideas: one was a minister from Georgia named Martin Luther King, Jr.; another was a Supreme Court justice from Maryland named Thurgood Marshall. But, mostly, it was ordinary citizens, like Rosa Parks, who marched and voted and hoped and dreamed—and made things happen.

So, in 1994, when newspapers told of an 81-year-old woman who was attacked and robbed in her apartment, people gasped. It was Rosa Parks, and, once again, she made people aware of a national sickness. This time the malady was crime, and it affected everyone.

Back in the 1950s (when Parks was protesting bus segregation), parents in Alabama didn't usually worry when they sent their children out to play. Boys and girls walked to school, walked to their friends' houses, and walked to the store—on their own.

By 1994, many parents had to take their children everywhere. They were scared that something might happen to them if they were out alone. Ten-year-olds were carrying guns, and killing people. Almost nowhere did people feel completely safe. Crime had become the leading concern for all of America's citizens. It was a special concern for young people; nearly one in four of the victims of violent crime was now a juvenile (under 18).

This was a crisis, and Rosa Parks wasn't ready to retire. In 1997,

Hardly anyone is a better symbol of the changing times than Oprah Winfrey, who went from a tough childhood to superstardom in films, on TV, in her own magazine, and in the world of books. She's a celebrity who is a big-time reader.

Some statistics:

In 2002, handguns were used to murder 11,789 people in the United States; 19 in Japan; 151 in Canada; 373 in Germany; and 54 in England and Wales. In 2005 there were 33,000 gun related deaths in the U.S., more than half were suicides. Compare that number with the total of 47,364 American deaths during the 10-year Vietnam War.

209

Kids and Guns in America: Some Facts

"Liberty without learning is always in peril," said John F. Kennedy, *"and learning without liberty is always in vain."*

The U.S. has the highest rates of childhood homicide, suicide, and gun-related deaths of all the world's industrialized countries.

The homicide rate for U.S. children is 5 times higher than for children in the other 25 industrial countries combined.

The suicide rate for American kids under 15 is twice as high as in the rest of the industrialized world.

The gun-related death rate for U.S. children under 16 is 12 times higher than for all of the other 25 industrial nations combined.

Every day, 14 Americans under age 19 are killed by guns, and 56 are wounded.

It is illegal in the U.S. for anyone under 21 to buy a handgun, or for anyone under 18 to buy a rifle or shotgun.

In a 1995 survey, 2 out of 25 high school students admitted bringing a gun to school in the last month.

In the 1998-1999 school year, more than 3,500 students were expelled for bringing guns to their public schools. And these figures include only the students who got caught.

Guns kept at home are 43 times more likely to be used to kill a family member or friend than to be used to kill in self-defense.

at age 84, she launched a Detroit school program intended as a national model. It was for parents as well as children, and included training in nonviolence, civil rights, and language arts. Can education fight crime and racial hatred? Is it enough? How do we attack the culture of violence? And what about guns?

In 1994, Congress passed the Gun-Free Schools Act, requiring states to enact laws ordering school districts to expel any student who brings a firearm to school. All states did. In the 1996–1997 school year, 6,093 students with firearms were expelled from public schools. (Most had handguns; some had grenades and bombs.) But that didn't end the violence. In a 15-month period in 1997 and 1998, 18 people were shot dead in school incidents. In Jonesboro, Arkansas, an 11-year-old and a 13-year-old took guns to school, shot and killed four classmates and a teacher, and left 10 wounded. In Oregon, a high-school student went on a rampage, killing his parents and two students; at Columbine High School, near Denver, 13 people were shot to death.

When 16 children and their teacher were gunned down in Dunblane, Scotland, the British Parliament enacted tough gun laws. They then spent $245 million paying for guns that citizens turned in.

But in America, gun enthusiasts say their right to bear arms is part of what makes them American, and that the right is enshrined in the Second Amendment, which says that *A well regulated militia being necessary to the security of a free State, the right of the people to keep and bear Arms shall not be infringed.*

Is the right to bear arms in our homes a sacred American right? Should school students be encouraged to learn the safe use of guns? Many experts see adolescence as a time when self-control is not easy. "There have always been kids willing to lose control and be impulsive and be hurtful and cruel. That is the nature of adolescence. The difference is, when we were kids, it was harder to find a weapon," says Jeff Butts of the Urban Institute.

And Delbert Elliott, a specialist in youth violence at the University of Colorado, says, "The end used to come after fists caused bloody noses and bruises—now it's not the end until someone is shot dead." How should we handle guns? What about violence in our movies and on TV?

44 A Boy from Hope

Newly elected President Bill Clinton plays his saxophone at one of the Inauguration Night balls. Clinton loves music, especially jazz, and is a strong supporter of music education in public schools.

The bus trip begins at Thomas Jefferson's home, Monticello, turns down a winding road, and heads on through softly undulating hills shadowed by the crests of Virginia's aptly named Blue Ridge mountains. There are 15 buses, but the one that draws waves from those who line the roadsides has a license plate that says HOPE 1.

William Jefferson Clinton, from Hope, Arkansas, is about to become the 42nd president and, at the age of 46, the third youngest in American history. He is the first Democratic president in 12 years.

With an impressive grasp of history and symbolism, Clinton is starting his inaugural ceremonies at the home of the man who wrote the Declaration of Independence.

The buses head northeast, retracing the path Jefferson followed to his inauguration in 1801. Through Brandy Station and past Manassas they roll—a route haunted by the Civil War.

Those in the buses have worked hard for this moment. But no one has worked harder than the president-elect himself. That a small-town boy from one of the poorest of states could make it to the nation's top job is what America is all about. Those who know him best are not surprised. His second-grade teacher predicted it, his mother believed in him, and so did many who met the gifted boy in the years

Bill Clinton's father, William Blythe, died in a car accident a few months before his son was born. His mother went off to study to become a nurse and left Bill with his grandparents. They taught him to read before he was three. When his mother remarried, she chose Roger Clinton, who was an alcoholic and abusive. Billy Blythe took his stepfather's name. In contrast with Clinton, Vice President Al Gore, who is the son of a Tennesse senator, was a child of privilege.

211

Bill Clinton was a terrific student and a school leader. It was that leadership ability that got him chosen as a delegate to Boy's Nation (a program sponsored by the American Legion that sends outstanding young people to Washington to learn about their government). The delegates were invited to the White House to meet President John F. Kennedy. Clinton, aged 16 and already 6 feet 3 inches tall, was first in line to get a presidential handshake. He made sure he got his picture taken so he could bring it home to his mother.

Invective is harsh, insulting language.

that followed. Now this man, with his engaging friendliness, who has wanted to be president since he was a young boy, has made it.

On the bus, the complexities of the presidency begin descending on him—a special phone rings and he is briefed on affairs in Bosnia and Haiti and elsewhere.

Few men have arrived at the presidency with a background to match Clinton's. A graduate of Georgetown University's School of Foreign Service, he has been a Rhodes scholar at Oxford University in England, he has a law degree from Yale University, and for 12 years he was governor of Arkansas. Everywhere he has left an impression of vigor, compassion, and astonishing ability—along with evidence of another side of his personality that is troublesome: stories abound of about-faces under pressure from wealthy interests, and other less-than-principled actions.

The woman sitting with him has, like her husband, awed people with her intellect and ability. As president of the Wellesley College student council, she was the first student there to address a commencement. *Life* magazine lauded her as one of the promising members of her generation. She, too, is a lawyer, and has held a series of jobs where her intensity and intelligence made her stand out. (She served on the legal staff that investigated Watergate. She has devoted much of her career to issues of health and child care.) Some of her generation believe that Hillary Rodham will be the first woman president.

Then she fell in love, submerged her own ambition in Bill Clinton's, and became half of what was to be an incredible political partnership. On the surface they are very different, but they share difficult childhoods. His included beatings, calls to the police for help, and the heartache of a home where an alcoholic father and an abused mother traded invective. Given the South's tradition of gentility, and the mores (MOR-aze—it means customs and accepted behavior) of a time when all this was too embarrassing to face, mother and son learned to smile, and cover up, and not tell the whole truth about the horrors they endured.

Hillary's childhood, in an affluent Chicago suburb, had a different kind of pain. Someone who knew her father, Hugh Rodham, described him as "tight-fisted, hard to please, and always in command." Someone else said the house he ran was "a boot camp." When little Hillary proudly brought home a report card with all A's, her father commented, "It must be a very easy school you go to." "My father was confrontational, completely and utterly so," said Hugh Rodham, Jr.

But whatever the stress they felt at home, both Hillary and Bill excelled in school. For both, church was important and fulfilling. Hillary became a Girl Scout with an impressive array of badges. Bill became one of the state's best high-school saxophone players. Members of a generation of rebels, they were surprisingly conformist.

Vice President–elect Albert Gore, Jr., and his wife, Mary Elizabeth "Tipper" Gore, are also on the bus. Dark-haired and square-shouldered, Gore is often described as stiff and formal, but his wry humor keeps Clinton and others chuckling. After graduating from Harvard College and Vanderbilt Law School, Gore spent two years as a soldier in Vietnam. He has been a newspaperman, and a congressman and a senator from Tennessee. Tipper was a news photographer.

The Gores have been through a terrible experience. In 1989, their six-year-old son was hit by a car as they left a baseball game. Now recovered, he struggled for his life. "The single horrifying event triggered a big change in the way I thought about my relationship to life itself," Gore said later. Political writer Elizabeth Drew will call Al Gore "the most influential vice president in history."

The buses head on, until the spike of the Washington Monument cuts the sky and they realize: they have arrived.

Now the celebrations begin. Thomas Jefferson walked from a boarding house to his inauguration, but that was before TV and mass media. Clinton's inauguration is carefully scripted by a Hollywood producer friend. At the Lincoln Memorial, a symphony plays a fanfare, jets fly overhead, and rock stars sing "We Are the World." The ceremonies—paid for by more than 200 corporations—continue for four days. White stretch limos and opulent galas are part of the scene. "Democrats look just like Republicans," writes a society columnist. "The two parties are now stylistically inseparable."

Clinton, whose good humor and exuberance are contagious, gets out his saxophone and toots. Known for long speeches, he keeps his inaugural address short. "The era of deadlock and drift is over," he says. "Let us resolve to reform our politics, so that power and privilege no longer shout down the voice of the people....Let us give this capital back to the people to whom it belongs." Hope fills the air.

President-elect Bill Clinton with his vice president, Al Gore, celebrate on Election Night, 1992. Al Gore was the most influential vice president until Dick Cheney came along in the Bush administration.

"Even Republicans," reports the *Wall Street Journal* at the time of Clinton's inauguration, "sense that the nation is almost desperate for things to start working better."

The *New York Times* warns the new president about Washington, "where the public interest gets ground into the midway dust of a circus of greed."

45 Politics and Values

Sometimes the White House seems like a palace. Sometimes it seems like a prison.

Historians around the year 2025 are going to begin making sense of Clinton's presidency. They can use the wisdom of hindsight. They'll have diaries and documents that are secret now. I don't know what they'll conclude, but of one thing I'm sure: those future historians will be fascinated by this administration and the public's reaction to it. They'll have a lot to write about.

What kind of president was Bill Clinton? He turned out to be the most conservative Democratic president since Grover Cleveland (president from 1885 to 1889 and from 1893 to 1897). He cut welfare, put more police on the streets, built prisons, stepped up the war on drugs, expanded the death penalty, and, after passage of a deficit reduction bill (without any Republican votes), balanced the budget. For the first time in 30 years, instead of a budget deficit, the country had a surplus! All that helped bring about a stock-market surge, low unemployment, minimal inflation, and general prosperity.

But Clinton was unable to get health insurance for all Americans, or to change the way we paid for political campaigns, or do much for public schools. The gap between the rich and the middle class grew wider and wider (and that caused alarm among those who believe that a strong middle class is essential in a democracy).

In foreign affairs, the Clinton administration brought warring parties from Serbia, Croatia, and Bosnia to Dayton, Ohio, where they sat down and agreed to stop killing each other. Former President Jimmy Carter was sent to Haiti and helped that impoverished island get its first fairly elected president, Jean-Bertrand Aristide, into office. In the Middle East, Clinton helped negotiate agreements, signed at the White

President Clinton brings Israeli Prime Minister Yitzhak Rabin (left) and PLO Chairman Yasser Arafat together for a historic handshake after the signing of the Israeli–PLO peace accord at the White House in 1993. Not since the Camp David accords of 1978 had people felt such hope for peace in the Middle East.

House in 1993, 1994, and 1998, between Israel and its Arab neighbors. In Ireland, where Protestants and Catholics had been fighting for centuries, the administration again acted as a mediator in the effort to achieve a historic peace agreement. Trade treaties—lowering tariffs and bolstering international free trade—were negotiated by the administration and ratified by Congress. And Clinton made a historic trip to the land of the ancient dragon—China—where he charmed the Chinese with his willingness to answer hard questions.

President Clinton poses with his daughter, Chelsea, and his wife, Hillary Rodham Clinton, during their state visit to China in 1998. They are touring an important archaeological site: the 2,000-year-old army of 6,000 terra cotta soldiers buried with the first Ch'in emperor.

All that should have made Bill Clinton one of the most popular presidents— and he did have high approval ratings in polls—but it isn't likely he'll be remembered for those accomplishments. This man, despite his gifts of unusual intelligence and charm, threw away the chance to be a great president.

Clinton's presidency, begun with so much promise, turned into a personal and national disaster. The ancient Greeks wrote tragic dramas about great leaders who had fatal flaws. It was hubris (HEW-briss—pride) that usually destroyed Greek heroes. Yet Clinton's fall was more soap opera than Greek tragedy. It was about personal gratification. It was also about lying. There was nothing heroic about it.

But the story is still more complicated—and that's what will make this administration so interesting to future historians. Even before he took office, Bill Clinton was accused of all kinds of wrongdoing. Some of his accusors were funded by wealthy enemies of the Democratic Party. Many of Clinton's critics seemed to have no purpose other than to bring down the president. His Republican opponents in Congress were intensely partisan (politically biased). The scandal-mongering kept talk show hosts very busy.

The attorney general chose a special prosecutor to investigate questions about a real-estate investment (called Whitewater) in Arkansas that Clinton had made while he was that state's governor. A special-prosecutor law had come out of the Watergate era. The idea was to find someone independent—outside politics— if the executive branch (the presidency) had to be investigated.

But, from the beginning, the law didn't work as it was intended. It became a political tool for the party that was not in the White

The 1st Amendment to the Constitution guarantees freedom of the press. The government cannot censor or control what the press publishes. (Today "the press"—often called "the media"—includes much more than newspapers and magazines produced on printing presses. It includes TV, radio, and the Internet.) Most Americans believe fiercely in the importance of that guarantee of freedom of the press. But is there a place for civility (good manners and good taste) in media coverage? Should there be limits on what we can know about the private lives of public officials? Or is it important to learn everything possible?

President Clinton with Monica Lewinsky, who met him when she was an intern working in the White House. What storybook character grew a long nose? Why?

To **impeach** is to accuse a public official of wrong conduct before a proper tribunal (a place of judgment, usually a court). The Constitution gives the House of Representatives power to impeach the president. Then the Senate must conduct a trial to consider the charges brought by the House. Only two presidents have been impeached: Andrew Johnson and Bill Clinton. Neither was found guilty of the "high crimes and misdemeanors" necessary for removal from office.

House to employ against the party that was. Democrats used it against Ronald Reagan and George Bush. Republicans took off after Clinton. The special prosecutors held power without checks, balances, or limits. They spent millions of public dollars, with no one overseeing them.

When Whitewater didn't produce any evidence of wrongdoing, special prosecutor Ken Starr turned the investigation from one direction to another. In the process of doing that, he ignored long-cherished legal traditions—such as the privacy of lawyer-and-client confidences—with chilling power. But he did find Clinton's flaw.

Bill Clinton was president when we were still trying to understand new attitudes about morality and sex. Television and films were bombarding us with images that had once been seen only in private. At the same time, tough, relentless journalists began telling us about the intimate private lives of politicians. We learned exact legal and financial details of our leaders' business dealings. In the past we hadn't known those things. Now there was a legion of experts—lawyers, journalists, public officials—in the investigative business. They had access to modern mass communications, which spread their opinions and information (and misinformation) everywhere—and quickly.

In the case of President William Jefferson Clinton, the special prosecutor and the press went far beyond the bounds of good taste or legal necessity in describing the president's relations with a woman who worked in the White House. We learned details of his private life that no one wanted to know. But the dangers of a runaway prosecutor seemed less important than something the president did. When faced with disturbing accusations about his personal life, Clinton was not honest. He lied to the American public and he lied to members of his administration. He wounded himself, his family, and the nation.

In December of 1998, Bill Clinton was impeached in the House of Representatives. In the Senate trial that followed, the President was found not to have committed "high crimes and misdemeanors." His private behavior was *not* deemed a constitutional offense (no matter how inappropriate). It was an example of constitutional democracy at work.

Covering Up . . . Or Just Plain Lying

"The whole of government," Thomas Jefferson wrote, "consists in the art of being honest."

We began our national adventure with a president who was known for his truth-telling. No one could imagine George Washington telling a lie. And for the next 100 years or so, our presidents were all expected to be truthful.

When Franklin Roosevelt wanted to send military aid to Russia under Lend-Lease he told a white lie. He said that the Soviet Union's constitution granted religious freedom. He knew that wasn't true, but some congressmen were attempting to block wartime aid to Russia. Roosevelt thought that Russia's might was essential to fight Nazism.

The Cold War was raging when a spy plane was shot down over Russia. President Eisenhower couldn't bear to lie, so he got his secretary of state to do it for him. He said it was a weather research plane. The truth soon came out—it usually does—and everyone knew they'd been told a flat-out lie. Why do you think our leaders felt they couldn't tell the truth? Were they right to cover it up?

John F. Kennedy lied about the buildup of American military forces in South Vietnam. "National security" was the reason for secrecy and deception. Is it a good one? Are there times when a president needs to lie?

Lyndon Johnson's lie may have been the most destructive of all. He said the North Vietnamese attacked an American ship in the Gulf of Tonkin. He knew that wasn't true. But Congress didn't, they voted to give him extraordinary military powers, which he used to turn the action in Vietnam into a serious war.

Richard Nixon's lying about the Watergate burglary was a national embarrassment. President Nixon believed and said that his political plan was more important than the law he had sworn to uphold. Congress and the American people didn't agree.

Reagan administration officials secretly sold weapons to Iran and secretly gave weapons to Nicaraguan Contra fighting forces—while the president was saying he would never do such a thing. Lieutenant Colonel Oliver North, called before the congressional investigating committee, said, "I will tell you right now, Counsel, and all the members here gathered, that I misled Congress." North seemed to believe that he (an unelected military officer) was doing the right thing for his country by lying. Should some government officials be able to operate outside the law? That wasn't the intent of the founding generation of Americans, but do today's different times justify some lies?

Two hundred years after the founding generation, Bill Clinton went on television and spoke a lie. ("I did not have sexual relations with that woman.") Clinton was attempting to cover up personal behavior that was embarrassing.

In the *Wall Street Journal*, Al Hunt quoted an author who cited lies by the George W. Bush administration, including "the president's claim that there already were 60 separate stem-cell lines sufficient for medical research, when he'd been told there were far fewer; the false claims that his tax cuts were aimed mainly at working-class Americans . . . and the numerous misrepresentations before the Iraq war."

John Adams, the first president to live in the White House, had this inscription put over the fireplace in the State Dining Room: *May none but honest and wise men ever rule under this roof.* Are there valid reasons to keep the truth from a nation's citizens?

Abraham Lincoln (known as "Honest Abe") didn't think so. At Gettysburg he said, "we here highly resolve . . . that this nation, under God, shall have a new birth of freedom—and that government of the people, by the people, for the people, shall not perish from the earth." You can't have a successful people's government without informed citizens. How do we become informed? Active courageous journalists, writers, and broadcasters can do that job. They may be our best hope for honesty in government.

217

46 Electing the 21st Century's First President

The year 2000 sounded special—it was a new century and a new millennium— and it made people hope for a new kind of politics. They didn't get it. The two candidates, George Walker Bush and Albert Gore, seemed plucked from earlier eras. They had a few things in common: both were privileged boys, each had lost a sister and under- stood grief, and for both the family business was politics. Other- wise they weren't much alike.

The morning after the 2000 presidential election, a New York newspaper prematurely proclaims a winner. The final result would not be official for weeks.

Al Gore grew up in Washington, D.C., where his father served as a Democratic senator from Tennessee. A serious kid, he went to St Albans (a select prep school), and to Harvard, and, though he objected to the war, to Vietnam. Then Gore worked himself up the political ladder from congressman to senator to vice president. His personal life was squeaky clean and he was an early voice on environmental issues like global warming. Still, when it came to political savvy, he didn't have as much as he needed. He seemed a '60s man who shared many of the goals of that liberal era, but hadn't gone overboard with them.

George W. Bush seemed straight out of the '50s. That was part of his appeal. Those were remembered as uncomplicated times. And Bush came across as a straightforward, uncomplicated guy. Descended from a patrician New England family with substantial wealth and a tradition of public service, he too lived with the expectation that he would be an achiever.

In 1948 Prescott Bush was a Republican senator from Connecticut when his son, George Herbert Walker Bush, moved to Midland, Texas, with his wife, Barbara, and their 2-year-old son George W. Young George grew up in West Texas amid oil rigs, desert dust, and wildcat oil men.

Big George Bush (that's how he came to be known) had come to Midland to make money on his own—away from the family connections in banking and railroads and Wall Street. He not only hit oil—hit real gushers—he soon seemed to head every committee in town as well as coach little league, serve as a deacon and then an elder in the Presbyterian church, and, with Barbara, be a PTA leader. "The King of the Roost," was the way his brother described it. And always he was interested in politics and in organizing for the Republican Party.

But making it as a Republican in Midland, which had long been Democratic territory, was close to hopeless. So, when the oil boom there began to subside, the senior Bush, looking to offshore oil opportunities, packed up his family and moved to Texas's largest city, Houston. George W., now an 8th grader, was enrolled in the exclusive Kinkaid school.

From there it was on to Phillips Academy in Andover, Massachusetts (where his father had gone to school), Yale (where all the Bushes went), and Harvard Business School. Despite the impressive schools, he failed in several business ventures (until he bought a baseball team and did well), and then lost in his first foray into politics, running for Congress from Texas. But he had more political acumen than his critics understood. Way back in 1888, Scotsman James Bryce noted the importance of that in his classic three-volume study, *The American Commonwealth:*

> *The ordinary American voter . . . likes his candidate to be sensible, vigorous, and, above all, what he calls "magnetic," and does not value, because he sees no need for it, originality or profundity, a fine culture, or a wide knowledge.*

George Bush's political genes were waiting to be tapped. At age 40, after he looked hard at himself, he changed. He made religion an important part of his life, and began working seriously on his father's

Vietnam certainly matured me in a hurry. It also gave me a tolerance for complexity that I don't think I had before. I didn't change my conclusions about the war being a terrible mistake, but it struck me that opponents to the war, including myself, really did not take into account the fact that there were an awful lot of South Vietnamese who desperately wanted to hang on to what they called freedom.

—Al Gore in 1988, quoted in *Inventing Al Gore* by Bill Turque, 2000

My faith frees me. Frees me to put the problem of the moment in proper perspective. Frees me to make decisions that others might not like. Frees me to try to do the right thing, even though it may not poll well.

—George W. Bush, *A Charge to Keep,* William Morrow, 1999

This was the Christmas card sent by the Bush family in 1972. Two people in the picture would become president of the United States. Can you pick them out?

Laura Welch Bush, who was born in Midland, Texas, was a librarian and a schoolteacher before marrying George W. Bush.

Every day, Americans eat 7 million pizzas and 4,400 tons of potato chips. Every day, some 35,000 people worldwide die of starvation.

—Figures from Russell Ash, *The World in One Day*

political campaigns. (Big George was now a big-time Republican candidate, soon to be president.) George W. kept his easygoing, affable personality, which made him easy to underestimate. He was a born leader and thrived in the public arena. He decided to run for governor of Texas, won and won again, and, at a time when the American people were looking for new faces, decided to run for president. He became the Republican candidate. Gore, the Democratic.

The election was about issues (polls showed that most Americans preferred Gore's platform: paying down the national debt, concern for the environment) and about values and behavior (polls showed Americans trusted Bush to best turn away from Clinton's unacceptable example). There were other issues too, although they were downplayed in the campaigns. The Republicans wanted to regulate morality, offer expanded opportunities to corporations, and lower taxes. The Democrats were interested in protections for the environment, wanted some controls on business, and believed that taxes and government services need balancing.

It was the longest and most expensive campaign in the history of the nation. How did it turn out? In a dead heat. After that, it took 36 days to find out who had won.

In 2005, Lance Armstrong won the Tour de France, a grueling two-week bicycle race with competitors from around the world and long stretches of pedaling in Europe's towering Alps mountain range. It was the seventh win in a row for Armstrong. No one had ever done that before. It was an especially heroic achievement as Armstrong was a cancer survivor.

47 Of Colleges and Courts

Because of modern technology, the two most important developments in American politics were the use of polling and television coverage, both of them joined together in zeroing in on and then manipulating what the voting public thought at a given moment.

—David Halberstam,
War In A Time of Peace, 2001

On January 18, 2001, President-Elect George W. Bush and his wife Laura, with Vice President-Elect Dick Cheney and his wife Lynn, wave from the steps of the Lincoln Memorial in Washington, D.C.

The Electoral College is not part of a university. It has nothing to do with a school. It has no buildings. (Look up the word "college" in a good dictionary, you may be surprised by all its meanings. It comes from the same root as "colleague," which means?) But when the members of the Electoral College vote, it is a weighty occasion. Those college members are called "electors." Their vote decides who will be president.

Every four years, each state chooses its electors. The number of electors in a state equals its number of representatives and senators in Congress. Electors never actually get together. What they do is send their votes for president and vice president to Washington. They vote for the rest of us. This is how they do it:

They check the popular vote in their state. Then—even if the vote is very close — usually all the electors' votes in that state go to the winning candidate. That means if you are running for president and you come in a close second in all the big states and win most of the small states and have the largest total vote across the nation, you may still lose the election. It's a winner-takes-all system.

The virtual tie in Florida was a once-every-few centuries proposition, and so was a presidential election that hinged on a single deadlocked state. It was a longshot wrapped in a longer shot. And so it happened that laws and institutions built for the press of the commonplace were called on to face the extraordinary.

—From *Deadlock, The Inside Story of America's Closest Election*, by the staff of the *Washington Post*

For more details

on the election, you might want to read *36 Days: The Complete Chronicle of the 2000 Presidential Crisis*, compiled by correspondents of the *New York Times*. Or *Deadlock: The Inside Story of America's Closest Election* by the political staff of the *Washington Post.*

Studying the year

2000 election, scientists at the Massachusetts Institute of Technology found that 4 to 6 million of the 100 million votes cast were not counted. No one had expected a number that large. (Gore had a popular vote margin of half a million votes.) The MIT study did not try to see if the uncounted votes would have changed the outcome of the presidential race. The report recommended that optical scanners rather than the punch cards and lever machines be used in future elections. The second choice recommended for reliability was low-tech hand-counted paper ballots.

Why do we elect our chief executives that way? We do it because that's what the Constitution says to do. (See Article II, Section I.)

The decision to have electors came, in part, because of jealousies between North and South at the time the Constitution was written. A direct popular vote — with only free males voting — would have given the North the choice of the president because it had a much greater free population. So the Founders came up with a system for picking electors similar to that for picking senators and representatives. That way the South was able to more than hold its own in selecting presidents. Having an Electoral College had a lot to do with balancing power.

There was another reason for it; it was equally important. Law professor Ronald Dworkin says, "The Constitution's authors did not trust the people to elect the president directly; they expected the members of the Electoral College to be distinguished and independent citizens who would make up their own minds, after collective deliberation, about who the president and vice president should be. . ."

It hasn't worked that way. Electors don't make up their own minds. Republican electors vote for Republican candidates. Democratic electors vote for Democratic candidates. Do you think we should have an Electoral College or should we vote directly for the president? Here's what 9-year-old Mitchell Phillips wrote in a letter published in the *Washington Post* on November 21, 2000. "I would make the winner of the popular vote our president. I don't think it is fair that each state gets a different number of electoral votes. I feel this way because no matter what the population of the state is, everyone's vote should count. It would be a lot easier to just count up the votes and whoever has the most votes wins and is president of the United States."

Ronald Dworkin agrees with Mitchell. In a long impassioned article in the *New York Review of Books* (December 14, 2000) he argued for a reform of the election process eliminating the Electoral College. Its original purpose had long ago been lost, said the professor:

Now we embrace the very different principle that the point of elections—and particularly the election of a national president, the one office we elect all together — is to determine and reflect the people's will.

But historian Douglas Brinkley doesn't agree:

The United States needs its Electoral College now as much as ever, for the very reason its critics deny: the traditional system does not so much encourage as demand that presidential candidates campaign in as many states as possible, rather than in just the most populous ones. . . The system also continues to protect the interest of regional groups such as small farmers. . .abolishing the Electoral College would deny small-yield and family farmers the voice the process makes audible to the national candidates who come calling every four years.

No one knows what would happen if we abolish the Electoral College. It has helped mold the American political system. It forces politicians to pay attention to small states. But sometimes it seems to thwart the will of the people. What should we do? It's not an easy decision. It's one that needs to be considered.

Now, as to the year 2000, Al Gore won the popular vote, nationwide, by about half a million votes out of about 100 million cast (a tiny .5% or half of one percent of the total). If you count numbers of voters, not percentage, it was the largest margin since Ronald Reagan in 1984.

The electoral vote was split with Florida's 25 electors holding the key to the election. Whoever got those 25 votes would become president. George Bush seemed the winner by a slight majority, but Florida's votes were being disputed. Substantial numbers of voters—especially African Americans—had been turned away from the polls for reasons that were

Top : As the votes in Florida were tallied, a judge tries to figure out who the ballot was punched for. Was it Bush? Was it Gore? Sometimes it was hard to tell. Bottom: On December 5, 2000, supporters of Al Gore march in protest outside of the courthouse in Tallahassee, Florida.

President-elect George W. Bush with retired General Colin Powell at Bush's Texas ranch in November 2000. A month later, Bush named General Powell as his secretary of state.

Our nation has never decided a presidential contest the way it decided the election of 2000. Never before has an election hung on the judgment of the United States Supreme Court, let alone on a decision that split the court into bitter camps and was settled by a single vote. Not in 124 years has a presidential election result been so disputed. Never in all those years have so many Americans believed that the winner of the White House actually lost the election. Nor in all those years has the winning side been so convinced that the losing candidate was intent on "stealing the election."

—E.J. Dionne, Jr., and William Kristol, from *Bush V. Gore*, 2001

The unprecedented decision of the five justices to substitute their political judgment for that of the people threatens to undermine the moral authority of the high court for generations to come.

—Alan Dershowitz, *Supreme Injustice*, 2001

later found to be invalid. Besides that, antiquated voting machines had failed in many locales. The ballot in one county was so confusing that many voters voted for a third party candidate without meaning to do so. Some punch ballot machines needed cleaning. If the voter didn't punch hard enough (sometimes the machine wouldn't let him do so) the ballot was left with a dimple (an indentation) or a hanging bit of paper called a "chad," instead of a clean hole. Sometimes chads from previous voters piled up in the machine and made other votes uncountable.

That's not all. Thousands of absentee ballots (ballots sent in by voters who were not in the state at the time of the election) had been treated in different ways in different parts of the state. The governor of Florida, Republican Jeb Bush, was the brother of candidate George W. Bush; the Republicans didn't think that made a difference, the Democrats did. There was still more. TV election night coverage was a disaster. The major networks predicted a winner before all the polls were closed, then changed their minds, then changed again. That may have influenced many voters.

In brief, the situation in Florida was a mess.

The first thing both sides did was to bring in armies of lawyers. It was War— and the stakes were very high.

Florida state law called for automatic machine recounts in close elections. But the machines were the problem. The Democrats wanted to recount votes by hand in several disputed counties (especially where they thought they could gain votes). Florida law talked about finding the "intent of the voter." The Florida Supreme Court agreed to specific hand recounts. The Republicans didn't want any hand recounts. Both sides sent protesters to Florida. Things got nasty.

Finally, the U.S. Supreme Court stepped into the fray—and by a five to four vote—took the

The Supreme Court in early 2005: William H. Rehnquist (center) is chief justice and two of the nine are women.

action away from the Florida Supreme Court in the case of *Bush* v. *Gore*. The court stopped all hand recounts and that decided the election. George W. Bush became the 43rd president.

But that didn't end the turmoil. For the first time in American history, a presidential election had been decided by the Supreme Court—and by one vote. That court—with its nine unelected justices appointed for life—is the most powerful court in the world. Did it have a sound legal basis for this decision? Or had the system gone awry? One of the four dissenting justices, John Paul Stevens, wrote, "Although we may never know with complete certainty the identity of the winner of this year's presidential election, the identity of the loser is perfectly clear. It is the Nation's confidence in the judge as an impartial guardian of the rule of law."

Others felt the Court had acted properly and were relieved to see an end to five weeks of tumult. Almost everyone agreed that the machinery of voting needed reform. And the importance of every vote was made very clear. Civics had come alive as it rarely had before.

Our nation is an experiment—it always has been so—we see no shame in making mistakes because we have the means to correct our flaws.

"What began in Florida as an argument about who will be the next president has become something much larger and more lasting—an argument about the proper sources of government in this republic," wrote syndicated columnist George F. Will.

James Bryce was prescient when, in 1888, he wrote;

A presidential election is sometimes. . .a turning point in history. In form it is nothing more than the choice of an administrator. . . In reality it is the deliverance of the mind of the people upon all such questions as they feel able to decide."

When the court issues an opinion, the justices ordinarily take the bench and the majority gives a brief oral description of the case and the holding. Today, after darkness fell and their work was done, the justices left the Supreme Court building individually from the underground garage, with no word to dozens of journalists from around the world . . . By the time the pressroom staff members passed out copies of the decision, the justices were gone.

—Linda Greenhouse, the *New York Times*, December 13, 2000

Prescient means seeming to have knowledge of events before they take place. (It's pronounced PRESH-ee-unt or PRESS-ee-unt. Both are acceptable.)

225

48 Big Ideas

Physicist Albert Einstein was horrified by the rapid spread of nuclear weapons technology and the stockpiling of arms after World War II. He often spoke out against the arms race.

What do you think schools will teach when they deal with 20th-century America a hundred years from now? Will the focus be on the parade of presidents? The flamboyant politics? The horrendous wars? I don't think any of those will be on the top of the list. I believe the 20th century's big story is the fight for fairness and justice for all people. The story of Martin Luther King, Jr., and the civil rights marchers, and the women and new Americans who broke down the old ways—that's what will be in every schoolbook. When people talk of that freedom story in the United States, they'll say it was paralleled by freedom movements in other countries—like Soviet Russia—where citizens overthrew repressive governments. So, as the new century began, almost no one could claim that anything less than freedom for all was just or desirable.

But that isn't the only big story of the time. There's another dazzler, and it has to do with science. The 20th century was an age of marvels with leaps of understanding and technological wonders arriving at a stunning pace.

When the century began, scientists weren't sure that atoms actually existed. They thought the stars and planets revolved in orbit, but didn't move beyond that. They thought the universe was static—that it had no history of change.

Then along came Albert Einstein—who began his career as a Swiss patent clerk and ended it as an American citizen. Einstein got 20th-century thinking going, in 1905, when he published his first paper on special relativity. (It changed our ideas on time, space, energy, and mass—which is just about everything.)

He followed that with work that made it clear atoms do exist (research Brownian motion for details); he also laid the foundations for quantum theory. (The smaller-than-atoms quantum world follows its own unique rules.) Quantum physicists were experimenting with tiny particles called electrons, which led to computers, fax machines, and the electronic goodies we all enjoy.

But Einstein wasn't finished. In 1916 he published a paper on general relativity, which was a new theory of gravity (and that would lead us to space travel and the Moon).

Then American astronomers discovered that ours is not the only galaxy. We learned that we're just a speck in the total picture. Edwin Hubble found that the galaxies are racing through space, away from each other, and very fast. Our universe is not static at all; it's expanding, and it has a history.

There was more to 20th-century science. A whole lot more. Richard P. Feynman (pronounced FINE mun), one of America's great scientists, had this to say about modern atomic theory:

If. . .all of scientific knowledge were to be destroyed, and only one sentence passed on to the next generations of creatures, what statement would contain the most information in the fewest words? I believe it is. . .that all things are made of atoms—little particles that move around in perpetual motion, attracting each other when they are a little distance apart, but repelling upon being squeezed into one another.

Edwin Hubble looked through a telescope at Mt. Wilson in California and discovered something no one knew: ours is not the only galaxy. In 1929 he found that all the galaxies are moving – away from each other. The Hubble telescope, launched into space in 1990, was soon showing us detailed pictures of the heavens only imagined before. Then it needed repairs; in May 2009 an astronaut crew spent two weeks in orbit replacing and rebuilding Hubble's sensitive equipment. The result: Hubble is again sending out stunning cosmic postcards.

Physicist Richard Feynman worked on the atomic bomb, taught at Cornell, and came up with a way to visualize the interactions of tiny particles that inhabit the smaller-than-atoms quantum world.

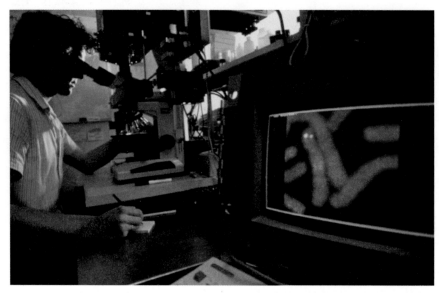

Dr. Peter Lichter of Yale Medical School uses a light microscope to do fine mapping of long DNA fragments on human chromosomes. The chromosomes appear red on the monitor screen, while the DNA fragments (called probes) appear yellow/green. By mapping chromosomes we find the location of genes and other markers. A map of the human genome was completed in 2006, giving us a blueprint of genetic information that should lead to improved drugs and a better understanding of genetic diseases (among other things).

Science is neither good nor evil. It is the way it is used that can be either. Twenty-first-century citizens will face major ethical questions involving science and technology. The use of cloning is one of them. Suppose someone wants to make a dozen copies of himself or herself. Do you see any problem with that? Knowledge of DNA will allow us to "engineer" the genes in future humans. It might be possible to eliminate debilitating diseases. But are there ethical problems with bio-engineering?

Understanding atoms lets us begin to understand the science of ourselves and our fellow creatures. In 1953, James Watson (an American) and Francis Crick (an Englishman) discovered a code inside each of our cells. Known as DNA it led, in 2001, to a grand map of all of our genes called the human genome. (If you don't know what genes are, look in a good encyclopedia or science book. This is an important subject.)

Albert Einstein had an idea that there is a connection between big (the whole universe) and small (the world of tiny particles). He began looking for a way to link all the forces and particles in the universe. That quest is for a theory nicknamed TOE, or "a Theory of Everything." When we find it, it will unravel many scientific puzzles and lead to ever more useful technology. What is clear is that discovery leads to discovery, and 21st-century science, building on that of the 20th, should reach spectacular heights.

Which brings us back to the freedom that we Americans take so seriously. You can't have real science without it.

"Doubt is not to be feared," said Feynman. "If you know that you are not sure, you have a chance to improve the situation, I want to demand this freedom for future generations."

Freedom of inquiry and thought is what our Founders believed to be the most precious gift they could give us. We've not only held on to it for more than two centuries, we've expanded it. That's quite an achievement.

Watch That Briefcase!

If you had your TV set tuned to CNBC, the financial news channel, on August 21, 2001, two commentators were watching Alan Greenspan get out of a car and head to his office. They discussed the color of his tie (maroon) and the brand of shoes he appeared to be wearing (Rockports). But what they really wanted to see was his briefcase.

"Hard to get an angle on it," said Mark Haines, one of the commentators."I wish he'd wear a contrasting suit jacket," he added. "That's pretty full. It's not bulging, but it's pretty full."

Mr. Greenspan is a 75-year-old who wears dark suits and a hang-dog expression. His lips permanently purse into a carefully constructed poker face. Every word he says is picked over by reporters and experts on television, in newspapers, and on the Internet. But his words are often puzzling. He speaks in a calm monotone in sentences like this:"We must ask whether the aggregate ratio of net worth to income is a sufficient statistic for summarizing the effect of capital gains on economic behavior or, alternatively, whether the distribution of capital gains across assets and the manner in which those gains are realized also are significant determinants of spending."

"Excuse me?"

Mr. Greenspan was named the head of the Federal Reserve, the central bank of the United States, in 1987. In 2001, he was still in the driver's seat. Think of "the Fed"—as it is known—as the nation's financial steering wheel. Think of Alan Greenspan as the man behind the wheel. Here is what the Fed does. When the nation is in a boom time, when stock prices are rising fast and businesses are producing plenty of cars and computers, Mr. Greenspan tries to provide a reali-

Alan Greenspan

ty check. He tries to prevent people and businesses from being too optimistic, because that could lead to a collapse down the road. When times are bad, when many people lose jobs, and businesses cut back on the cars and computers they produce, Mr. Greenspan tries to make sure bad times don't last. In short, he tries to keep the nation's economy humming along slowly and steadily.

So how does he do this?

First, the Fed was established in 1913 by the U.S. government to help ensure that the nation's economy and financial system avoided crises. It is made up of 12 regional banks in places like Atlanta and San Francisco, and a seven-member board that is appointed by the president. Mr. Greenspan is the chairman of the Federal Reserve board.

To poke and prod the economy, the Fed can do several things, including buying or selling government bonds—called Treasury bonds—seen as one of the safest investments there is (because they are backed by the federal government). By choosing when

to buy or sell large amounts of the bonds, the Fed can affect other "interest rates" like the interest regular banks charge people who need loans to buy houses.

In the 1990s, the Internet caused the nation's economy to surge. Hundreds of new companies and hundreds of thousands of jobs were created and stock prices rose to unimagined levels. Many experts believed the country had a "New Economy" and the stock market could grow at a pace that defied experience.

Mr. Greenspan was skeptical. His most famous saying warned against "irrational exuberance": that is, the danger of getting caught up in exciting trends like the Internet before Internet companies actually proved they could make money. To control the nation's enthusiasm, the Fed kept raising interest rates in the late '90s. By 2001, it was clear that even the Internet could not change normal boom and bust cycles. Stock prices plummeted, workers were laid off, and many new companies went out of business. The Fed began lowering interest rates, trying to make it cheaper for banks to lend to struggling businesses.

By August 21, 2001, the Fed had cut a key interest rate six times in little more than a year. Would they do it again? That day was one of the Fed board's big meetings. According to the Briefcase Indicator, if Mr. Greenspan carried a full briefcase into the meeting, he had been poring over data and would cut rates."I'd say the briefcase is calling for 25 points," said T.V.'s Mr. Haines, meaning that he thought the Fed would cut interest rates by 0.25 percent. And so it did. The briefcase spoke the truth.

—Danny Hakim,
reporter,
the *New York Times*

49 Catastrophe, War, and a New Century

People flee the scene near New York's World Trade Center after terrorists crashed two planes into the 110-story towers on September 11, 2001.

"Not in history has a modern imperial city been so completely destroyed. San Francisco is gone," wrote author Jack London. It was April of 1906 and an earthquake had ripped through California killing 3,000 people and leaving another 200,000 homeless. In San Francisco, at the earthquake's epicenter, buildings had tumbled, gas mains and electrical lines split, and fires consumed what had been, minutes before, a proud city. Forty miles away, Jack London could see a "lurid tower" of flame, it "swayed in the sky, reddening the sun, darkening the day, and filling the land with smoke."

Ninety-two years earlier, in 1814, the city of Washington was, according to a soldier who was there, "wrapt in one sheet of fire." The British had torched the city, burning the Capitol, the White House, and most of the public buildings. When a British soldier threw a fire-tipped pole into a well, without knowing that the well held gunpowder, he blew himself and others away. Then a storm raged in with hurricane-force winds, and finished the destructive job for the British.

Before that, in 1793, a natural form of bio-terror struck the then U.S. capital: Philadelphia. In a few awful months, more than 4,000 people died (a tenth of the population) of a horrible disease — yellow fever — that no one understood. Alexander Hamilton, who was there, told in a letter of "undue panic which is fast depopulating

The Statue of Liberty and the twin towers of the World Trade Center stood as dual beacons: one symbolizing American freedom, the other American business initiative. Then came 9/11/01.

the city and suspending business, public and private."

Printer Mathew Carey wrote a book on the epidemic, which he published himself in November 1793. He titled one chapter, "General despondency. Deplorable scenes." No one knew what to do or how the disease was spread. (We now know it's a virus spread to humans by mosquitoes.) Carey wrote, "The old custom of shaking hands fell into such general disuse, that many shrank back with affright at even the offer of a hand."

Those weren't the worst disasters we've faced on U.S. ground. There was the one day, in 1862, when 6,000 men died at Antietam. (Where's Antietam?) The nine months in 1918 when more than 500,000 Americans died of influenza (21,000 in October alone). And December 7, 1941 when Japanese bombers—without any warning—dropped bombs on the U.S. Naval Base at Pearl Harbor, Hawaii, sinking 19 ships, killing 2403 Americans, and getting us into World War II. (It was, said President Franklin Delano Roosevelt, "a day that shall live in infamy.")

Our response to all these disasters was similar. We took some deep breaths, grieved for those who perished, fought enemies where they existed, built anew, and went back to being Americans—which means we were optimistic, energetic, more free than any people anywhere, and dedicated to that freedom.

When the 21st century emerged, we were enjoying a breezy, confident, promising time of affluence and achievement. After a long and tortuous Cold War, it seemed to the average American as if the world's problems were on the way to being solved and that democracy would soon be universal. How could there be a contest? How could oppression triumph over freedom?

Most of us were very sure of ourselves, but we were underestimating the power of demons: of anger, jealousy, poverty, and ignorance. We were the world's superpower, and often so self-absorbed that we hardly paid attention to what was going on in the rest of the world (aside from wanting global customers). We knew that a world-wide terrorist network, Al Qaeda (pronounced *al kay duh*), was training a generation of young men in tactics of violence, but we didn't do much about it. We'd forgotten that freedom is a delicate flower that needs nurturing or rough feet will trample it.

On September 11, 2001, something happened that jolted us from our complacency, and we and the whole world shuddered. That day, nineteen terrorists hijacked four airliners, ramming two of them into the World Trade Center in New York City, one into the Pentagon in Washington, D.C., while the fourth crashed in a Pennsylvania field after a heroic takeover by passengers and crew. Officially, more than 3,000 people died (including citizens from 80 nations), thousands of others were injured, many seriously. Most were just ordinary people—but very special to the children, parents, friends, and lovers they left behind.

It was, as President George W. Bush announced, a declaration of war by international terrorists based in the Muslim world. "This is the world's fight," said the president. The "civilized world," he said, was pitted against a terrorist network intent on "remaking the world—and imposing its radical beliefs on people everywhere."

Making September 11th still worse, we learned that the hijackers blamed us, and the world's free nations, for most of their problems. And they hated us so much, they were willing to die themselves in order to kill our citizens. Being hated isn't easy to take. Especially as it was our deep beliefs—the freedom and pluralism and religious openness we so cherish—that they especially abhorred. Terrorist organizations (Al Qaeda, the political/religious Taliban in Afghanistan, and others) were teaching armies of followers to be haters, too.

These people were using the language of the Islamic religion to justify murder. They were preaching that we were Satan's children, that only they and their followers knew the truth about God, and that God would reward them for murdering us. They were religious zealots and—history shows—zealotry is uncompromising.

Robert F. Kennedy once said, "What is dangerous about extremists is not that they are extreme, but that they are intolerant. The evil is not what they say about their cause, but what they say about their opponents."

The terrorists' message was a perversion of Islam, which rests on a foundation of peacefulness and respect for others. It was also a smokescreen that was hiding the real problems of a portion of the world where people were hurting. Much of the Middle East, despite oil riches, was an economic disaster. It was a region aching for answers.

But the terrorists were destroyers, not

Civil liberties is not only about protecting us from our government. It is also about protecting our lives from terrorism.

—Lawrence Tribe, professor of law, Harvard University

It isn't easy to respect ideas you don't like. But our kind of government demands it. The First Amendment makes civic respect part of our legal system. (There's a limit on this, ideas and actions have to be lawful; they can't harm anyone.)

On September 14th, more than a thousand Arab-American worshippers gathered at the Passaic County Mosque in New Jersey. They came to pray for America and for victims of the World Trade Center and Pentagon terrorist attacks.

David Goldemberg was on his way to work when the World Trade Center in New York City was attacked. He happened to have his camera with him and quickly began to use it. This photo was taken shortly after the planes flew into the towers. In less than two hours they had collapsed. Several of David's friends were among the dead. David said we could use this picture if we made a donation to the fund that was set up to assist the victims' families. That's what we did.

builders. They said the killing of innocent people was a tribute to Allah (God). Around the world, religious leaders, including Muslims, recoiled in horror.

The Al Qaeda leader, a Saudi named Osama bin Laden, had been disowned by his family and kicked out of his own country. He had defiled the spirit of Islam's holy book, the *Quran* (also written Koran), with other acts of terror. Three years earlier, he had issued an unholy edict which said: "To kill Americans and their allies, both civil and military, is an individual duty of every Muslim who is able, in any country, where this is possible. . ." Bin Laden was calling for what he said was a *jihad*, or holy war, against America. But there is nothing holy about war (it is sometimes necessary for protection or to end criminality). Many Muslim leaders made it clear that bin Laden did not speak for them and that their religion is respectful of life and of all peoples and that, according to Islamic teachings, it is unholy to start a war or to kill the innocent. More than that, some Islamic scholars insist that the word *jihad* is often misused. It means to strive or struggle for a worthwhile purpose. To call killing innocent people a *jihad* is a distortion of its meaning, say many Muslims. (But, others, throughout Islamic history, have called for *jihads* against non-believers. Words are important and disagreement over them often leads to conflict.)

Why do some people hate? Why are some arrogant enough to believe that they have the right, and even the "religious" duty, to kill others? It is an old illness, the cruel nasty brutality of those who believe they, and only they, know what is right and true. Hitler thought he was of a superior race and he convinced many in his nation that they were, too. Then almost anything they did was justified.

Some medieval Christians supported murderous Crusades (in the 11th to 13th centuries) to capture Jerusalem from Muslims (who had taken it from Jews and Christians in a 7th-century murderous *jihad*). The Crusades were followed by Inquisitions (in the 13th to 15th centuries) to find heretics or non-believers (mostly Jews and Muslims) in Christian lands and often burn them in "the name of God." Those who lit the fires were convinced that they alone understood God's mind. (Religious wars, crusades, *jihads*—call them what you will—they are never pretty.)

234

And so the Islamic hijackers were just another example from a parade of misguided humans willing to kill because their leaders tell them they are carrying out God's wishes.

"Few things have done more harm than the belief on the part of individuals or groups (or tribes or states or nations or churches) that he or she or they are in sole possession of the truth. . .and that those who differ from them are not merely mistaken, but wicked or mad, and need restraining or suppressing," wrote British philosopher Isaiah Berlin.

Most of us, in our democratic society, think differently. Because we are free to read history, we know about witch burnings, crusades, and false *jihads*. We also know of Europe's Dark Ages when Islam was the leading world civilization and Christians and Jews participated in its affluent, tolerant multi-cultural cities and universities. It was Islamic scholars who preserved Greek art and science when Western nations had discarded them. And all the world became richer for it.

And then something happened, and fairly quickly, so that, today, most Islamic nations are poor and troubled. Bernard Lewis, an expert on the Middle East, writes: "By all the standards that matter in the modern world—economic development and job creation, literacy, educational and scientific achievement, political freedom and respect for human rights—what was once a mighty civilization has indeed fallen low."

When things go wrong you can do two things: blame others, or face problems and do something about them. The killers who destroyed the World Trade Center blamed the West for troubles in their nations. Many voices, Islamic and others, saw that as cowardly. Pakistani businessman, Izzat Majeed, writing in the Pakistani daily, *The Nation*, had this to say:

"We Muslims cannot keep blaming the West for all our ills. . . Without a reformation in the practice of Islam that makes it move forward and not backward, there is no hope for us Muslims anywhere. . . True Jihad today is not in the hijacking of planes, but in the manufacturing of them."

Why is there misery in so many Muslim nations? Most experts tie it to the absence of freedom. Bernard Lewis says, "It is precisely the lack of freedom—freedom of the mind from constraint and indoctrination, to question and inquire and speak; freedom of the economy from corrupt and pervasive mismanagement, freedom of women from male oppression; freedom of citizens from tyranny—that underlies so many of the troubles of the Muslim world."

Zealots, fanatics, and extremists are people who hold an intense belief and sometimes they will do almost anything to further that belief. Give them weapons and they can become very dangerous. Militant extremists are found in all the major religions. That doesn't make sense, because all the great religions are built on themes of love and peace. Some extremists reject the rule of law when it comes to beliefs. Christian extremists have gunned down doctors and nurses in abortion clinics in the United States. Muslim extremists killed Egypt's president for negotiating with Israel. A Jewish extremist murdered Israel's prime minister because he wanted to achieve peace with Palestinians. In three southern provinces of Thailand, where extremists want a separate Muslim state, thousands have been killed because they are Buddhist. And it was militant Islamic extremists who crashed planes into the Pentagon and the World Trade Center.

Terrorists aren't always religious zealots. Timothy McVeigh killed 168 of his fellow citizens when he blew up a government building in Oklahoma City. His hatreds were political.

235

50 New York and the American Way

In 1949, E.B. White, author of *Charlotte's Web*, wrote a small book, *Here Is New York*, about the city he loved. Here is some of it:

"The city, for the first time in its long history, is destructible. A single flight of planes no bigger than a wedge of geese can quickly end this island fantasy, burn the towers, crumble the bridges, turn the underground passages into lethal chambers, cremate the millions.
All dwellers in cities must live with the stubborn fact of annihilation; in New York the fact is somewhat more concentrated because of the concentration of the city itself, and because, of all targets, New York has a certain clear priority. In the mind of whatever perverted dreamer might loose the lightning, New York must hold a steady irresistible charm. . .this riddle in steel and stone is at once the perfect target and the perfect demonstration of nonviolence, of racial brotherhood, this lofty target scraping the skies and meeting the destroying planes halfway, home of all people and all nations, capital of everything. . ."

"This is the world's fight. . .This is civilization's fight," said President George W. Bush, speaking before a joint session of Congress on September 20, 2001. Then he warned other nations, "Either you are with us, or you are with the terrorists." Neutrality was not possible.

Why did the terrorists pick on New York? Walk down New York's streets and you'll rub elbows with Pakistanis, Puerto Ricans, Japanese, Scots, Poles, Afghans, and Nigerians (many on their way to citizenship), as well as American citizens of every hue and faith and origin. Name any country you want, and you'll find someone from there in New York. And all those diverse people manage to live and work together in a free society with astonishing harmony. What a marvelous example for the world. And that's just what the zealots were attempting to destroy. Their narrow vision said there is only one way to live: their way.

We Americans reacted to the mass murders of September 11th with forceful, effective action. President George W. Bush immediately made it clear that we have no tolerance for terrorism and wrongdoing. Citizens gave him their overwhelming support. "Bush is now my commander-in-chief," said Al Gore, of the man he had fought so fiercely.

Almost unnoticed was our astonishing response to the unprecedented emergency. Several thousand commercial airlines in the air on September 11th had to find places to land in an instant shuffle between airports. The nation's air-traffic-control system handled things easily.

New Yorkers and volunteers from around the nation respond-

ed without hesitation. Firefighters rushed to the World Trade Center and 343 died heroically trying to save others. Subways, water pipes, electricity, phone lines and other elements of the city's infrastructure were hard hit, but workers quickly repaired them. A U.S. Navy hospital ship pulled into New York harbor and provided meals, medicine, and care. Hospitals set up emergency trauma units. TV reporters hurried to what was called "ground zero" with cameras whirring and provided informative, sensitive reporting. Schoolchildren made sandwiches for rescue and cleanup crews. Donors lined up to give blood. So many volunteer workers turned up that most had to be sent away. Relief agencies, mental health workers, the U.S. government, and compassionate individuals rolled up their sleeves and opened their pocketbooks. *The New York Times* attempted an obituary for each of the victims. '. . . the reason the response was so swiftly effective—the human response was so commanding. . .was our freedom," said writer Frederick Allen.

Firefighter Steve Gaudet said, "There was a chief telling us to go . . . that we'd lost enough men. Nobody listened." Three hundred forty-three firefighters died, leaving more than 600 children. This picture shows firefighters at ground zero days later.

Perhaps most poignant was the platform erected at ground zero so that families and others could visit the site, pray, and pay respects. Those who came left messages and notes:

"Andrew—I've been here twice looking for your beautiful smile and that twinkle in your eyes and both times God has let me know you are with Him in a safer place."

"To my dearest love, life has no meaning without you, Angela, you were appropriately named. Kind, sweet and gentle. Love you forever, Elliott"

"Daddy, a piece of me died with you on Sept. 11. You were the most important man in my life. You were my strong point. You were my daddy."

"What lies behind us and what lies before us are tiny matters compared to what lies within us," wrote the 19th century philosopher, Ralph Waldo Emerson. After September 11th we knew that what lies within us is civic spirit, compassion, unselfishness, love, and a large measure of heroism.

Desperate relatives posted pictures of their missing loved ones. Most were not to be found.

237

51 War in Iraq

George W. Bush, speaking to sailors on the flight deck of the USS Abraham Lincoln on May 1, 2003, said, "Today we have the greater power to free a nation by breaking a dangerous and aggressive regime."

In December 2002 the nation of Iraq delivered a 12,000-page report to the United Nations. It was a little more than a year after the September 11th attacks and the report—packaged in forty-three volumes along with six folders and twelve CD-ROMs (all written in English)—claimed that Iraq did *not* possess nuclear bombs or other weapons of mass destruction (known as WMDs).

Was it true? No one knew. And no one trusted Saddam Hussein, Iraq's dictator. Saddam lived in opulent palaces and ruled brutally, killing Iraqis who opposed him or whom he viewed as a threat, often just because they were from a different ethnic group. No one could predict what he might do, especially if he had WMDs.

The United States was fighting one war in the Middle East after 9/11, targeting the terrorist al Qaeda and Taliban militias in Afghanistan, both of which operated under the influence of the radical Osama bin Laden, who had funded and developed training camps for terrorists. Bin Laden was still at large, but now President George W. Bush was turning his attention to Iraq and what he and his administration viewed as a major threat to the world: the possibility that Saddam Hussein had deadly weapons of mass destruction and a willingness to share them with terrorists.

On the same December day that he delivered those documents to the UN, Saddam's information minister read a speech from Saddam addressed to the Kuwaiti people apologizing for invading their country in 1990 and then asking their "young believers" to "stand up to the foreign occupier with arms . . . . Why don't the believers, loyalists, and holy warriors get together with their counterparts in Iraq . . . to discuss first and foremost jihad against the occupying infidel armies?" he said. (Infidels are non-believers.) That Saddam would be supported by religious Muslim activists seemed laughable to most Middle East experts. Saddam had been known for his lack of religious faith. What was going on?

Saddam was calling for help. Now that he was threatened he hoped to ally himself with the "holy warriors." Kuwait's Information Minister, Sheikh Ahmad, answered with disdain, "The speech contained incitement and encouragement of terrorist acts which the whole world has rejected and condemned."

Meanwhile, President Bush was challenging Saddam Hussein to let UN investigators into Iraq to search for WMDs. And Saddam wasn't cooperating. More than two decades earlier, Iraq had built a nuclear reactor with help from France. The reactor was not yet "hot" (operational) in June 1981 when Israel carried out a carefully planned bombing attack that destroyed the reactor and with it Iraq's nuclear program. Had Saddam rebuilt that program? There was no information that said he had. But it was known that Iraq had experimented with chemical and biological weapons. Did Saddam still have them? No one seemed to know. Much of the information concerning Saddam's capabilities and intent was classified and not available to the public. Within the government itself there was a raging debate and no agreement as to whether Iraq had the capability and the intent to use WMDs.

After Iraq invaded Kuwait in 1990 (see page 196) the peace terms called for Iraq to destroy (under UN supervision) all world-threatening weapons. UN inspectors entered Iraq and found and dismantled some biological facilities, but Saddam kicked them out before they were sure they had them all and before they could be sure there was no nuclear program. Because of their lack of cooperation ("non-compliance" with the terms of the peace treaty) the United Nations imposed sanctions, which kept Iraq from buying and selling a variety of goods on the world market, especially military supplies. Under President Clinton, the U.S. dropped bombs on targets in Iraq.

In September 2002, Iraq said that UN inspectors could return, but then wouldn't agree to the UN's conditions. Three months later, Iraq produced the 12,000 page report. The UN inspectors said there was nothing new in it, but asked for more time to negotiate. President George W. Bush wasn't willing to wait.

On March 20, 2003, a U.S.–led force invaded Iraq. On television, the action sometimes seemed like a video game, with artillery and bombs lighting up the night. As American and British soldiers marched from Kuwait to Iraq's capital, Baghdad, reporters traveled with the troops at the military's invitation (they were known as "embedded" reporters).

Bush was still baffled about the countries that produced ideologies and people with the goal of killing Americans in terrorist attacks. He wondered how the U.S. could reform such societies, and wanted to advocate the promotion of democracy and women's rights in the Muslim world. No president had said that before.

—Bob Woodward, in the *Washington Post*

On the third day of U.S. raids on Baghdad, explosions lit the night sky triggering giant fireballs, deafening explosions, and a huge black cloud. Saddam Hussein's opulent palace was a major target. Here is what it looked like the next day, March 22, 2003.

Baghdad is an unrelievedly earth-colored city, its drab vistas broken only by the occasional peacock blue and gold domes of mosques, which glisten prettily in the sun, and by the dusty strands of eucalyptus and date palms that seem to grow everywhere [. . .]

—From *The Fall of Baghdad*
by Jon Lee Anderson, 2004

"As we sped through a gap in the giant sand berm that separates Kuwait from Iraq, the screaming engines of dozens of Assault Amphibious Vehicles filled the night air with a gruesome sound—and must have filled anyone ahead of us with utter dread," wrote NBC correspondent Chip Reid. "These were the first minutes of the ground war, and my unit was at or near the front, a fact that they repeated with pride."

Baghdad fell twenty-one days later, on April 9, 2003. On April 15, Saddam's hometown, Tikrit, surrendered. On May 1, President Bush declared that "In the battle of Iraq, the United States and our allies have prevailed." On December 13, a bearded, bedraggled Saddam

In the United States We're Free to Disagree
Senator Robert C. Byrd speaks out on March 19, 2003

I believe in this beautiful country. I have studied its roots and gloried in the wisdom of its magnificent Constitution. I have marveled at the wisdom of its founders and framers. Generation after generation of Americans has understood the lofty

Robert C. Byrd

ideals that underlie our great Republic. I have been inspired by the story of their sacrifice and their strength.

But, today I weep for my country. I have watched the events of recent months with a heavy, heavy heart. No more is

the image of America one of strong, yet benevolent peacekeeper. The image of America has changed. Around the globe, our friends mistrust us, our word is disputed, our intentions are questioned. ...

The brutality seen on September 11th and in other terrorist attacks we have witnessed around the globe are the violent and desperate efforts by extremists to stop the daily encroachment of western values upon their cultures. That is what we fight. It is a force not confined to borders. It is a shadowy entity with many faces, many names, and many addresses.

But, this Administration has directed all of the anger, fear, and grief which emerged from the ashes of the twin towers and the twisted metal of the Pentagon towards a tangible villain,

one we can see and hate and attack. And villain he is. But, he is the wrong villain. And this is the wrong war. If we attack Saddam Hussein, we will probably drive him from power. But, the zeal of our friends to assist our global war on terrorism may have already taken flight. ...

What is happening to this country? When did we become a nation which ignores and berates our friends? When did we decide to risk undermining international order by adopting a radical and doctrinaire approach to using our awesome military might? How can we abandon diplomatic efforts when the turmoil in the world cries out for diplomacy?

Why can this President not seem to see that America's true power lies not in its will to intimidate, but in its ability to inspire? ...

Goodbye to Saddam! A statue of the brutal Iraqi dictator is toppled in Baghdad's Firdaus Square on April 9, 2003. On May 29th, on the same spot, a group of Iraqi artists, actors, and students, calling themselves *Al Najeen* (the survivors), raised a new statue, this one celebrating freedom.

Hussein was captured. He'd been hiding in a hole in the ground on a relative's farm.

As for those WMDs, the U.S. troops couldn't find any. It was all baffling, especially to the British and American leaders. Military historian John Keegan commented, "Iraq in 2003 demonstrate[s] that classical military theory applies only to the countries in which it was made . . . Elsewhere, and particularly in the artificial, ex-colonial territories of the developing world, usually governed as tyrannies, it does not."

Iraq was one of those artificial territories. It was also one of the earliest centers of human civilization. The Iraqi land between the Tigris and Euphrates Rivers was home to the ancient Sumerians, the Babylonians, and the Assyrians. A very old epic (a great story called *The Epic of Gilgamesh*) tells us it is where King Gilgamesh wept when his friend Enkidu died. The *Bible* says it was the land where Abraham, the patriarch of three great religions (Judaism, Christianity, and Islam), was born.

In 334 BCE, the Persians controlled the region. That's when Alexander the Great swept in with his conquering army and the land fell under Greek rule. After that it became a kind of borderland between the Persian and Roman empires and was known as Mesopotamia (a Greek word for the land between the rivers).

Sitting between East and West, it was an inviting place for invading armies. In the 8th century CE, Islamic Arabs arrived, conquered, and stayed. Two centuries later, Baghdad had become a gorgeous city and a center of mathematics, science, poetry, and affluence. This is the era described in the magical tale *Arabian Nights*, in which Scheherazade captivated the caliph (the ruler) and saved her own life by telling him a thousand and one stories. It was also the time and place where Arabic numerals (the numbers from 0 to 9 that we use today) were developed.

The creative ferment of this golden age came to an end when Mongols rode out of the steppes, terrorizing and conquering. A few cen-

Iraq: in Arabic the word means the shore of the great river ·and the land surrounding it.

A *steppe* is a semi-dry grass-covered plain. Central North America is sometimes described as a steppe (but prairie is the more common term). When you hear *the* steppes, it usually means the vast treeless grasslands of Eurasia, extending from the Danube River in Europe to southwest Siberia.

Sunni and Shi'a (or Shiite). What's the difference? Briefly, it's about leadership and the way their holy book, the Qu'ran, is to be understood. Sunnis are a majority (about eighty-five percent of all Muslims) in most Muslim nations, except in Iran and Iraq. Sunnis usually believe in a literal interpretation of the Qu'ran. Shi'ias look to their religious leaders, the Imams, as God's infallible voice on religious truth.

Army Specialist Eric Barrett watches for insurgent (rebel) activity at Al-Radwnea, Iraq in July, 2005. A young Iraqi friend tags along. Barrett is a member of Bravo Company, 2nd Battalion, 121st Infantry Regiment.

turies after that, Ottoman Turks captured the great city of Constantinople (today Istanbul, Turkey). That was in 1453, and it finished the Byzantine (eastern Roman) Empire. The Ottomans soon ruled an enormous empire of their own, stretching from southeast Africa to the Balkans. With the help of a strong imperial army and slaves, known as *mamelukes*, the Ottomans divided, conquered, taxed, and controlled.

In what is now Iraq, the Ottomans set up three separate states and, to this day, they have represented three different entities, never unified in outlook. Sunni Muslim Arabs people a central region, with Baghdad as its capital. In the south, Shi'a Muslim Arabs dominate; Basra is its central city, with ties to nearby Shi'a Iran and its religious leaders. The third province, in the Kurdish north, has the city of Mosul as its center. Kurds, mostly Sunni Muslim, are not Arabs. Many have longed for an independent Kurdish state.

The Ottomans relied on powerful local tribal families to keep order and run things. Those families were happy to hold power and keep everything as it was. So the region became a kind of backwater. In the mid-19th century, with democratic movements in Europe and some agitation in Iraq, Turkey allowed a few Western reforms in the provinces of Baghdad, Mosul, and Basra. Then World War I came along and Turkey entered the war on the side of Germany. Allied forces attacked the Ottoman lands. By 1918 all of Iraq was under British occupation. The British, who were interested in the oil, set up a puppet monarchy and used military force to counter an insurgency. Airplanes bombed villages to punish insurgents and establish order. It was one of the first times aircraft was used in this role.

At the end of World War I, the modern Iraqi nation was pasted together from the three regions—Baghdad, Mosul, and Basra—that seemed to have little in common. The Kurds wanted independence from their Arab neighbors, and the Sunnis and the Shi'as (competing branches of Islam) each wanted to dominate the other. There's a whole lot more to this tale, but the main idea is that this is a region with a short history of nationhood and a long history of tribal and religious conflict and a distaste for foreign invaders.

So, almost as soon as President George W. Bush declared the battle of Iraq officially over in May of 2003, another battle began. This was not army vs. army, it was suicide bombers and car bombs blowing up innocent bystanders. It was an insurgents' war, which is a rebellion against those in control.

The American and British forces were trying to establish a democracy in Iraq and turn the nation over to Iraqi leaders. But like most wars, this one didn't go as intended.

For the most part the insurgents were Sunni extremists, who were a minority in Iraq but, under Saddam, had been a ruling elite. They were caught up in anti-American and anti-Western hatreds as well as centuries-old religious and regional conflicts and a desire to regain power. (Keep in mind, these insurgents were Muslim *extremists*. Surveys showed that most Muslims, including most Sunnis, disapproved of the violence.) Complicating things was the oil, and its riches, that went to those in power. U.S. and coalition forces, hampered by poor intelligence and little knowledge of Islamic culture, made some bad mistakes, which didn't help things. President Bush was clear about his goal. Talking to reporter Bob Woodward he said, "I believe the United States is *the* beacon for freedom in the world. And I believe we have a responsibility to promote freedom that is as solemn as the responsibility is to protect the American people, because the two go hand-in-hand."

Our intentions were good; was that enough? To exercise power conscientiously we needed to know and understand the greater world and its peoples. That was the challenge of the 21st century. This was to be an era where knowledge and information dominate.

As to the war in Iraq, some people were calling it a clash of cultures. But that was too simplistic. Most Muslims clearly preferred peace to war and freedom to tyranny. This was about terrorists, people with a fervent belief that they want to impose on others usually by violent means. It was a civil war with religious groups fighting for power and old anti-Western feelings complicating things.

For the United States and its allies there was a timely question: How do we to deal with cultures that have completely different traditions, laws, and ways of organizing themselves from ours?

"We are a people who have made a religion of liberty," says historian Walter McDougall. Can we impose our treasured concepts of freedom and democracy on others? Perhaps at bottom there's an old philosophical question to consider: does the end (the goal) justify the means (the way in which you try to attain the goal), even if the means are violent?

Rumsfeld, needing a Cultural Interpreter

"Liberation! Liberation! Liberation!" says America's Secretary of Defense, Donald Rumsfeld, who is pictured as a tourist in Iraq by cartoonist Ann Telnaes. An Arab hears "liberation" and thinks "occupation."

Iraq's past is the world's past, its awesome art objects are a cultural heritage that we all share. Iraqi laws protecting its ancient treasures had been seen as a model for the region. But wars bring unexpected destruction and the losses in the Iraq War were devastating to the worlds of art and history. With no one to stop them, looters stripped the National Museum of Antiquities of its major treasures and burned the National Library. Paul Zimansky, a professor of archaeology at Boston University, compared the loss of the library to the burning of the library at Alexandria (in Julius Caesar's time) that destroyed original texts from the ancient world—the work of Aristotle and others—that have never been recovered.

52 Blowing in the Wind

John Kerry is pictured testifying before the Senate Foreign Relations Committee on April 2, 1971. Kerry, who had been a Navy Lieutenant Junior Grade in Vietnam, made a moving plea to end the war, which he said was a "mistake." Kerry was director of the Vietnam Veterans Against the War. His action was controversial, many veterans didn't agree with him.

The 2004 presidential election pits tall solemn Massachusetts senator John Kerry against friendly affable President George W. Bush. During the Vietnam War, Kerry was captain of a PCF (Patrol Craft Fast), usually known as a Swift boat. Those aluminum-sided 50 foot boats carry little protective armor; they rely on machine guns, grenades, and their speed for safety. In Vietnam, Swift boats patrolled the rivers trying to disrupt Viet Cong supply routes.

When John Kerry asked to be assigned to a PCF it was as dangerous a wartime job as you could find. He was wounded three times and got awarded Silver and Bronze Stars for bravery, which made him a war hero. But there were some who called him a traitor. That's because, when he came home, Kerry spoke out against the war in hearings before Congress; then he joined a group of veterans who threw their medals over a fence at the U.S. Capitol to protest the war while it was still being fought.

All that had happened almost 30 years before Kerry ran for president, but the Vietnam War was still an unhealed national wound. George Bush had done home duty with the National Guard during that war; his service records disappeared mysteriously.

In 2004, Bush's campaign strategist, Karl Rove, labeled Kerry a flip-flopper, accusing him of changing his mind on issues; flip flop sandals were waved at campaign events. There were serious matters to be discussed and argued, but the campaign turned noisy and shallow—and Kerry wasn't a candidate who connected well with people.

Once again it was a close election. This time, instead of Florida as the deciding state, it was Ohio, and no one was sure, until early morning the day after the election, who had actually won. Then the country found that George W. Bush had been reelected as president of the United States and Dick Cheney as vice-president.

Bush's agenda for the second term? According to his press secretary, Scott McClellan: To reform Social Security (a government insurance program for the elderly and disabled), to bring the Iraq War to an end turning the Middle East into a region of peace and prosperity, to lay the groundwork for a permanent Republican majority that would dominate national politics.

None of those goals is achieved. Meanwhile, in a rush to begin a war in Iraq, the president ignores intelligence reports that say there are no WMDs. He doesn't share that information with Congress. In wanting his way, Bush isnt being different from many other chief executives.

In a 1791 letter to George Washington, Thomas Jefferson wrote, "Delay is preferable to error."

How much privacy should public officials have? Remember, they are our employees, we citizens are paying their salaries. You'll hear talk of "transparency" in government. That's the idea that there should be no dark closets holding government policy and actions from citizens. Except, and this can be a big exception, when we are dealing with national security.

Almost all of the 20th century presidents, starting with Franklin D. Roosevelt, had attempted to acquire executive power beyond that described in the Constitution. Usually the claim was that national security, or war, or other emergencies, made enhanced executive power necessary. Back in April 1952 the United Steel Workers demanded a raise in wages for its workers; the steel industry refused, and a steel strike was called. Harry S. Truman was fighting the Korean War: he is-

The 2007 Nobel Peace Prize was awarded to former Vice President Al Gore and the Intergovernmental Panel on Climate Change "for their efforts to build up and disseminate greater knowledge about man-made climate change, and to lay the foundation for the measures that are needed to counteract such change." The Nobel Committee was calling attention to our shared environment on Earth, the spaceship that we all ride.

sued an executive order directing the Secretary of Commerce to seize the steel mills to prevent the strike. The president said, during a national emergency (in this case a war) the executive branch becomes supreme and does not need approval from Congress for actions in the national interest. The steel companies were outraged, they went to court in protest. The U.S. Supreme Court thought the case important enough to take up immediately. Within two months they handed down a decision in the case of *Youngstown Steel & Tube Co.* v. *Sawyer* (known as the "Steel Seizure Case"). They decided, 6-3, that the president is not all-powerful even in wartime and that he could not seize the steel industry.

In 2004, when President George Bush claimed that he has the power to hold suspected terrorists without giving them a hearing, Supreme Court Justice Sandra Day O'Connor disagrees. She cites the Steel Seizure Case. "We have long since made clear that a state of war is not a blank check for the president when it comes to the rights of the nation's citizens," the justice writes.

In 2005 and 2006, Congressional hearings are held to examine the Bush administration's domestic surveillance (at home spying) programs. Again the Steel Seizure Case is cited and especially the opinion of Supreme Court Justice Robert H. Jackson, who wrote in 1952: "What is at stake is the equilibrium established by our constitutional system." That equilibrium, or balance of powers, is sometimes hard to resolve. How much power and flexibility should the chief executive have in a crisis or emergency?

Before that question gets answered, some fast-blowing winds make Americans focus on state and local issues. In August of 2005, a hurricane forms over the Bahama Islands. Named Katrina, it moves over Florida as a moderate Category 1 hurricane causing a few deaths and some flooding. Any hurricane means serious winds, damage, and usually floods. A Category 1 is the mildest; a Category 3 can be really bad; a Category 5 is the worst. After leaving Florida, Katrina picks up speed and strength as it travels over unusually warm currents in the Gulf of Mexico. Roaring and blowing it heads for a swath of land that stretches from Texas to Louisiana.

On Friday, August 26th weather centers tracking the storm say it could be very destructive and that landfall in New Orleans is highly likely. Some New Orleans residents begin to board up their homes and leave. Later, the National Hurricane Center and the National Weather Service will be commended for their accurate forecasts, which give coastal residents ample warning of what is heading their way.

On Saturday evening, with Katrina bearing down, New Orleans Mayor Ray Nagin calls for a voluntary evacuation of the city.

On Sunday, August 28, the National Weather Service's New Orleans/Baton Rouge office issues an urgent bulletin predicting "devastating damage." Katrina, still over the Gulf, has become a Category 5, its ugly potential is now clear. Mayor Nagin orders a mandatory evacuation of the city. The weather bureau says the region could be "uninhabitable for weeks." More than a million people leave New Orleans in

What's the Blow on Hurricanes?

Hurricane Katrina in the Gulf of Mexico; those pretty swirls can be deadly.

Just think of a hurricane as a big heat-pumping system. It usually starts with tropical ocean water warmed by a burning hot sun to at least 80 degrees Fahrenheit (27 degrees Celsius). Now picture winds coming from different directions over the ocean and meeting over that pocket of hot water: humid air rises, cooling and condensing into storm clouds that drink up a lot of latent heat energy from ocean water.

Add a high-pressure area above the storm clouds and it will push the rising air out and away, which means more hot humid air gets sucked into the space below and the potential storm grows.

The whole thing sucks in tropical ocean air,

condenses its moisture into powerful storm clouds, and pushes the air away so that more can rush in to take its place. Meanwhile the rotation of the Earth is spinning this windy pump around, which helps form an "eye" and pushes the clouds into a pinwheel shape.

If the steamy, sea-churning storm stays over warm ocean water, a hurricane may keep pumping for days. Over cool land it quickly falls apart. Even a Category 5 hurricane, without hot air to pump, can weaken into a tropical storm in hours. But don't count on it, stay away from the water when a hurricane is brewing, and if the storm heads for land, find some place safe to take cover.

the largest mass evacuation from a major American city ever.

But not everyone leaves. For some there is no transportation; others, who don't understand the urgency, think they can make it through the storm, a few, without radios, never realize what is coming. Looters, with criminal intent, think they can outwit the storm.

New Orleans sits in a bowl at the mouth of the Mississippi River (the delta), stretching from the river to big round Lake Pontchatrain. The original city was built on rare high land at the river's edge. As the city grew, waterways were opened to Pontchatrain to promote boat

Note the white strand stretched across a broken levee. Those are plastic bags filled with sand, an attempt to hold back the waters. You can see how effective the sandbags were.

commerce. Then, in the 1940s, the state filled those waterways and homes and buildings were put on the filled land. Further low land got developed when large areas of marshland and swamp were drained. Meanwhile the town's underlying water table fell drastically. So New Orleans began to sink. By 2001, 51% of the land surface in greater New Orleans subdivisions (called parishes) is at or below sea level. (Much of the Netherlands is below sea level; people like to live near water.)

Federally built levees were designed to keep the water out and the city dry, but over time there were many warnings that in a major storm the levees might not hold, almost everyone knew they needed to be strengthened. Flooding was not unusual in parts of the city.

Katrina hits Gulf Coast communities east of New Orleans early Monday, August 29th as a Category 3 fury with sustained winds that reach 125 mph (205 km/h). At 9 A.M., the eye passes slightly to the east of New Orleans, over Lake Pontchatrain. Lake water surges 15 feet above the norm and the levee walls, meant to protect New Orleans, aren't able to hold back Katrina's wrath. The federal flood protection system fails at 50 places. Water pours through breaks in the levees quickly flooding the city. Then those walls keep the water from draining away.

By late afternoon New Orleans is dark, it has no electricity, and there is no fresh water to drink. Bodies of drowned people and animals float in what, the day before, had been city streets. Some people have climbed on to rooftops to escape flooded homes and are calling for help. The Louisiana Superdome is an evacuation center, but Katrina has torn two holes in its roof and wind and water damage make it a stinking mess.

A day of sunshine after the flood: Are these looters picking up whatever they can find? Or are they men trying to salvage some of their own things? Who might have had fun on the bicycle before the flood? Where is it going? The only thing certain is that for many, life in New Orleans will never be the same.

At Memorial Hospital, the electricity fails and the auxiliary power goes down. The August heat registers 100° F and there is no air-conditioning or power for vital medical equipment to function. Windows are blown out and water fills the hospital's ground floor. No one has prepared personnel for the choices and action necessary in a major emergency, by the time rescuers get to the hospital some patients are dead, in some cases because of decisions made in a fearful pressured situation.

FEMA (Federal Emergency Management Agency) is the government agency empowered to respond to emergencies. Director Michael Brown, in Washington, D.C., waits 5 hours on Monday before asking his boss, Michael Chertoff, to send a thousand Homeland Security employees to New Orleans. Then he gives them two days to get there.

Meanwhile, oil refineries (there are lots of them in Louisiana) are sloshing oily ooze into the water. They stop refining oil, which sends oil prices up around the globe.

Without working phone lines, there is no way to communicate with those outside the area or those stranded in their homes. Cell phones go dead as does the Internet (base stations were destroyed). Local TV and radio are down.

By Tuesday, floodwaters cover 80% of New Orleans and they don't recede. Houses, shops, restaurants, and office buildings are stuck inside a deep dirty toxic moat. The water will stay for weeks. Now evacuation helicopters begin rescuing people from rooftops and buildings. Rescuers in rowboats bang on rooftops and wait for a response.

At least 1,836 people die in what is one of the deadliest natural disasters in American history. It is the costliest. (Check out the Galveston flood of 1900. No one knows how many died then, but at least 6,000.) New Orleans in 2005 produces incredible examples of heroism and selflessness, but there is also looting and criminal disorder. Mostly, for days, no one seems to be in charge. (The United States Coast Guard gets widely commended for its response.)

That same Tuesday morning the president's phone rings at 5 A.M.; he is given details on the crisis. President Bush is in San Diego preparing remarks he will make to veterans of World War II. After a 9 A.M.

By August 31, 2005, eighty percent of New Orleans was flooded, with some parts under 15 feet (4.5 m) of water. On September 15, 2005, the inundation had been reduced from 80% to 40%, which means there were still a whole lot of flooded areas that would not be habitable for a very long while.

New Orleans is known for music and good times. But it wasn't easy to sing about Katrina. After the water did its damage, people had to deal with insurance companies and government bureaucracies.

speech, the president and his entourage climb aboard Air Force One. The president has decided to return to Washington to deal with the emergency, but first he will spend the night at his home in Crawford, Texas. On the way back to Washington he flies over New Orleans, viewing the disaster from the window of Air Force One.

Later, *Washington Post* investigative reporter Bob Woodward, who published four books on the president, wrote, "As we know now, Bush said he didn't get the weather report and there's video of him getting the weather report, whether it sunk in or not. And that was a symbol."

Slowly New Orleans begins to recover: its heroes are mostly ordinary people who roll up their sleeves and help their neighbors. Downed trees, wet mattresses, destroyed homes, decayed food, and noxious mold clutter the soggy city; before there can be any rebuilding the debris has to be collected and bagged. From across the nation, and the world, people respond to the city's tragedy with astonishing generosity. Some come to New Orleans to do what they can to help. Many communities, like Houston, open their homes and halls to Katrina refugees.

Eventually the president approves more than $110 billion in disaster relief funds and visits the Gulf region more than a dozen times. But the slow response to Katrina becomes a public relations disaster for the administration. For those in New Orleans it is a human and city disaster, for the nation as a whole, it is a devastating example of the cost of bureaucratic indifference to known problems. And four years later, thousands of Katrina victims in Mississippi and Louisiana are still living in temporary trailers.

Are you interested in doing some hurricane research? See what you can find about the Great Hurricane of 1780, the Galveston Hurrican of 1900, the 1928 Okeechobee Hurricane, and 1998's Hurricane Mitch.

251

53 The Iraq War Continues

Roadside bombs and suicide bombers are terrorist stealth weapons; they are hard to stop. Here an Iraqi soldier, with a rocket-propelled grenade, passes a burning British vehicle hit by a roadside bomb in Basra, Iraq's second largest city.

On January 21, 2009, President Barack Obama issued an executive order saying that those held at Guantánamo Bay "have the constitutional privilege of the writ of habeas corpus."

Habeas Corpus is a latin phrase meaning "you[may] have the body."

The Iraq War, which was supposed to be quick and clean with no cost to the American taxpayer (oil revenue was expected to pay for it), goes on and on. By 2007 it has lasted longer than World War II. By the end of 2009, it has cost more than the Vietnam War. Over four thousand American soldiers have been killed, over one hundred thousand Iraqis are dead, hundreds of thousands in the Middle East are displaced, and the war's cost—hundreds of billions of dollars— begins impacting the American economy.

Information emerges slowly making it clear that there were no links between the 9/11 terrorists and Iraq. Saddam Hussein's cruel dictatorship had one plus: he kept terrorist groups out of Iraq. Now terrorists are setting off roadside bombs with regularity. While the addition of thousands of American soldiers (called "the surge") does bring some safety to Iraqi streets, for the most part, at home and abroad, things aren't going well.

Under the Bush administration the basic constitutional right of *habeas corpus* for prisoners of war has been ignored. The guarantee of *habeas corpus*, a foundation of British and American law, is provided for in our Constitution (it means if you are arrested someone must inform you of charges and allow you to defend yourself in court). The rule of law has been central to American beliefs. But political prisoners are being held, without access to lawyers or free trials, at an American-run prison in Iraq called Abu Ghraib, at the Guantánamo Bay Naval Base on the island of Cuba, at a prison at the Bagram Air Base in Afghanistan, and elsewhere.

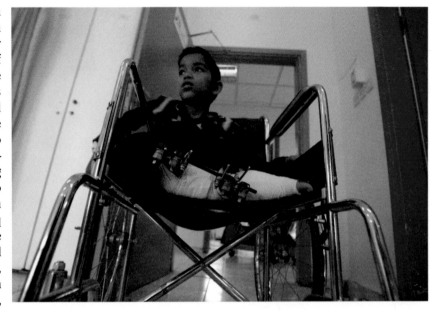

Abdullah, a nine-year-old Iraqi injured in the war, has had multiple surgeries in a hospital in Amman, Jordan.

Some are tortured, despite international and U.S. laws that condemn torture. According to the *New York Times* columnist Frank Rich, "torture was a premeditated policy approved at our government's highest levels. . .and, that, in the assessment of reliable sources like the F.B.I. director Robert Mueller, it did not help disrupt any terrorist attacks."

Administration spokespersons say that the war on terror has changed global ground rules and that new tactics are essential. (This is an issue on which there was, and is, much disagreement.) But nations that had once looked to the United States for inspiration and moral leadership are beginning to produce suicide bombers eager to kill Americans.

At the same time, our soldiers are making astonishing sacrifices for their nation and for people in the Middle East. Many are dedicated to rebuilding Iraq and helping turn it into a vibrant democracy. But back in the United States, polls show that most Americans are tired of the war and its many costs. Needs at home, like health care and education funding, are being neglected. The bipartisan politics of earlier congresses is hard to find. A vision for 21st-century America seems to be lacking.

The end of the Cold War left us as the most powerful country the world has known. We took on a role as the world's peacekeeper—but is that something that Americans really want?

The United States
was well into the Iraqi War when Americans learned that their leaders had ignored, or refused to believe, intelligence sources that told them there were no weapons of mass destruction or biological weapons in Iraq. Several sources document this in detail. One of them is *The Way of the World*, a book by Pulitzer Prize winner, Ron Suskind a former *Wall Street Journal* writer.

253

Bombs, death, and army convoys are part of daily life in war-ravaged Iraq. Above, an Iraqi woman weeps over the body of her sister, killed by a roadside bomb in 2009. Right, U.S. Army soldier Pete Lopez observes Iraqi traffic control in Baghdad. Opposite, U.S. Army soldiers are on their way to Basra province to provide urgent humanitarian aid.

A 2008 Pentagon inventory of U.S. military bases lists 865 facilities in more than 40 countries and U.S. territories (with American personnel in 6 additional countries where we don't even have bases). Some 99,295 people connected to U.S. military forces were living and working in Japan alone. The Department of Defense calls itself "one of the world's largest landlords." *Newsweek International* editor, Fareed Zakaria, says the U.S. "military effort against Islamic extremism has received close to $1 trillion of funding."

Americans were beginning to ask: Can we afford the expense of a huge global military empire? Should other wealthy nations be sharing costs when there is a crisis that demands military intervention? Does an American military presence create conflict inside nations that resent foreign troops? Do our troops truly act as peacekeepers? The Bush administration doesn't clarify or answer these questions.

As he leaves the presidency in January 2009, George W. Bush's disapproval rating (in a Gallup poll) is 61%. Eight years earlier, in 2001, when Bill Clinton stepped down the American public gave his performance as president an astonishingly high 66% approval (despite his

impeachment). It was a rosy time for America. The Cold War had ended; the nation was at peace; instead of a national debt, there were nearly $6 trillion in monetary surpluses that were expected to grow in the years to come. America was enjoying great power status.

By 2009, all that had changed: the United States was fighting two major wars (in Iraq and Afghanistan), the debt was astronomical, and the economy was in the worst tailspin since the Great Depression. Where was the nation heading? Where should it head? No one seemed to know.

In his First Inaugural Address, Thomas Jefferson said,

"Freedom of religion; freedom of the press, and freedom of person under the protection of the habeas corpus, and trial by juries impartially selected. These principles form the bright constellation which has gone before us. . . The wisdom of our sages and the blood of our heroes have been devoted to their attainment. They should be the creed of our political faith. . . and should we wander from them in moments of error or alarm, let us hasten to retrace our steps and to regain the road which alone leads to peace, liberty, and safety."

Benji McHugh, a member of the 238th Aviation Regiment, watches for enemy activity from the ramp of a Chinook helicopter over Sharano, Afghanistan in June 2009.

255

54 A Very Brief History of a Very Complex Place

The giant Buddhas of Bamyan, carved into a cliff in the 6th century, were among the world's artistic treasures. In 2001, the Taliban dynamited them.

A British newspaper reporter, in Afghanistan in 2009, noticed a young Afghani pedaling a bike while drinking a can of American beer. That seemed unusual in this land where consumer goods are not abundant, and drinking liquor is outlawed in some regions. So he asked his driver about it. The driver laughed, "That," he told the reporter, "is democracy."

Democracy gets defined in many ways, but as a can of beer? Yes. Some people see democracy as a cultural thing: a way of life that includes sleek cars, skinny blue jeans, violence-filled movies, fast foods, and canned beer. What about America's founding ideas? We're a nation "of the people, by the people, for the people." How about our freedom of religion (that allows us to respect and live with people who don't believe as we do)? How about our courts and civil rights laws (that have made bigotry illegal)? Most of us see those ideas as central to our democracy, but we haven't done a great job explaining them, and sometimes (as when we've tortured prisoners) we haven't lived up to our ideals. Can we send soldiers to fight for an abstract belief in democracy, when some Americans, as well as those in other lands, don't understand it?

These were questions some Americans were asking as the Afghanistan war entered its ninth year. It was clear that military force was not working. The more soldiers we sent, and the more airpower we used, the more suicide bombers responded by blowing themselves up, along with innocent civilians and public buildings.

We had gone to war in Afghanistan in response to the destruction of New York's twin towers. In Afghanistan, Osama bin Laden, leader of the terrorist organization, Al Qaeda, claimed credit for that horrendous event (much of the actual planning for 9/11 was carried out by an Al Qaeda group in Hamburg, Germany).

United States officials knew bin Laden. In the 1970s, when Afghanis were fighting Russia, bin Laden had trained Muslim volunteers to fight the Russians, with American support. Some background here might help.

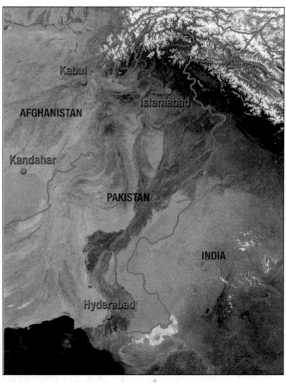

Afghanistan is located at a crossroads, between India, Iran, and central Asia, where Europe and Asia find passageway to each other (check the map here and on page 303). Alexander the Great and his mighty Greek army marched from Persia (today Iran) into Afghanistan in 320 B.C.E. There, Alexander faced his fiercest battles and gravest losses. (He did fall in love with a local chief's daughter, Roxanne, and married her.)

Even then, Afghanistan was a country with an ancient heritage: some of the world's first farming communities had appeared there tens of thousands of years earlier. Alexander's army learned what others would learn later: Afghanis will fight foreign forces just because they are foreign.

Its people have a tradition of taking what they want from invaders—there have been many—and using it in their own ways. Some left their languages: Pashto (Afghani) and Farsi (Persian). An Arab-Muslim conquest in the 7th century made Islam the common religion of the region, wiping out a Greek, Hindu, Buddhist, Mongol past.

In 1747 a Pashtun leader, Ahmad Shah, established an Afghani state in the south and east; that state gradually conquered nearby Tajik, Hazara, and Uzbek areas to the north and west. Today Pashtuns make up about

This satellite photograph shows the Indus River valley running north and south and the snow-capped Himalaya mountains in the northeast. The valley held one of the world's first urban cultures from about 2500 B.C.E. to 1500 B.C.E., which was when the Egyptians were building pyramids. Traders and artisans lived in well-planned cities; farmers raised domesticated crops in rural areas. Today the region may be less civilized. The overlay on the western side of the map shows the rugged, mountainous region between Afghanistan and Pakistan, a training ground for terrorists and often the scene of intense fighting.

half of the population, Tajiks about 25 percent. (Statistics are shaky as there has been no official census in Afghanistan since 1979.)

During the 19th century Britain and Russia, fighting for dominance in Asia, sent armies and set up power bases in the region (the Persian/Iranians sent warriors too). The British tried to rule the unruly Pashtuns, which led to disaster after disaster. On August 19, 1919 the British finally left, and today Afghans celebrate that as their independence day. In the 20th century Pashtuns led a modern monarchy; periods of corruption alternated with moderately representative government.

Then, in 1978, in a big coup, Afghanistan became what was labeled a democratic republic (most Americans called it communism). In some regions, men were forced to cut their beards, women couldn't wear the traditional long dress called a *burkha*, and many mosques were closed. Thousands were arrested and imprisoned. Devout Muslims were soon fighting liberal Muslims in a civil war over issues of modernization, power, and foreign influence. The Soviet Union sent troops and money with the hope of gaining power in the region. The U.S., under President Jimmy Carter, sent massive aid to support anti-Russian guerilla efforts. Osama bin Laden, a Saudi living in Afghanistan, was among those whose efforts were financed by the U.S. No one realized that he would form a terrorist group: Al Qaeda. Other anti-Russian fighters included the Taliban, an organization led by conservative Muslim scholars and religious leaders with a medieval agenda (they thought women should have almost no rights and everyone should pray to Allah exactly as ancient Afghanis did). The Taliban's radical extremists learned how to be terrorists. The Russians, expecting to rule Afghanistan, stayed for a decade (1979-89), finally leaving in defeat, having lost 15,000 soldiers.

Even in wartime people must shop and carry on with daily activities. In this street scene in Afghanistan, Muslim women are wearing beautiful blue *burkhas* (also *burqa* or *burka*), an outer garment that covers them from head to toe. Their faces are veiled with a *purdah*, a word meaning "curtain." The *burkha* had its origins in desert times to help protect men and women from sand on windy days. Today it's a Muslim issue of modesty.

By the year 2000, the Taliban controlled 90% of the country, providing free schooling for Afghani boys (not girls), in schools called *madrassas*, where students were taught to memorize the Qu'ran and hate all things "western" or "democratic." In early 2001, Taliban militia destroyed all statues in the nation, including two ancient giant Buddhas in Bamian, near Kabul. Taliban religious leaders said the figures were idolatrous and un-Islamic; much of the international community, including some Islamic nations, said they were historic treasures.

When the United States and its allies invaded Afghanistan after 9/11, we were determined to capture Osama bin Laden. But bin Laden, who wasn't

Afghani and had only a small following there, soon moved to neighboring Pakistan, a nation with nuclear weapons and an unstable government. Suicide warfare and extremist tactics began to threaten Pakistan as the Taliban spread there too.

Back in Afghanistan the Taliban (mostly Pashtun) controlled most of the rural regions, while the Northern Alliance (dominated by Tajiks) received diplomatic recognition from the United Nations. The Taliban terrorized and the Northern Alliance seemed hopelessly corrupt.

We had walked into a civil war where there didn't seem to be any reasonable alternatives. Writing in the *New York Times* on October 29, 2009, Nicholas Kristoff suggested that if we wanted to reach Afghanis, we should build schools, not send troops. "For the cost of a single additional soldier stationed in Afghanistan for one year, we could build roughly 20 schools there," he wrote. Kristoff cited the work of Greg Mortenson, who had opened 39 schools in Afghanistan and 92 in Pakistan, "The aid organization CARE has 295 schools educating 50,000 girls in Afghanistan, and not a single one has been closed or burned by the Taliban," said Kristoff.

Schools can't solve all the problems of the region, but neither can foreign soldiers. Afghanistan has a long history of resisting outside forces. The more foreign soldiers, the more determined the suicide bombers become. There's another issue: Afghanistan is one of the world's poorest nations. Its women are badly mistreated. This is a nation that needs help achieving a reasonable standard of living for its citizens. If democracy means a decent lifestyle—rather than an invading army—could any nation resist?

Al Qaeda is a terrorist network, a group that operates between nations, but has no national home. Its members are fundamentalist Sunni Muslims (most Sunnis don't approve of its terrorist ways) whose goal is global jihad that would remove all foreign influences from Muslim countries.

Village elders in Afghanistan speak at a *shura* (meeting) with the governor of Zabul province (he's not pictured) about education, security, road construction, and other issues of importance to them. It is November 2009. This is local democracy in action. A U.S. soldier listens.

55 The Great Panic

by Danny Hakim

Many of the newly jobless have no choice but to live in a tent. Tammy Day, using a plastic crate for a chair, is one of them. This photo, taken in March 2009, shows one of three homeless encampments, known as tent cities, near Sacramento, California.

In 1849, prospectors pitched tents alongside the American River in northern California, searching for fortunes during the height of the gold rush.

In the beginning of 2009, a much different city of tents arose near the same river, outside Sacramento, as hundreds of homeless people took shelter at a sprawling, makeshift encampment.

This tent city was born out of desperation. There were blue tents and red tents and camouflage tents, there was no electricity or running water, and there were many residents who had never before been homeless or imagined they would be.

"This is the bottom of the barrel here," one resident, an unemployed construction worker, told NBC News. "I don't think it can get any worse than this."

Such tent cities sprang up across the country in late 2008 and early 2009, from Nashville to Portland, as the nation and the world were gripped by a paralyzing financial crisis. The crisis was sparked by the collapse of the housing market in the United States. For decades, housing prices had gone up and up, and banks had found new and more inventive ways to lend Americans money to buy bigger homes.

Some critics of the practice said America had become addicted to borrowing money. Not only were average Americans borrowing more money than they could afford, but major banks and lending companies were making too many loans that would never be paid back and taking far too many risks, putting the entire financial system in jeopardy.

By 2008, the housing market had collapsed. Home prices began to fall for the first time in decades, more and more people lost their jobs and many Americans were forced out of homes they could no longer afford to pay for.

It soon became clear that America was facing its worst financial crisis since the Great Depression. News reports seized on parallels to the 1930s. The *New York Times*, in a story on a tent city in Fresno, California, proclaimed that such camps presaged "the arrival of modern-day Hoovervilles," referring to the shantytowns that emerged during the early days of the Depression, while Herbert Hoover was president.

"We cannot look away and pretend like this does not happen, because it *is* happening," said California Governor Arnold Schwarzenegger,

During the Great Depression in the 1930s, homeless camps sprouted up across the country. Seattle's "Hooverville" (pictured in this photo) had more than 2000 shacks, created from scrap wood, scrap metal, bricks, cardboard and other junk.

261

after the state announced that the Sacramento tent city would be closed and its residents relocated. "These are people that have not chosen to be in this condition, it's because the economy's down, a lot of them lost jobs, their money, belongings, everything."

The collapse of the housing market would have been bad enough, but then the nation's major investment banks began to falter. That was a serious problem indeed. Generally speaking, investment banks are not like the community banks where Americans across the country keep their money. Traditionally, investment banks do not accept deposits or make loans to individuals, though there are exceptions. But investment banks like Merrill Lynch and Goldman Sachs play an essential role in American capitalism.

They help private businesses become public corporations by selling shares of stock. When towns and cities need to build new schools or parks or offices, they need investment banks to help them issue and sell bonds. What is a bond? When someone buys a bond, they are essentially loaning money to a government or a corporation with the understanding that they will be paid back, with interest, at a later date.

In short, American commerce depends on investment banks. But the industry was on the brink of collapse in 2008. Over the previous decade, investment banks had taken millions of home loans made by other banks and lenders, bundled them together and resold them. Large batches of loans were sold and resold so many times that investors lost sight of how risky many of them were.

So long as housing prices were rising, this was all immensely profitable. And when the housing market collapsed? It was disastrous. The trouble began with Bear, Stearns, a firm founded in 1923 that was the second most admired securities firm in the world, at least according to a ranking by *Fortune* Magazine in its March 19, 2007 issue.

On Monday, September 15, 2008, a young woman holds a sign in front of Lehman Brothers headquarters in New York. That day, the 165-year-old investment bank devastated by falling real estate values, poor investment decisions, and a credit crisis, filed for bankruptcy protection. It was the biggest bankruptcy filing ever.

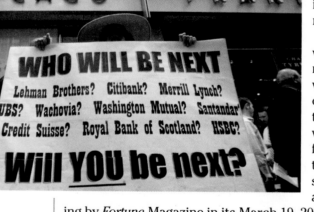

Bear was known as a scrappy firm where bond traders still wore suspenders and chomped cigars, a throwback to an earlier Wall Street era. But Bear had made many of the riskiest bets, and as its troubles became known, investors rushed to pull their money from the bank, similar to the runs on more traditional banks during the Depression.

Worse, a story in the *Wall Street Journal* implied that Bear's chief executive, James Cayne, wasn't paying attention while his company was on the verge of collapse. In the summer of 2007, when Bear's troubles were first coming to a head, the paper reported that Mr. Cayne "wasn't near his Wall Street office."

Where was he? "Playing in a bridge tournament in Nashville, Tennessee, without a cell phone or an email device." The paper discovered he had spent nearly half of the workdays in July either playing bridge or working on his golf game.

That lightning-strike line? It's the path the German stock index is taking on Sept 16, 2008, and it's mostly downhill. A broker at the Frankfurt Stock Exchange in Frankfurt Main, Germany, looks stressed. Has he lost a lot of money? Or is it his customers who have?

By March of 2008, a year after the *Fortune* ranking, Bear was sold at a fire sale price, $10 a share, to JPMorgan Chase. If you had owned 1,000 shares of Bear Stearns in January of 2007, when the stock traded for as much as $172, it would have been worth $172,000. That same investment would have been worth just $1,720 when the company was sold, a devastating loss.

Bear would not have survived at all if the Federal Reserve had not intervened and provided the company an emergency loan. The Fed, as it is known, is an enormous bank run by the government that lends money to private banks. Traditionally, the Fed never lent money to investment banks, but made an exception in this case, fearing Bear's collapse would lead to others.

But Bear was lucky compared to Lehman Brothers. As the crisis escalated, the Fed decided it could not rescue every major bank. In September 2008, Lehman Brothers, a 165-year-old investment banking giant, declared bankruptcy, a loss that made clear how serious the financial crisis had become.

There were many dark chapters during the financial crisis.

While Merrill Lynch, another giant investment bank, teetered on the brink of insolvency, its chief executive, John Thain, spent more than $1 million to redecorate his office. He even had his company spend $87,000 on a new rug. Not that he got to walk on it for very long—he resigned shortly after news of his redecorating led to public outrage.

Bernard Madoff, who ran a multibillion dollar investment firm, was discovered to have operated the largest Ponzi scheme in history, a fraud named for the swindler Charles Ponzi. Basically, Madoff took people's money, lied to them about what he was doing with it and ended up stealing much of it, while promising he was investing it.

In Detroit, General Motors and Chrysler, two of the three American automakers, declared bankruptcy, costing tens of thousands of workers their jobs and sending Pontiac, one of the nation's oldest car brands, to the scrap heap.

By the fall of 2009, the nation's unemployment rate had climbed to 10 percent, meaning that one out of every 10 adults were out of work. Such statistics don't even count people who were too frustrated to look for work. Still, things were worse in the Great Depression, when the unemployment rate reached 25 percent.

Perhaps most worrisome about the financial crisis was that so few of the nation's leading financial experts saw the trouble coming. In October of 2007, Ben Bernanke, the chairman of the Federal Reserve, proclaimed "the banking system is healthy." Within months, the financial system required a government bailout that cost taxpayers trillions of dollars.

David Wessel, in his book *In Fed We Trust*, said that "where the Great Panic was concerned, almost no one got a gold star for guessing the future right."

President Obama, in a speech to Wall Street in September 2009, vowed that changes would be made in the hope of preventing more financial crises. "Those on Wall Street cannot resume taking risks without regard for consequences," the president said, "and expect that next time, American taxpayers will be there to break their fall."

President Obama and his administration are spending stimulus money to create and save jobs and prevent financial collapse. The deficit is rising. So is the possibility of inflation. Conservatives, who agreed to a bailout under President Bush, are now protesting. Everyone is worried.

56 Both Lucky and Ready

Barack Hussein Obama, a mostly un-known Illinois state legislator, is running for a seat in the U.S. Senate when he gets a telephone call from John Kerry's campaign manager asking if he will deliver the keynote speech at the Democratic convention in 2004. Obama thinks for a few minutes and says, "I know exactly what I want to say. . . I really want to talk about my story as part of the larger American story."

And that's exactly what he does a few months later when he tells those at the convention, and a larger audience watching on television, about his Kenyan father who herded goats as a child, about his Kansas-born mother, his grandfather who enlisted in Patton's army during World War II, and his grandmother who worked on a bomber assembly line.

Here's Barack Obama with his wife, Michelle, and daughters Sasha (6) and Malia (3), at election night headquarters in Chicago in 2004. He's just won a seat in the Senate and is both lucky and happy.

I stand here knowing that my story is part of the larger American story, that I owe a debt to all of those who came before me, and that, in no other country on earth, is my story even possible.

Obama doesn't tell them about his inner struggles. He is an African-American raised in a white family and that left him searching for his identity. "I was attempting to raise myself to be a black man in America, and beyond the given of my appearance, no one around me seemed to know exactly what that meant," he writes in an autobio-

265

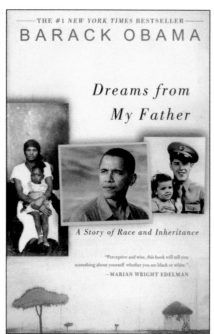

THE #1 *NEW YORK TIMES* BESTSELLER

BARACK OBAMA

Dreams from My Father

A Story of Race and Inheritance

"Perceptive and wise, this book will tell you something about yourself whether you are black or white."
—MARIAN WRIGHT EDELMAN

Barack Obama was elected the first black president of the *Harvard Law Review* and a book publisher asked him to tell his story. So this book is not about politics. Rather, it is a beautifully written memoir about a boy with a white mother from Kansas and a black father from Kenya, who had to struggle to figure out his identity. He saw his father once, when he was ten and in school in Hawaii. Before he could see him again, his father had died in an automobile accident. This is an only-in-America story of a young man given remarkable opportunities, and making the most of them.

graphical book. Growing up he was conflicted: he tried drugs and drink, but he also read widely in books that ranged from Saint Augustine to the works of the civil rights movement.

In college at Columbia University he decided he wanted to be a community organizer. "When classmates in college asked me just what it was that a community organizer did, I couldn't answer them directly. Instead I'd pronounce on the need for change. . .Change won't come from the top, I would say. Change will come from a mobilized grass roots."

But when he tries to find a job where he can initiate changes, no one was interested in his resumé. So he works for a business organization to help pay off his student loans until, finally, he becomes a community organizer for a church-based association in Chicago. It offers job training and tenants' rights programs to people living in public housing.

After three years he realizes that, if he has a law degree, he can do more for those he wants to help. So he goes off to Harvard Law School in 1988, works hard, and becomes the first African American elected president (that means editor-in-chief) of the *Harvard Law Review*. That gets him some publicity and a contract for a book on his life that he calls, *Dreams from My Father: A Story of Race and Inheritance*. When he graduates from Harvard Law it is magna cum laude (those Latin words mean "with high honors).

Back in Chicago, he joins a law firm that specializes in civil rights work, he teaches constitutional law at the University of Chicago, he leads an effort to register African-American voters, and he marries Michelle Robinson, a graduate of Princeton University and Harvard Law School. They know, first hand, the power of education to open the doors of opportunity.

"My presence on this stage is pretty unlikely," Obama tells the audience at the Democratic National Convention. Then he explains how it happened, "My parents shared not only an improbable love; they shared an abiding faith in the possibilities of this nation. . . They imagined me going to the best schools in the land, even though they weren't rich, because in a generous America you don't have to be rich to achieve your potential. . ."

It is a speech full of ringing oratory and patriotism:

Tonight, we gather to affirm the greatness of our nation, not because of the height of our skyscrapers, or the power of our military, or the size of our economy. Our pride is based on a very simple premise, summed up in a declaration made over two hundred years ago, "We hold these truths to he self-evident, that all men are created equal. That they are endowed by their Creator with certain inalienable rights. That among these are life, liberty and the pursuit of happiness."

This Illinois congressman, who describes himself "as a skinny kid with a funny name," is a gifted speaker; his audience cheers him on. By 2004, many Americans are tired of war and tired of divisive politics; the speech focuses on what we all share: a belief in the ideas that have made the United States unique. Among them, he says is "God's greatest gift" to Americans, "the audacity of hope."

That is the true genius of America, a faith in the simple dreams of its people. . .for alongside our famous individualism, there's another ingredient in the American saga. A belief that we are connected as one people. . . that makes this country work. It's what allows us to pursue our individual dreams, yet still come together as a single American family. E pluribus unum. *Out of many, one.*

The audience at the Democratic convention can barely contain itself. Polls will show that, in their homes, the television audience is also captivated. Obama continues:

Yet even as we speak, there are those who are preparing to divide us, the spin masters and negative ad peddlers, who embrace the politics of anything goes. Well, I say to them tonight, there's not a liberal America and a conservative America; there's the United States of America. There's not a black America and white America and Latino America and Asian America; there's the United States of America.

Even before Barack Obama finishes it is clear that with this powerful speech he has catapulted himself onto the national scene. Almost immediately, television pundits begin talking about an "Obama phenomenon." In Illinois he will capture white votes as no other racial minority candidate has ever done and be elected as a U.S. Senator. Just four years later, this "skinny kid with a funny name who believes that America has a place for him too," will win the Democratic nomination for president.

Workers install Shepard Fairey's portrait of President-elect Barack Obama on a wall that says, "New Arrivals." That seems appropriate. As does the word "Hope" on the image. Obama campaigned on a platform of change; many who voted for him hoped he would bring a new kind of politics to Washington and a new, more responsive government.

267

Not Your Ordinary Parents

In 1959, Barack Obama was the first African student to attend the University of Hawaii. Thirty-six years later his son, named for him, will write, "He had been selected by Kenyan leaders and American sponsors. . .joining the first large wave of Africans to be sent forth to master Western technology and bring it back to forge a new, modern Africa."

Kenya's Barack Obama studied hard and graduated at the top of his class. In a Russian course he met an 18-year-old American girl, Ann Dunham whose parents lived in Hawaii but had roots in Kansas and, way back, in England. The two students fell in love, got married, and, in August 1961, had a son. This was a biracial marriage at a time when that was illegal in some states, but not in Hawaii. For these two it didn't seem to be an issue.

Ann Dunham was a young woman who focused on big ideas, she wanted to do something with her life; she had no time or inclination for the nonsense of prejudice.

Her African husband, a man who impressed everyone he met, didn't tell her that he had a wife in Kenya, where multiple marriages are acceptable. When she found out, she thought he was divorced. That wasn't true.

You can sense the energy and vitality in Barack Obama Sr., father of a future president.

In 1963, when Barack Obama Sr. chose to go to Harvard to get a PhD, Harvard offered no funds to support his American family. The marriage was doomed. Obama returned to Kenya where he fathered six African children. His American son, Barack Obama II, would know his father mostly through pictures in an album; it was his mother who shaped his character.

Ann Dunham, now a young single mother, is determined to get a bachelor's degree, which she does from the University of Hawaii in 1967. About the same time she meets and marries another student. He is an Indonesian, Lolo Soertoro. Soon after they are married, Lolo is unex-

pectedly called home because of political turmoil in his country. A year later, Ann joins him in Jakarta (the capital of Indonesia on the island of Java), taking her 6–year-old son, Barack, with her. There she has a daughter, Maya, gets a job, and falls in love with Indonesian culture. She soon speaks Indonesian well. Barack (everyone calls him Barry) and his easygoing Muslim stepfather get along. Lolo has an ape, which is part of a small zoo in their backyard that includes chickens, ducks, a big yellow dog, two birds of paradise, a cockatoo, and two baby crocodiles.

Barry's mother wakes him at 4 a.m. each morning to give him lessons in English before he heads to an Indonesian public school. When her son objects, or fakes a stomach ache, she is firm, "This is no picnic for me either, buster."

Her lessons go beyond the English language. "If you're going to grow into a human being, you're going to need some values," she says. Values for Ann Soertoro means honesty, fairness, straight talk, and independent judgment. Then Barry passes an admissions test for the elite Punahou School in Hawaii; he can live with his grandparents, and his mother and sister will visit. So off he goes, on his own, flying across the Pacific Ocean on a journey from one world culture to another.

Meanwhile Lolo Soertoro wants a wife who will stay home and have babies. Ann wants to work and study and make an impact on the world around her. Lolo and Ann part, but remain friends.

Ann Dunham Obama Soertoro is now determined to be an anthropologist (a student of human beings and their surroundings), which means she needs a PhD. She will get that doctorate.

Barry is 10, in school in Hawaii, when he learns that his African father is coming for a visit. He has no memory of his father; he doesn't know what to expect. Obama, Sr. is asked to speak at the Punahou School: his son is scared, will his father embarrass him? But when Obama Sr. tells the students about life in Kenya, everyone is impressed with his intelligence, his directness, and his vivid descriptions. Barack Obama Sr. stays a month—that's all his son will ever see of him.

Ann Soertoro continues her studies, which take her back to

Ann Dunham Obama holds her two-year-old son, Barack, in Hawaii in 1962.

Asia to do research. A weaver in college, she is fascinated with craftspeople. Her 800-page dissertation (a long paper necessary to get a doctorate) focuses on village industries, especially blacksmithing. It is really a study of independent working people in a third world country. Her conclusion is that lack of credit (money) is the major factor holding back small busi-

nesses; that people everywhere have similar goals.

Ann gets a job as a consultant for the United States Agency for International Development and focuses on ways to bring credit to small villages. Most banks like to give big loans to known borrowers; she is interested in getting small loans to those who have never borrowed before. Then she joins Indonesia's oldest bank and works on a microfinance program, opening credit and savings opportunities to the poor. Today Indonesia has one of the world's largest microcredit programs. Yale anthropologist Michael Dove says "it was pretty radical stuff when Ann Soertoro was doing her work. But then, she had a habit of swimming against the current."

"She was a very, very big thinker," said Nancy Barry, a former president of Women's World Banking, an international microfinance network.

Neither Ann Soertoro (who died of cancer) nor her first husband, Barack Obama, (who died in an automobile accident) live to see their son become a candidate for president of the United States.

57 Yes, We Can!

Bruce Springsteen crooning for his candidate in Cleveland, Ohio on November 2, 2008.

It is November 2, 2008, the place is Cleveland, Ohio, and rock star Bruce Springsteen, known for his liberal politics and his song "Born in the U.S.A.," is leading 80 thousand people in singing "This Land is Your Land." He is warming up the crowd for Barack Obama who, later that same day, will speak to 60 thousand cheering supporters in Columbus and 25 thousand in Cincinnati. Then the Democratic Party candidate for president of the United States will head off for a final day of campaigning that will take him to Florida, North Carolina, and Virginia. Even without a celebrity musician on the podium, the crowds will be enormous.

The morning of November 3rd, Obama learns that his grandmother, Madelyn Dunham, who helped raise him in Hawaii, has died (he had flown to Hawaii to see her during her final illness). It is a heart-wrenching moment in a campaign that began slowly and is finishing with a crescendo of popular participation: two contenders are drawing crowds and excitement that matches and often exceeds the pull of rock stars.

Obama began well behind the Democratic Party front-runner, Hillary Clinton, who seemed to have the important financial backing, the key political support, and the political savvy to capture the Democratic nomination. Many expected, and hoped, that she would become the first woman president.

In contrast, Obama's appeal is to ordinary people who are usually small donors. He has been a community organizer in Chicago, a law school professor, an Illinois congressman, and briefly a U.S. senator. It isn't a whole lot of experience, but that is part of his appeal: He doesn't seem to be part of the Washington scene at a time when most Americans disapprove of what has been going on in the capital city.

The Iraq War is an important campaign issue. Hillary Clinton and John McCain voted to authorize war along with a majority in the U.S. Congress. Barack Obama was a member of the Illinois state senate, on Oct. 2, 2002, when he gave a speech that warned against sending troops into Iraq. (It was 18 days before the invasion began.) He said he did not oppose "all wars," but he opposed "dumb wars." He predicted that "even a successful war against Iraq will require a U.S. occupation of undetermined length, at undetermined cost, with undetermined consequences."

Obama is exceptionally eloquent, and he campaigns as a candidate of change. He puts together a talented and disciplined campaign staff; they will try to bring as many new people to the polls as possible. They register millions of potential voters, especially young people, and are successful in expanding the electorate. Using the Internet effectively, they raise money from a broad swath of Americans. Obama, with a big smile and amazing composure, climbs up and up in the polls. He finds a catch phrase to inspire his followers: "Yes, we can!" he shouts.

The Republican candidate, John McCain, is a weathered senator with a reputation for doing his own thing. He calls himself a "maverick." McCain was a prisoner-of-war in Hanoi during the Vietnam War and responded to torture and other indignities with strength and integrity. He seems to represent the best when it comes to traditional American values. But in 2008 most Americans

Campaign activity before the 2008 election, from top to bottom: Volunteers in Nashua, New Hampshire carry signs for presidential hopeful Senator Hillary Clinton. Senators Clinton and Obama, fighting for the Democratic nomination, check notes during a Democratic primary debate in South Carolina. Republican candidates John McCain and Sarah Palin together at a Pennsylvania rally. Presidential candidate Obama and Vice Presidential Candidate Joseph Biden just after Biden's speech at the Democratic National Convention.

271

"The 2008 presidential campaign could have provided the opportunity for a national discussion of the new world we live in," wrote Fareed Zacharia in *The Post-American World*. Zacharia complained that instead of that discussion there was much irresponsible fear-mongering meant to scare Americans. "They hate you!" said one candidate describing the opposing party. Both John McCain and Barack Obama resisted the temptation to engage in hate-speech. In his book *Courage Matters*, McCain urged his readers to participate in daily life in America without fear: "Calculate the odds of being harmed by a terrorist. It's still about as likely as being swept out to sea by a tidal wave," he wrote.

aren't looking for traditions, they want new faces and new ideas and it is McCain's running mate, Alaska's governor Sarah Palin, who begins to draw cheering crowds that rival those of Barack Obama. Palin is controversial and quirky and she doesn't have much background in national politics, but she adds fire and excitement to the campaign. Calling herself a "hockey mom," she is soon a superstar. She not only energizes the Republican base, she also hikes ratings of the television show Saturday Night Live when they do a spoof of her.

Dealing with the press and answering tough questions is another story; Palin doesn't have the experience, and she and John McCain seem to have problems with each other. A *Washington Post*/ABC poll taken near election day shows that while Palin has intense fans, McCain's choice of her as a possible vice-president has left a majority of potential voters questioning his judgment.

On November 3rd, Obama makes his final campaign appearance at Manassas, near Bull Run creek, the site of the first big battle of the

---

Presidential Guidance: Debate Is The Breath of Life

President Dwight D. Eisenhower had a letter on his desk from World War II veteran Robert Biggs. The president, a great general during the war, was a hero to Biggs, who now expressed some disappointment. He told the president that he "felt from your recent speeches the feeling of hedging and a little uncertainty." He added, "We wait for someone to speak for us and back him completely if the statement is made in truth."

Here are the president's words in response, written on Feb. 10, 1959: "I doubt that citizens like yourself could ever, under our democratic system, be provided with the universal degree of certainty. . .and the clear guidance from higher authority that you believe needed," Eisenhower continued, "Such unity is not only logical but indeed indispensable in a successful military organization, but in a democracy debate is the breath of life."

It was a defense of the American founding ideal of an open society where the press is free, debate is treasured, and certainties are always open to question. But thoughtful debate demands educated citizens. Thomas Jefferson made that clear when he wrote, "If a nation expects to be ignorant and free, in a state of civilization, it expects what never was and never will be."

Civil War. This is an important stop; Virginia has not voted to elect a Democratic presidential candidate since 1964. Rain and traffic congestion delay the candidate. But more than 80 thousand people wait patiently at Manassas to hear Obama speak. Joel Achenbach of the *Washington Post* describes the crowd as "an artificial lake of humanity." Whatever they are looking for, the sea of people believe they have found it in this candidate.

After 20 months of organizational efforts, phone calls, money-raising, and speeches, the Bull Run hurrah is the wrap up. The campaign is over. Obama flies home to Chicago to vote. On the plane he thanks members of the press who have followed him on this journey. "It will be fun to see how the story ends," he says.

A year earlier most pundits didn't think Obama had a chance to capture the Democratic nomination. Hillary Clinton was a formidable candidate. After that, John McCain fought in what was a tight race, but the seemingly endless Iraq War, the erupting financial crisis, and the appeal of a candidate who focused on change, began to swing undecided voters. By election day, Nov 4th, it is the size of the Obama victory that many believe is uncertain.

Yet only as the voting returns are tabulated, does what is happening seem to hit TV commentators and people across the country. The United States, with its lofty ideals, has lived with a nasty reality that it has often tried to ignore, but the awfulness of racism and other prejudices has impacted America since its beginnings. Now the United States is electing an African-American as chief executive. That means that any American, whatever his or her background, has a chance to rise to the top. Can that really be true?

Georgia's civil rights leader John Lewis is speaking at Ebenezer Baptist Church in Atlanta when the returns tell him that Barack Hussein Obama will be president. Later Lewis describes his emotions to reporters Dan Balz and Haynes Johnson, "I just felt so good. And then. . . I cried. I just cried."

Congressman John Lewis was one of the most courageous of the civil rights leaders of the 1960s. From 1963-1966 he was Chairman of the Student Nonviolent Coordinating Committee. In this photograph, taken in Selma, Alabama on March 7, 1965, Lewis, on the ground, attempts to ward off a blow from the club of an Alabama state trooper. For more on the march to Selma, see Chapter 25 (pages 120 to 123).

President-elect Barack Obama arrives at Grant Park, Chicago with his wife, Michelle, and their daughters, Malia (in red) and Sasha, on the night of November 4, 2008. He has just won the presidency and, after a long hard campaign, the whole family and their supporters are ready to celebrate.

That evening, John McCain's words conceding defeat are gracious and inspiring. He says, "This is an historic election. . . . A century ago, President Theodore Roosevelt's invitation of Booker T. Washington to visit—to dine at the White House—was taken as an outrage in many quarters. America today is a world away from the cruel and prideful bigotry of that time. There is no better evidence of this than the election of an African-American to the presidency of the United States. Let there be no reason now for any American to fail to cherish their citizenship in this, the greatest nation on earth."

Not long after that, President-elect Barack Obama, his wife Michelle, and their daughters Sasha and Malia, stand onstage at Chicago's Grant Park. To an excited crowd of well wishers he says, "If there is anyone out there who still doubts that America is a place where all things are possible, who still wonders if the dream of our founders is alive in our time, who still questions the power of our democracy, tonight is your answer." Then he tells the crowd the story of Ann Nixon Cooper, age 106, who voted for him earlier that day.

"She was born just a generation past slavery; a time when there were no cars on the road or planes in the sky; when someone like her couldn't vote for two reasons, because she was a woman and because of the color of her skin. And tonight, I think about all that she's seen throughout her century in America: the heartache and the hope, the struggle and the progress, the times we were told that we can't, and the people who pressed on with that American creed: Yes, we can."

And the crowd roars back, "Yes, we can."

Joining the Supremes

The headline in New York's Spanish language newspaper, *El Diario de Nueva York*, shouts out: "Exemplary Son of El Barrio Becomes Prosecutor." Edwin Torres has been named an assistant district attorney. He is the first Puerto Rican in that role in New York City and probably in all of the United States. El Barrio (a part of the city also known as Spanish East Harlem) bursts with pride. It is 1959 and the job pays $60 a week.

Fifty years later, in August 2009, Judge Sonia Sotomayor is confirmed by the U.S. Senate as the first Hispanic justice on the Supreme Court. That achievement makes headlines in the *New York Times* and in newspapers worldwide. Edwin Torres, now retired from careers as a jurist and novelist, is 78 and glowing. "It was beyond anyone's imagination when I started that a Puerto Rican could ascend to that position, to the Supreme Court."

But this is America and it has happened. Puerto Ricans (according to a 2004 report) have the highest poverty rate among Latinos nationwide. Yet Sonio Sotomayor, raised by a single widowed parent (her mom) in a Bronx housing project (a stone's throw from Manhattan's Harlem), worked hard in high school, got into an Ivy League college (Princeton), became a lawyer (at Yale Law School), and then a judge. She has conquered towering obstacles to make it to the top of the legal world. President Barack Obama says, "With this historic vote the Senate has affirmed that Judge Sotomayor has the intellect, the temperament, the history, the integrity and the independence of mind to ably serve on our nation's highest court." He calls it another step that moves the nation closer "to a more perfect union."

It was done as the Constitution directed, but not without some controversy. Article II of the U.S. Constitution says the president "shall nominate, and by and with the Advice and Consent of the Senate, shall appoint Ambassadors, other public Ministers and Consuls, Judges of the Supreme Court, and all other Officers of the United States, whose Appointments are not herein otherwise provided for."

Sonia Sotomayor

That means the president gets to make important appointments, but the Senate has final approval (or disapproval) of those appointments. It was a way to check and balance power. Alexander Hamilton explained that the Senate, "may defeat one choice of the Executive and oblige him to make another; but they cannot themselves choose."

When Sonia Sotomayor is nominated by President Obama as a Supreme Court justice she faces tough questioning from a number of senators. Some of it is about her ideas on the law; some of it is just political. There is nothing new about that.

In 1795 President George Washington appointed John Rutledge as chief justice of the Supreme Court while the Senate was in recess. He took office immediately. When the senators came back to work they considered Rutledge's nomination. He had been South Carolina's delegate to the Constitutional Congress and was one of the new nation's leading lawyers, but he had used extra-strong language to criticize a treaty that most senators supported. So he only served as our second chief justice from July to December (in 1795); then the Senate rejected his nomination.

58 Where Are We Going? It's Up to Us

Does this look like a picture of a mad scientist working on a crazy experiment for a TV spoof? It happens to be a real physicist, Walter Houser Brattain,engaged in a real experiment: he was trying to find a way to replace vacuum tubes with something more efficient. And he did it. Brattain, along with John Bardeen and William Shockley, all working at Bell Laboratories, invented the transistor (it was done by 1947). In 1956 they shared the Nobel Prize in Physics for that achievement. That wasn't so long ago, although it seems so. Their small-sized invention changed the world we live in. It made tiny—as in cell phones and computing devices—possible. Brattain grew up on a cattle ranch in the state of Washington, and went to Whitman College in that state.

At 9 A.M., April 21, 1952, representatives from some 30 companies check in at the Bell Laboratories in Murray Hill, New Jersey. Each has paid $25,000 (a lot of money in 1952 dollars) to be there. They will stay for six days of instruction and conversation on the transistor (see page 201). Until this meeting transistors have mostly been used by the military. Now Bell Labs is going to license the technology to commercial firms. That $25,000 includes the right to use transistors in any way they wish.

Bell Labs is an appropriate place for this meeting. It was founded by Alexander Graham Bell who, in trying to develop a device to help the deaf hear, created the telephone and changed the world of communication.

Does anyone at that 1952 meeting realize that the transistors they are seeing will spawn microchips (micro means small) with tiny implanted transistors, sometimes thousands of them? Do any of them guess that by the end of the century, those information-packed chips will be ubiquitous (that means found almost everywhere) and used to program devices from dishwashers to hand-held games?

Probably not. Without a crystal ball no one can see where this microtechnology will lead, even though the group assembled in New Jersey includes plenty of visionaries. They will take part in a crescendo of innovation and help create an everyday world powered, in good part, by computerized chips. Because they have chosen to be at this meeting, some of these individuals and their firms will have a big future.

They are part of an American tradition that combines inventiveness with business savvy. That mixture has enriched the nation, and helped individuals prosper. America's inventor-in-chief, Thomas Edison, famously remarked: "Anything that won't sell, I don't want to invent."

By the 21st century, when the 1952 meeting of entrepreneurial tinkerers is mostly forgotten, life around much of the globe has been transformed by computer chip technology. Laptop computers, cell phones, programmable TV, and global positioning devices (GPS), are just some of the wonders it has spawned.

The next step is nanotechnology (think really small). A nanometer (nm) is one billionth of a meter. The smallest life form, of which we know, is a bacterium that is about 200 nm in length. Put another way, a nanometer is to a meter, as a marble is to the earth, or smaller than one-thousandth of a human hair.

Using atomic force or scanning microscopes to see and manipulate atoms, we are now building nano-scale machines, atom by atom. Does any of this affect you? Yes, many new products have nanocomponents; they include gecko tape, sunscreens, paints, disinfectants, fuels, and much more. Nano-medicine, and nanodiagnostics, are expected to transform medical care, building on the assumption that no two humans are alike and so medical care should be personalized. Nanotechnology, like microchip technology, is growing explosively.

Meanwhile, in the macro (big) world, computers are talking to each other, and the conversations are becoming a way of life. Before the 1990s, a computer roadway existed for military and university use. When that networking avenue opened its doors to everyone, it became the information superhighway known as the Internet. It

Some scientists, thinking small, are coming up with powerful new ideas and products and no one, yet, is quite sure where they will lead. Here are "Nano Trees" made from wires about one thousand times smaller than a human hair. The wires of silicon carbide grow from tiny droplets of a liquid metal (Gallium) that condenses on a silicon surface after methane flows over that surface. (The chips inside a home computer are silicon.) By changing temperature and pressure the growth process can be controlled to form a range of structures, including these flower-like materials. Possible applications for Nano Trees: water repellent coatings and a base for a new type of solar cell.

Way back, in the 1880s, some techno buffs were trying to figure out ways to improve city life. The big urban problem was horse manure. Cities were getting buried in horse manure, and it seemed as if it would only get worse. So if you wanted to clean up, an efficient shovel seemed to be something worth inventing. No one imagined that horseless carriages would replace horses in the century that was ahead. It isn't easy to predict the future.

grew, and grew, at what seemed almost the speed of light, spreading information, opportunities, and mayhem too.

The Internet could do much that traditional media did, but do it faster and often at no cost to the consumer. Newspapers and magazines were soon in trouble. So were other traditional information venues. But the emerging opportunities on the Internet were dazzling and hard to resist.

For centuries, the wisdom of the ages, along with the newest thinking, clustered in great cities and their big institutions. With the Internet, someone living on a lonely farm, far from a big university or cultural center, can have access to the riches of the Library of Congress. That farmer can take almost all the courses MIT and many other universities offer, for free.

The Internet and the whole Information Revolution is leveling the knowledge playing field. One writer describes it as flattening the earth. He means there are no longer mountain-like barriers keeping most people from information. The Internet is being called the greatest democratic innovation ever, surpassing even the advent of the printing press. (Of course, in large parts of the world there are still people who have never made a phone call, or eaten a good meal, or heard of the Internet.)

President Barack Obama tours an alternative energy research laboratory with Professor Vladimir Bulovic at Massachusetts Institute of Technology in October 2009.

In the United States, President Barack Obama seemed determined to support these technological revolutions—to maintain and augment America's role as a nation of innovators.

On September 21, 2009, speaking at the Hudson Valley Community College in Troy, New York, the president makes a powerful announcement: "I have set a goal of putting a full three percent of our Gross Domestic Product—our national income—into research and development," he says, "surpassing the commitment we made when President Kennedy challenged this nation to send a man to the moon." He intended that his administration focus on science and technology and education.

"Our strategy begins where innovation so often does: in the classroom and in the laboratory—and in the networks that connect them to the broader economy," he says, announcing a national "first-ever Chief Technology Officer, charged with looking at ways technology can spur innovations that help government do a better and more efficient job."

Hector Ruiz is sitting in the audience at the community college, along with political dignitaries, students, business people, and reporters. Ruiz, chair of Global Foundries Inc., is building a $4.2 billion computer chip manufacturing plant nearby. The Hudson Valley Community College is developing a curriculum to train technology workers for that plant.

His First Day on the Job

President Obama holds his first full Cabinet meeting. Here he's flanked by his Democratic rival, now Secretary of State Hillary Rodham Clinton, and a Republican from the Bush administration, Secretary of Defense Robert Gates.

On January 21, 2009, his first full day as president, Barack Obama revoked Executive Order 13233, saying he was encouraging transparency and accountability in government by giving the American people greater access to historic presidential and vice-presidential documents.

The issue of openness in government is argued with great passion. Some say that America's three-branched government, with its checks and balances, is dependent on an informed citizenry. American historian Henry Steele Commager wrote that, "The generation that made the nation thought secrecy in government one of the instruments of Old World Tyranny and committed itself to the principle that a democracy cannot function unless people are permitted to know what their government is up to."

But some say that the 18th century was a horse and buggy era and its concepts aren't always appropriate in today's world where small groups of terrorists can disrupt a nation. They argue that broad disclosure of government information could endanger the nation and that government officials heirs should be the decision-makers.

Technology may be leading us to direct democracy, with more and more issues decided directly by citizens who may vote from their computers. Our founders believed in representative democracy, most of them worried that direct democracy could mean mob rule. They thought that elected representatives would have the time and opportunity to study issues carefully before making decisions. Today, with pressure groups often controlling the media and instant polls swinging voters back and forth like kids on a seesaw, an intelligent, educated electorate is essential to the future of our nation.

How can you get ready for what's to come (whatever it may be)? In an information-based society, those who have knowledge, who are educated, have a big head start. So study and read and learn as broadly as you can.

After President Obama visits an industrial wiring class the excitement in the school is palpable. "I hear people downplaying nanotechnology," says New York State Senator Neil Breslin, "to hear our message reinforced by the president was amazing."

President Obama notes that in the past 20 years, New York has lost half its manufacturing work, a loss of almost half a million jobs.

"We will not fill those jobs—or keep those jobs on our shores—without graduating more students, including millions more from community colleges," says the president. Ruiz says, "This to me is the beginning of manufacturing coming back."

The president returns to his theme, "Our great challenge will be to ensure that we do not simply drift into the future, accepting less for our children and less for America. Instead, we must choose to do what past generations have done: shape a brighter future through hard work and innovation."

"You Campaign in Poetry, You Govern in Prose" *

Being president isn't easy. Here, President Obama is depicted as "The Joker" on a protester's sign saying *I'll keep my guns, freedom, & money... YOU CAN KEEP THE "CHANGE."*

Congress is supposed to give a new president a honeymoon: a few first months where members of both parties cooperate and let him get off to a good start. President Obama's honeymoon was brief. Then his plans to reform health care unleash an intense partisan backlash. After that, almost everything he suggests meets with some kind of political attack. Even a speech he gives to schoolchildren, about the importance of education and the need to work hard in school, is criticized by his foes. This president keeps his calm, maybe that's because he knows his history. The American habit of attacking the president began with George Washington. While Thomas Jefferson said of Washington, "Never did nature and fortune combine more perfectly to make a man great," not everyone agreed. One newspaper of the time called our first president a "scourge and a misfortune." Benjamin Bache, Ben Franklin's grandson and a leading Republican newspaper publisher (of Philadelphia's *General Advertiser* and the *Aurora*), accused Washington of nepotism, of wasting public funds, of wanting to be a monarch, of trying to go to war against France (and there was more). Whew! No president has been spared newspaper or media criticism. That's the American way. Under our Constitution we can dissent, satirize, parody, and even be mean-spirited in our criticism of public officials. In most countries it would be called seditious—we consider it our birthright.

*Attributed to Mario Cuomo, former Governor of New York State

"A Call to Action"

19th century Swedish chemist Alfred Nobel invented dynamite, which he thought was so dangerous it would end all wars. It didn't, but it did earn a lot of money for Nobel, who got called the "merchant of death."

Maybe that's why, a year before he died, he changed his will, leaving his fortune to establish prizes in physics, chemistry, medicine, literature, and peace. The peace prize was to go to "those who, during the preceding year, shall have conferred the greatest benefit on mankind."

From the beginning, the prizes raised controversy. Nobel's relatives were shocked that they didn't get the money. His Swedish countrymen were upset that he chose a committee from the Norwegian parliament (the Storting) to pick the Peace Prize winner. (Swedish committees pick the other prize winner; in 1969 a prize in economics was added in Nobel's memory.)

The prizes have always carried tremendous prestige (along with a handsome check). Peace Prize winners have included South Africa's Nelson Mandela and India's Mother Teresa. No one fussed about those choices. But when President Woodrow Wilson was selected in 1919, for his work promoting the League of Nations, his political opponents howled. Something similar happened in 2002 when ex-President Jimmy Carter got the prize for his work promoting peace worldwide. In 2009 Barack Obama was given the prize for his "extraordinary efforts to strengthen international diplomacy and cooperation between peoples." The committee lauded "Obama's vision of and work for a world without nuclear weapons." Most Americans were proud, but some felt he hadn't been president long enough to have solid achievements in the field.

Obama himself said,

[...] To be honest, I do not feel that I deserve to be in the company of so many of the transformative figures who've been honored by this prize—men and women who've inspired me and inspired the entire world through their courageous pursuit of peace.

But I also know that throughout history the Nobel Peace Prize has not just been used to honor specific achievement; it's also been used as a means to give momentum to a set of causes. That is why I've said that I will accept this award as a call to action, a call for all nations and all peoples to confront the common challenges of the 21st century. These challenges won't all be met during my presidency, or even my lifetime. But I know these challenges can be met so long as it's recognized that they will not be met by one person or one nation alone.

This little boy wanted to know if the president's hair felt like his own. President Obama let him feel for himself. Being president means being cheered, booed, given medals, and, in this case, patted on the head.

This award—and the call to action that comes with it—does not belong simply to me or my administration; it belongs to all people around the world who have fought for justice and for peace. And most of all, it belongs to you, the men and women of America, who have dared to hope and have worked so hard to make our world a little better.

So today we humbly recommit to the important work that we've begun together. I'm grateful that you've stood with me thus far, and I'm honored to continue our vital work in the years to come.

Thank you,
President Barack Obama

Chronology of Events

1945: Harry S. Truman becomes 33rd president on the death of Franklin D. Roosevelt

1945: Japan surrenders; World War II is over

1947: President Truman launches the Marshall Plan

1947: First baseman Jackie Robinson joins the Brooklyn Dodgers, ending segregation in major-league baseball

1948: Truman defeats Republican Thomas E. Dewey

1950: Senator Joseph McCarthy stirs up anti-communist hysteria with a nationwide witch-hunt

1950: American-led UN forces enter the Korean War

1952: World War II general Dwight D. Eisenhower elected 34th president, the first Republican in 24 years

1953: The Korean War ends; Korea remains divided in two

1954: In *Brown* v. *Board of Education*, the Supreme Court finds "separate but equal" unconstitutional in schools

1954: France pulls out of French Indochina (Vietnam); the U.S. sends in a small number of military "advisers"

1955: Dr. Martin Luther King, Jr., leads a successful black boycott of segregated city buses in Montgomery, Alabama, in response to the arrest of Rosa Parks

1957: Eisenhower sends federal troops to enforce high school desegregation in Little Rock, Arkansas; Sputnik launched by the Soviet Union

1959: Alaska and Hawaii become 49th and 50th states

1960: Democrat John F. Kennedy, a Roman Catholic, becomes the youngest elected president

1962: African-American students and teachers across the South stage anti-segregation sit-ins at lunch counters

1962: In the Cuban missile crisis, JFK refuses to let the Soviet Union install nuclear missiles in Cuba

1963: Around 250,000 people march on Washington, D.C.; Dr. King delivers his "I have a dream" speech

1963: On November 22, President Kennedy is assassinated in Dallas; Lyndon Johnson becomes 36th president

1964: The Civil Rights Act bans discrimination; Johnson is elected president by the biggest majority ever

1964: Dr. King receives the Nobel Peace Prize

1965: The Voting Rights Act outlaws practices designed to prevent black people from voting

1965: President Johnson launches his Great Society anti-poverty programs such as Medicaid and AFDC

1968: Martin Luther King, Jr., is assassinated by James Earl Ray, an escaped convict who is later captured

1968: Robert F. Kennedy is assassinated while campaigning for the presidency in California

1968: Republican Richard Nixon elected 37th president; he begins by withdrawing some troops from Vietnam but later expands the war into Cambodia

1969: The space program lands a man on the moon

1971: 26th Amendment gives 18-year-olds the right to vote

1972: Nixon is the first president to visit communist China; he is reelected president by a large majority

1973: North and South Vietnam sign a peace agreement

An African American man ascends a staircase to the segregated balcony of a movie theatre. It was 1939, when separate was supposed to be equal, but never was.

1973: To avoid being impeached over the Watergate scandal, Nixon becomes first president to resign. Gerald Ford becomes 38th president and pardons Nixon

1976: Jimmy Carter defeats Ford; he is 39th president

1979: Inflation hits double digits, and a Middle East oil embargo creates an energy crisis in the U.S

1979: Muslim fundamentalists seize power in Iran and keep 52 Americans hostage for more than a year

1980: Republican Ronald Reagan de feats Carter tobecome 40th presi dent; the Iranian hostages are freed

1985: Mikhail Gorbachev, the new Soviet leader, begins the process that leads to democratization of the U.S.S.R.

70 years later the first African American president, and perhaps the world's most powerful individual, ascends the staircase to Air Force One.

1988: George H. W. Bush elected 41st president

1989: A series of "peaceful revolutions" frees eastern Europe from Soviet domination; the Cold War is over

1990: Iraqi president Saddam Hussein invades Kuwait; U.S.–led international troops drive him out in the Gulf War

1992: Democrat William (Bill) Clinton defeats Bush to become the 42nd president

1996: Bill Clinton re-elected president

1998: Bill Clinton becomes the second president ever impeached; he is acquitted in his Senate trial in 1999

2000: George W. Bush is proclaimed 43rd president in a decision by the U.S. Supreme Court

2001: Terrorists attack U.S., destroying the World Trade Center in New York City and damaging the Pentagon in Washington D.C. Terrorists are pursued in Afghanistan

2003: The U.S launches war in Iraq; Iraq's capital, Baghdad, falls after twenty-one days; Saddam Hussein is later captured

2004: George W. Bush defeats John F. Kerry for a second term as president

2005: A powerful hurricane strikes the Gulf Coast causing devastation in New Orleans and other cities

2007: October: Ben Bernanke, Chairman of the Federal Reserve declares "The banking system is healthy."

2008: September: Lehmann Brothers, investment banking giant, declares bankruptcy. Stock market plunges

2008: November: Senator Barack Obama is elected President of the United States, the first African American to hold the office

2009: January: President Obama is inaugurated. Invokes Lincoln, calls for national unity

2009: September: U.S. Bureau of Labor Statistics reports unemployment rate of 9.8 percent. Up from 4.8 percent in September 2007

2009: October: President Obama is awarded the Nobel Peace Prize "for his extraordinary efforts to strengthen international diplomacy and cooperation between peoples"

More Books to Read

I love to read stories of people's lives. I used to think it was because I was a newspaper reporter (which means being a kind of professional snoop),but I now know that most people are fascinated by personal tales. In the 20th century, memoirs (which tend to be informal autobiographies) became a special art form. Of course the rich and famous had interesting stories to tell, but so did ordinary people. When an underpaid New York schoolteacher wrote of his wretched childhood as a poor immigrant boy, it flew to the top of the bestseller list, made him a whole lot of money, and turned the teacher into a celebrity. Here are a few memoirs I especially like.

Places Left Unfinished At the Time of the Creation, John Phillip Santos, Penguin Books 1999. Santos, from San Antonio, Texas, was the first Mexican-American Rhodes scholar. This is a story of immigration —from Mexico to El Norte. It's funny, poetic, and poignant.

An Hour Before Daylight, Memories of A Rural Boyhood, Jimmy Carter, Simon & Schuster 2001. How the 39th president grew up in Depression times on a rural Georgia farm. It's more interesting than you might think.

An American Childhood, Annie Dillard, Harper Collins 1997. This is the work of a terrific writer who is very tuned into the world of nature.

Falling Leaves, Adeline Yen Mah, Broadway Books (Random House) 1997. A Cinderella story: about a little girl who was not wanted by her familybut grew up to be a physician and a writer.

When I was a Puerto Rican, Esmeralda Santiago, Vintage,1993. Esmeralda lived in a metal shack in Puerto Rico, came to the United States, and got a degree at Harvard. It wasn't as easy as that sounds.

Rocket Boys, by Homer H. Hickam, Jr., Dell Publishing 1998, and *The Coalwood Way,* by Homer H. Hickam, Jr., Delacorte Press 2000. Two wonderful books by a boy from a coal-mining town who had a dream —to build rockets—and went for it. The first book inspired an equally great movie, *October Sky,* which is available on video. Be sure and see it.

American Chica, Marie Arana, Random House 2001. Arana writes of her mother's "All-American Hollywood face alive with expectation. At her side is my Peruvian father—black-haired,handsome, smiling and shouting Spanish over his shoulder." This bicultural memoir is for everyone, no matter their background.

Escape From Slavery: The True Story of My Ten Years in Captivity—and My Journey to Freedom in America, Francis Bok, St Martin's Griffin 2003. Here is the first sentence in this book: "I have told the story many times about that day in 1986, when my mother sent me to the market to sell eggs and peanuts:

the day I became a slave." Francis is captured and sold into slavery in southern Sudan in Africa. How he makes it to the United States is a story to remember.

Wait Till Next Year, Doris Kearns Goodwin, Simon and Schuster 1997. This is about a Catholic girl growing up in the New York suburbs with a father who was a big-time baseball fan.

Lazy B. Growing Up on a Cattle Ranch in the American Southwest, Sandra Day O'Conner and H. Alan Day, Random House, 2002. Sandra Day O'Conner and her brother grew up on a cettle ranch on the Arizona-New Mexico border. It "was no country for sissies," she writes in this memoir of a childhood with cowboy friends, a tough father, and a mother who cared about books. They helped prepare her to be the first woman to serve on the U.S.Supreme Court.

A few other great memoirs: *Angela's Ashes*, by Frank McCourt, Touchstone edition 1999. (This is the book by the NY schoolteacher.) *Personal History*, by Katharine Graham, Vintage Books 1998. (Do you think being part of an important family makes life easy? Read this book by the publisher of the *Washington Post* and find out.) *Five Finger Discount*, Helene Stapinksi, Random House 2001. (Do you sometimes think your family is weird? Helene's relatives were crooks, swindlers, bookies, and worse.) Also look for memoirs by these authors: Maya Angelou (*I Know Why the Caged Bird Sings*), Claude Brown (*Manchild In the Promised Land*), Frank Conroy (*Stop-Time*), Jill Ker Conway (*The Road from Coorain* and *True North*), Moss Hart (*Act One*), Charlise Lyles (*Do I Dare Disturb The Universe),* Malcolm X (*The Autobiography of Malcolm X*), Willie Morris (*North Toward Home*).

Picture Credits

AP / WW: Associated Press / Wide World Photos
CB: Corbis-Bettmann
DDE: Dwight D. Eisenhower Library, Abilene, Kansas

HST: Harry S. Truman Library, Kansas City, Missouri
JFK: John F. Kennedy Presidential Library and Museum, Boston, Massachusetts

Cover: Bruce Davidson, March on Washington, 1963, Magnum Photos; 5: Stock Market; 6: CB; 7: LOC; 8: State Historical Society of Wisconsin (Wi [X3] 36638, CF 6797); 9 (top): Jack Lambert, *Chicago Sun-Times*; 9 (bottom): NA/Women's Bureau; 10: CB; 11: Philadelphia Convention and Visitors Bureau; 12: Roy Justis, *Minnesota Star*, 1947; 13–16: HST; 17: CB; 18: National Baseball League; 19: William Gladstone; 20 (top): National Baseball League; 20 (bottom): Los Angeles Dodgers, Inc., Maurice Rerrell; 21 (left and right): CB; 22: LOC; 23: *Lenin at the Tribune*, 1947 (oil on canvas), Gerasimov, Aleksandr Mikhailovic (1881-1963)/Tretyakov Gallery, Moscow, Russia/© DACS/Alinari The Bridgeman Art Library International; 24 (left and right): The Granger Collection, New York; 25: CB; 26 (top): Front cover of 'John Bull', August 1956 (colour litho), English School, (20th century)/Private Collection/© The Advertising Archives/The Bridgeman Art Library International; 26 (bottom left): *Arkansas Gazette*, June 14, 1953; 26 (bottom right): *Indianapolis Star*, 1949; 27: LOC; 29 (left): Hulton-Deutsch Collection/Corbis; 29 (right): Burt R. Thomas, *Detroit News*; 30 (top): HST; 30 (bottom): *Krokodil*; 31: NA; 32: Milton Ackoff, *Wipe Out Discrimination*, 1949, LOC; 33: Abbie Rowe/NPS/HST; 35 (left): LOC; 35 (right): United Nations; 36: *A Good Man is Hard to Find*, lithograph poster by Ben Shahn for the Progressive Party, 1948, The Granger Collection, New York; 37: Abbie Rowe/NPS/HST; 38: CB; 39 (inset): Mercantile Library Association, St. Louis; 39 (bottom): Abbie Rowe/NPS/HST; 40: Michael Barson Collection; 41 (top left): CB; 41 (top right): LOC; 41 (bottom left and right): CB; 42 (right): Xinhua News Agency, Beijing; 43 (top and bottom): NA; 44: LOC; 45: CB; 46: AP/WW; 47 (top): CB; 47 (bottom): LOC; 48: Rue des Archives/The Granger Collection, New York; 49 (top left): DDE; 49 (right): CB; 49 (bottom): Archive Photos; 50 (left): CB; 50 (right): NA; 51 (top): DDE; 51 (bottom): CB; 52 (top): Herblock, *Washington Post*; 52 (bottom): CB; 53: NA; 54 (top): *St. Louis Post Dispatch*; 54 (bottom): LOC; 55: CB; 56 (top): PIX, Inc.; 56 (bottom): Car Culture/CB; 57 (top): motelpostcards.com; 57 (bottom): Allan Grant; 58: Sandy Felsenthal / Corbis; 59: © Curtis Publishing Co.; 60 (top): Ngo Vinh Long Collection; 60 (bottom): War Resisters League; 61, 63 (top): U. S. Navy; 63 (bottom): Ngo Vinh Long Collection; 64: CB; 65 (top and bottom): LOC; 66 (bottom): LOC; 66 (top) and 67: Alaska State Library and Archives, Juneau; 68: photo by Alex Rivera; 69: NYPL, Picture Collection; 70: Ben Shahn, *Integration, Supreme Court*, 1963, Des Moines Art Center, purchased with funds from the Edmunson Art Foundation (1964.6); 71 (top): NYPL, Picture Collection; 71 (bottom): Granger Collection, New York; 72: The *New York Times*, December 24, 1961; 74 (top): CB; 74 (bottom): AP/WW; 75: LOC; 76: NYPL, Picture Collection; 77: LOC; 78: Schomburg Center for Research in Black Culture, NYPL; 79: National Portrait Gallery, Smithsonian Institution/Art Resource, NY; 80: Charles Moore/Black Star; 81: LOC; 82 (top): Schomburg Center for Research in Black Culture, NYPL; 82 (bottom): LOC/The Granger Collection, New York; 83: NYPL, Picture Collection; 84, 85 (top): LOC; 85 (bottom): CB; 86, 87: LOC; 88–90: JFK; 89 (center): LOC; 91: Underwood & Underwood/CB; 92 (top and bottom): CB; 93: AP/WW; 95 (top): JFK; 95 (bottom): Richard Yardley, *Baltimore Sun*, 1962; 96 (top): LOC; 96 (bottom left): *Prensa Latina*; 96 (bottom right): AP/WW; 97 (top left): Fred Powledge; 97 (right top): Bob Adelman/Magnum Photos; 97 (bottom): Danny Lyon/Magnum Photos; 98 (top): State Historical Society of Wisconsin (Wi [X3] 36638, CF 6797); 98 (bottom): Bob Adelman/Magnum Photos; 99: AP/WW; 100: CB; 101 (top left and right), 102 (top): NA; 102 (bottom): CB; 103 (top): LOC; 103 (bottom): Federal Bureau of Investigation; 104 (top): LOC; 104 (bottom): NA; 105–106: JFK; 107 (top): AP Photo/Ike Altgens; 107 (bottom): Wally McNamee/Corbis; 108 (top and bottom): JFK; 108 (right): AP/WW; 109 (top): Yoichi R. Okamoto/LBJ; 109 (bottom): LBJ; 110–112: LBJ; 113: *Austin Statesman*/LBJ; 114:Patrick Byrd/Science Faction/Corbis; 115: Cecil Stoughton/LBJ; 116: Karl Hubenthal; 117: CB; 118 (top): Gib Crockett/LOC; 118 (bottom): Yoichi R. Okamoto/ LBJ; 119 (top): CB; 119 (bottom): Yoichi R. Okamoto/LBJ; 120: CB; 121: Ed Hollander; 122: photo © James H. Karales; 123 (top): CB; 123 (bottom): T. L. Blair/Camera Press/Retna; 124: Flip Schulke/Corbis; 125 (top and bottom): CB; 127: CB; 128: David Levine, © *The New York Review of Books*, 1971; 129 (top): CB; 129 (bottom): Eddie Adams/AP/WW; 130 (bottom): Bill Canfield, *Newark Star Ledger*; 131: Joy Hakim; 132 (top): CB; 132 (bottom): photo by Ben Fernandez, Marquette University Memorial Library, Department of Special Collections and University Archives, Milwaukee, Wisconsin; 133 (top): David Levine, © *The New York Review of Books*, 1966; 133 (bottom): NA; 134 (top left and right): CB; 134 (bottom left): AP/WW; 134 (inset): NYPL, Picture Collection; 135 (top): Yoichi R. Okamoto/LBJ; 135 (bottom): LBJ; 136 (top and bottom): CB; 137 (top): LOC; 137 (bottom), 138: NYPL, Picture Collection; 139: CB; 140 (left): LOC; 140 (right): Robert R. McElroy/*Newsweek*; 141: Diana Mara Henry/*Viva*; 142 (top): LOC; 142 (bottom): CB; 143: CB; 144: Walker Evans/LOC; 145:

LBJ: Lyndon B. Johnson Library, Austin, Texas
LOC: Library of Congress
NA: National Archives

NPS: National Parks Service
NYPL: New York Public Library

CB; 146: NYPL, Picture Collection; 147: Dorothea Lange/LOC; 148 (left): JP Laffont/Sygma/Corbis; 148 (right): Bill Gillette/NA; 149: Cornelius Keyes/NA; 151: Joy Hakim; 152: Dorothea Lange/LOC; 153: Herbert Orth; 155 (top): Robert Knudsen/LBJ; 155 (bottom): CB; 156: Georg Gerster/Ralpho/Photo Researchers; 157 (left): CB; 157 (right): LOC; 158: Yoichi R. Okamoto/LBJ; 159: Joseph Louw/Time & Life Pictures/Getty Images; 160: Flip Schulke/Corbis; 161: CB; 162 (top): CB; 162 (bottom): NYPL, Picture Collection; 163 (left top and bottom, middle center and right): LOC; 163 (middle left): Jeff Reinking; 164 (top and bottom): CB; 165 (top): Wally McNamee/Corbis; 165 (bottom): Bonnie M. Freer/Photo Trends; 166 (top): CB; 167 (left): The Granger Collection, New York; 167 (right): *New York Daily News*; 168 (left): NA; 168 (right): Rue des Archives/The Granger Collection, New York; 169 (left): Rue des Archives/The Granger Collection, New York; 169 (right): Michael Ochs Collection; 169 (bottom): Redferns; 170: LOC; 171 (top): Magnum Photos; 171 (right): Cummings Prentiss Studios; 173 (top): Corbis; 173 (bottom): Joy Hakim; 174: LOC; 175 (top): Oliphant © 1974 Universal Press Syndicate; 175 (bottom): CB; 176: NASA; 178: LBJ; 179 (left): Gerald R. Ford Library; 179 (right): Nixon Presidential Materials; 180 (top): Gerald R. Ford Library; 180 (middle left): Jimmy Carter Library; 180 (bottom right), 181 (top): CB; 181 (bottom): Jimmy Carter Library; 182: Ronald Reagan Library; 183: CB; 184 (left): Ronald Reagan Library; 184 (right): Smithsonian Institution; 185: © Mazzotta/Rothco; 187: Dean Wong/Corbis; 188: Ronald Reagan Library; 191 (bottom): CB; 191 (top): Fairfax County Public Library; 193 (bottom): The Stock Market; 194: AP/WW; 195: Reuters/Corbis; 196: George Bush Presidential Library; 197: Peter Turnley/Corbis; 198 (top): Reuters/Corbis; 198 (bottom): CB; 199: Joy Hakim; 200: CB; 201: Rosenfeld Images Ltd./Photo Researchers; 202: National History Day; 203: Christie's Images; 204: Tom McHugh/ Photo Researchers; 205 (top): CB; 205 (bottom): CB; 207: American Demographics; 208: (top and bottom): LOC; 209: Harpo Productions; 211: Donna Binder/Impact Visuals; 212: Reuters/CB; 213: Arnie Sachs/Consolidated News Pictures; 214: Reuters/Corbis; 215: © Tribune Media Services, Inc., all rights reserved, reprinted with permission 216: Barry Blitt/*The New Yorker*, August 10, 1998; 218: Archive Photos; 220: (top) CB; 220: (bottom) www.shutterstock.com; 221: NA; 223 (top): Najilah Feanny/Corbis; 223 (bottom): Corbis; 224: Archive Photos; 225: Collection, Supreme Court Historical Society/Steve Petteway; 226: NA/Courtesy AIP Emilio Segre Visual Archives;

227: NASA; 228: Peter Menzel/Photo Researchers; 229: Reuters/Corbis; 230: AP Images/Diane Bondareff; 231: Kit Kittle/Corbis; 233: Najlah Feanny/Corbis; 236: Ron Sachs/CNP/Corbis; 237 (top): Matthew McDermott/Polaris Images; 237 (bottom): Corbis; 234: David Goldemberg; 238: AP/WW; 239 (bottom and inset): Reuters/Corbis; 240: Allison Shelley; 241: AP/WW; 242: Department of Defense; 243: Ann Telnaes; 244: CB; 245: Adam Zyglis; 246: U.S. Embassy Norway; 247: GOES 12 Satellite, NASA, NOAA; 248: Bob McMillan/FEMA Photo; 249: Jez Coulson/Panos Pictures; 250: U.S. Coast Guard, Petty Officer 2nd Class Kyle Niemi; 251: Nate Beeler; 252: Atef Hassan/Reuters/Corbis; 253: Ali Jarekji/Reuters/Corbis; 254 (left): Ali Mohammed/epa/Corbis; 254 (right): Department of Defense, U.S. Air Force photo by Tech. Sgt. Andrew M. Rodier; 255 (top): Department of Defense, U.S. Army photo by Spc. Maurice A. Galloway; 255 (bottom): Department of Defense, U.S. Army photo by Sgt. Prentice C. Martin-Bowen; 256 (left): Ian Griffiths/Robert Harding World Imagery/Corbis; 256 (right): Alison Wright/Corbis; 257: Jacques Descloitres, MODIS rapid Response Team, NASA/GSFC (overlay: Nancy Rose); 258: Peter van Agtmael/Magnum Photos; 259: Department of Defense, U.S. Air Force photo by Staff Sgt. Christine Jones; 260: Justin Sullivan, Getty Images News; 261: Washington State Digital Archives; 262: AP Photos/Mary Altaffer; 263: Boris Roessler/dpa/Corbis; 264: Dario Castillejos, El Imparcial de México; 265: John Gress/Reuters/Corbis; 267: Jewel Samad/AFP/Getty Images; 268 and 269: Obama For America/Handout /Reuters/Corbis; 270: Brooks Kraft/Corbis; 271 (top to bottom): Justin Lane/epa/Corbis; Matt Campbell/epa/Corbis; Matthew Cavanaugh/epa/Corbis; Rick Friedman/Corbis; 273: CB; 274: Gary Hershorn/Reuters/Corbis; 275: Christy Bowe/Corbis; 276: Bell Laboratories, courtesy AIP Emilio Segre Visual Archives; 277: Science Source; 278: The White House flickr website (Official White House Photo by Pete Souza); 279: Ron Sachs/Pool/CNP/Corbis; 280: DCpages.com; 281: Pete Souza/White House/Handout/ CNP/Corbis; 282: Photo by Marion Post Wolcott for the Farm Security Administration, 1939, LOC/The Granger Collection; 283: AP Photo/Pablo Martinez Monsivais; 297 (top): Bodleian Library, University of Oxford. MS. Pococke; 375: folios 3v-4r.; 297: (bottom): Planetary Visions Limited/German Aerospace Center; endpaper: (front): Prayer Pilgrimage for Freedom, 1957, Bob Henriques/Magnum Photos; (back): Chicago, November 04, 2008, Brooks Kraft/Corbis.

Index

A Abdullah II, 232
Abernathy, Ralph, 82, 97, 121, 127, 159
abortion, 143, 235
absentee ballots, 226
Abu Graib, prison, 253
Abzug, Bella, 141
Adams, John, 217
Aeschylus, 160
Afghanistan, 181, 238,253, 256-259;
    schools and, 258
African Americans, 9, 64–67, 113, 202,
    265,266,273,274. *See also* civil
    rights movement
Agamemnon, 160
Agnew, Spiro, 175, 179
Ahmad, Sheikh 238
Aiken, Howard Hathaway, 201
Al Qaeda network, 232, 233, 238, 257-259
Alabama, 120–23, 124–27
Aldrin, Edwin E. "Buzz," 177
Aleuts, 66, 156
Alexander the Great, 241, 257
Alexandria, 242
Allen, Frederick, 237
Anderson, Jon Lee, 240
Angelou, Maya, 163
Anthony, Susan B., 141, 142
Arabian Nights, 241
Arafat, Yasser, 214
Aristide, Jean-Bertrand, 214
Aristotle, 242
Armstrong, Lance, 220
Armstrong, Neil, 177
atoms, 227, 228, 277

B Baez, Joan, 168
Baghdad, 240, 242
Bailyn, Bernard, 252
Bagram Air Base, prison, 253
Bakker, Jim, 142
Bakker, Tammy, 142
balanced budget, 214
Baldwin, James, 163
Ball, Lucille, 137–38, 143
bnakruptcy, 264
banks. See investment banks.
Bardeen, John, 276
baseball, 18–22
Basra, 242, 2544
Bates, Daisy, 84, 85
Bay of Pigs, 93–94, 95
Bear, Stearns, investment bank, 262, 263
Beatles, 168–69
Begin, Manachem, 181
Bell, Alexander Graham, 276
Bell Laboratories, 276
Ben-Yehuda, Eliezer, 34
Berlin, Germany, 28, 188–89
Berlin, Isaiah, 235
Bernanke, Ben, 264
Bevel, James, 99, 100
Biden, Joseph R., 271
Bill of Rights, 11, 45, 46, 48, 252
Bin Laden, Osama, 234–235, 238, 257, 258
Birmingham, Alabama, 97, 98
Black Muslims, 123
Black Panthers, 162
Blackwell, Elizabeth, 142
Bloomer, Amelia Jenks, 142

Boston Tea Party, 239
Bourke-White, Margaret, 140
boycotts, 76, 78–82, 79–80
Brattain, Walter Houser, 276
Bray, Rosemary, 118
Briggs v. *Clarendon County,* 68
Brinkley, Douglas, 225
Brooklyn Dodgers, 19, 22
Brown, Henry Billings, 64
Brown, Linda Carroll, 68
Brown, Minnijean, 84
Brown v. *Board of Education,* 68–73, 83,
    87, 185, 202
Bryce, James, 225
Buddhas of Bamyan, 256, 258
Bunche, Ralph, 35, 126, 127
burkha (also burqa or burka), 258
Bush, George H. W., 195–96, 205, 216,
    219–20

Bush, George W., 218–25, 232, 233, 236,
    238–43, 244-251, 254
Bush, Jeb, 226
Bush, Laura Welch, 221
Bush, Prescott, 219
Bush v. *Gore,* 225
Byrd, Robert C., 239
Byzantine Empire, 241

C Caesar, Julius, 242
California, 17, 184, 191, 200, 260, 261
Calley, William, 136
Camp David accords (1978), 214
campaign finance reform, 214
campaigns. *See* elections
Campbell, Ben Nighthorse, 156
Carey, Mathew, 232
Carmichael, Stokely, 134
Carson, Rachel, 90–91
Carter, Jimmy, 214, 281
Castro, Fidel, 93, 96, 198
Catt, Carrie Chapman, 142

censure, 48
census, 206–7
Central Intelligence Agency (CIA), 181
Challenger space shuttle, 186
Chapman, Mary Jim, 154, 156
Chávez, César, 148–52, 149, 151, 155, 164
Cheney, Dick, 221, 245
Cheney, Lynn, 221
Chief Technology Officer, 278
Chiang Kai-shek, 41–42
China, 41, 42, 43, 96, 128, 172, 173, 195, 200, 215, 218
Chou El-lai, 172
Chow-wah-what-yuk, 154
Christianity, 235
Chrysler, 264
Churchill, Winston, 27
cities. *See* suburban culture
Civil Rights Act (1964), 118, 121
civil rights movement, 32–33, 83–87, 96, 98, 101–4, 144, 202, 226, 266, 273; cartoon on, 52; Emmett Louis Till, 145; Martin Luther King, Jr., 7; red scare and, 40; Truman and, 36; women's movement and, 139
climate change, 245
Clinton, Chelsea, 215

Clinton, Hillary Rodham, 212–13, 215, 270, 271 273, 279
Clinton, William Jefferson, 211–13, 214–18, 254
Cold War, 29, 30, 43, 93, 170, 232, 255
Collins, Francis, 230
Collins, Michael, 177
communism, 12, 24, 26, 40–43, 45, 93, 128, 172, 197, 258
community organizer, 266, 270

Communist Party, 45
computers, 201, 204, 277
Congress for Racial Equality (CORE), 101, 102
Connally, John, 107
Connor, Eugene "Bull," 97, 98, 99, 120, 121
conservatism, 183
Constantinople, 241
Constitution, 70, 122, 222, 240, 252, 275, 280
Constitutional Amendments:
    1st Amendment, 45, 48, 196, 215
    2nd Amendment, 210
    14th Amendment, 64, 68–73
    15th Amendment, 11, 121
    24th Amendment, 118, 122
    26th Amendment, 172
Coolidge, Calvin, 70, 183, 185
Cooper, Anne Nixon, 274
cotton gin, 144
counterculture, 165
Crick, Francis, 53, 228
Crusades, 234
Cuba, 93, 253
Cuban missile crisis, 93, 95–96
Cuomo, Mario, 280

Dallas, Texas, 106, 107–8
Dallas County, Alabama, 121
Dark Ages, 235
Davis, John, 127
Davis, John W., 70–71
Davis v. *County School Board of Prince Edward County*, 172
Day, Dorothy, 132
death penalty, 214
democracy, 10, 12, 200, 256
Democratic National Convention (2004), 265–267, 271
Denton, Jeremiah A., Jr., 131, 173
Department of Defense, 254
Dershowitz, Alan, 224
Detroit, Michigan, 56, 134, 169
Dewey, Thomas, 36–39
Dinkins, David, 208
Dionne, E. J., Jr., 224
disease, 230, 232
DNA (deoxyribonucleic acid), 53, 228
Domestic Surveillance Program, 245, 246
drug culture, 166
drug use, 130, 214
DuBois, W. E. B., 103
Dunham, Madelyn, 270
Durr, Clifford, 80
Durr, Virginia, 80
Dworkin, Ronald, 222
Dylan, Bob, 167–68
Dyson, Freeman, 226

Eckford, Elizabeth, 84, 85
ecology, 90–91
economics, 105, 115, 153–55, 194–95, 203–4, 214, 229, 269
edge cities, 191–93
Edison, Thomas, 277
education, 214, 253, 266, 278
Egypt, 35, 181
Einstein, Albert, 226–27
Eisenhower, Dwight D., 49–53, 62, 63, 71, 85, 89, 96, 113, 129, 172, 181, 217, 272
elections, 43, 115, 164, 218–25, 244-246, 270-274, 280
Electoral College, 221–25
Ellison , Ralph, 162–63
employment, 214
environment, 90–91
equal rights movement, 137–43

equality, 208–9
Eskimos, 66, 156
Euphrates, 241
Europe, 28
European Union, 194–95

Fair Deal, 40
Falwell, Jerry, 142
Farm Workers Association, 149–52
Farsi, 257
Federal Bureau of Investigation (FBI), 40, 253
Federal Emergency Management Agency (FEMA), 249
Federal Reserve, 229, 263, 264
feminism, 139–40

Feynman, Richard P., 227
15th Amendment, 11, 121
financial crisis, 260-264, 273
1st Amendment, 45, 48, 196, 215
Flanders, Ralph, 48
Florida, 225–26, 246-251
Ford, Betty, 179, 180
Ford, Gerald, 179, 180
14th Amendment, 64, 68–73
France, 60–63, 239

Franklin, Aretha, 169
freedom of religion, 255
freedom of speech, 48
freedom of the press, 255
freedoms, 235
Friedan, Betty, 137, 138–39, 139–40, 141
Friedman, Thomas J., 232
Frost, Robert, 89
Fulbright, J. William, 106, 130

G Galveston flood, 250
Gandhi, Mohandas (Mahatma), 36,
76, 121, 152
Gates, Bill, 204
Gates, Henry Louis, Jr., 73, 87, 98
Gates, Robert, 279
Gaudet, Steve, 237
General Motors, 264
general relativity (1916), 227
genetics, 53, 228
G.I. Bill of Rights, 37
Gilgamesh, Epic of, 241
Goldman Sachs, investment bank, 262
Goldwater, Barry, 129, 175
Goodman, Andrew, 103

Gorbachev, Mikhail, 188, 189
Gordy, Berry, 169
Gore, Albert, 211, 213, 218–25, 236, 245
Gore, Mary Elizabeth "Tipper," 213
Great Depression, 255, 261, 264
Great Migration, 144–46
Great Society program, 113, 115, 117–18,
119, 128, 133, 183
Green, Ernest, 84, 87
Greenhouse, Linda, 225
Greenspan, Alan, 229
Grenada, 190
Gruening, Ernest, 66, 67
Guantánamo Bay, prison, 253
Gulf of Tonkin, 115, 130, 131, 133
Gun-Free Schools Act (1994), 210
guns, 209

H habeas corpus, 252, 255
Haines, Mark, 229
Hakim, Danny, 229, 260
Hamilton, Alexander, 230, 275
Hammond, John Henry, Sr., 166–67, 168
Harlan, John Marshall, 64–65
Harvard Law Review, 266
Harvard Law School, 266, 268
Hawaiian islands, 91, 266, 268
Hayes, George E. C., 87
Headstart, 118
health-care reform, 214, 253, 280
Hellman, Lillian, 48
Hersh, Seymour, 136
Herzl, Theodore, 34
Heschel, Abraham, 126
Himalaya mountains, 257
hippies, 133, 165–69
Hiss, Alger, 41
Ho Chi Minh, 60–63, 129
Hoffman, Abbie, 132
Holiday, Billie, 167
Hoover, J. Edgar, 40, 158
Hoover, Herbert, 261
Hoovervilles, 261
Hopper, Clay, 21
Houston, Charles Hamilton, 64, 65
Howard University, 65
Hubble, Edwin, 216, 227
Hubble telescope, 227
Hudson Valley Community College, Troy,
278
Hughes, Langston, 208–9
hula hoops, 49
Hungary, 29
hurricanes, 247; hurricane Katrina
(2005), 246-251; Galveston flood
(1900), 250
Hurston, Zora Neale, 163
Hussein, Saddam, 196, 238–40, 252

I Love Lucy, 137
Imams, 241
immigrants and immigration, 10,
198–202, 203, 206–7. See also
migrant labor
impeachment, 178, 216, 255
Indonesia, 268
Indus River, 257
inflation, 214
Information Age, 192–93, 204, 208, 278,
279
Inquisitions, 234
Insurgency, 242, 245, 252-255
Internet, 229, 271, 277, 278
Investment banks, 262, 263
Iran, 181
Iran-Contra investigation, 217
Iraq, 35, 196–97, 238–243, 245, 252-255,
271, 273
iron curtain, 27–28
Islam, 123, 232–35, 258, 259
Israel, 35, 239
Israeli-PLO peace accord, 214
Istanbul, 241

J Jackson, Jimmy Lee, 124
Jakarta, Indonesia, 268
jazz, 167
Jefferson, Thomas, 11, 45, 46, 116, 117,
121, 126, 153, 171, 218, 239, 245,
255, 272, 280
jihad, 234, 235, 238, 259
Jim Crow laws, 18–22, 65, 66, 70, 78, 153
Job Corps, 118
Jobs, Steven, 204
Johns, Barber Rose, 68–69
Johnson, Andrew, 112, 178, 216
Johnson, Lady Bird, 107, 109, 112
Johnson, Lyndon B., 96, 106, 108, 109–11,
112, 113, 158, 217; antiwar protests

I LIKE IKE

and, 133–36; campaigning, 115, 117; cartoon, 116, 133; Coles on, 114; with MLK, 119; Thurgood Marshall and, 135; Vietnam War and, 128; on voting rights, 123
Johnson, Samuel, 239
Jones, LeRoi, 134
Jordan, Barbara, 178
JPMorgan Chase, 263
Judaism, 235

KKatrina, hurricane, 246-251
Keegan, John, 240
Kennedy, Jacqueline, 88, 92, 107, 108
Kennedy, John F., 88, 91, 92, 93, 95, 100, 105, 113, 176, 185, 210, 212, 217, 278; assassination, 106–7; civil rights movement and, 102; in Fort Worth, Texas, 106; Vietnam and, 129
Kennedy, Robert, 96, 100, 108, 155, 159–60, 161, 164, 232
Kent State University, 166
Kenya, 265, 266, 268
Kerensky, Alexander, 24
Kerner Commission, 134
Kerry, John, 217, 244, 265
Khomeini, Ruhollah (Ayatollah), 181
Khrushchev, Nikita, 51, 53, 93, 95, 96
Kim Il Sung, 41, 43
King, Billie Jean, 141
King, Coretta Scott, 74, 81, 82, 120, 123, 127, 160

King, Martin Luther, Jr., 74–77, 82, 97–100, 101–4, 120–23, 127, 152, 155, 157–60, 161–62, 209, 226, 239; anti-war protests and, 133–35; arrested for boycott, 80; assassinated, 159; funeral procession, 161; "I have a dream" speech, 103–4; on Jackie Robinson, 101; with LBJ, 119; Montgomery, Alabama, 81; quote, 8
King, Martin Luther, Sr., 74
Knight, Gladys, 169
Koran (also Quran), 234, 241, 258
Korean War, 42–43, 51, 52
Kroc, Ray, 58
Ku Klux Klan, 97, 103
Kurds, 241
Kuwait, 196, 238, 240

LLaden, Osama bin. *See* Bin Laden, Osama
La Follette, Robert, Jr., 44
Lander, Eric, 230
Landis, Kenesaw Mountain, 19
Lebanon, 35, 190
Lee, Cager, 124
Lehman Brothers, investment bank, 262, 264
Lenin, Vladimir Ilyich, 23, 24
levees, 248
Levitt, William, 55
Levittown, New York, 54, 55
Lewinsky, Monica, 216
Lewis, Bernard, 235
Lewis, John, 122, 273
liberalism, 183
Little Rock, Arkansas, 83–87

London, Jack, 230
Los Angeles, California, 134
Louisiana Superdome, 246
Louisville, Kentucky, 71
lying by public officials, 41, 216, 217

MMacArthur, Douglas, 32, 43
Majeed, Izzat, 235
Malcolm X, 123, 162, 163
Manassas, 272, 273
Mandela, Nelson, 281
Mankiller, Wilma, 156
Mao Zedong, 41–42
Marshall, George C., 30–31, 32, 51
Marshall, Paule, 163
Marshall, Thurgood, 65, 69, 70, 87, 101, 135, 164, 209
Marshall Plan, 30–31, 172
Marx, Karl, 24, 26, 194
Massachusetts Institute of Technology, 222
McCain, John, 173, 271-274
McCarthy, Joseph, 44–48, 51, 93, 172
McCarthyism, 44–48, 239
McDonald, Dick, 57, 58
McDonald, Maurice, 57, 58
McDonald's, 57–59
McDougall, Walter 242
McNamara, Robert, 130
McVeigh, Timothy, 235
Medicaid, 118
Medicare, 11
Memphis, Tennessee, 157–60
Mendoza family, 147–49
Merrill Lynch, investment bank, 262, 264
Mexican Americans, 113
Mexican workers, 147–52
microchip technology, 276, 277

Microsoft Corporation, 204
Middle East, 214–15, 232, 238–243, 245,
    252, 253
migrant labor, 147–52
Miller, Judith, 239
Mississippi, 32, 33
Mississippi River, 248
Monroe, Marilyn, 49, 50
Montgomery, Alabama, 77, 80–81, 24–27
Moreno, Graciela, 150
Morrison, Toni, 163
Mortenson, Greg, 259
Morton, Kathryn Harris, 73
Mosul, 242
motels, 57
Mother Teresa, 281
Mothershed, Thelma, 84
Moyers, Bill, 217
Murrow, Edward R., 46–47
Muslim culture. *See* Islam

My Lai, South Vietnam, 136

Nabrit, James, 87
nano technology, 277
NASA, 176
Nation of Islam, 123
National Association for the
    Advancement of Colored People
    (NAACP), 69
National Human Genome Research , 228
National League of Women Voters, 142
National Library (Iraq), 242
National Museum of Antiquities (Iraq),
    242
National Organization for Women
    (NOW), 140
National Security, 245
Native Americans, 66, 156
Nature magazine, 230

Negro-leagues (baseball), 18–22
Neighborhood Youth Corps, 118
New Deal, 40, 89, 113, 183
New Frontier program, 105, 106, 113
New Orleans, 246-251
"New Right," 142–43
New York City, 231–35, 247
New York Times, 225, 229, 237, 239, 253,
    259, 261
Nixon, E. D., 79, 80, 82
Nixon, Richard M., 41, 62, 170–78, 179,
    217
Nobel, Alfred, 120
Nobel Prize, 35, 120, 126, 161, 245, 281
nonviolence, 77, 99, 120, 149, 152, 158, 189
North, Oliver, 217
Northern Alliance, 259

Obama, Barack Hussein, 278-281;
    childhood, 268, 269; children of,
    265, 274; Illinois congressman and
    state senator, 264-267, 271; par
    ents of, 268, 269; U.S. president,
    267, 270-275
Obama, Barack, Sr., 268
Obama, Michelle, 265, 266; First Lady,
    274
Obama, Anne Dunham Soertoro, 268, 269
oil, 56, 242, 249, 252
Oklahoma City, 235
Olympic Games, 36, 164
O'Neil, Buck, 21
Operation Headstart, 118
Osama bin Laden. *See* Bin Laden, Osama
Oswald, Lee Harvey, 108
Ottomans, 241–42
Owens, Jesse, 20

Paige, Satchel, 18
Pakistan, 257, 259
Palestine, 34
Palin, Sarah, 271, 272
Panama Canal, 181
Parks, Rosa, 78–82, 127, 209–10, 239
Pashto, 257
Pashtuns, 257, 258
Pattillo, Melba, 83–85, 86, 87
Peace Corps, 89, 90, 115
Pearl Harbor, Hawaii, 232
Pentagon in Washington D.C., 130,
    232–35, 254
Peratrovich, Elizabeth Wanamaker, 67
Perez, Orestes Lorenzo, 198–99
perjury, 41, 217
Persian Gulf War, 196
Persians, 241
Phillips, Mitchell, 222
Plessy, Homer, 64
Plessy v. *Ferguson,* 53, 64–65, 70–71
Plutarch, 15
polio myelitis, 49, 50
Poor People's Campaign, 157
Population, 206–7
poverty, 109, 110–11, 115, 116–18, 141,
    147–52, 153–55, 187
Powell, Colin, 226
Presley, Elvis, 49, 52, 168
prisons, 253
prisoners of war, 131
Progressive Party, 36
Puerto Ricans, 275

Pulitzer Prize, 136
Punahou School, Hawaii, 268

Q Qaeda, Al. *See* Al Qaeda network
Quantum theory, 227
Quran (also Koran), 234, 241, 258

R Rabin, Yitzhak, 214
racism, 273
Randolph, A. Philip, 101–2
Ray, Gloria, 84
Ray, James Earl, 159
Reagan, Nancy, 183
Reagan, Ronald, 181, 182–89, 190, 195, 216, 225
Reeb, James, 126
Reid, Chip, 240
relativity, 227
religion, 226, 234, 235
Rhee , Syngman, 41
Rickey, Branch, 19–20, 22
riots, 161–62
Roberts, Terry, 84
Robertson, Pat, 142
Robinson, Jackie, 19–22, 101
Robinson, Jo Ann, 79, 81
Robinson, Mack, 20

Robinson Michelle, 266. See also Obama, Michelle.
Rockefeller, John D., Jr., 16
Roe v. *Wade,* 143
Roosevelt, Eleanor, 16
Roosevelt, Franklin Delano, 13, 36, 37, 50, 61, 89, 112, 118, 120, 217, 232, 245, 274
Rosenberg, Ethel, 41
Rosenberg, Julius, 41
Ross, Fred, 151
Ruby, Jack, 108

Ruiz, Hector, 279, 280
Rumsfeld, Donald, 242
Russia, 23, 24, 27, 28–29, 35, 95, 96, 176, 188, 194–97, 257, 258. *See also* Soviet Union.
Rustin, Bayard, 103, 121

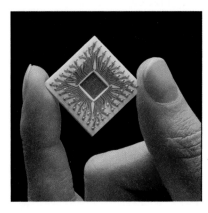

Rutledge, John, 275

S Sadat, Anwar, 181
Saddam Hussein. *See* Hussein, Saddam
Salk vaccine, 49, 50
San Francisco, 230
Scheherazade, 241
Schenck, Alberta, 66–67
Schlafly, Phyllis, 142
Schwartzkopf, Norman, 196
Schwarzenegger, Arnold, 261
science and technology, 226–28, 278
2nd Amendment, 210
segregation, 18–22, 32, 53, 64–65, 66, 68–73, 77, 78–82, 83–87, 145, 153–55, 209
Selma, Alabama, 121, 124–27, 273
Seneca Falls, New York, 141, 142
September 11, 2001 attacks, 232, 240, 252, 258
sharecropping, 144–45
Shattuck, Allen, 67
Shepard, Alan B., 176
Shi'a, 242
Shi'ite, 242
Shockley, William, 201, 276
Sirhan Sirhan, 164
sit-in demonstrations, 8, 98–100
Smiley, George, 82
Smith, Margaret Chase, 46, 47
Smithsonian Institution, 154, 156

Soertoro, Lolo, 268
Somalia, 196–97
Sotomayor, Sonia, 275
South Carolina, 146
South Pacific (Rodgers and Hammerstein), 230
Southern Christian Leadership Conference (SCLC), 101, 121
Soviet Union, 12, 23, 26, 27, 28–29, 32, 35, 52, 128, 181, 194–97, 258
space program, 176–77
special relativity (1905), 227
spies, 40–43, 44–48
Springsteen, Bruce, 270
Sputnik, 176, 178
Stalin, Joseph, 15, 24, 25, 26, 29, 41, 50
Stanton, Elizabeth Cady, 10–11, 141-142
Starr, Ken, 216
starvation, 220
Statue of Liberty, 231
Steel Seizure Case, 246
"A Statute for Religious Freedom," 250
Steppe, 241
Stevens, John Paul, 225
stock market, 214, 262, 263
Stoppard, Tom, 239
Student Nonviolent Coordinating Committee (SNCC), 101, 121, 272
suburban culture, 54–59, 139–40, 191–93
suicide bombers, 242, 252, 253, 257
Sumeria, 241
Sunni, 241, 242
"supply-side economics," 183
Supreme Court, 53, 69–70, 82, 226–27, 245, 275
Suskind, Ron, 253

T Taliban, 234–235, 238, 256, 258
Teacher Corps, 118
technology, 201, 204
television, 49–50, 87, 127–28, 137–38,

137–40, 177, 205
tennis, 143
terrorism, 190, 232–37, 238, 240, 245, 257, 258, 279
Texas, 178
"Theory of Everything" (TOE), 228
Thomas, Clarence, 164
Thomas, Jeff, 84
Thompson, Hugh, Jr., 136
Thoreau, Henry David, 239
Tigris, 241
Tikrit, 241
Till, Emmett Louis, 145
Tinker v. *Des Moines Independent School District*, 71
Tito, Marshall, 29
Torres, Edwin, 275
torture, 253, 257
totalitarianism, 12, 27
transistors, 201, 276
Tribe, Lawrence, 233
Truman, Bess, 37

Truman, Harry, 13–17, 30, 32, 33, 39, 42, 50, 62, 135; cartoon, 9; communism and, 29; Korean War and, 43, 245; re-election of, 36–39; red scare and, 40; Vietnam and, 129; Zionist movement and, 35
Truman Doctrine, 29, 30
Turkey, 242
24th Amendment, 118, 122
26th Amendment, 172

U Underground Railroad, 239
unemployment, 214, 264
unions, 157, 186
United Farm Workers, 152
United Nations, 238, 240, 259
United States Agency for International Development, 269
United Steel Workers strike (1952), 245
Upward Bound, 118
U.S. census, 206–7
U.S.S.R. *See* Soviet Union

V vaccines, 49, 50
Veeck, Bill, 19
Venter, Craig, 230
Vietnam, 42, 96, 200
Vietnam War, 60–62, 71, 118, 128–32, 165–66, 217, 244, 252, 271; antiwar protests, 118–19; cost of, 128; Ford and, 179–80; Kennedy and, 106; LBJ and, 115, 133–36, 154–55, 158; Nixon and, 172–73; Tet offensive, 170
Vo Nguyen Giap, 194
voting machines, 226
voting rights, 11, 118, 121–23, 127
Voting Rights Act (1965), 118

W Walker, Alice, 163
Wallace, George, 124–25
Walls, Carlotta, 84
Wall Street, 262-264
Wall Street Journal, 263
war on drugs, 214
war on terror, 253
War Powers Act, 217
Warren, Earl, 71
Washington, Booker T., 274

Washington, George, 217, 245, 275, 280
The Washington Post, 221, 238, 239, 251, 273
Watergate investigation, 174–75, 180, 217
Waterston, Robert, 230
Watson, James, 53, 228, 230
Weapons of mass destruction (WMDs), 238, 239, 241, 245, 253
Weizmann, Chaim, 35
welfare, 214
White, E. B., 236
White, Edward H., 176
Whitewater investigation, 215
Wilder, Douglas, 208
Will, George F., 225
Willard, Emma, 142
Williams, Hosea, 125, 127
Wilson, Alex, 85
Wilson, Kemmons, 56, 57
Wilson, Teddy, 167
Wilson, Woodrow, 281
Winfrey, Oprah, 209

Wollstonecraft, Mary, 142
women's rights, 137–43, 204, 234
Women's Rights Convention, 142
Woodward, Bob, 238, 242, 251
World Trade Center, 230–37
World War I, 242
Wozniak, Stephen, 204, 205
Wright, Richard, 146, 162, 163

Y Yeager, Chuck, 36
yellow fever, 230
Yugoslavia, 29, 197

Z Zimansky, Paul, 242
ZIP codes, 105
zoning laws, 192
Zumwalt, Elmo, Jr., 194

A Note from the Author

Dear Reader,

As soon as I began writing **A History of US** I realized this was a job I couldn't handle alone. I needed help. From the beginning lots of people were willing to give it, and they've never stopped. I wish I could thank everyone who has encouraged me or who spread the word about these books, because they made all the difference. At first, it was tough going. For some reason, the style of the books was seen as something very new. And innovation is scary to people in the publishing world.

We had entered a new era — the Information Age — but most schoolbooks were still reflecting the goals of the Industrial Age. They were non-thinking books that stressed memory and forgot stories and the ideas that make history an intellectual venture. I quickly realized that my readers had eager minds and no patience with boring books; given solid concepts, they devoured them. I had found the most exciting audience any writer could hope for.

Writing books is one thing, getting them published is another. Byron Hollinshead at American Historical Publications made the books happen and has supported and encouraged them with continuing wisdom and an incredible dedication to history and schools. Oxford University Press became publisher; its president, Laura Brown, had faith in a new approach to history for young readers.

The AHP team that originally produced the books includes: Tamara Glenny, Mervyn Clay, Sabine Russ, and Mary Blair Dunton, with Wendy Frost and Elspeth Leacock providing the beautifully drawn maps. At Oxford, Casper Grathwohl, Martin Coleman, Rosely Himmelstein, Susan Buckley,

Jackie Ball and Damon Zucca are among those who have provided support. Oxford created solid teaching guides that include assessments and student activities. Then the Talent Development Middle School team at Johns Hopkins University developed their own wonderful materials working in actual classrooms. Susan Dangel, Maria Garriott, and Cora Teter are the writers. (Those materials are available from OUP.)

Recorded Books provided an audio version of the books with a fine reading by Christina Moore. That's not all. Kunhardt Productions decided to do a PBS TV series, *Freedom: A History of US*, based on the books. That spawned an amazing website: www.pbs.org/wnet/historyofus/. The Kunhardt videos are available for classroom use from PBS Video (http://shopPBS.org/teachers).

When you write for young readers the best people want to help you. I don't have room to list all those who encouraged and participated, but I thank you all, especially the eager readers who have sent wonderful letters, including my new teacher friend in Turkey, Yucel Kalem.

Diane Brooks's input has been unique. She was head of social studies in California when I first met her and she read what was then a manuscript looking for a publisher. Diane made no-nonsense suggestions and I went home and rewrote. Then Oxford asked her to correlate the books with the California standards. She did far more than that. The document she wrote (available from OUP) is an insightful look at how history should be presented in the classroom. Christina Cocek Anderson also created a thoughtful and engaging correlation to the Virginia standards.

Ruth Wattenberg and Liz McPike at the American Federation of Teachers, along with Al Shanker, encouraged me even before these books were published (and never stopped with that encouragement). The amazing Elaine Reed helped make the NCHE (National Council for History Education) a special force in history education (Peter Seibert has taken over as executive director). National History Day, an organization that turns students into historians, has been a friend. The Gilder Lehrman Institute, which makes superb seminars available for teachers, sponsored a traveling exhibition to coordinate with *Freedom: A History of US*. The NCSS (National Council for Social Studies) hosted me as a speaker on more than one occasion. David McCullough has been both an inspiration and a cheerleader (read his books to learn how history should be written). The Lounsbery Foundation, Elihu Rose, and the Virginia Center for the Creative Arts all helped me when I needed it. My brother, Roger Frisch, and his wife, Patti, were sounding boards, as was my husband, Sam, and our favorite team: Ellen, Jeff, and Danny.

And then there are the educators: Barbara Dorff, Anita Robinson, Tom Adams, Dennis Denenberg, Melissa Matusevich, Janet Allen, Stephanie Harvey, Merrill Watrous, Christopher Naze, Frank Wang, and Victoria Hollister are just a few of them. I'm constantly awed by the teachers, administrators, and educational consultants that I meet.

But perhaps most of all I'd like to thank Paul Gagnon for being who he was and doing what he did. Paul, who was a teacher and dean at the University of Massachusetts, died in 2005. I don't know anyone who was more dedicated to schools and to history. Perhaps the best tribute I can give to Paul is to let him speak for himself. Here are a few of the words that he wrote:

When students and school boards ask, "Why history? What are we supposed to be getting out of this?" the best answer is still that one word: judgment. We demand it of all professionals: doctors, lawyers, chefs, and quarterbacks. And we need it most in the profession of citizen, which, like it or not, exercise it or not, we are all born into.

—*"Why Study History"* November 1988,
Atlantic Monthly

As the years pass, we become an increasingly diverse people, drawn from many racial, national, linguistic, and religious origins. Our cultural heritage as Americans is as diverse as we are, with multiple sources of vitality and pride. But our political heritage is one—the vision of a common life in liberty, justice, and equality as expressed in the Declaration of Independence and the Constitution two centuries ago.

—*Education for Democracy:
A Statement of Principles*,
from the Education for
Democracy Project, a
joint effort of the AFT,
Freedom House, and the
Educational Excellence
Network, 1987.

ATLAS
Being Up to Date

Way back in time, when we didn't know much about the world, mapmaking was a form of artistry and maps were often gorgeous works that only the elite could afford. Then, as we explored unknown areas, more and more maps got drawn. You couldn't develop land, or settle on it, if you didn't know where you were. Accurate maps were in demand. Usually there was no time to be artistic.

Early in the 20th century, photographers climbed into airplanes and began taking aerial photographs of the land. Those photographs were not maps, but they helped make ever-more accurate maps. So did satellites when they were fired into the atmosphere, sending back stunning and precise earth portraits. Landsat 1 was the first satellite with eyes for global mapping. A single Landsat 1 scene (115 miles by 115 miles) included more than thirty million observations. Each scene took 25 seconds to complete. Landsat 1, launched in 1972, was followed by ever-more sophisticated satellites. The total amount of information sent by Landsat satellites was, and is, staggering.

You're looking at the world upside down (north is at the bottom), the way Moroccan mapmaker al-Idrisi saw it in the twelfth century.

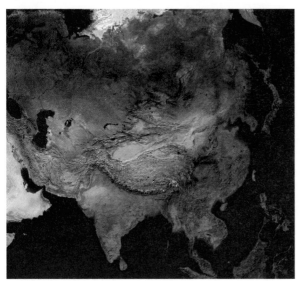

But, astonishing as satellite photography is, it doesn't tell the whole story. A whole new level of cartography came along when computers entered the field. Mountains of information can be processed in a computer, making for an incredible variety of maps. Computer-based mapping is known as GIS: it stands for Geographic Information Systems. GIS maps usually have a scale of 1:1,000,000 or better. That means we can now map tiny bits of land along with vast areas of space.

Computer mapping can show earthquakes throughout history, current fault lines, weather (past and present), temperature, population. . . the possibilities are endless. Computers keyed to satellites can locate you and your vehicle wherever you are and chart a route to your destination.

Cameras sometimes distort space; computers can make corrections. Computers have done something no one expected. They have helped make maps gorgeous again. Today, cartography is a "hot" science. And you don't have to be elite to have access to great maps. Just start on the Internet with the U.S. Geological Survey maps at http://www.usgs.gov.

ARCTIC OCEAN

Greenland
(Denmark)

Arctic Circle

Alaska
(U.S.)

60N

Canada

NORTH
AMERICA

40N

United States

ATLANTIC
OCEAN

Azores Is.
(Port.)

Midway Islands (U.S.)

Canary Is. (Sp.)

Western
Sahara
(Mor.)

Tropic of Cancer

Hawaii (U.S.)

Mexico

Cuba
Haiti
Jamaica
Puerto
Rico (U.S.)
Belize
Honduras
Dominican
Republic
Guatemala
El Salvador
Nicaragua
Costa Rica
Panama

Cape Verde

Maur

Gambia
Senegal
Guinea-Bissau
Sierra Leone
Gui
Liberia

PACIFIC OCEAN

Venezuela

Guyana
Suriname
French Guiana
(France)

Colombia

0   Equator

Galápagos
Islands
(Ecuador)

Ecuador

SOUTH
AMERICA

Peru

Brazil

ATL
OC

Samoa

American
Samoa
(U.S.)

Tonga

20S

Bolivia

Paraguay

Tropic of Capricc

Chile

Uruguay

Argentina

N

40S

Falkland
Islands
(U.K.)

W   E

S

60S

South
Georgia
(U.K.)

Antarctic Circle

120W

60W

80S

Inset map (Europe)

20W

70N

0   N

20E

40E

W   E

S

Iceland

Arctic Circle

Norwegian Sea

Scale
0   250   500 Miles
0   250   500 Kilometers

Sweden

Finland

60N

Norway

Estonia

Russia

United
Kingdom

North
Sea

Latvia

50N

Denmark

Baltic

Lithuania

Russia

Ireland

Netherlands

Belarus

Belgium

Germany

Poland

Ukraine

50N

ATLANTIC
OCEAN

Luxembourg

Czech
Republic

Slovakia

Moldova

Liechtenstein

Austria

Hungary

Romania

Black
Sea

Switzerland

Slovenia

Croatia

Serbia &
Mont.

60S

France

Monaco

San
Marino

Bosnia
& Herz.

Bulgaria

40N

Andorra

Corsica
(Fr.)

Italy

Macedonia

Turkey

Portugal

Sardinia
(It.)

Vatican
City

Albania

Spain

Balearic Is.
(Sp.)

Mediterranean
Sea

Greece

Gibraltar
(U.K.)   0

10E

Sicily
(It.)   Malta

20E

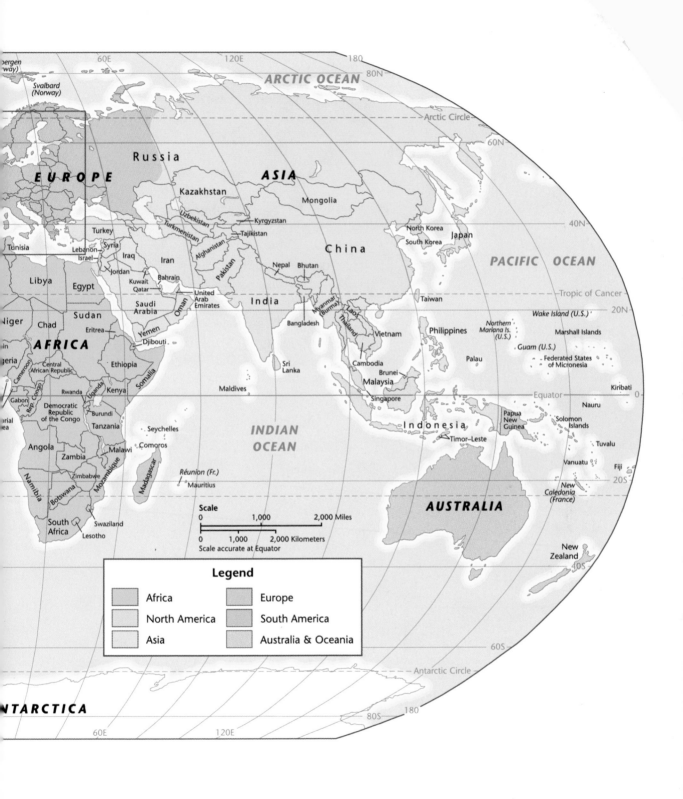

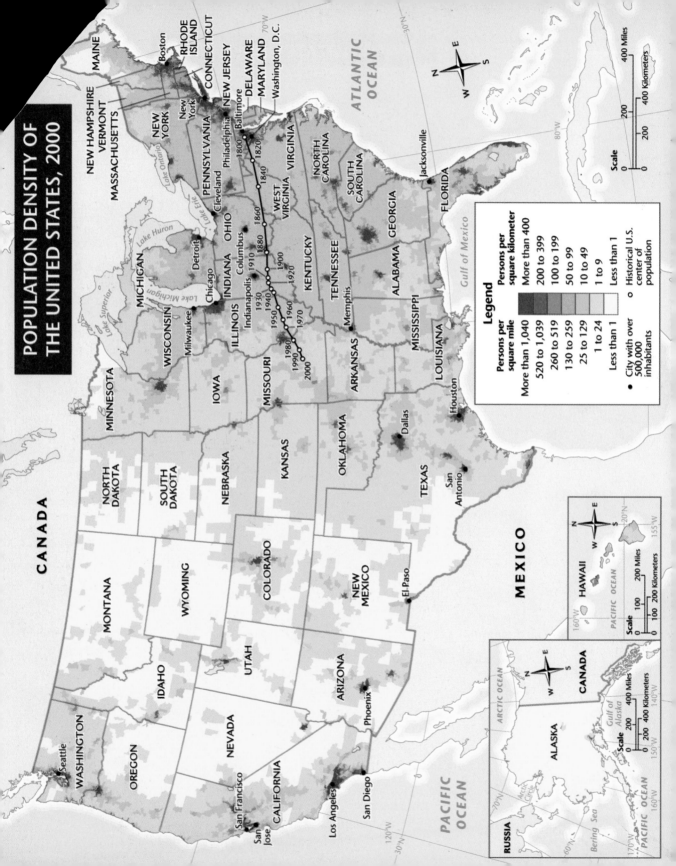

POPULATION DENSITY OF THE UNITED STATES, 2000

Legend

Persons per square mile

More than 1,040
520 to 1,039
260 to 519
130 to 259
25 to 129
1 to 24
Less than 1

Persons per square kilometer

More than 400
200 to 399
100 to 199
50 to 99
10 to 49
1 to 9
Less than 1

● City with over 500,000 inhabitants
○ Historical U.S. center of population